Cut!

Cut!

Hollywood murders, accidents, and other tragedies

BARRON'S

First edition for the United States, its territories, and Canada
published in 2006 by Barron's Educational Series, Inc.

First published in 2005 by Global Book Publishing Pty Ltd
This publication and arrangement
© Global Book Publishing Pty Ltd 2005
Text © Global Book Publishing Pty Ltd 2005
All photographs credited on page 337
Captions for preliminary pages and chapter openers listed
on page 337

All inquiries should be addressed to:
Barron's Educational Series, Inc.
250 Wireless Boulevard
Hauppauge, New York 11788
www.barronseduc.com

ISBN-13: 978-0-7641-5858-2
ISBN-10: 0-7641-5858-9

Library of Congress Catalog Card No.: 2005924768

Project manager	Dannielle Doggett
Foreword	John-Michael Howson
Contributors	Andrew Brettell
	Bruce Elder
	Denise Imwold
	Damien Kennedy
	Dr. Noel King
	Warren Leonard
	Prof. Toby Miller
	Heather von Rohr
Cover and	Cathy Campbell
page design	Stan Lamond

Printed in China by Sing Cheong Printing Co. Ltd
Color separation Pica Digital Pte Ltd, Singapore
9 8 7 6 5 4 3 2 1

Contents

Foreword

It's been said by cynics observing the vagaries of stardom that "dying young is a great career move." Heartless, perhaps, but it has an element of truth. James Dean, for instance, remains the eternal rebellious youth with whom an audience born decades after his untimely death can still identify. And we never saw a shimmering Marilyn sag into a wrinkled decline with small parts or no parts or chubby mother roles in television sitcoms, the fate that befell many of her contemporaries. Elvis left the building on the cusp of becoming a pitiful wreck, so that the Elvis icon millions worship is still that of a handsome country boy from Tennessee singing "Jailhouse Rock" and "Blue Suede Shoes" way before his final few years as "Fat Elvis." Bobby Darin departed before fulfilling his ambition to become the new Frank Sinatra, but when we recall how, in his closing years, "Old Blue Eyes" had to read his lyrics from "idiot" sheets attached to the stage floor, we can only be thankful Bobby was spared that humiliation.

Can one imagine an old Natalie Wood, an aging Steve McQueen, a graying Sal Mineo, a withered Rudolph Valentino, or a decrepit Jean Harlow? Forever they will flicker across the silver screen at their peak, a time when millions around the world adored them and before they were asked "Didn't you used to be someone famous?"—a fate that befell an aged Joan Crawford and sent her into reclusive decline.

Because the world focuses on Hollywood—more a mythical state of mind than a geographical location—its stories are larger than life. Combining fame, fortune, beauty, glamor, wealth, and all the things that sell magazines and lift television ratings, the tales become a confusion of fact and fiction. Hollywood's real-life dramas read like screenplays: a writer's fiction rather than the media's fact. Real-life tragedy played out before lenses and microphones becomes confused with entertainment, something that Billy Wilder captured in the quintessential Hollywood story *Sunset Boulevard* (1950). Millions have daydreamed of being stars and having a life far removed from that of mere mortals. But stardom has a price that those chosen to enjoy its success have to pay. The question is whether any felt it was worth it.

John-Michael Howson

From Porsches to Pavements— Hollywood Deaths

Death in Hollywood is something that exercises a powerful attraction for both Hollywood insiders and, more particularly, for Hollywood outsiders—the many fans who follow the comings and goings of their favorite Hollywood players. In recent times we have become accustomed to watching that section of the annual televised broadcast of the Academy Awards® in which we see a montage of movie stars and other members of the Hollywood fraternity who have died during the previous year, each image drawing varying amounts of applause according to the level of continuing recognition attached to the deceased film personality.

Why do we care about these people and how they died? Let's consider the nature of "celebrity." The idea has existed for eons, but it gained currency during the nineteenth century when democracy and capitalism transferred esteem from churches and kings to commodities and commoners. The fleeting fame that ensued has, of course, always been criticized for its lack of lasting value. But it evokes important cultural and social debates about the differences between public and private life, natural and manufactured beauty, apparent and authentic personality, ideal and average ability, and good and bad behavior.

The Fascination with Celebrity Deaths

A celebrity is like a personal acquaintance, yet simultaneously a stranger, a figure who is known through media intimacy rather than human interaction. Many fans invent connections with film stars and other celebrities in ways that mimic friendship and allow them to make sense of their everyday lives, and delight in sharing their devotion with others through forums such as audience conventions, web pages, discussion groups, quizzes, and books. In the United States, E! Television is a cable network that is entirely dedicated to celebrity gossip, which itself dominates much of the "current affairs" on both cable news stations and the broadcast networks. There is a seemingly insatiable hunger for information about actors and actresses, and the more morbid the better—Google offers about 27.5 million "hits" under the category "celebrity death."

ABOVE Fans of Elvis Presley are perhaps the most dedicated of all. As well as dressing like "The King of Rock 'n' Roll," many make a pilgrimage to his home in Memphis, Tennessee, to mark the anniversary of his death.

As the list of stars who died young (such as James Dean) or at least while still *acting* young (like Errol Flynn) grows in number, so do the stories of their excesses—Fatty Arbuckle and orgies and sexual violence; George Reeves finding his own personal Kryptonite in a weird marital triangle; Jean Harlow's mysterious demise as she was embodying a stereotype that found its epitome in tragic Marilyn Monroe; the curse of the Barrymores; Irving Thalberg leaving just the trace of an F. Scott Fitzgerald character; John Gilbert's feminine voice and ambiguous sexuality seeing his career corroded by the advent of talking movies and a taste for drink; the cancer of Bogie, as product placement by tobacco companies claimed its inevitable and ongoing toll; the "It" girl,

Clara Bow, traipsing down the slippery slope to mental illness; the advent and seeming demise of *kung fu* via Bruce Lee; Robert Donat's beautifully aspirated tones tragically marking his struggle with asthma; the gruesome Manson Family murder of Sharon Tate and friends (in a house whose very number has reportedly been obliterated to erase the memory); and Rudolph Valentino's last tango with his adoring fans. How these Hollywood legends died, at what age, with what effect—such concerns have become the fodder of gossip columns and water-cooler discussions around the globe.

ABOVE Rudolph Valentino lies in state in New York after his death in 1926 at just 31 years of age. About 80,000 fans lined the streets to watch his funeral procession.
LEFT Jean Harlow also died at an early age—she succumbed to kidney failure and uremic poisoning in 1937 at 26 years old.

The Effect of Hollywood Deaths

Sometimes we are prepared for a Hollywood death—think of the recent passing of Marlon Brando and how the press reported his careful preparations for his funeral in the months immediately preceding his demise. But at other times the person dies at a young age, seemingly gone in an instant, "like a fist when you open your hand," as Sam Spade says in Dashiell Hammett's novel, *The Maltese Falcon*. These two extremes generate particular kinds of sorrow in the mourning fans—the loss of a person whose work we have lived with and admired for so long is sad because it means there will be no more new work to await so keenly; and the person who dies young denies us all the later work we were anticipating with such excitement.

Sometimes the imminence of death is incorporated into a film, and becomes a lasting reminder to film fans of the star's mortality. Think of the pained face of Steve McQueen in *Tom Horn* (1980) and *The Hunter* (1980), each released in the year that "The King of Cool" succumbed to lung cancer, and consider the sadly tender scenes between James Stewart and John Wayne in Don Siegel's *The Shootist* (1976), when Stewart's character, Dr. Hostetler, has to tell Wayne's character, John Bernard Books, that he has inoperable cancer—Wayne himself died from cancer just three years later.

Spencer Tracy doubted whether his health would be robust enough for him to finish the shooting of *Guess Who's Coming to Dinner* (1967), and for Tracy fans the final scenes

ABOVE Steve McQueen looked tired and drawn in his last role, as Ralph "Papa" Thorson in The Hunter *(1980). The film was released in the United States in August 1980—three months later, McQueen was dead from lung cancer.*

LEFT An evocative image of Marlon Brando appeared on the cover of Time *magazine in January 1973 to promote the film* Last Tango in Paris *(1972). Brando passed away in 2004 at the age of 80.*

ABOVE Spencer Tracy (left), Katharine Hepburn, and Cecil Kellaway in Guess Who's Coming to Dinner *(1967). Tracy was ill during the making of the movie, and he suffered a fatal heart attack just 17 days after filming finished.*

of him in that film are heart-breaking, not least because we see Katharine Hepburn look with such tenderness on the love of her life, knowing this would be the last time they would appear on screen together. When Hepburn heard she would be receiving an Oscar® for her performance in that film, she asked if "Mr. Tracy" was also receiving one. When told he wasn't, she said, "That's alright, I'm sure mine is for both of us."

Often, death will have no dominion over the Hollywood person we have lost. In his 1957 article, "The Death of Humphrey Bogart" (translated by Phillip Drummond), legendary French film critic André Bazin asked, "Who does not mourn this month for Humphrey Bogart, who died at fifty-six of stomach cancer and half a million whiskeys?," before going on to describe how this cinema icon seemed able to "make us love and admire in him the very image of our own decomposition." For Bazin, Bogart typified with poetry and modernity the main actor-myth of the years from 1940 to 1955: Bogie played both good guys and bad guys, but the distilled image is one that typified stoicism, "distrust and weariness, wisdom, and scepticism," and conveyed "an existential maturity" that seemed to transform life into "a stubborn irony at the expense of death." As we now know, Bogart's persona lived on in all kinds of posthumous worship. Jean-Luc Godard's famous 1960 film *A bout de souffle* (known to UK and US audiences as *Breathless*) refers to Bogart's image in two ways—as Jean-Paul Belmondo's character draws his finger across his own lips while looking at a movie poster for *The Harder They Fall* (1956), and when the end of the film quotes the end of *High Sierra* (1941). Years later, Woody Allen's *Play It Again, Sam* (1972) would draw on the Bogart myth—encompassing everything from *Casablanca* (1942) to *The Big Sleep* (1946)—and consolidate the legend for all time.

The Dean Legacy

Perhaps it is the death of James Dean that stands as the most representative sample of what it can mean for a culture at large when a member of one of its entertainment professions dies young and the circuits of media mythologizing leap into action. In Dean's case, many of the earliest responses came from high culture. Frank O'Hara wrote his poem, "For James Dean"; French sociologist Edgar Morin's *The Stars* appeared, with a chapter offering a case study of James Dean; and in *Midcentury: A Novel of Our Time*, John Dos Passos (who would lose an eye and his wife in his own automobile accident) says, "There is nothing much deader than a dead motion picture actor," as he probes the cultural consequences of James Dean's

RIGHT Humphrey Bogart was the quintessential tough guy in movies of the 1940s and 1950s, appearing in many film noir classics such as The Enforcer *(1951). Sadly, his career was cut short by his untimely death from throat cancer in 1957.*

death at the wheel of his Porsche, wondering how the life of a remote, glamorized Hollywood star can have such a widespread popular cultural effect.

Nicholas Ray directed James Dean in *Rebel Without a Cause* (1955), and many of the other young actors in that film (Natalie Wood, Sal Mineo, and Nick Adams) died in their thirties or forties. In another Nicholas Ray film, *Knock on Any Door* (1949), John Derek's character, Nick Romano, expresses a commonly quoted philosophy—"Live fast, die young, and leave a good-looking corpse"—that could symbolize many Hollywood deaths. When he fell to the pavement outside Johnny Depp's The Viper Room nightclub in Los Angeles and allegedly said, "I'm gonna die, dude," it is not hard to imagine that River Phoenix looked pretty much the way he did throughout *My Own Private Idaho* (1991). But the car crash corpses of James Dean, Jayne Mansfield, or Françoise Dorléac (decapitated in an accident after filming 1966's *Cul-de-sac* with Roman Polanski) would certainly not meet that "good looking" esthetic criterion. Nor would an airplane death like Carole Lombard's (whose plane crashed into Table Rock Mountain outside Las Vegas in 1942).

ABOVE After James Dean's fatal car accident in September 1955, there was an explosion of media interest in the talented young actor.

LEFT Carole Lombard posed on the landing gear of a small airplane in 1935. Ironically, she died in a plane crash only seven years later.

FAR LEFT The Viper Room, a nightclub in West Hollywood, will forever be associated with the death of River Phoenix in 1993.

A Morbid or Motivating Interest?

Hollywood has long been the main focus insofar as entertainment and celebrity are concerned, and star deaths from Judy Garland to Christopher Reeve attract our attention because the same circuits of publicity that push far too much information about live movie stars at us continue the publicity after they die, especially if the life has been controversial and the death mysterious. Was Thelma Todd's death suicide or murder? Did Carole Landis really kill herself because of her dalliance with actor Rex Harrison? We might occasionally wonder whether all this media coverage promotes some sort of populist *Schadenfreude* principle, one that expects—even hopes for—celebrity success to be followed by a spectacular fall.

Do we need to separate what might be considered a morbid interest in Hollywood deaths from a continuing interest in celebrity deaths more generally, when film, television, and pop star deaths rub shoulders with the deaths of presidents (Abraham Lincoln and John F. Kennedy), civil rights leaders (Martin Luther King, Jr.), politicians (Robert Kennedy), pacifists (Gandhi), and princesses (Diana)? Or

is it the case that celebrity deaths from all arenas frequently perform a similar post-death function in the culture at large, generating other activities from fans or general mourners. The fact that a pop song (by Australian group T.I.S.M., short for "This is serious, Mum") could come out called "(He'll Never Be An) Ol' Man River" and contain a line like "I'm on the drug that killed River Phoenix" shows us what kind of era we now inhabit, a decidedly post-Dead Kennedys world. Marilyn Monroe dies, and her passing is immortalized

in documentaries, books, plays, and songs, one of which, "Candle in the Wind," is later tweaked by co-creator Elton John into a song that mourns the death of another blonde celebrity, Princess Diana.

However much in bad taste some of these acts of commemorative homage might seem, they testify to the survival of a spirit of communal creativity between the lost cult figure and surviving, bereft fans. Even those of us who see ourselves as standing a little apart from such things still benefit from the increase in the number of new cultural arti- facts (novels, plays, poems, videos, films, songs, paintings) that we can consume. Of course, trauma and tragedy have long proven key resources for *making* art, and for stories that are told *about* art. They provide, in a sense, guides to living—and dying. In genre terms, think of the Western, the combat film, action adventure, horror, tragic biopics, film noir, the hospital drama—lives lost poetically early on screen. Think *Spartacus* (1960), *Love Story* (1970), *My Life* (1993), *Titanic* (1997), *Saving Private Ryan* (1998), *Stepmom* (1998), or *Gladiator* (2000).

We get as many stories about the "real" people who perform in these dramas. Think of the clichés that have emerged to describe young people who become famous fast only to have their star fall from the sky at an early age—"flying too close to the sun," "it is better to burn out than it is to rust." These trite sayings are both warnings and entice- ments. They tell us about the fun and the peril to be had from a heady lifestyle, urging us to weigh the pluses and minuses for our own conduct. And they allow us to peek at the excesses of others without direct exposure to them. This is vicarious pleasure at its height, in addition to a kind of etiquette book that tells us about what we should and shouldn't do. It's fun and furtive at the same time that it's instructive and public.

LEFT Orange Marilyn, *a 1964 silkscreen painting by Andy Warhol based on a 1952 publicity still of Marilyn Monroe, was sold at a 1998 Sotheby's auction in New York for over $17 million.*

ABOVE Grace Kelly went from being an Oscar®-winning actress to a sophisticated mem- ber of a European royal family. Her death in 1982 was mourned not only by the people of Monaco, but also by her legion of film fans.

LEFT Comedian and actor John Belushi believed in living his young life to the full. Fame and partying went hand in hand, until a fatal drug overdose at the age of 33 put a stop to his wild ways.

The Big Sleep

Cancer … pneumonia … septicemia … cerebral hemorrhage.…Being a Hollywood celebrity does not make you immune to medical problems—and sometimes the stress of stardom can lead to the biggest sleep of all. A range of diseases has afflicted the Hollywood elite, from the age-old scourge of tuberculosis—which claimed the lives of Renée Adorée, Colin Clive, Vivien Leigh, and Mabel Normand—to the modern threat of HIV and AIDS, which played a major role in the death of Rock Hudson and Anthony Perkins, and may have hastened the demise of Michael Jeter and Robert Reed.

Cancers of all types have ravaged Hollywood stars over the years. Ovarian cancer has cut a swath through the females of Tinseltown, with Sandy Dennis, Diana Dors, Joan Hackett, Cassandra Harris, Madeline Kahn, Alice Pearce, and Gilda Radner succumbing to this disease. Lung cancer is another silent killer, taking out Betty Grable, Steve McQueen, Silvana Mangano, Agnes Moorehead, and Robert Taylor, among others.

Some performers never even made it into their teens before a fatal illness struck them down. Lawrence "Sunny" McKeen died of blood poisoning in 1933 at the age of eight, and 12-year-old Heather O'Rourke suffered a cardiopulmonary arrest in 1988.

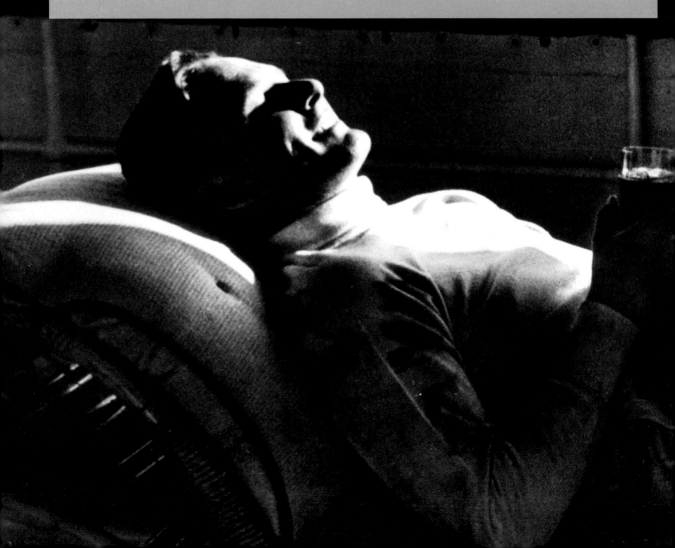

Renée Adorée

Born September 30, 1898
Died October 5, 1933

Renée Adorée was a French circus performer who became a beloved silent screen star before tragic illness wore her down. It is impossible to tell if Adorée's career would have survived the transition to sound, because by 1933, at the age of 35, she had passed away.

Born Jeanne de la Fonte in Lille, France, Adorée learned her trade in the circus with her parents from the age of five. By 12, she was a headline performer in the small, nomadic circuses in which her family traveled. Adorée later commented that in one season she appeared as a toe dancer, acrobat, equestrienne, and clown! Just after her 15th birthday she left the circus and joined a company of pantomimists on a tour of Europe. She gained the attention of movie producers while performing and emigrated to the United States in the great actor rush to establish a career in early film. At the time of her first movie appearance, Adorée spoke five languages but had never attended school.

In 1920, she was given the name Renée Adorée and performed in the film *The Strongest*. In the same year she met actor Tom Moore, 15 years her senior, on New Year's Eve in New York, and the two married six weeks later. They appeared in *Made in Heaven* in 1921, but the relationship did not last and she divorced Moore in 1924. Adorée would marry one more time—in 1925, to Sherman Gill, who would remain her husband until her death.

ABOVE Renée Adorée as Petra comforts Paul Ellis as Ramon in the 1924 drama-romance, The Bandolero, *directed by Tom Terriss.*

Adorée appeared in minor roles until 1922, when MGM placed her in *West of Chicago*, where she received second billing in the role of Della Moore. In *Daydreams* (1922), Adorée played opposite comic genius Buster Keaton as a young girl who reads letters by Keaton and fantasizes about the successful employment he's found. Adorée's character daydreams, and then with bitter juxtaposing irony we see the truth: she imagines he is a surgeon when he is really assisting a veterinarian; when she sees him "cleaning up" on Wall Street he is actually working as a janitor.

RIGHT Renée Adorée at a costume party thrown by actor Basil Rathbone in 1923. Adorée was a popular member of the early Hollywood community.

But it was Adorée's role as Melisande in King Vidor's melodrama *The Big Parade* (1925) that made her a star. During the tumultuous years of World War I, James Apperson, played by John Gilbert, befriends the tobacco-chewing Karl Dane while stationed in France. Apperson falls madly in love with Melisande but, tragically, must leave her to fight on the front lines. Adorée's sensuousness and penetrating eyes, as well as Gilbert's solid performance, found a large audience, making *The Big Parade*

MGM's most successful film until *Gone with the Wind* in 1939. The studio peddled the pair's star power, and Adorée and Gilbert starred in nine films together, including *La Boheme* (1926) and *The Cossacks* (1928).

When Hollywood moved to sound, many foreign stars were reduced to supporting work as comic relief and clichéd French maids. The transition to sound slowed Adorée's career but did not destroy it, her voice broadcasting well on the primitive recording devices of the early talkies. Adorée, like fellow foreign stars Olga Badanova, Paul Lukas, Greta Garbo, and Dolores del Rio, worked hard to learn English. Despite this, MGM did not renew Adorée's contract, so First National picked her up and gave her a memorable role as a struggling carnival manager in *The Spieler* (1928). Adorée's circus training certainly held her in good stead for this part.

During production of the 1930 film *Call of the Flesh* (also known as *The Singer of Seville*), Adorée, playing support to Ramon Novarro, developed a respiratory illness. Against the advice of her physicians, she continued working on the picture. Once shooting wrapped, Adorée was rushed to a sanitarium in Prescott, Arizona, where she lay flat on her back for two years in an effort to regain her health. Six months before her death Adorée was released from the sanitarium, thinking she had recovered sufficiently to attempt a screen comeback. Almost immediately, however, her health failed again, and she passed her time recuperating in the Tujunga Hills, California.

Renée Adorée died of tuberculosis five days after she turned 35, in Tujunga. Her funeral was held at 11:00 A.M. on Saturday, October 7, 1933, at the Hollywood Forever Cemetery. She is interred in a mausoleum in the Hollywood Cemetery Chapel, Abbey of the Psalms, #119, and her crypt is often decorated with her photograph. In 1939, archival footage of Renée Adorée was included in a celebration of the silents and transition to sound, *March of Time: The Movies Move On*. Besides Adorée, other luminaries of the silent screen such as Charlie Chaplin, Douglas Fairbanks, Mary Pickford, and Adorée's leading man, John Gilbert, were featured.

Adorée has a star on the Hollywood Boulevard Walk of Fame.

LEFT A studio assistant delivers fan mail to Renée Adorée during a break in filming. Her gentle beauty and vulnerability made her a favorite with audiences.

BELOW Glamorous Renée Adorée poses for a publicity shot taken a few months before her untimely death at the age of only 35.

Frank Albertson

Born February 2, 1909
Died February 29, 1964

While stars stole the limelight during Hollywood's golden era, the backbone of cinema performance was provided by the character actors. These were typecast performers who were immediately recognizable to audiences and saved scriptwriters unnecessary exposition. Frank Albertson was one such actor, shifting from leads to character roles in the 1930s. Few people remember character actors; Albertson is almost entirely forgotten and appears in next to no film histories and biographies. Yet he has given solid comic and dramatic performances in some of the best-loved films of the American cinema.

Frank Albertson was born in Fergus Falls, Minnesota. He entered the film industry in the humble position of prop boy in 1922 and made an uncredited appearance in *The Covered Wagon* (1923), but it wasn't until five years later that he achieved his first credited appearance in the comedy feature *Prep and Pep* (1928). Albertson's film work put him on a path that converged with many of the greatest directing talents working in Hollywood's Golden Age: John Ford, George Stevens, Frank Capra, Alfred Hitchcock, Fritz Lang, and Frank Borzage, to name just a few. In most of his roles he played the perennial juvenile, lighting up the screen with his youthful exuberance.

Albertson appeared in Paramount's semidocumentary combat film *Wake Island* (1942). He was also in *Alice Adams* (1935) as Katharine Hepburn's well-meaning but annoying brother, Walter Adams. He appeared in *Room Service* (1938) as the confused hayseed playwright, and in Frank Capra's *It's a Wonderful Life* (1946) as Sam Wainwright. He played opposite Joan Crawford in *The Shining Hour* (1938), and opposite Clark Gable in *The Hucksters* (1947). In Alfred Hitchcock's *Psycho* (1960), he was, quite simply, a plot device with a lecherous demeanor and a Texas accent. He played Tom Cassidy, the rich oil tycoon, who gives Lowery $40,000 to buy a house for his daughter's wedding present. Lowery asks Marion Crane to bank the money and so, inadvertently, begins Marion's fateful journey to the shower at the Bates Motel.

Frank Albertson's final screen appearance represents the contradiction of his career. He gave a standout performance as Sam, the mayor, in the Janet Leigh vehicle, *Bye Bye Birdie* (1963), yet the appearance was uncredited.

Frank Albertson died in 1964 in Santa Monica, California, ending a 40-year tenure in Hollywood. He is buried in Holy Cross Cemetery, Culver City, Los Angeles. His plot is Section P, Lot 284, Grave 4. He had well over 100 screen appearances to his name.

ABOVE During 1930, when this photograph was taken, Frank Albertson appeared in eight films, including The Big Party, Born Reckless, *and* Son of the Gods.

RIGHT Frank Albertson watches as adjustments are made to Lucille Ball's outfit before they film the next scene in the Marx Brothers' 1938 comedy, Room Service.

Agnes Ayres

Born April 4, 1898
Died December 25, 1940

ABOVE *Agnes Ayres in the arms of Rudolph Valentino in* The Sheik *(1921). Five years after this film was released, Valentino was dead after succumbing to peritonitis and septicemia.*

Agnes Ayres was born Agnes Eyre Hinkle (sometimes spelled Henkel) in Carbondale, a small town in Illinois. In the 1920s she became a popular star, especially with her performance in *The Sheik* (1921), but when the Hollywood executives tired of her, she retreated to obscurity and died alone.

In 1914, Ayres was noticed by a staff director at the local Essanay Studios, and she was placed in a crowd scene for three dollars a day. A year later, Vitagraph Pictures star Alice Joyce noted a resemblance between herself and Agnes Ayres, and Ayres was eventually cast in the role of Joyce's sister in *Richard the Brazen* (1917).

Paramount executive Jesse Lasky saw Ayres in 1920 and became enamored of her, giving her a starring role in a Civil War tale, *Held by the Enemy* (1920). Lasky then persuaded Cecil B. DeMille to give Ayres leading roles in several productions. Ayres played opposite Wallace Reid in four features, including *Clarence* (1922), but she became obsessed with Reid and engaged in long and frequent visits to the actor's home until his wife threatened to throw acid in Ayres's face.

Of course, Ayres's most famous role was Lady Diana Mayo, the terrified English heiress carried into actor Rudolph Valentino's desert tent in *The Sheik* (1921). Ayres's Lady Diana is described as "beautiful, unconventional, spurning love as a weakness," but Valentino immediately forces her to exchange her riding breeches for a dress and to rediscover her womanhood. Agnes Ayres played the sheik's wife in the sequel, *The Son of the Sheik* (1926).

In 1923, Ayres's romance with Lasky ended, and she stopped receiving the best scripts and having her choice of directors. Losing work in Hollywood, Ayres married Mexican diplomat Manuel Reachi in 1924, and they had a daughter in 1925, but the marriage faltered and they were divorced by 1927. Ayres's failing career should not have raised financial concerns because she invested carefully in real estate. However, she lost a lot of money in the stock market crash in 1929. Penniless, she was forced to play vaudeville, touring in one-night stands.

Ayres returned to Hollywood in 1936, but never again achieved star billing. Her final feature film appearance was an uncredited role in Henry Hathaway's *Souls at Sea* (1937). Ayres grew despondent and was committed to a mental hospital for emotional problems. Then in 1939, to make matters worse, Reachi, now a film producer, gained custody of their daughter. Ayres died, in total isolation, of a cerebral hemorrhage in her home in West Hollywood at the age of just 42.

Star Shot

Agnes Ayres and Gloria Swanson were great friends, and even shared the same dressing room when they both worked at Essanay Studios.

Lex Barker

Born　May 8, 1919
Died　May 11, 1973

Lex Barker, the tenth actor to play Edgar Rice Burroughs's Tarzan in Hollywood, was built like a Greek god. He was the perfect picture of health, right up until he suffered a heart attack on a New York street at the age of 54.

ABOVE His strapping physique guaranteed Lex Barker's status as a sex symbol. He is pictured riding an elephant for a charity function held in the late 1940s.

Barker came from a wealthy banking family; born Alexander Chrichlow Barker, Jr., he was a direct descendant of Roger Williams, the founder of Rhode Island. He served five years in the Army and was discharged as a major, earning three medals during his service.

Lex Barker's film debut was in *Doll Face* (1945), and the football and track athlete was soon discovered by Sol Lesser, who was looking for someone to play the famous character of Tarzan. This role had been filled by Olympic swimming star Johnny Weissmuller for the previous 17 years. Barker's first Tarzan movie was *Tarzan's Magic Fountain* (1949). *The New York Times* described Barker as "a streamlined apeman with a personable grin and a torso to make any lion cringe," but was less than favorable about the picture. Barker's other Tarzan films, such as *Tarzan and the Slave Girl* (1950) and *Tarzan's Peril* (1951), did not fare much better.

Barker had five marriages, including one to Lana Turner. Gossip columnists at the time reported Barker and Turner divorced after a fight in a parking lot, but later on Barker's gentlemanly image was forever tarnished. Turner's daughter, Cheryl Crane, revealed in an autobiography that Barker had raped her repeatedly. The abuse went on for three years before Turner found out and gave Barker 20 minutes to clear his things from her Beverly Hills home.

After his career as Tarzan ended, Barker made many westerns before heading for Europe in 1957. There he appeared in a number of motion pictures in Italy, France, and especially Germany, where he became a box office star. Barker even appeared in Federico Fellini's *La Dolce Vita* (1960), though by far his strangest film was *The Girl in the Kremlin* (1957). In this film, the plot features Stalin escaping death and secretly traveling to Greece, where he satisfies his desire for bald women.

On May 11, 1973, two women with whom Lex Barker had made a luncheon date became concerned when he did not appear. They reported their concerns to the East 67th Street Police Station in New York. Barker was found unconscious on Lexington Avenue near 61st Street about midday on May 11. He was taken to Lenox Hill Hospital, where he was pronounced dead.

Diana Barrymore

Born March 3, 1921
Died January 25, 1960

iana Barrymore started at the top and rapidly descended. Despite her pedigree, she fell victim to the Barrymore curse of excessive drinking and public scandal.

Diana Barrymore was the daughter of John Barrymore, the great Shakespearean actor, and Blanche Oelrichs Thomas, better known under her pen name of Michael Strange. Strange was going to name their daughter Joan Strange Blythe, but at the christening changed it to Diana.

As a teenager, Barrymore signed on for the part of Ann in the touring company of the play *Outward Bound*. Her father was ecstatic with her performance, stating that she was "the best thing I ever produced." This was a rare moment of interest from her father; the two Barrymores were often estranged, although he made sure to introduce her to the drink Brandy Alexander.

Universal executives were aware that she had an exploitable name, so a contract was rapidly negotiated giving the 20-year-old $1,000 a week for six months. Her fee was soon raised to $2,000 a week. But her sudden rise was bittersweet. While Diana attended the preview of her first credited film, *Eagle Squadron* (1942), on May 29, 1942, her father died.

After several below-par performances, Universal asked Barrymore to play a small part in an Abbott and Costello feature, but she refused, claiming it would cheapen the family name. Such

ABOVE Actress Diana Barrymore dances with her second husband, tennis player John R. Howard. The marriage lasted all of six months.

an attitude did not stop her from displaying her personal life with much-publicized debauchery. Universal placed Barrymore on suspension and later gave her only a secondary role in *Ladies Courageous* (1944). In early 1947, immediately after splitting with her first husband, Bramwell Fletcher, she flew to Boston to meet with tennis pro John R. Howard, and they were married on January 17, 1947. This marriage ended almost immediately with a drunken fight in Louisville, Kentucky. Universal dropped Barrymore. By the time she was 23, Barrymore's screen career was over. She received screen credits in only six films.

Barrymore finally reclaimed her life, co-writing an autobiography in 1957, *Too Much Too Soon*, with Gerold Frank, and soberly rehearsing and playing in *The Ivory Branch* for $30 a week. The final pages of her autobiography are filled with hope: "Perhaps I have begun to find my way."

A maid discovered Diana Barrymore's dead body in her second-floor rear apartment at 33 East 61st Street in New York City. Aged 38, she had died of heart failure brought on by a mixture of alcohol and sleeping pills.

Star Shot

Diana Barrymore was one of over 400 young hopefuls who auditioned for the role of Scarlett O'Hara in *Gone with the Wind* (1939). The part eventually went to Vivien Leigh.

LEFT Diana Barrymore in a 1945 promotional shot. Barrymore had a lifelong problem with alcohol and attended meetings at Alcoholics Anonymous for a time.

John Barrymore

Born February 14, 1882
Died May 29, 1942

By the time John Barrymore died in 1942, he had already killed his career through alcohol and womanizing. Barrymore had become more associated with tabloid gossip and theatrical self-parody than his masterful performances of Shakespearean heroes.

Barrymore was born in Philadelphia, the son of Georgie Drew and Maurice Blyth (who adopted the surname of Barrymore). His two siblings, Lionel and Ethel, also pursued successful careers in acting. By 1909, he was on Broadway with the comedy *The Fortune Hunter*. But it was Shakespeare that earned him critical and public adoration, especially his performance of *Hamlet* in 1922. While treading the boards, Barrymore pursued a successful screen career, starring most notably in *Dr. Jekyll and Mr. Hyde* (1920).

Once entrenched in Hollywood, Barrymore had his

ABOVE MGM's Grand Hotel *(1932) boasted a stellar cast. John Barrymore and Greta Garbo were supported by Joan Crawford and Wallace Beery.*

choice of any film script Warner Bros. could offer him. The coming of sound was a boon for the rising star with his deep baritone voice, and he appeared in many prestigious pictures such as Oscar®-winner *Grand Hotel* (1932) for MGM. However, Barrymore's personal life was a mixture of marriage, sudden divorce, and alcoholism. He was married four times, and his affairs and breakups were always tumultuous and well-publicized. As he grew older, the public grew less fond of his hell-raising ways.

In 1935, when Barrymore became smitten with Elaine Jacobs (her stage name was Elaine Barrie), the tabloid press had a field day reporting on their public quarrels and reconciliations.

Last Words

John Barrymore's last words are reputed to be: "I guess this is one time I miss my cue." However, his final word was simply "hello" to his brother when he came out of his coma.

RIGHT John (left) and Lionel Barrymore in 1932. The brothers appeared with their sister, Ethel, in only one film, Rasputin and the Empress *(1932).*

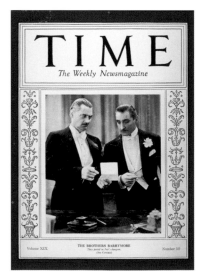

Eventually Barrymore, convinced the relationship was over, abandoned Jacobs and took the train from New York to California. A newspaper paid for Jacobs to pursue Barrymore across the country. All this had a huge impact on John Barrymore's public image: he was tarnished as an aging satyr.

Barrymore's life became even more tumultuous after his divorce from his third wife, Dolores Costello, and his marriage to Elaine Jacobs. He retreated to a sanitarium after an argument with his wife, and filed for bankruptcy early in 1937.

A period of calm followed, and Barrymore released the films *Bulldog Drummond Comes Back*, *Night Club Scandal*, *Bulldog Drummond's Revenge*, and *True Confession*, all in 1937. Because of his drinking, he had difficulty remembering lines and often

required dialogue to be written on a blackboard. In 1939, Barrymore gave an affecting performance in RKO's *The Great Man Votes*. He appeared to be recovering from his tarnished image, until he made a fateful decision that destroyed the last vestiges of his credibility.

Elaine Jacobs pressured the sickly Barrymore to star opposite her in the theater production *My Dear Children*, by all accounts a lightweight script. On opening night in 1939 Barrymore stuck to the script until he forgot his lines. When the prompt whispered his lines, he called out, "Just a little louder darling. I couldn't hear you." At the curtain call he was greeted with a five-minute ovation. This adoration continued to cloud his judgment, and he toured *My Dear Children* with occasional breaks until May 18, 1940. It was obvious the crowds did not come to see the great actor at the height of his prowess, but to watch the aging has-been unpredictably step out of proceedings and joke about his own personal life. This performance paved the way for film roles caricaturing himself in *The Great Profile* (1940), where he played Evans Garrick, an alcoholic Shakespearean actor, and, even more obviously in his final film, *Playmates* (1941), a lighthearted mix of big-band and Shakespeare, where he played the role "John Barrymore."

On May 19, 1942, John Barrymore was at a rehearsal on the Rudy Vallee radio program and uttered the line from *Romeo and Juliet*: "Soft! What light through yonder window breaks." This was the last line he spoke as an actor. He collapsed soon after and was rushed to Hollywood Presbyterian Hospital, where he was diagnosed with bronchial pneumonia and complications involving the liver and kidneys. A priest arrived, accompanied by a nurse, to administer the last rites. Barrymore was asked if he had anything to confess. Barrymore replied, "Yes, Father. I am guilty at this moment of having carnal thoughts."

The priest was shocked. "About whom?"

"About her." Barrymore pointed at the nurse.

On May 29, 1942, John Barrymore awoke momentarily to acknowledge his brother, Lionel, before lapsing into a coma. He was pronounced dead at 10:20 P.M.

Among the pallbearers at Barrymore's funeral on June 2, 1942, were Louis B. Mayer, David O. Selznick, and W. C. Fields. Like Tyrone Power's tombstone, Barrymore's crypt bears the inscription "Good night, sweet prince."

LEFT Errol Flynn played John Barrymore, pictured here in 1942, in the 1958 film Too Much Too Soon, *based on the 1957 autobiography by Barrymore's tragic daughter, Diana.*

BELOW John Barrymore appeared as Svengali in the 1931 motion picture of the same name. He liked to disguise his good looks with bizarre makeup and costumes.

James Baskett

Born February 16, 1904
Died September 9, 1948

Since Hattie McDaniel won the award for Best Actress in a Supporting Role for her portrayal of Scarlett O'Hara's loyal mammy in *Gone with the Wind* (1939), few African-American actors and actresses have won Oscars®. In the year of his death, James Baskett would become one of only two African-American actors in the history of the Oscars® to receive an honorary Academy Award®. Yet his achievement was not without controversy.

A leading African-American actor in New York, Baskett was cast as Gabby Gibson on the *Amos 'n' Andy* radio show before moving into B-grade movies. After appearing in films such as *Harlem is Heaven* (1932), *Policy Man* (1938), *Straight to Heaven* (1939), and *Revenge of the Zombies* (1943), Baskett answered an advertisement for a voice actor to play a butterfly in Disney's live-action and animated film, *Song of the South* (1946). Walt Disney was so taken with Baskett's voice that he cast him as the philosophical storyteller Uncle Remus, and Baskett was the first actor to be hired by Disney for a full-length, live-action feature.

Song of the South (1946) is set in the 1870s and deals with a troubled boy who comes to spend a summer with his grandmother on her plantation. There the boy meets Baskett's Uncle Remus, who comforts him with tales of Brer Rabbit, Brer Bear, and Brer Fox. The most famous sequence of the film features Uncle Remus singing the Oscar®-winning song "Zip-A-Dee-Doo-Dah" in a cheery woodland populated by animated animals.

James Baskett received an honorary Oscar® in recognition of his "able and heart-warming characterization of Uncle Remus, friend and storyteller to the children of the world," but African-American reaction to the award was anything but "Zip-A-Dee-Doo-Dah." An angry editorial in

ABOVE Ingrid Bergman presents James Baskett with his honorary Oscar® in 1947. Baskett could not attend the premiere of Song of the South *in Atlanta, Georgia, as no hotel would give the African-American actor a room for the night.*

the African-American magazine *Ebony* described the character of Uncle Remus as an "Uncle Tom-Aunt Jemima caricature complete with all the fawning standard equipment thereof: the toothy smile, battered hat, gray beard, and a profusion of 'dis' and 'dat' talk." Hedda Hopper, the film industry gossip columnist, attacked such critics, saying they think "that Negroes should play only doctors, lawyers, and scientists." Upon its release in 1946, *Song of the South* was picketed more heavily than any other film since *Birth of a Nation* (1914). Despite the controversy, the film was Disney's most successful that year.

Just two years after the release of *Song of the South*, James Baskett died at the age of 44 from heart problems on September 9, 1948 (some sources say July 9, 1948). He was buried in Crown Hill Cemetery in Indianapolis, Indiana.

Warner Baxter

Born March 29, 1889
Died May 7, 1951

RIGHT Handsome Warner Baxter in 1945. His last motion picture role was as Roger Manners in State Penitentiary *(1950).*

BELOW Warner Baxter with co-star Myrna Loy in Frank Capra's 1934 horse-racing comedy, Broadway Bill. *Baxter was once reported as being afraid of horses.*

Jim Tully in *Picturegoer Magazine*, 1936, described Warner Baxter as "a Valentino without a horse. He is the chap the lonely woman on the prairie sees when she looks at the men's ready-to-wear pages in the latest mail-order catalogue." This sums up Baxter's dependability and unostentatious star quality. Baxter is hardly remembered nowadays, but during the silent and early sound era he was a matinee idol who always gave solid performances when he had good material to work with.

Baxter's early life was not easy. His father died when he was five months old. In 1905, the family moved to San Francisco just in time for the 1906 earthquake, which destroyed all their possessions. At a young age, Baxter revealed a fascination for show business: "I discovered a boy a block away who would eat worms and swallow flies for a penny. For one-third of the profits, I exhibited him in a tent." Baxter's mother did not encourage his theatrical aspirations, but his tenacity won the day.

Warner Baxter played the leading man in many silent films, including opposite Clara Bow in *The Runaway* (1926), but his springboard to fame was on the back of actor Raoul Walsh's misfortune. Walsh was in line to direct and star as the Cisco Kid in one of the first talkie westerns, *In Old Arizona* (1928). When Walsh was involved in an accident and lost an eye, the studio desperately sought a replacement. After dozens of actors tested for the part of the Cisco Kid, Baxter got the role. Baxter's exuberant acting won him the Best Actor Academy Award®.

With *I'll Give a Million* (1938), Warner Baxter's career as a star was at an end. He was absent from the screen in 1942 when Fox dropped his contract and he suffered a nervous breakdown. He spent the rest of his career in B-grade pictures for Columbia, and during this time played Dr. Robert Ordway in the *Crime Doctor* series. Baxter spent his last years in Malibu, where he was active in civic affairs. He had suffered from arthritis for years, which made eating difficult and led to malnutrition. He died from bronchial pneumonia.

Baxter and his second wife, Winifred Bryson, had celebrated their 33rd wedding anniversary in January 1951, just months before he died. Baxter is interred at Forest Lawn Memorial Park, Glendale, California, in the Gardens of Memory where Mary Pickford, Sam Wood, and Humphrey Bogart were also laid to rest.

William Bendix

Born January 14, 1906
Died December 14, 1964

RIGHT William Bendix (middle) with Alan Ladd, during the filming of China *(1943). Bendix guest starred in the television shows* Burke's Law *and* Mr. Ed.

William Bendix was one of the great character actors of the 1940s. He was usually cast as a brutish yet soulful, inarticulate thug, in a film career that took him to every studio. But Bendix is best remembered for his radio and television performances as the crisis-prone lug, Chester A. Riley.

Bendix generally played supporting parts that allowed other film stars to shine, but he achieved fame with several roles. He earned himself an Oscar® nomination for the role of Private Randall in Paramount's semidocumentary combat film, *Wake Island* (1942). However, it was his role in the film *The Hairy Ape* (1944), based on Eugene O'Neill's play, that made him famous. In *The Hairy Ape,* he plays steamship stoker Hank Smith, Brooklyn's reincarnation of Neanderthal man, obsessively trying to find "someplace in the world I belong." In the same year, Bendix played another moving role— Gus Smith, the seaman whose leg is amputated in Alfred Hitchcock's *Lifeboat* (1944).

However, Bendix is best remembered as Chester A. Riley, the everyman who deals with crises of his own making with the catchphrase "what a revoltin' development dis is." Bendix became Riley on radio in 1944, and in the 1950s Bendix so impressed Howard Hughes that he succeeded Jackie Gleason in *The Life of Riley* on television. Bendix played Riley for eight seasons and 217 segments, giving him more national recognition than his film roles ever did.

William Bendix's career declined after *The Life of Riley*. A proposed television series in 1964, *Bill and Martha*, was canceled, and Bendix sued both CBS and its president, James T. Aubrey, for $2,658,000, maintaining he was capable of completing his work and was not, as the network insisted, in poor health.

Bendix's last two films were both B-grade westerns: *Law of the Lawless* (1964) and *Young Fury* (1965), which was released posthumously. On December 8, 1964, he experienced yet another "revoltin' development" when he was taken to the hospital suffering from lobar pneumonia. He died on December 14 and was buried on the grounds of San Fernando Mission Cemetery, Mission Hills, California. Bendix had been married to his wife, Theresa, for 37 years and had two daughters, Lorraine and Stephanie. In an interview in 1960, William Bendix summed up his life: "I've had a long, varied, pleasant, eventful career. I don't hate anybody and I don't have any bitter thoughts. I started out without any advantages, but I've been lucky and successful and I've had fun."

Star Shot

As a teenager, William Bendix was a batboy for the New York Yankees and knew Babe Ruth. Bendix later played the great baseballer in *The Babe Ruth Story* (1948).

LEFT As Reuben "Wahoo" Jones in Streets of Laredo *(1949). William Bendix had a fascinating heritage: he was a descendant of famous German composer Felix Mendelssohn (1809–1847).*

Constance Bennett

Born October 22, 1904
Died July 24, 1965

With the coming of sound, screen actresses were no longer only mesmerizing visions but were defined by the lilt, register, and style of their voices. Constance Bennett had a voice that purred intrigue, and fans considered her the last word in sophistication. Despite her intelligence, the studio still sold Bennett as a clothes horse. She quipped: "I'm a lot more sartorial than thespian. They come to see me and go out humming the costumes."

Unlike most stars of her time, Bennett had no background on stage. Instead, the young society debutante appeared in bit parts on screen before meeting producer Samuel Goldwyn at an Equity Ball in 1922. He suggested she test for a featured role in *Cytherea* (1924). While Bennett specialized in sob-and-sex stories, she is remembered best as a light comedienne, especially in *Topper* (1937), with Cary Grant, and *Merrily We Live* (1938). Constance Bennett became famous as the highest paid actress in Hollywood after agent Myron Selznick brokered her a deal of $30,000 a week to star in *Bought* (1931) at Warner Bros. For *Two Against the World* (1932), her salary broke records again, this time reaching $150,000 for four-and-a-half weeks' work.

Because Bennett was independent and outspoken, the press often attacked her luxurious lifestyle. An article in a film magazine reported that Bennett spent a quarter of a million dollars on her wardrobe in one year. She flatly denied this, saying she would have to buy diamond-studded dresses and emerald-trimmed kimonos to waste money so foolishly. She was no stranger to lawsuits, fighting in court with Willy Pogany, a painter she commissioned to do her portrait. She refused to pay him, complaining that he had made her waist and thighs too thick. Bennett's last film appearance, still looking stylishly chic, was in *Madame X* (1966), as Lana Turner's mother. It was her 56th film.

Constance Bennett died in 1965 of a cerebral hemorrhage. Her husband, Colonel (later Brigadier General) John Theron Coulter, was present. As a colonel's wife, and because of her organization of stage shows entertaining occupying forces in Europe during the Berlin Airlift, she was buried in Arlington National Cemetery in Virginia. Until her death, she remained slim and did not change her long blonde hairdo or abandon her gold cigarette holder, both of which were her trademarks. More importantly, she steadfastly challenged Hollywood traditions with her irreverent wit until the very end.

ABOVE Constance Bennett is embraced by co-star Clark Gable in After Office Hours *(1935). In 1940, Bennett made her stage debut in Noel Coward's play,* Easy Virtue.

Humphrey Bogart

Born December 25, 1899
Died January 14, 1957

RIGHT Humphrey Bogart loved boating. His yacht was called Santana, which was also the name of the yacht in his 1948 film, Key Largo.

BELOW A scene from The Barefoot Contessa (1954), in which Humphrey Bogart plays a film director who casts Ava Gardner in his next movie.

One of the true greats, Humphrey Bogart was blamed for establishing gambling, alcohol, and tobacco as the true accouterments of the rugged antihero after his role in the classic film noir *Casablanca* (1942). As café owner Rick Blaine, Humphrey DeForest Bogart nursed a Scotch as he plaintively muttered, "You played it for her, so you can play it for me. If she can take it, I can. Play it Sam, play 'As Time Goes By.'" That one line summarized Bogie's screen persona: alone, depressed, but free.

Prior to *Casablanca* (1942), Humphrey Bogart drifted in the bit-player Hollywood wilderness after signing a contract with Fox in 1930. He was shuttled into an assortment of films as studios attempted to predict cycles of fickle audience interest. Bogart established his tough-guy credentials playing a district attorney opposite Bette Davis in *Marked Woman* (1937). Goldwyn borrowed him from Warners to play antagonist "Baby Face" Martin in the prestigious motion picture, *Dead End* (1937), from a screenplay by Lillian Hellman. It was a huge success, earning $1.4 million at the box office, and it garnered the actor some much-needed exposure. He was then shunted into the social-problem film *Black Legion* (1937), playing an embittered factory worker who joins the Ku Klux Klan. In 1939, monster movies were big, and Bogart received the eponymous role of *The Return of Doctor X*. Bogie played a doctor who is electrocuted, but then keeps himself alive as a vampire zombie by sucking blood from others.

Bogart shot to stardom in the 1940s, playing a string of redeemed antiheroes in *High Sierra* (1941); *Sahara* (1943), a huge hit that made $2.3 million at the box office; and *Passage to Marseille* (1944). He also created timeless classics like John Huston's films *The Maltese Falcon* (1941) and *The Treasure of the Sierra Madre* (1948). In the taut economical thriller *To Have And Have Not* (1944), Bogart's sheer chemistry with his 19-year-old co-star Lauren Bacall sparked rumors that his marriage to third wife Mayo Methot was on the rocks. It was. On May 10, 1945, Bogart divorced Methot, and on May 21, he married Bacall, dubbed "The Look" by gossip columnists.

Warners reteamed the famous couple in Howard Hawks's *The Big Sleep* (1946), in which Bogart portrayed Raymond Chandler's hardboiled private investigator, Philip Marlowe. New scenes were shot and the film was recut to focus on the sparks between Mr. and Mrs. Bogart, including the notoriously euphemism-laden racehorse conversation. "I like to be ridden," purrs the sultry Bacall.

Bogart was in the Top 10 Distributors' moneymakers for almost an entire decade (1943–1949), then again in 1955. The 1950s were a relatively slow period for Bogart, who was inextricably linked with 1940s wartime movies. Jack Warner released him from his studio contract in 1950, while Ronald Reagan was kept on. Bogart finally won a Best Actor Oscar® for his role as crusty boatman Charlie Allnut opposite Katharine Hepburn in *The African Queen* (1951). Again, John Huston directed. Bogart's role as the unstable Captain Queeg in *The Caine Mutiny* (1954) reinvigorated his career briefly, but he would die just three years later. His final role was in the boxing film *The Harder They Fall* (1956).

During the last two years of his life, Bogart was increasingly on the defensive with the gutter press about the condition of his health. At one point he jumped on the phone to one columnist and yelled, "Do I sound as if I'm fighting for my life? God damn it, don't you check your stories? You just allow that bitch to print anything!"

But a biopsy came back positive—he had malignant cells in the esophagus, or throat cancer. Bogart immediately switched to filtered cigarettes. In the hospital, he gave the press typically boisterous sound bites like: "It's a respectable disease, nothing to be ashamed of, like something I *might* have had." Rumors abounded that he called for Scotch, a portable chess set, and newspapers.

Bacall recalls that she spent Bogart's last night of consciousness sleeping on the bed next to him in their home. He scratched at his chest in his sleep, twitched, and rolled around. Bacall thought she smelled medication and disinfectant, then realized that it was decay. Bogart had been married to Bacall for almost 12 years when he finally slipped into a coma and died on January 14, 1957. To this day he is survived by the venerable Lauren Bacall, who is still making motion pictures.

Bogart has a star on the Hollywood Walk of Fame at 6322 Hollywood Boulevard. His hand and footprints are immortalized on the forecourt to Grauman's Chinese Theatre in Los Angeles. In 1999, the American Film Institute paid tribute to Bogart's screen immortality when they modestly named him the Greatest Male Star of All Time.

ABOVE Humphrey Bogart with the love of his life, model turned actress Lauren Bacall. Bacall is the mother of Bogart's only children, his son, Stephen, and daughter, Leslie.

Last Words

"Goodbye kid. Hurry back."

LEFT One of the best-loved movies of all time, The African Queen *(1951) teamed Humphrey Bogart with screen legend Katharine Hepburn.*

Ward Bond

Born April 9, 1903
Died November 5, 1960

Ward Bond played the trustworthy and grizzled companion to John Wayne, both on and off screen, for three decades. From Bond's first appearance with the Duke in John Ford's *Salute* (1929), Bond, Wayne, and Ford remained inseparable, drinking and creating films together until Bond's untimely death from a massive heart attack. Among the trio's many collaborations are *The Long Voyage Home* (1940), *They Were Expendable* (1945), *The Quiet Man* (1952), and *The Searchers* (1956).

Bond was a student at the University of Southern California, where he played on the university football team alongside "Duke" Morrison, who would become known as John Wayne. Originally, Wayne did not want to be teamed with Bond because he perceived Bond to be too ugly for movies. Ford insisted, and soon Wayne and Bond became close friends. Ironically, Ward was singled out for his performance in *Salute* (1929), while no one noticed John Wayne's brief appearance. Before long, Wayne became a star in John Ford's *Stagecoach* (1939), and Bond became a key member of Wayne's Stock Company Players. Bond was considered one of filmdom's most reliable supporting players.

ABOVE Ward Bond appeared in some of Hollywood's greatest films, including The Maltese Falcon *(1941) and* It's A Wonderful Life *(1946).*

The early 1950s were not kind to Bond, after his strident anti-Communist affiliation with the Un-American Activities Committee. But the television series *Wagon Train* (1957–61) saw Bond shift finally from character actor to star, playing Major Seth Adams. This transformation exacted a toll as Bond became involved in casting and editing the show, while smoking, drinking, and eating excessively. According to fellow character actor Harry Carey, Jr., Bond popped "amphetamines as if they were candy" to control his ballooning weight.

Bond spent his last day in Dallas, Texas, discussing Communist plots and John F. Kennedy with conservative millionaire Clint Murchison. When he returned to his room at the Baker Hotel, he suffered a heart attack. Bond's wife, Mary Louise, called Wayne from Dallas, and he immediately flew there to accompany the body home and deliver the eulogy at Bond's funeral. John Wayne also attended the scattering of Bond's ashes into the Catalina Channel, an act stipulated in Bond's will because "I loved lobster all my life, and I want to return the favor."

Star Shot

On November 5, 1960, Ward Bond was due to meet singer Johnny Horton, to offer him a role on *Wagon Train*. Horton was killed in a car accident early that morning, and Bond died later that day.

On the night of November 23, 1960, a particularly poignant episode of *Wagon Train* aired. Bond had persuaded Wayne to appear on the show as General William Tecumseh Sherman and even convinced Ford to direct. It was the last time the three would work together.

RIGHT Ward Bond (left) appeared with veteran character actor Charley Grapewin and a very young Gene Tierney in the 1941 comedy, Tobacco Road.

Olive Borden

Born July 14, 1907
Died October 1, 1947

O live Borden was one of Mack Sennett's bathing beauties by the age of 15, and earned $1,500 a week at the height of her career in 1926, but a fateful decision led this star to a life of uncertainty and poverty.

Born Sybil Tinkle in Richmond, Virginia, and educated in the Baltimore convents, Borden's career quickly took off when she appeared in several Hal Roach comedies. Her rising star took her to just about every major studio in Hollywood in the early 1920s. Tom Mix, the silent screen cowboy, asked her to work for Fox as a leading lady in *My Own Pal* (1926) and *The Yankee Señor* (1926). She continued to work for Fox in *Pajamas* (1927), *Come to My House* (1927), and *Gang War* (1928), until she refused to take a salary cut from Fox and left the studio in 1928. She then made four pictures for Columbia, *Wedding Rings* (1929) for First National, and she was listed as one of RKO's favorite actresses.

Endowed with jet black hair and dark brown eyes, Borden was said to have the most perfect figure in Hollywood. In February 1928, *Motion Picture Magazine* described Borden thus: "Having the longest and blackest locks in Hollywood, it's only natural that Olive Borden should go violently gypsy every so often. She could play Lady Godiva and still look respectable. She divides herself impartially between Boudoir and Wilderness roles, both of which call for a slight disorder in the dress. If you've seen the delectable Olive, you know why."

Later in life, Borden fell on hard times. Her final appearance was in *Chloe, Love Is Calling You* (1934). She disappeared from Hollywood in the late 1930s and joined the WACs in 1943. After her discharge, she attempted to re-ignite her failing career but had no luck. "Since I've got out of the Army I've gone from job to job; something always goes wrong," she once said in an interview.

Borden spent the remaining years of her life on skid row in Los Angeles, scrubbing floors at the Sunshine Mission, a home for destitute women, and helping out in stage pageants. In 1947, she was found in a cheap hotel seriously ill from a stomach ailment and died at the age of 40. Among her possessions was a glossy 3 by 5 inch (7.6 by 12.7 cm) photograph of herself, signed in white ink: "Sincerely, Olive Borden."

ABOVE *Beautiful Olive Borden in 1927, at the height of her fame. Borden is thought to have been married twice, to John Moeller and Theodore Spector.*

Clara Bow

Born July 29, 1905
Died September 27, 1965

Clara Bow entranced audiences by introducing a new level of honesty into screen performance. She was the original "It" girl, the irrepressible flapper who embraced her freedom—yet Bow was anything but free. Her past haunted her, and the Hollywood machinery that allowed young women little range in their film roles exploited her. Bow's story, however, is one of survival, not death.

Bow's childhood was a nightmare. Born to Robert Bow, a sexually abusive father, and the mentally ill Sarah Bow, she lived in abject poverty in Brooklyn's tenements. In one interview, Bow said shortly: "We just lived, and that's about all." Bow saw her grandfather die from a heart attack while he played with her on a swing, witnessed one of her few friends burn to death, and was threatened at night by her mother wielding a kitchen knife—an event that undoubtedly led to her chronic insomnia.

To survive, Bow embraced the moving pictures. She would watch films and mimic stars like Mary Pickford in front of her mirror. In 1921, the 16-year-old won The Fame and Fortune Contest sponsored by *Motion Picture Magazine*, *Motion Picture Classic Magazine*, and *Shadowland Magazine*. The prize was a small part in the 1922 feature *Beyond the Rainbow*, though she was cut from the initial print.

In Hollywood, the rising producer B. P. Schulberg exploited Bow economically and sexually. Bow was grateful to be working in motion pictures and would constantly give more vivaciousness and charm than most of her films deserved. One highlight of her career was starring in the first Best Picture Oscar®-winner, *Wings*, in 1927.

ABOVE Clara Bow could express emotions on request. She claimed that in order to cry, she only had to think about her childhood.

RIGHT With Rex Bell. Clara Bow once said, "All the time the flapper is laughin' and dancin', there's a feeling of tragedy underneath."

Men were mesmerized by Bow's overt sexuality, and women tried to mimic Bow's fashion. In 1927, B. P. Schulberg, never one to miss a marketing opportunity, consolidated Bow's talents and the public's tastes with the film *It*. The movie featured the popular romance novelist and chief proponent of "It," Elinor Glyn, discussing what exactly "It" was: "that quality possessed by some which draws all others with its magnetic force….The possession of 'it' must be absolutely un-self-conscious and must have the magnetic 'sex appeal' which is irresistible." Bow had "It" in spades, and it became her undoing.

The same honesty found in her performances colored her public demeanor, so she was incapable of censoring herself. She was involved in affairs, or "engagements" as she called them, with Victor Fleming, Bela Lugosi, Gary Cooper, and Gilbert Roland.

Whenever the pressure got too much, she would have a nervous breakdown, retreating to the privacy of her bedroom.

It wasn't long before Hollywood and the majority of the press turned on Bow. A series about Clara Bow in the *Coast Reporter* had one issue conclude by advising: "You know Clara, you'd be better off killing yourself." In one year Bow faced three major scandals featuring her "engagements" with men, gambling, and tax evasion. These scandals came to a head in 1931 when Clara Bow's former secretary, close friend, and confidante, Daisy DeVoe, tried to blackmail her. Bow sued DeVoe for embezzlement, and in retaliation Daisy DeVoe announced in great detail every vice her former employer was engaging in.

Hounded by the tabloids and abandoned by Paramount, Bow concentrated on her screen career. But she was forever typecast as the "It" girl: innocent and seductive, shamelessly hunting for a man. Tired of scandal, Bow sought protection elsewhere. She married cowboy actor Rex Bell in 1931 and decided to isolate herself from the public eye. She had two sons, Rex Jr. (in 1934) and George (in 1938), but she finally fell victim to the mental illness that had plagued her mother and grandmother. She spent the rest of her life in and out of sanitariums.

When Bell became Lieutenant Governor of Nevada in 1954, Bow retreated from even family life and lived her final 11 years in near total seclusion. She lived in a Culver City bungalow and did not emerge until Bell died from a heart attack in 1962 while he was chasing the governorship of Nevada. Because Clara Bow believed that public exposure was synonymous with humiliation, she did not attend Bell's funeral in Las Vegas. However, she did attend a second service in Los Angeles. It was her first public appearance in 15 years.

Bow became convinced that she was near the end. She made preparations for her departure in infinite detail. She collected photographs, newspaper clippings, and fan mail for her sons. She meticulously considered her funeral service: the clergyman, the pallbearers, the lining of the casket, and even her hair and makeup.

On September 26, 1965, Bow was watching a late-night telecast of *The Virginians* on television when she passed away sometime during the night. Despite her horrific childhood, her difficult career, and her mental illness, Clara Bow did not succumb to suicide, but to heart disease. The impression she left on film and society in the 1920s is remembered even today. She is considered cinema's first sex symbol.

Star Shot

Between the time of her marriage and the birth of her first son, Clara Bow made two films—*Call Her Savage* (1932) and *Hoop-La* (1933), her last film. Bow made enough money from them to retire.

ABOVE A silver-screen luminary, Clara Bow was the first actress to openly revel in her sexuality. As well as "The 'It' Girl," she was also known as "The Brooklyn Bonfire."

Stephen Boyd

Born July 4, 1928
Died June 2, 1977

ABOVE The Big Gamble (1961), which was filmed on location in Ireland, teamed Stephen Boyd with the stunning French actress Juliette Gréco.

RIGHT Stephen Boyd (right) with Hope Lange and Brian Aherne in The Best of Everything (1959). The film also featured Joan Crawford and Louis Jourdan.

Stephen Boyd was a supporting actor in several historical epics including *The Fall of the Roman Empire* (1964) and *The Bible* (1966), but is best remembered as the vicious Messala chariot-racing against Charlton Heston in *Ben-Hur* (1959). Boyd always had a predisposition for roles in fantasy and adventure films but, after the lucrative 1960s, his career rapidly descended into playing parts in foreign horror productions and other forgettable films.

Stephen Boyd was born William Millar in Glengormley, Northern Ireland. The youngest of nine children of James and Martha Millar, Boyd's mother nicknamed him "Poison," because she'd been carrying poison in her stomach when he was born. He adopted his mother's maiden name of Boyd when he left school to embark on a professional acting career.

Stephen Boyd's acting success was a long time coming. By 1950, after garnering acting and radio work in Ireland, Boyd was in England working as a cafeteria attendant and doorman at a London cinema. He nearly died of influenza during the deadly London fog of 1952, but fortune finally smiled on the desperate young actor when thespian Sir Michael Redgrave introduced him to the director of the Windsor English Repertory Company.

After a few small roles in British films, such as *An Alligator Named Daisy* (1955), Boyd won a seven-year contract with 20th Century Fox. His first role for them was as the Irish spy in *The Man Who Never Was* (1956); Hollywood stalwart director William Wyler was so impressed by Boyd that he asked 20th Century Fox to lend him out. Wyler cast him in the role of Messala in *Ben-Hur* (1959), opposite Charlton Heston.

Filming *Ben-Hur* was not easy for Boyd, as he was brought in late in the production. To contrast with Heston's blue eyes, Boyd had to

LEFT With actors Stuart Whitman (left), Fabian (center), and Hope Lange. In early 1960, Stephen Boyd was the subject of a This Is Your Life special.

wear contact lenses to tint his eyes brown, and he could see only straight ahead through tiny peepholes. This compounded the difficulty of learning to drive a team of Yugoslavian black horses for the famous chariot-race scene. Several times the horses bolted, once crashing Boyd through a high wall.

To make matters worse, Boyd's armor was made of heavy steel and became so hot under the sizzling Italian sun that wardrobe assistants had to wear gloves just to remove it. After shooting Messala's death scene, it took three men three hours to strip off the rubber adhesive and red goo, Boyd's skin often coming with it.

Writer Gore Vidal concocted a backstory of a homosexual affair between Messala and Ben-Hur, and in typical Vidalian fashion he told Boyd but kept the homophobic Heston in the dark. Boyd injected shared looks between the two characters, charged with erotic devotion, and was honored with a Golden Globe® for Best Performance by an Actor in a Supporting Role.

We can only hypothesize how Stephen Boyd's career would have progressed had he consolidated his performance in *Ben-Hur* (1959) with the role of Marc Antony in *Cleopatra* (1963), but Boyd was one of several victims of the most disastrous production in history. Shooting originally began in England and Boyd was announced as the male lead, while Peter Finch landed the part of Julius Caesar. When Elizabeth Taylor contracted pneumonia, production was halted and the two male leads, honoring prior commitments, pulled out. Richard Burton replaced Boyd as Marc Antony, the role that would lead to Burton and Taylor's tumultuous and much-publicized affair.

In the 1960s, Boyd appeared in other historical features, including *The Fall of the Roman Empire* (1964) and *Genghis Khan* (1965), but his performances suffered when he shifted away from epics. He had the dubious honor of starring in *The Oscar* (1966)—one of the worst inside-Hollywood films ever to be made—as Frankie Fane, a big-mouthed yet irresistibly charming actor. Fane destroys everyone in his effort to gain the golden statuette.

By the 1970s, Boyd's career had fallen away after a succession of poor roles, such as Brad Killian in Romain Gary's *Kill! Kill! Kill! Kill!* (1971), opposite James Mason and Gary's wife, Jean Seberg. In this truly awful thriller, Stephen Boyd catatonically interrogates Seberg by swinging her around and around under some gelled lights. He followed this with *Evil in the Deep* (1976) and *Lady Dracula* (1978), while appearing in a series of West German horror films.

Boyd was married twice. In 1958 he tied the knot with an MCA executive, Mariella di Sarzana, but the marriage only lasted 24 days. His second wife was Elizabeth Mills, a secretary at the British Arts Council whom he had met in 1955. Mills supported Boyd throughout his career, following him to the United States in the late 1950s and becoming his personal assistant and secretary. Their marriage took place less than a year before Boyd's death.

Stephen Boyd died of a heart attack while playing golf with Mills at the Porter Valley country club. His grave is located at Oakwood Memorial Park in Chatsworth, California.

Star Shot

Stephen Boyd was nominated for a Golden Globe® for Actor in a Leading Role (Musical or Comedy) for the 1962 film *Billy Rose's Jumbo*, Busby Berkeley's last film project.

BELOW Stephen Boyd had a guest role in an episode of the popular show Hawaii Five-O, *but died before it was shown on television.*

Alice Brady

Born November 2, 1892
Died October 28, 1939

Alice Brady rose to stardom during the silent period of film history before disappearing from the screen in 1923. She returned to Hollywood to become one of the best-loved comediennes of the 1930s before her early death from cancer during the production of *Young Mr. Lincoln* (1939).

Alice Brady was the daughter of William A. Brady, the Director-General of the World Film Corporation. The appealing and enchanting brunette made her screen debut in her father's production, *As Ye Sow* (1914), and quickly became the romantic lead in features.

The shooting of silent films could be a pleasant process. Sideline musicians would play music to inspire the cast; Alice Brady preferred pieces from the opera *Madame Butterfly*. Yet filming could also be an extremely dangerous process when, in an effort to capture exciting realism, film sets were doused with kerosene, set alight, and the actor was told to escape. Alice Brady was caught in one such conflagration, shooting a scene from *Maternity* (1917): "I lost a big bunch of hair from the very top of my head, together with a part of one eyebrow, the sleeve and shoulder of the waist I wore, and about a third of my skirt."

Alice Brady was one of many top-billed stars, earning $5,000 a week, when she quit films in 1923 to appear on the stage. Ten years later, when she reappeared on screen, she no longer played heroines, but her career didn't wane. Brady is remembered as one of the finest comediennes of the time, playing zany characters with a gift for malapropisms. Her first talkie was *When Ladies Meet* (1933), before playing imperious Aunt Hortense in *The Gay Divorcee* (1934) opposite Fred Astaire and Ginger Rogers. With comic perfection she delivered lines such as: "You know, you're beginning to fascinate me, and I resent that in any man."

Alice Brady played comedy until the end of her career, when she created the dramatic role of Molly O'Leary in *In Old Chicago* (1937), winning an Academy Award® for Best Actress in a Supporting Role. At the same time she learned she had terminal cancer. Her last role was opposite Henry Fonda in John Ford's *Young Mr. Lincoln* (1939), playing old, widowed Abigail Clay. Screenwriter DeWitt Bodeen described her trial scene as "one of the profoundest manifestations of humanity's frightened bafflement before an inexplicable universe ever recorded by the camera."

Alice Brady died in New York City, before the release of *Young Mr. Lincoln*. She was five days shy of her 47th birthday.

ABOVE Before becoming a Hollywood actress, Alice Brady had considered an operatic career—she sang in a number of Gilbert and Sullivan operettas.

Star Shot

Alice Brady never received her Oscar® for *In Old Chicago* (1937). She was at home with a broken ankle, so a well-dressed man accepted the award for her. He and the statuette were never seen again.

RIGHT Alice Brady (left) has something to say to Anita Louise in Lady Tubbs *(also known as* The Gay Lady*). Brady played the title role in the 1935 comedy.*

Geraldine Brooks

Born October 29, 1925
Died June 19, 1977

Geraldine Brooks was one of many actresses who rose to fame in the 1940s with Warner Bros. Brooks was mismanaged and constantly typecast as the "troubled daughter," despite her obvious range.

Brooks began taking dancing lessons when she was two years old. Brooks's father, James Stroock, the owner of Brooks Costume Company, gave Brooks a five percent royalty interest in the successful Broadway musical *Oklahoma!*, allowing Brooks the financial freedom to study and look for acting jobs.

Warner Bros. offered her a contract to play Julie Demarest, the hysterical niece who commits suicide in *Cry Wolf* (1947), starring opposite Barbara Stanwyck and Errol Flynn. Brooks did not enjoy the experience: "Barbara Stanwyck was cold as ice. Throughout the whole film, she treated me as though I were a piece of the furniture.... Errol Flynn worked beautifully in the morning, but in the afternoon he was pretty drunk and stumbled over his lines.... He once told me, 'I have to—they expect me to.'" Brooks was rewarded for her pains with $850 a week, despite the average starting wage being only $75 to $100 a week.

After receiving disappointing roles in lamentable films (the lowest point of her career was MGM's *Challenge to Lassie* in 1949), Brooks moved to Italy where she made *Ho Sognato Il Paradiso* (1949), which was released in the United States as *Streets of Sorrow.* Following *Ho Sognato Il Paradiso,* she made *Vulcano* (1950) with director William Dieterle. After appearing in *The Green Glove* (1952) with Glenn Ford, she returned to the United States but appeared rarely in films, spending most of her time on live and recorded television. Geraldine Brooks is probably best remembered for her role as E. G. Marshall's romantic interest in *The Defenders* and her appearance on the last episode of *The Fugitive,* which aired on February 21, 1967.

Brooks's life and interests were eclectic. After the Watts riots of 1965, Brooks and second husband Budd Schulberg, the writer of *On the Waterfront* (1954), established a writers' workshop for underprivileged African-Americans. In 1975, she published a book of bird photographs with accompanying essays by Schulberg. Her final screen appearance was in *Mr. Ricco* (1975), opposite Dean Martin.

Despite the fact that Brooks had cancer, it was actually a heart attack that killed her at the age of 51. She is buried in Washington Memorial Park Cemetery in New York.

ABOVE Brooks guest starred in many of the top television shows of the 1960s and 1970s, including Dr. Kildare, Get Smart, Ironside, Kung Fu, and Baretta.

Star Shot

In 1970, Geraldine Brooks was nominated for a Tony® for the role of Sara Brightower in the play *Brightower*, written by film producer, scriptwriter, and playwright Dore Schary.

Richard Burton

Born November 10, 1925
Died August 5, 1984

ABOVE With Roddy McDowell (left) in 1963's Cleopatra. *Richard Burton was paid $250,000 for his work in the film.*

Star Shot

In the late 1970s, on a flight from Mexico to California, Richard Burton met a marketing professional who wanted to become an actor. Burton advised the young man, Kevin Costner, to commit full-time to his dream.

RIGHT Richard Burton and Elizabeth Taylor are the parents of a daughter, Maria, born in 1964 in Germany.

*W*hen I played drunks I had to remain sober because I didn't know how to play them when I was drunk.

So said Richard Burton, one of the most talented Welshmen and alcoholics ever to grace the stage and screen. He also said, "I have to think hard to name an interesting man who does not drink." Burton holds the joint record for the most Academy Award® nominations without a win with drinking pal Peter O'Toole, but during his career he bagged a British Film Academy Award, two Golden Globes®, a Theatre World Award, a Tony®, and even a Grammy®. He was decorated with a British CBE in 1970, and in 2002 Burton was honored with inclusion in the BBC-sponsored List of 100 Great Britons.

The second youngest of 13 children, Richard Walter Jenkins often claimed that his escape from a destitute childhood was due to reading, as he would consume one book a day. Born in Pontrhydyfen, Wales, Burton took his stage name from teacher and inspiration Philip Burton, who also legally adopted him. English was his second language, as he spoke Cymraeg, the Welsh language, as his mother tongue. Wales was always the key to Burton's attitude, and he said once of his screen persona: "I rather like my reputation, actually, that of a spoiled genius from the Welsh gutter, a drunk, a womanizer; it's rather an attractive image." At the age of 16, Burton left school and worked as a shop assistant, but due to Philip Burton's influence he received a six-month scholarship to Exeter College, Oxford, reading drama. This was as part of the university's commitment to wartime cadets.

Burton made his stage debut at Maesteg Town Hall in Wales, but his career did not really commence until his term in the British Navy concluded in 1947. Burton's first British screen part was in *The Last Days of Dolwyn* (1949); he later moved to Broadway, and in 1952 he made his way to Hollywood, appearing as the male lead opposite Olivia de Havilland in

My Cousin Rachel. The success of this film led to other important motion pictures like *The Robe* (1953), and he utilized his famous Welsh brogue as narrator of the radio production of *Under Milk Wood* (1954), a role which he would reprise in the film version 18 years later. Richard Burton's first film with fellow marriage-addict Elizabeth Taylor was the mega-production *Cleopatra* (1963), where he played Marc Antony. He was married five times, including twice to Elizabeth Taylor—in 1964 for ten years and again in 1975 for another torrid year. Burton and Taylor played semibiographical roles in the successful screen adaptation of *Who's Afraid of Virginia Woolf?* (1966), where a cynical yet highly educated couple spend a dinner party verbally lashing each other before mesmerized guests.

ABOVE Richard Burton (left) and Billy Connolly appeared together in Absolution *(1978). Burton played a priest who has heard a very worrying confession.*

Burton starred in reputable British movies in the late 1950s, including *Look Back in Anger* (1958), but his home was always the stage, and he gave a brilliant performance in the Broadway musical *Camelot* in 1960. Burton was often accused of accepting lesser film roles for the money, to which he responded: "I've done the most awful rubbish in order to have somewhere to go in the morning." His salary moved swiftly from $50,000 in 1952 to $1 million in the 1960s—a substantial amount in those days—including a percentage of the gross of *Where Eagles Dare* (1968).

Ever ebullient, in 1974 Richard Burton was notoriously banned from BBC productions for attacking Winston Churchill's role in World War II: "What man of sanity would say on hearing of the atrocities committed by the Japanese against British and Anzac prisoners of war, 'We shall wipe them out, every one of them, men, women, and children'….Such simple-minded cravings for revenge leave me with a horrified but reluctant awe for such single-minded and merciless ferocity."

One of Burton's final parts was opposite daughter Kate in the television miniseries *Ellis Island* (1984). At that point he was sober, yet his years of chronic alcoholism were catching up. The man nicknamed "Rich" died shortly after the wrap of *1984* (1984), and four days before he was to commence shooting *The Wild Geese II* (1984), a sequel to the popular 1978 thriller. The film was shot and subsequently dedicated to Burton's memory.

On August 5, 1984, wife Sally Hay woke up to find Burton in a coma beside her in bed. She called a doctor and Burton was taken to Cantonal Hospital in Geneva, Switzerland. At 1:15 P.M. Richard Burton died of a massive cerebral hemorrhage. His death graced the front page of every newspaper in Britain, and his daughter read a poem by Welsh poet Dylan Thomas as he was buried in red, the Welsh national color, at Protestant Churchyard in Céligny, Switzerland. Richard Burton once said, regarding his liquid weakness, "My father considered that anyone who went to chapel and didn't drink alcohol was not to be tolerated. I grew up in that belief."

RIGHT Richard Burton played a number of historical figures during his career, including Marc Antony, Thomas á Beckett, Henry VIII, Leon Trotsky, and Richard Wagner. He was well-read and had an outstanding knowledge of English poetry.

John Candy

Born October 31, 1950
Died March 4, 1994

O ne of a galaxy of comedy stars to emerge from Canada over the past two decades—including Jim Carrey, Mike Myers, Dan Aykroyd, Eugene Levy, Martin Short, and Leslie Nielsen—John Candy was a rotund, talented, slightly melancholic actor who rose to star in a number of his own Hollywood comedy vehicles. He was born in East York, a suburb of Toronto, and attended Holy Cross Catholic School, graduating from McNeil Catholic Secondary School. His father, Sidney, suffered a fatal heart attack at age 35 when Candy was only five years old, which should have sounded warning bells in the young John's ears. However, the imposing 300-pound (136-kg) frame Candy carried his entire adult life gave him the confidence to be a bankable "funny fat man."

ABOVE John Candy (right) with legendary comedian George Burns. Candy's success was in part due to his amazing ability to portray an "everyman."

Candy honed his comic timing with Toronto's Second City comedy troupe and on *SCTV* in the 1970s and 1980s. He worked on several Canadian films—including *It Seemed Like a Good Idea at the Time* (1975), *Find the Lady* (1976), and *The Silent Partner* (1978)—breaking through to Hollywood with minor parts in *1941* (1979), the cult hit *The Blues Brothers* (1980), and *Stripes* (1981), in which film critic Pauline Kael defined his performance affectionately as "the big blob farmer from the Second City." Candy rejected numerous offers to join *Saturday Night Live*, demonstrating remarkable loyalty to his fellow *SCTV* comedians, as *Saturday Night Live* was the biggest comedy show on television at the time. Ironically he appeared in ten motion pictures with *Saturday Night Live* alumni, more than any other non-*Saturday Night Live* actor.

Candy fared best in strong supporting roles: *National Lampoon's Vacation* (1983), *Splash* (1984), and *Little Shop of Horrors* (1986). He participated in the Canadian ensemble Northern Lights on the immensely successful album *We Are The World (USA for Africa)*. He perhaps foolishly turned down the role of Louis Tully in the blockbuster *Ghostbusters* (1984), the part eventually going to his diminutive *Little Shop of Horrors* co-star Rick Moranis (although he scored a cameo in the "Ghostbusters" music video). It is interesting to reflect on how Candy would have interpreted the role of "Keymaster" to Sigourney Weaver's "Gatekeeper."

Comedy rode a huge wave of success in the 1980s through a legion of talented directors, writers, and comedians, exploiting narratives of situation, impeccable timing, and tight writing. Director John "Blues Brothers" Landis called the phenomenon the "behavioral humor of outrage," a rebellion against affluent Reaganite suburban culture. Unfortunately, poor script choices undermined many Candy vehicles, while the fame of other comedians like Steve Martin continued to rise. Candy's *Summer Rental* (1985), *Armed and Dangerous* (1986), *The Great Outdoors* (1988), *Who's Harry Crumb?* (1989), and *Delirious* (1991) were not well received. One film that did do well was the bittersweet *Planes, Trains and Automobiles* (1987). Director John Hughes teamed Candy (as Del) with Steve Martin (as Neal), and the result is a hilarious and touching film that offers Candy fans this favorite dialogue exchange:

[Waking up after sharing the same bed in a motel]

Neal: Del….Why did you kiss my ear?

Del: Why are you holding my hand?

Neal: Where's your other hand?

Del: Between two pillows….

Neal: Those AREN'T PILLOWS!!!

LEFT With Chevy Chase in National Lampoon's Vacation *(1983). At the time of his death, John Candy had appeared in more movies directed by John Hughes than any other actor.*

As with many comic actors struggling to migrate to more dramatic roles (and the associated industry respect they yearn for), by the end of the 1980s Candy's movies were not grossing as much as they should, and he resorted to delivering cameos in *Home Alone* (1990) and *Career Opportunities* (1991); as the desolate cop in *Only the Lonely* (1991); bizarrely yet effectively as a sunglassed New Orleans lawyer in Oliver Stone's *JFK* (1991); and as a Chicago sportscaster in *Rookie of the Year* (1993). This brief period in the doldrums ended when he starred in the based-on-a-true-story *Cool Runnings* (1993), as an ex-Olympian who coaches the Jamaican bobsled team. In 1994, he milked his northern heritage in *Canadian Bacon* (released posthumously in 1995) and directed the television movie *Hostage for a Day.*

John Candy succumbed to a fatal heart attack on location in Mexico for *Wagons East* (1994). He told actress Catherine O'Hara just before departing that he feared going to Mexico because "something bad is going to happen there." Candy had been warned by doctors to lose some weight as he was genetically prone to heart disease, but he refused, stating that his girth gave him screen roles. John Candy's cult status generated many U.S. and international tributes upon his death. The eccentric rock outfit Ween dedicated their album *Chocolate and Cheese* to him, while *Blues Brothers 2000* (1998), the Spanish film *¿Quién mató a Dr. Pus?* (2003), and his last two acting roles were also dedicated in memoriam to a fine comic actor.

Candy is survived by his wife, Rosemary Hobor, and two children, Jennifer and Christopher. He is interred at Holy Cross Cemetery, Culver City, California, in the Mausoleum, Room 7, Block 1.

Star Shot

John Candy's funeral was held on March 9, 1994, and broadcast live on Canadian television. Mourners included Tom Hanks, Rick Moranis, and Dan Aykroyd, who delivered the eulogy.

FAR LEFT John Candy was more than just a comic and dramatic actor. He took on the role of executive producer for a number of films, including Who's Harry Crumb? *(1989).*
RIGHT James Belushi (left), Cybill Shepherd, John Candy, Ornella Muti, Richard Lewis, and Sean Young in a publicity shot for the comedy thriller Once Upon A Crime *(1992).*

Jack Carson

Born October 27, 1910
Died January 2, 1963

BELOW A scene from The Jack Carson Show. Carson also appeared in notable films such as A Star Is Born *(1954) and* Cat on a Hot Tin Roof *(1958).*

Carson, a veteran of vaudeville and a prominent member of the Warner Bros. stock company, was yet another character actor hamstrung by the Hollywood system that, in Jack Carson's own words, "typecast a guy and left him to rot." He was the perennial goofball, a 6 foot, 2 inch (1.88 m), good-natured meathead who occasionally shone when he was allowed to play more subtle dramatic roles.

After an unbilled debut in United Artists' *You Only Live Once* (1937), Carson was signed on as a featured player with RKO. The studio gave him bit parts opposite Fred Astaire in *Carefree* (1938) and opposite Ginger Rogers in *Having Wonderful Time* (1938). Carson quickly decided he would get nowhere in the factory system of RKO and chose to freelance instead.

By 1941, Carson had established himself on screen and had earned a Warner Bros. contract. He became known for his on-screen roles as the big affable guy who loses the girl in the final reel, or the loyal pal providing comedy relief. Carson's favorite role was in Michael Curtiz's *Roughly Speaking* (1945), which cast him against type as a husband with big business ideas. He was constantly infuriated after this appearance when cast and crew approached him and said, "Why didn't you say you could act?"

Another high point in Jack Carson's career was his role in Curtiz's *Mildred Pierce* (1945), the motion picture that turned Joan Crawford's career around and garnered her an Academy Award® for Best Actress. Whenever Carson's film career dwindled, he could always rely on television gigs, especially *The Jack Carson Show* which he hosted from 1954 to 1955.

In 1962, Carson returned to the stage, but on August 26 he collapsed during a rehearsal of the play *Critic's Choice*. Carson never regained his health, but he did become involved in one more project, acting in Disney's *Sammy, the Way-Out Seal* (1962).

In late 1962, Carson entered hospital to be treated for a stomach malignancy. On New Year's Day, 1963, Carson's fourth wife, Sandra Jolley, watched the Super Bowl Game with the ailing actor. On January 2, 1963, Frank Stapel, Carson's agent of 25 years, talked with Carson about upcoming projects. After Stapel left, Jolley returned to Carson's room and found him dead. He died only four hours before fellow actor Dick Powell. Both were victims of stomach cancer.

Services for the 52-year-old Carson were held in a replica of Anne Laurie's Church at the Wee Kirk o' the Heather, Forest Lawn Memorial Park, Glendale, California. Among the pallbearers were his ex-vaudeville partner Dave Willock, as well as on- and off-screen buddy Dennis Morgan.

Nell Carter

Born September 13, 1948
Died January 23, 2003

Despite being only 4 foot, 11 inches (1.5 m) tall, Nell Carter had a huge voice that commanded stage, television, and film audiences alike. Carter survived cocaine and alcohol addictions, diabetes, and two brain operations, but eventually died at the age of just 54.

Nell Carter first performed professionally at the age of 11 on a weekly radio show in her home town of Birmingham, Alabama. Despite a bumpy beginning in the appalling television soap opera *Ryan's Hope* and the even worse *Misadventures of Sheriff Lobo*, she starred in 1977 in the stage revue show *Ain't Misbehavin'*. She carried her role from off-Broadway to Broadway and then television and was rewarded in each field with an Obie®, a Tony Award®, and finally an Emmy®. Carter was also nominated for two Emmys® for her role as motherly housekeeper Nell Harper in the television series *Gimme a Break* (1981–87).

Carter's most recent work on the Broadway stage was playing Miss Hannigan in the 20th anniversary revival of *Annie* for a year from January 1997. There was some controversy when Carter expressed her dismay and disappointment that the show's producers used the old television commercial featuring Marcia Lewis to promote the revival. The producers claimed it was too costly to shoot a new commercial, but Carter rebutted this by saying, "Maybe they don't want audiences to know Nell Carter is black."

Carter had already had to fight cocaine and alcohol addictions with 12-step programs in the 1980s, but she faced even more difficult challenges in the following years. Carter was diagnosed with Type II diabetes and underwent two brain operations in 1992 to fix aneurysms. When she was first diagnosed with diabetes, she denied it. "Being diabetic was not what I thought of as being normal, and I feared the stigma of having to take medicine and having people stick me with a needle."

Before she died, Nell Carter saw fellow singer and friend Whitney Houston in a television interview with Diane Sawyer, tearfully discussing her crippling drug addiction. Carter made a commitment to help Houston into the Hazelden rehabilitation clinic in Minnesota, but she was never able to make good on her promise.

The day before she died, Carter was rehearsing for a play, *Raisin* (a musical version of the play *Raisin in the Sun*), in Long Beach, California. Carter collapsed and died from heart disease and diabetes complications in her Beverly Hills home. She was found dead by her 13-year-old adopted son, Joshua.

ABOVE Nell Carter converted to Judaism when she married her first husband, Georg Krynicki, in 1982. The union lasted 10 years. They adopted two sons.

LEFT A born entertainer, Nell Carter made guest appearances on television hits such as Jake and the Fatman, Reba, *and* Ally McBeal.

Star Shot

Despite her long career in show business, Nell Carter was broke when she died. She had less than $200 in her bank account, and had filed for bankruptcy the previous year.

Katrin Cartlidge

Born May 15, 1961
Died September 7, 2002

ABOVE Katrin Cartlidge appeared in Rosanna Arquette's Searching for Debra Winger *(2002), which examined the pressures on women over the age of 40.*

RIGHT Katrin Cartlidge on the set of No Man's Land *(2001), with Georges Siatidis (center) and Simon Callow. The film explores the Balkan conflict during 1993.*

Only two years before her death, Cartlidge, in an interview, said: "I actually love getting older. I hated my twenties; I couldn't wait to be 30. I'm really looking forward to turning 40, if I get there....So roll on. I can't wait." Cartlidge would make it to 40, but would die a year later. Her death shocked the film community, particularly in Europe.

Katrin Cartlidge quickly gained a reputation as a versatile, spirited, and controversial actress. She is best known for roles as downtrodden, streetwise, abused women who survive through sardonic and subversive insolence. Cartlidge was always attracted to intelligent roles and chose directors who she felt would "produce something original, revealing, and provoking." Cartlidge proved her absolute commitment to screen art by becoming an outspoken member of many European film festival panels.

In 1982, she was cast in the United Kingdom's groundbreaking television show *Brookside,* but it was her performance as the drug addict Goth, Sophie, in *Naked* (1993)—a scathing indictment of Prime Minister Margaret Thatcher's Britain—that saw her receive international attention. This also began a long professional relationship with director Mike Leigh. Eschewing Hollywood, Cartlidge worked with Mike Leigh twice more in *Career Girls* (1997) and *Topsy-Turvy* (1999), in Milcho Manchevski's *Before the Rain* (1994), Lars von Trier's *Breaking the Waves* (1996), Lodge H. Kerrigan's *Claire Dolan* (1998), and Danis Tanovic's black comedy *No Man's Land* (2001). Each film presented a bleak, uncaring world with little justice.

Katrin Cartlidge's sudden death reflected the same unforeseen speed with which misfortune struck her film characters. In early September 2002, Cartlidge complained of suffering from flu symptoms. When they became more pronounced, her boyfriend, actor Peter Gevisser, took her to a hospital near their North London home. She was diagnosed with pneumonia, and it wasn't long before septicemia set in. Cartlidge's condition continued to deteriorate, and she died on September 7.

In his obituary, Mike Leigh spoke eloquently of Cartlidge's contribution to his life and art in general. "I find it impossible to believe she is gone, that I will never again meet for lunch and have that special free-flowing Katrin conversation, at once profound and hilarious. But the hardest thing of all is to face the unbearable truth that Katrin Cartlidge will never again make her magical contribution to my films."

Cartlidge was survived by her parents, Derek and Bobbi; a sister, Michele; a brother, Tony; and her boyfriend, Peter Gevisser.

Ted Cassidy

Born July 31, 1932
Died January 16, 1979

ABOVE Ted Cassidy as Lurch at the wheel of the Addams Family car. The television series aired from 1964 to 1966, and succeeded because of its offbeat approach to family life.

Which cult actor played characters with such magnificently campy names as Metallus, Frankenstein, Jr., Igoo, Meteor Man, The Giant, Big Donnie, Goliath, Godzilla, Brainiac, The Thing, and Demon Balzaroth?

The towering 6 foot, 9 inch (2 m) tall Theodore Crawford "Ted" Cassidy played a plethora of giant characters, both in front of the camera and as cartoon voices, including a remarkable number of superheroes and their evil nemeses. For trivia buffs, Metallus was the villain in television's *Space Ghost* (1966), the only cartoon character to go on to host his own chat show. Cassidy's acting career spanned two decades until the year before his death, but he first lumbered in front of the cameras in 1964 in his most famous role, the monosyllabic butler Lurch in the television show *The Addams Family*.

Cassidy was born in Pittsburgh, Pennsylvania, but was raised in Philippi, West Virginia. He played a single season of basketball at Stetson University and averaged 17 points and 10 rebounds per game, simply because there was no one else who could reach that high. Cassidy married after graduating in 1956 and remained so for 20 years. After he finished college, he worked at a radio station in Jacksonville, then Pensacola, Florida, where his two children, Sean and Cameron, were born. Both are now lawyers.

Ted Cassidy moved east to Dallas, Texas, to work as an announcer for WFAA radio and was integral to WFAA's coverage of the assassination of President Kennedy in 1963. Cassidy became one of the first journalists to interview witnesses William and Gayle Newman. His resonant bass voice landed him offers to do voice acting, although it was his contacts at WFAA who led to his audition for *The Addams Family*. Lurch was originally conceptualized as a mute, but during the pilot's production Cassidy improvised his trademark catchphrase "You rang?" and suddenly Lurch became a speaking role—just. A little-known fact is that Ted Cassidy also played the scuttling hand monster, Thing, in *The Addams Family*, and there is a certain irony that a voice actor had two low-dialogue roles on the same show! He was also cast in motion pictures like *Butch Cassidy and the Sundance Kid* (1969), opposite the inimitable duo of Paul Newman and Robert Redford.

Ted Cassidy died in 1979 in Los Angeles, California, from complications following open-heart surgery. His girlfriend cremated his remains; some ashes were scattered and some were buried in the garden of his Woodland Hills home, evidently in a very large urn.

Star Shot

Ted Cassidy co-wrote the screenplay for *The Harrad Experiment* (1973) with Michael Werner. It was based on the Robert H. Rimmer novel, and Cassidy appeared in the film in an uncredited role as a diner patron.

Peggie Castle

Born December 22, 1927
Died August 11, 1973

Peggie Castle was a leading lady of B-grade movies during the 1950s. She retired from making films in the early 1960s and died in obscurity.

Castle was born in Appalachia, Virginia. Her family moved to Hollywood when Castle's father became studio manager of the Goldwyn studios. A tall blonde with green eyes, Castle started out as a magazine model before debuting in *When a Girl's Beautiful* (1947).

Two years later Peggie Castle was discovered by a talent agent at a restaurant in Beverly Hills. She was contracted to Universal International, where she starred in numerous second features. In the following years Castle played gangsters' molls, cowboys' love interests, and murderesses in films such as *The Prince Who Was a Thief* (1951), *Harem Girl* (1952), *Wagons West* (1952), and *Jesse James' Women* (1954). The last movie features a memorable catfight between Castle and Lita Baron. Two of her most unusual roles were in *Invasion USA* (1952) and *Back from the Dead* (1957). In the former, Castle plays one of five people in a tavern guiltily watching Communists take over America. In *Back from the Dead,* Castle plays a new bride possessed by the evil spirit of her husband's first spouse.

Castle did appear in more creditable films, such as *I, the Jury* (1953) and her last motion picture appearance in *Arrivederci Roma* (1958), before playing Lilly Merrill on the television western *Lawman* (1958–1962). She quit show business altogether in 1962.

Castle did not have a successful marital life. On her first day at the Universal studio she met casting director Robert H. Rains and fell in love. She divorced her first husband, Los Angeles businessman Revis Call, and married Rains, but their marriage would only last three years. She divorced Rains and married her assistant director on *Overland Pacific* (1954), William McGarry, 22 years her senior. This marriage continued until 1970 but, by the end of it, Castle was suffering from chronic alcoholism. Her final marriage to businessman Arthur Morgenstern lasted three years before Morgenstern died in April 1973, the same month as Castle's mother. It was only four months later that Castle followed suit.

Suffering from alcoholism and losing her grip on reality, Castle had been discharged from Camarillo State Hospital a few months before her death. On August 11, 1973, former husband William McGarry found Castle dead from cirrhosis of the liver and a heart condition in her Hollywood Boulevard apartment. She was only 45.

ABOVE Peggie Castle keeps her cool when Biff Elliot, as hard-boiled private eye Mike Hammer, points a gun at her in the 1953 thriller I, the Jury.

John Cazale

Born August 12, 1935
Died March 12, 1978

LEFT On the set of the war film The Deer Hunter *(1978). From left, John Cazale, Chuck Aspegren, Robert De Niro, John Savage, and Christopher Walken.*

A talented Italian-American character actor, John Cazale only starred in five feature films during his short lifetime—arguably the five most important films of the 1970s. He studied drama at Oberlin College and Boston University, and before his screen debut he won several awards for stage performances. Cazale broke through in the tragic role of forgotten son Fredo Corleone in Francis Ford Coppola's *The Godfather* (1972), after Al Pacino invited him to audition. Cazale and Pacino had been friends since they were teenagers.

John Cazale starred with Gene Hackman and little-known Harrison Ford in Coppola's *The Conversation* (1974), as Hackman's assistant Stan. Cazale played the struggling underling to a dominant protagonist in a near-reprise of Fredo. Cazale played a character named Stan in two films: *The Conversation* (1974) and *The Deer Hunter* (1978). Coppola was so impressed with Cazale in *The Godfather* (1972) that in *The Godfather Part II* (1974) he expanded Fredo's character, hinging the plot on him. Fredo unwittingly betrays the family; he is then executed on the orders of his brother in one of the most infamous scenes in film history.

Cazale's fourth film, *Dog Day Afternoon* (1975), earned him a Golden Globe® nomination for Best Supporting Actor for his role as Salvatore, "Sal," the bank robber. Al Pacino played the leader of the operation, Sonny. Sal is gunned down in the film after following orders from Sonny; once again, John Cazale defined the weak, neurotic man surrounded by stronger personalities.

On location for *The Deer Hunter* (1978), everyone became ill in the wet heat of Thailand, except director Michael Cimino who "refused." Cazale was already ill with bone cancer, adding a poignant dimension to the cast's health issues. He met Meryl Streep while filming, and they became engaged. While Universal was unaware of Cazale's condition, Cimino was, and as Cazale weakened Cimino was forced to film his scenes first. As shooting slowed and the studio discovered Cazale's disease, they wanted him removed from the film—fortunately, Streep stood by him and threatened to quit if he was fired. John Cazale died not long after filming was completed.

Some twelve years after John Cazale's death, he appeared in *The Godfather Part III* (1990), in uncredited archival footage. As with the previous two films in the iconic trilogy, *The Godfather Part III* was nominated for the Best Picture Oscar®—but unlike the other movies, it did not win the award.

Star Shot

John Cazale is the only actor in the history of Hollywood who can lay claim to the fact that every film in which he appeared was nominated for the Academy Award® for Best Picture.

RIGHT John Cazale (left) in the pivotal role of Fredo Corleone, with Al Pacino as his brother, Michael, in The Godfather, Part II *(1974). Shooting of the film was delayed for four weeks when Pacino was diagnosed with pneumonia.*

Helen Chandler

Born February 1, 1906
Died April 30, 1965

Helen Chandler appeared delicate, even anemic, but was extremely headstrong. Her offbeat behavior was exacerbated by endless drinking that would end up destroying a promising career. Chandler always wanted to play *Alice in Wonderland* and Shakespeare's Juliet. But because of her alcoholism and personal problems she achieved neither of these goals.

Helen Chandler began impressively enough. She was on the stage by the age of eight. At age 12 she played one of the princes murdered in the tower in *Richard III*, headlined by John Barrymore. By 16 she was playing the difficult role of Hedwig in Henrik Ibsen's

ABOVE Helen Chandler (far right) in Fanny Foley Herself *(1931). The film featured British character actress Edna May Oliver (second from left).*

The Wild Duck. Chandler was determined to become a film star so she went to Fox studios and asked to see Mr. Fox. Allan Duan saw her and gave her the role of Jenny in *The Music Master* (1927), with Alec B. Francis and Lois Moran.

Tod Browning saw Chandler on stage and cast her in *Dracula* (1931), the biggest money maker for Universal that year. The experience was not entirely pleasant for her: "In *Dracula*, I played one of those bewildered little girls who go around pale, hollow-eyed, and anguished, wondering about things…. I was! Wondering about when I could get to a hospital and part with a rampant appendix without holding up the picture."

Because of an inability to deal with personal problems and her debilitating alcoholism, by the mid- to late 1930s Chandler was relegated to secondary roles in films such as *It's a Bet* (1935) and *Mr. Boggs Steps Out* (1938). She lost her second husband, Bramwell Fletcher, to Diana Barrymore. Chandler's health and emotional problems meant that, while she completed occasional radio broadcasts, in August 1940 she was admitted to La Crescenta Sanitarium.

In 1950, the manager of Chandler's North Whitley Terrace Apartment had to pull the unconscious Chandler from her smoke-filled home. She was rushed to the Hollywood Receiving Hospital with multiple burns that disfigured her face. Investigators found quantities of sleeping tablets in Chandler's apartment and established that Chandler's latest husband, seaman Walter Piascik, had shipped out recently. Chandler was committed to California's DeWitt State Hospital for five years.

Star Shot

Helen Chandler was cremated, but no relative took possession of her ashes. They remain to this day in Chapel of the Pines Crematory in Los Angeles, California.

RIGHT Helen Chandler plays Nikki, the love interest of Richard Barthelmess, in William Dieterle's 1931 film, The Last Flight.

On April 30, 1965, Helen Chandler was admitted to hospital in a state of shock and underwent surgery for massive bleeding of an ulcer. She died the same day of a heart attack. On the afternoon of May 3, services were held at Pierce Brothers Funeral Home in Hollywood. Very few people attended.

Jeff Chandler

Born December 15, 1918
Died June 17, 1961

The death of rugged, gray-haired actor Jeff Chandler at the age of 42 due to "medical misadventure" shocked the film industry.

Chandler, born Ira Grossel in Brooklyn, New York, was raised by his mother. Like so many actors of his generation, his career was put on hold by World War II when he joined the Army and was stationed in the Aleutian Islands. Jeff Chandler was discovered by Dick Powell and given a small role in Powell's *Johnny O'Clock* (1947). Chandler then spent two years working on radio shows and had three other small film roles before being cast in Universal's *Sword of the Desert* (1949) as an Israeli leader.

Despite his Jewish background, Jeff Chandler would commonly play Native Americans, beginning with the part of Cochise in *Broken Arrow* (1950), starring James Stewart. For this role Chandler received an Oscar® nomination for Best Actor in a Supporting Role.

Chandler married actress Marjorie Hoshelle in 1946, and they had two daughters, Jamie and Dana, before separating in 1954. Hoshelle and Chandler would be separated and reconciled more than half a dozen times before 1957. The next year Chandler played opposite swimming actress Esther Williams in *Raw Wind in Eden* (1958), and they pursued a steamy affair. On the strength of this, Hoshelle decided to divorce Chandler, but by 1960, when the decree became final, Chandler and Williams had drifted apart.

Jeff Chandler suffered a slipped disk on location in the Philippines during the filming of *Merill's Marauders* (released posthumously in 1962), a World War II combat movie. The relatively simple surgery to fix his back at a Culver City hospital was complicated when Chandler suffered hemorrhages and infection. During an emergency seven-hour operation he was given 55 pints (26 liters) of blood while the surgeons repaired a ruptured artery. He survived, but a subsequent hemorrhage and infection weakened him. By the end, the gaunt Chandler had suffered for five weeks and had undergone three operations. When he died of generalized blood infection complicated by pneumonia, his mother, Ann Shevelow, his father, Philip Grossel, and his ex-wife, Marjorie Hoshelle, were present.

Funeral services were held on June 19, 1961, at Temple Isiah in Los Angeles; he was buried at Hillside Memorial Park. Among the pallbearers were Jeff's baseball friends, Hoby Landrith and Bill Rigeny, as well as actor Tony Curtis.

Less than two weeks after Jeff Chandler's death, 150 actors signed a petition demanding an investigation into the circumstances surrounding Chandler's death. Marjorie Hoshelle brought legal action against the hospital responsible, and an out-of-court settlement was reached.

ABOVE Jeff Chandler with his wife, Marjorie Hoshelle, at a screening of a 3-D film. Their two daughters both died from cancer: Dana in 2002 and Jamie in 2003.

Star Shot

As well as being a respected actor, Jeff Chandler was a successful singer, songwriter, and musician. He sang the theme song from his 1955 film, *Foxfire*.

Lon Chaney

Born April 1, 1883
Died August 26, 1930

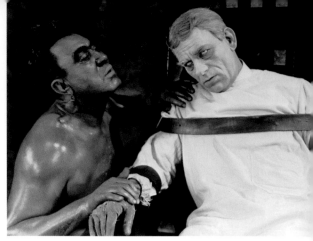

on Chaney was "The Man of a Thousand Faces." Cut off in his prime, very little of his work survives today, thanks to Universal's terrible system of archiving films.

Born to deaf parents, young Chaney developed communication via body movements and facial expressions that proved invaluable when he pursued work on the silent screen. Chaney received his first screen credit in Universal's *Poor Jake's Demise* (1913), beginning a career that spanned over 150 monstrous yet often pitiable faces.

For many film roles Chaney constructed elaborate prosthetics and went to great lengths to achieve a desired effect. In *The Penalty* (1920), he played a criminal whose legs had been amputated, so he constructed a complicated harness that forced him to walk on leather stumps. But Chaney's real gift was his insight into the psychology of the outsider. With each villain, he constructed the face of evil and yet retained the character's humanity.

Chaney's shift from Universal to MGM in the early 1920s turned him into a star. His two most memorable performances include Quasimodo in *The Hunchback of Notre Dame* (1923) and the title character in *The Phantom of the Opera* (1925).

Because of Chaney's visual yet silent style of performance, many, including the man himself, doubted he could make the transition to talkies. Chaney studied sound recording with the same commitment he'd shown to makeup. His first sound film, the 1930 remake of his 1925 hit *The Unholy Three,* proved that the man of a thousand faces could also be the man of a thousand voices. MGM immediately planned to put Chaney in *The Sea Bat* (1930) and *Cheri-Bibi* (1931). Tod Browning planned to cast Chaney in *Dracula* (1931), the film that made Bela Lugosi a star. But Chaney's career was cut short before he could conquer talkies.

Chaney caught pneumonia while working in the snow on *Thunder* (1929) and was unwell during the shooting of *The Unholy Three* (1930). He was rushed to Hollywood Hospital on August 1, 1930, when his throat started hemorrhaging due to cancer. According to some witnesses, he lost his voice and communicated via pantomime on his deathbed. Lon Chaney died on August 26, 1930.

Every Hollywood studio observed two minutes of silence. A squad of marines lowered the MGM flag. Wallace Beery, a fellow character actor, flew his plane over the funeral and dropped wreaths of flowers. Chaney was, and still is, considered irreplaceable by his legion of fans.

RIGHT London After Midnight *(1927) was promoted as starring "The Man of a Thousand Faces." Lon Chaney had a brilliant and much-sought-after ability to transform himself into truly memorable characters.*

ABOVE Walter James (left) taunts Lon Chaney in The Monster *(1925). Chaney's son, Lon Chaney, Jr., also became a famous horror star.*

Star Shot

Lon Chaney's first wife, singer and actress Frances "Cleva" Creighton, attempted suicide in 1913 by ingesting poison, which damaged her vocal chords. The couple divorced two years later.

Charley Chase

Born October 20, 1893
Died June 20, 1940

Charles Joseph Parrott, or Charley Chase, is an unsung comic legend, a star and director whose work deserves rediscovery in the same manner as Buster Keaton. This tall, slender, bespectacled comic was a man of many pseudonyms, credited variously as Charley Chan Chase, Charles Parrott, and, surreally, King Zang. He worked for influential producers such as Mack Sennett and Hal Roach, and was involved in over 240 films, mostly shorts.

Born in Baltimore, Maryland, Chase developed a vaudeville routine by the age of 16, which included monologues, song, dance, and banjo playing. He hit Broadway in 1912, and in 1914 Chase moved to Keystone where he learned to throw pies in Sennett films, and played opposite Charlie Chaplin in *The Knockout, The Masquerader,* and *Dough and Dynamite* (all released in 1914). Chase also co-directed with the controversial Roscoe "Fatty" Arbuckle.

In 1921, Chase took a director's job for Roach, yet was soon back in front of the camera with a series of two-reelers. Roach also hired Charley Chase's younger brother, James Parrott, who also became a prolific actor and director, later directing Stan Laurel and Oliver Hardy in several films, as well as his brother. By the mid-1920s, Chase was co-directing with Leo McCarey and starring in a string of comedies like *Bad Boy* (1925), *Mighty Like a Moose* (1926), and *Dog Shy* (1926).

ABOVE Kalla Pasha (right) bites Charley Chase's hand in one of the many comic short films Chase made during the 1920s and 1930s.

Unlike most vaudevillian comics, Charley Chase survived the transition to talkies: in 1929, he starred in the Universal film *Modern Love*. He also made a notable appearance in the Laurel and Hardy film *Sons of the Desert* (1933). When Roach tried to phase out shorts, Chase's feature film *Bank Night* flopped, and was cut to two reels for release as *Neighborhood House* (1936). In the same year Roach let Chase go due to Chase's continued resistance to features; he ended up at Columbia Pictures, starring in more shorts and directing stars like The Three Stooges. One of Chase's most renowned comedies, *The Heckler* (1940), was also one of his last. He was hired by MGM where he spent the rest of his career, drinking heavily.

Charley Chase had a serious alcohol problem, just like Buster Keaton, and died of a heart attack in Hollywood at the age of 46. His frustration at not reaching the heady heights of Chaplin can be attributed to his depression and death. Chase is interred at Forest Lawn Memorial Park, Glendale, California, on Sunrise Slope, L-72, next to Bebe, his devoted wife.

Montgomery Clift

Born October 17, 1920
Died July 23, 1966

RIGHT In Judgment at Nuremberg *(1961). Clift turned down the lead role in* Sunset Boulevard *(1950), the part eventually going to William Holden.*

BELOW Montgomery Clift on location for The Misfits *(1961). Although he appeared in fewer than 20 films, his legend lives on.*

On screen, Montgomery Clift exuded an aura of vulnerable masculinity, but in real life his underlying insecurities were too much for him to bear. Clift's gradual deterioration is described by one of his teachers, Bob Lewis, as "the slowest suicide in show business."

Born in Omaha, Nebraska, Clift was the son of William, a successful banker who never understood his son, and Ethel ("Sunny"), a woman with high social aspirations. Ethel was committed to raising Montgomery, his twin sister Ethel, and his older brother Brook like aristocracy.

Clift pursued a successful career on the stage but was reluctant to move to Hollywood, despite numerous efforts by producers to contract his talents. Yet he eventually accepted the part of Matt Garth opposite John Wayne in *Red River* (1948). Clift's fine elegant looks contrasted perfectly with the cowboy's more rugged handsomeness, and Clift soon became a star. During his career, he received Oscar® nominations for *The Search* (1948), *A Place in the Sun* (1951), *From Here to Eternity* (1953), and *Judgment at Nuremberg* (1961), though he never won.

Despite his acting talents, Montgomery Clift was utterly insecure; his mother controlled him till his early twenties, and he constantly tried to hide his homosexuality. His emotional difficulties were not helped by his sudden rise to stardom, and he became an alcoholic and habitual drug user. As a youth he'd been fascinated with pills. He would question pharmacists in detail about the concoctions they were making for his various ailments. Now his drug and alcohol use began to interfere with his work. His considerable professionalism meant that, at first, he never drank on the set—but by the time he was appearing in *From Here to Eternity*, cast and crew began commenting on his drunken behavior.

One evening, during the shooting of *Raintree County* in 1957, Clift dined at co-star Elizabeth Taylor's house. He was visibly shaking throughout the dinner. On his way home he veered off the road and crashed into a telephone pole. Taylor arrived at the crash scene and discovered the injured Clift was having difficulty breathing. She plunged her hand into his throat and pulled out two of his broken teeth that were blocking his throat.

The crash affected only his face, leaving him with a broken jaw and nose, a crushed sinus cavity, and severe facial lacerations. Plastic surgery prevented the crash from ruining Clift's looks and career, but his dependency on drugs and liquor continued to prop his frail ego. (James Dean wasn't so lucky; he died in a car crash in 1955.)

Clift had other problems apart from his self-destructive personality. He suffered from various illnesses including colitis and a thyroid disease, the symptoms of which were often indistinguishable from the effects of alcohol and drugs. When Clift co-starred in *The Misfits* (1961)—Clark Gable and Marilyn Monroe's final movie—Monroe said of

Clift: "He's the only person I know who is in worse shape than I am."

Clift then played the title role in John Huston's *Freud* (1962) and Universal sued him because he was incapable of remembering his lines. Studios were now in the habit of insuring their productions, and Clift's track record made him a liability. He didn't act for three years, until Elizabeth Taylor offered him a part in *Reflections in a Golden Eye* (1967). Clift was also offered a part in

The Defector (1966), which he felt was an inferior script, but he was so desperate to prove that he was worthy of *Reflections* he signed on. Throughout the shooting of *The Defector* Clift was ill but did his own stunts to show the studio that he was capable.

On Friday night, July 22, 1966, Clift drifted to sleep early at his New York townhouse. When his friend Lorenzo, who was caring for him, entered the bedroom he found Clift naked except for his glasses. Lorenzo was used to Clift's drunken states but when he scooped up his charge he was surprised at how comatose he was. He checked Clift's pulse. A doctor was called and pronounced that Clift had died sometime during the night. Although one would have expected that he would have succumbed to convulsions due to alcoholism, or perhaps a drug overdose, Clift had, in fact, died from a heart attack. Marlon Brando went on to star in *Reflections in a Golden Eye*.

All of Clift's one-time companions from his long career on stage and screen had encountered him once or twice before his inevitable demise; they each had a heart-wrenching story to tell about this once intelligent, talented actor debilitated by drugs, alcohol, and ill health. In 1997, *Entertainment Weekly* magazine voted Clift one of the "Hundred Greatest Stars of All Time."

LEFT Montgomery Clift with Elizabeth Taylor in A Place in the Sun *(1951). Clift and Taylor remained close friends until his death in 1966, at the age of just 45.*

RIGHT A 1950 studio publicity shot of Montgomery Clift. His handsome, sensual looks and appearance of vulnerability made Clift one of the hottest stars of the decade.

Last Words

"Absolutely not!" Clift shouted in response to his friend and live-in helper Lorenzo when he suggested they watch *The Misfits* (1961) on television.

*RIGHT Colin Clive
(left) contemplates the
futility of war in the
1930 motion picture,
Journey's End. His
characterizations were
often introspective.*

Colin Clive

Born January 20, 1900
Died June 25, 1937

Colin Clive, a talented actor with an expressive angular face who worked with director James Whale on four films, came to rely on alcohol to steady his nerves, and he quickly became reclusive on set. His career ended with his untimely death at the age of 37.

Clive was born in St. Malo, France. His father, Colonel Colin Clive-Greig, as well as his grandfather and uncles, all had distinguished military careers, but an accident in riding school spoiled Clive's future in the Army. Instead he became an actor and worked with James Whale on the phenomenally successful *Journey's End* (1930), playing Captain Stanhope. Clive struggled with the role, originally filled by Laurence Olivier, until the writer, R. C. Sheriff, suggested he have a couple of stiff drinks with lunch to calm his nerves. Clive's transformation during rehearsal was miraculous but the effect on his life would be disastrous.

In 1939, Clive went on to play his most memorable part in the title role of James Whale's *Frankenstein*. Whale elicited a wonderfully varied performance from the actor, saying "Colin is like a beautiful pipe organ. All I have to do is pull out the stops and out comes this glorious music." After the original shooting had wrapped, Whale, in an effort to soften the film, shot an epilogue that revealed Henry Frankenstein survived his fall from the mill. Clive was unavailable so an uncredited actor filled in. Again, on *Bride of Frankenstein* (1935), Whale shot a new ending that resurrected Clive's Frankenstein. Unfortunately, Colin Clive's addiction to alcohol meant that no one could save the actor himself.

By the time Colin Clive was working on *Bride of Frankenstein* his alcoholism had worsened. According to Valerie Hobson (who played Elizabeth), Clive had an ever-present dresser whose job was to make sure

*ABOVE Colin Clive
played the object of
Katharine Hepburn's
affections in 1933's
Christopher Strong,
Hepburn's second film.*

he did not drink. On the set of his final film, *The Woman I Love* (1937), all Clive's scenes had to be shot in the morning because he was drunk by midday.

Clive died of tuberculosis, exacerbated by his chronic alcoholism. At the crest of his fame he had appeared in 17 features and commanded a salary of $2,000 a week. Although best known for his horror films, Clive was also effective as the mysterious and romantic Edward Rochester in *Jane Eyre* (1934), and as the jealous husband in *History is Made at Night* (1937).

James Coco

Born March 21, 1930
Died February 25, 1987

Rotund and likable stage, screen, and television character actor James Coco followed in the footsteps of such comic luminaries as Oliver Hardy and the controversial Roscoe "Fatty" Arbuckle. Although not plagued by the tabloids during his life like the infamous Arbuckle, and not reaching the heady heights of stardom like Hardy, Coco built a diverse career that even included an entrance into the literary realm.

Coco was a familiar face in television commercials in the 1960s. He made his movie debut in *Ensign Pulver* (1964), and then went on to appear in a cavalcade of films including *End of the Road* (1970), *Tell Me That You Love Me, Junie Moon* (1970) starring Liza Minnelli, and *A New Leaf* (1971), a hilarious comedy starring Walter Matthau and Elaine May. In *Man of La Mancha* (1972), Coco was nominated for a Golden Globe® award for his supporting role as Sancho Panza, the sidekick of the renowned literary character Don Quixote, played by Peter O'Toole.

Restricting himself not only to the silver screen, Coco found time to star on Broadway in a role written especially for him by the great American comedy writer Neil *(The Odd Couple)* Simon, *The Last of the Red Hot Lovers* (1969). He was nominated for a Tony® award. Coco then returned to motion pictures in *The Wild Party* (1975), *Murder by Death* (1976), and *Only When I Laugh* (1981). For the latter, Coco had the unusual distinction of being nominated for an Oscar® and a Golden Globe®, as well as a Golden Raspberry (Razzie®) Award. Between stage jobs he went on to star in two television series during the hurly-burly 1970s: *Calucci's Department* (1973) and *The Dumplings* (1976).

Coco endeared himself to a new and younger audience when he made a guest appearance on *The Muppet Show* in 1978, and had a cameo role in *The Muppets Take Manhattan* (1984), the third in a succession of hugely successful films in the Muppet franchise.

Working right up until his sudden end, Coco had just commenced shooting the dubiously titled *Rented Lips* (1988) at the time of his shocking demise. In February 1987 he died of a heart attack in New York City, the place of his birth and the launching pad for his career.

Star Shot

Playing off his screen persona as the funny fat man and demonstrating his diverse talents, Coco wrote two cookbooks in the 1980s: *The James Coco Diet Book* and *Cooking with Coco*.

BELOW James Coco made many appearances on television shows, including Fantasy Island; Murder, She Wrote; and Who's the Boss?.

Gary Cooper

Born May 7, 1901
Died May 13, 1961

orn Frank James Cooper, Gary Cooper changed his name in 1925 on the advice of his agent. His incredible career garnered him five Academy Award® nominations for Best Actor (a one-time record), winning twice for *Sergeant York* (1941) and *High Noon* (1952), as well as receiving an Honorary Award in 1961. As stellar a star as they come, Cooper was one of the Top 10 Distributors' moneymakers in the 1940s and 1950s.

Cooper was born in Helena, Montana, but lived in England with his mother for seven years of his early life. At 13 he was injured in an automobile accident and relocated to his father's cattle ranch to recuperate. This was a turning point for young Gary; Montana is where he developed his horseriding skills and an affinity with the range. In 1924 he moved to Los Angeles with the notion of becoming a cartoonist, but after three months found work as an extra in Hollywood. In 1925 Cooper's boyish good looks gave him a role in a silent short opposite star Eileen Sedgwick, and after its release he accepted a studio contract at Paramount.

ABOVE Gary Cooper (center) starred with Ingrid Bergman in For Whom the Bell Tolls *(1943), based on the best-selling novel by Ernest Hemingway.*

He appeared in over a hundred films, most notably the very first Academy Award® winner *Wings* (1927) in which he plays an airman who flies to his death. Some of his career highlights include *The Virginian* (1929), *Seven Days Leave* (1930), *Only the Brave* (1930), *A Farewell to Arms* (1932), *Alice in Wonderland* (1933), *The Lives of a Bengal Lancer* (1935), *Mr. Deeds Goes to Town* (1936), *Beau Geste* (1939), *Meet John Doe* (1941), *Sergeant York* (1941), *The Pride of the Yankees* (1942), *For Whom the Bell Tolls* (1943), *The Fountainhead* (1949), *High Noon* (1952), and *They Came to Cordura* (1959).

Star Shot

"I'm just glad it'll be Clark Gable who's falling on his face and not Gary Cooper." Gary Cooper (in reference to Gable in the 1939 film, *Gone with the Wind*).

After tabloid-fodder affairs with Clara Bow (who believed them to be engaged), Lupe Velez, and socialite Countess Dorothy di Frasso, in 1933 Cooper married Veronica ("Rocky") Balfe, a New York socialite and actress who was billed as "Sandra Shaw." During his marriage Cooper had torrid and very public affairs with many of his leading ladies, notably Patricia Neal and Grace Kelly. Cooper and Rocky had one daughter—Maria—born in 1937.

RIGHT Director King Vidor cast newcomer Patricia Neal opposite Gary Cooper in The Fountainhead *(1949), based on the novel by Ayn Rand.*

The Virginian gave Cooper his iconic cowboy status. As the title character and foreman of Box H Ranch, Cooper must order and then lynch his best friend for cattle poaching. The film is a tragedy where an ambiguous moral system operates,

either choice leaving a dark shadow over
the character. Cooper's quiet nobility and
stoicism are the central defining character-
istics of his many heroes. The conservatism
he displayed in *The Virginian* was apparent
in Cooper's personality as well as his roles.
When questioned by the Communist witch
hunters, the House Un-American Activities
(HUAC), he said he didn't know much
about Communism, but as far as he could
tell, he was against it, because it didn't seem
to be "on the level."

The studio system was fickle in the
1930s and 1940s: cycle after cycle of fads
required stars to be versatile to take advantage of the next hot genre. Cooper was a heartthrob and star but also a tool of the studios,
and they used him shamelessly to usher in
every new movie production trend of the era.
During the cycle of "femme fatale" films, Cooper
played opposite Marlene Dietrich in *Morocco*
(1930) to introduce her to the American public.
The cycle of romantic films based on famous novels saw
Cooper play Ernest Hemingway's ambulance driver in *A Farewell to
Arms* (1932). The film was a mammoth success and gained Cooper prestige among
audiences and critics. Columbia borrowed Cooper from Paramount for *Mr. Deeds Goes to
Town*, to cash in on the screwball comedy cycle began by Frank Capra's *It Happened One
Night* (1934). Gary Cooper's most acclaimed role, as aging Marshall Will Kane, came in *High
Noon* opposite the luminous Grace Kelly, and he won an Academy Award® for Best Actor for
the role. Cooper was 24 years older than when he played *The
Virginian*, his face lined, his body worn down, but with an emo-
tional depth and increased wisdom that comes with experience.

In 1959, during the shooting of *The Hanging Tree*, Cooper found
that riding horses caused him pain. While shooting his last film,
The Naked Edge (1961) Cooper discovered he had spinal cancer;
by 1960 he had undergone two operations. His final public appearance was at a testimonial dinner in his honor in January 1961.
Gary Cooper, veteran of more than a hundred films and a screen
legend, died of cancer four months later and was interred in the
Sacred Heart Cemetery, Southampton, New York. He has a star on
the Hollywood Walk of Fame at 6243 Hollywood Boulevard.

BELOW With Raymond
Walburn (left) in Frank
Capra's Mr. Deeds Goes
to Town (1936).

RIGHT Lou Costello gives his daughter a piggyback ride, while Bud Abbott looks on. Abbott and Costello appeared in some 35 films together during their long partnership.

Lou Costello

Born March 6, 1906
Died March 3, 1959

L ovable stooge Lou Costello was the heart and soul of one of the most successful comedy teams in film history. Abbott and Costello offered their audiences comic relief from the harsh realities of the World War II era, but their pictures weren't just escapist fluff—they touched a chord with the American psyche. Fast-talking straight man Bud was slick and authoritative, with a punishing hand, while chubby, clownish Lou was a hapless Everyman whose immigrant heritage lent a social dimension to his persona. Bumbling out of every scrape, weathering every slap, Lou seemed to stand for the triumph—or at least survival—of the little guy.

Louis Francis Cristillo was born in Paterson, New Jersey, in 1906 to an Italian father and an Irish mother. A basketball player in high school, he later took up boxing, impressing the crowd with his ability to take a pounding. But his dream was to be a comic like his idol Charlie Chaplin, so he hitchhiked to Hollywood in 1927. After stints on studio labor crews, he was promoted to stunt work at MGM—weighing only 125 pounds (57 kg) at the time, he once doubled for Dolores del Rio. But the work was brutal, and he wasn't getting any breaks. After a year or so, Costello hit the road again, looking for another way to make his start.

The aspiring young comic soon got a job in a traveling burlesque show, and began touring the country, working on his stage schtick as a befuddled Dutch immigrant—and putting on weight. About 1935 he found himself in Brooklyn, sharing a bill with former lion tamer and race car driver Bud Abbott. Backstage, they started working up sketches together. Thus was born a partnership that would last for more than 25 years.

They set out as a team, developing (with writer John Grant) the classic routines that would eventually make "Who's on first?" and "I'm a ba-a-a-ad boy" household expressions. Key to their success was the avoidance of the bawdy material that was typical in burlesque, but forbidden in post-Hayes Code cinema. Abbott and Costello were good, clean fun—and after some radio and Broadway engagements, Hollywood took notice.

In 1940 they were signed at Universal, and appeared in

ABOVE Bud Abbott (wearing hat) and Robert Mitchum (right) appear to dislike the costume worn by their friend, Lou Costello, at an Easter party in 1946.

RIGHT In Abbott and Costello Meet Frankenstein (1948), the boys also find themselves at odds with Count Dracula (played by Bela Lugosi, at left).

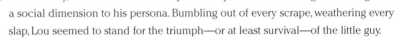

supporting roles as a couple of henchmen in an otherwise unremarkable B-musical, *One Night in the Tropics* (1940). It was their second film, *Buck Privates* (1941), that put them in the big time. Shot for a mere $90,000, the boot-camp comedy grossed $10 million. They followed with another blockbuster, *In the Navy* (1941), and in 1942 exhibitors named Abbott and Costello the country's number one box-office attraction.

Costello had married his wife Anne in 1934, and they had three children. Just when he had achieved fulfillment in his personal and professional life, tragedy struck. In 1943, the baby, Lou Jr., toddled into the family swimming pool and drowned. Costello kept a radio engagement that night, but fell to pieces afterward. His wife turned to the bottle for comfort, while Costello stuck with his usual vices—eating and gambling. More productively, he channeled his grief into charity. With Abbott's help, he founded the Lou Costello, Jr. Youth Foundation, a recreational center in Los Angeles. Friends and family later said the loss had left him a broken man.

In the mid-1940s, Abbott and Costello's popularity began to wane, and they were criticized for the repetitiveness of their routines. Looking for something new, they struck gold with *Abbott and Costello Meet Frankenstein* (1948). Taking advantage of Universal's experience with the genre, they dropped themselves into a classic horror movie, to hilarious effect. Their box office soared, and in 1952 they got their own television show. But by then the partnership had begun to unravel, largely due to Abbott's increasingly heavy drinking.

Costello called it quits in 1957, after Abbott showed up smashed for a 20th anniversary performance of "Who's on First?" embarrassing them in front of a roomful of NBC brass. There were also financial tensions—early on their 60/40 percentage split had favored Abbott, but later the tables turned. The bitter rivalry came to a head when Abbott sued Costello for $222,000 in earnings from their television show. By the scheduled date of the pre-trial hearing, however, Lou Costello was dead.

On February 26, 1959, Costello had a heart attack and was taken to Doctors' Hospital in Beverly Hills. He seemed to be recovering, but on March 3 he succumbed to a second heart attack. That morning he'd been joking around with his manager, Eddie Sherman, while eating an ice cream soda. He had spent the afternoon with his wife (she would die less than a year later of heart failure). Abbott, apparently, was sick himself and had not been told about Costello's hospitalization. Sherman maintained that despite their feuds, they "loved each other like brothers." When he was informed of Lou's death, Bud Abbott sobbed, "My heart is broken. I've lost the best pal anyone ever had." He had reportedly been watching their "Who's on First?" routine on television when he heard the news.

ABOVE Lou Costello (right) once said, "Comics are a dime a dozen. Good straight men are hard to find." His partnership with Bud Abbott (left) is a show business legend.

Last Words

"That was the best ice cream soda I ever tasted."

RIGHT Laird Cregar was educated in England. During his summer breaks, he worked as a bit player with the Stratford-on-Avon theater.

Laird Cregar

Born   July 28, 1916
Died   December 9, 1944

In 1942, shortly before his own untimely death, Hollywood royalty John Barrymore hailed Laird Cregar as "the one truly great young actor of the last ten years." An imposing 6 foot, 3 inches (1.9 m) and 300 pounds (136 kg), Cregar was "great" in more than one sense of the word, and through diligent hard work and sheer dedication to his craft, he won respect from some of the greatest Hollywood stars of his era. But while his talent may have warranted star billing, his physique defined him de facto as a character actor—with fatal results. Mustachioed, moody, and sinister, Cregar was always going to be the bad guy, establishing himself quickly in the same top-hatted, hand-wringing, evil chuckling antagonist group as Vincent Price, Christopher Lee, Peter Cushing, and George Zucco. Cregar was also gay, and his negative body image was an integral part of the obsessive weight loss that caused his tragic death.

BELOW As Slade in The Lodger (1944). Laird Cregar brought a cerebral intensity to this performance, making it a truly memorable film.

A native of Philadelphia, Pennsylvania, Samuel Laird Cregar was born in 1916 (some sources say 1914) and ventured out to California when he was 19 to study acting at the Pasadena Community Playhouse, a renowned theater and training ground for Hollywood stars. Drawn to motion pictures by the late 1930s, Cregar's debut on the silver screen came in 1940 with a walk-on in *Oh Johnny, How You Can Love* (1940), and Warner Bros. B-movie *Granny Get Your Gun* (1940). Laird Cregar accepted a studio contract from 20th Century Fox the same year, immediately garnering solid supporting parts as a clownish fur trapper in *Hudson's Bay* (1941), as a Spaniard opposite Tyrone Power in *Blood and Sand* (1941), and in *Charley's Aunt* (1941).

Comedy was not to be Cregar's destiny, and he would distinguish himself as an artist of Machiavellian villainy. His most memorable performances include a diabolically lovestruck detective who commits suicide by drinking poison in the early film noir classic *I Wake Up Screaming* (1941), and as Jack the Ripper who commits suicide by jumping out of a window and into a river in *The Lodger* (1944) opposite George Sanders and Merle Oberon. Between these bookends of a short but high-impact career, Cregar supported Veronica Lake and Alan Ladd in Ladd's breakthrough performance in *This Gun For Hire* (1942), based on a Grahame Greene novel, where Ladd shoots Cregar in the chest. He also worked with Tyrone Power in the swashbuckler *The Black Swan* (1942), and played opposite Gene Tierney in esteemed director Ernst Lubitsch's *Heaven Can Wait* (1943).

More than his looming physique, heavy brow, and intense features, Cregar's subtle psychological interpretations accounted for the power of his screen presence. He spoke eloquently of his techniques for varying each role, even as he was being typecast. In the year of his death he told the *New York Herald Tribune* with acerbic wit, "I have a feeling the studio is almost beginning to consider me an actor now, instead of a type." He did receive star billing for his next—and last—motion picture, but the role was that of yet another demented soul, murderous musician George Harvey Bone in the period mystery *Hangover Square* (1945), opposite Linda Darnell. The insane composer suffers from blackouts in which he cannot remember the murders taking place. The film opened posthumously, inspiring some of the best reviews of his career.

ABOVE As composer George Harvey Bone in Hangover Square (1945). Laird Cregar brought just the right amount of gothic madness to the role.

Longing to play romantic leads, Cregar had plastic surgery on his face, and became obsessed with weight loss. At the end of 1944 he checked into Good Samaritan Hospital for stomach bypass surgery, which was, in those days, a new procedure. He survived, but the operation and months of crash dieting had left his heart weak. Cregar managed to lose 100 pounds (45 kg) in near-record time, but his system was not built for such a concerted assault and he suffered two massive coronaries in the days that followed. Cregar passed away on December 9 at the youthful age of 28, although he always looked far older.

Cregar's compulsion to change his image wasn't about weight alone. He was gay, closeted

to the public, but his sexual orientation was more or less common knowledge in Hollywood. In the 1930s and 1940s, homosexuality was fatal for a burgeoning career, and Cregar was one actor who suffered more than most because he became obsessed with the leading men he constantly supported. Inseparable from his dream of becoming a matinee idol was the tragic necessity of suppressing his true nature. As with many Hollywood stars, Laird Cregar is interred at the Forest Lawn Memorial Park, Glendale, Los Angeles County, in the Eventide Section, lot 37, space 2. Another master of malice, Vincent Price, delivered the eulogy at Cregar's funeral. Laird Cregar's epitaph simply reads, "I am with you always," and for true aficionados of horror and adventure, he always will be.

Star Shot

When Laird Cregar was struggling to break into the movies, he produced and starred in a one-man stage show about famed writer and wit Oscar Wilde.

LEFT Laird Cregar exercising in his bedroom. The actor was often cast as characters who were much older than he was.

Richard Cromwell

Born January 8, 1910
Died October 11, 1960

Richard Cromwell's sincere demeanor and boyish good looks brought him great success as a juvenile actor throughout the 1930s. Born LeRoy Melvin Radabaugh, he moved to Hollywood when he was 15, leaving his family home in nearby Long Beach to study ceramics at Madame Chouinard's Art Institute. Cromwell worked his way through school doing odd jobs, including a brief stint as a movie extra, then opened his own shop, where his masks of film stars created a small sensation. His customers included Marie Dressler and Joan Crawford, who convinced him to take another shot at the movies.

When the call went out for an unknown actor to play the title role in *Tol'able David* (1930), young Radabaugh won the part. He was signed on at Columbia and given the new name Richard Cromwell. His debut was a popular and critical success, and

ABOVE Richard Cromwell (right) with Tom Brown in Annapolis Farewell (1935). Cromwell was earning $200 a week at the time.

Cromwell was rewarded with steady work portraying youthful sons, brothers, students and sidekicks. He was at his best acting with talented leads—most notably, Franchot Tone and Gary Cooper in *The Lives of a Bengal Lancer* (1935), Bette Davis in *Jezebel* (1938), and Henry Fonda in *Young Mr. Lincoln* (1939).

A number of Richard Cromwell pictures, particularly *The Lives of a Bengal Lancer* and *Tom Brown of Culver* (1932), cast him in a decidedly homoerotic light. Like many Hollywood "bachelors," he was, in fact, gay—and a frequent guest at director George Cukor's infamous boys' nights. Nonetheless, in 1942—on his return from three years of war service in the Coast Guard—he married 19-year-old Angela Lansbury. They divorced only six months later.

Star Shot

Richard Cromwell's co-star in *Young Mr. Lincoln* (1939), Alice Brady, also succumbed to cancer at an early age. She passed away in 1939, just before her 47th birthday.

As Cromwell outgrew his collegiate image, roles became scarce. He retired from the screen, happily resuming his first career, ceramics, under his given name. It's doubtful that Roy Radabaugh ultimately regretted the demise of his motion picture career much more than that of his marriage. In the years that followed, he distinguished himself as a ceramic artist, creating a bold, modern style based on Native American and Aztec imagery. His tile work was acclaimed by designers and architects, and became a popular adornment in the hotels of Los Angeles.

RIGHT Richard Cromwell and Ann Sothern in a Columbia Studio publicity shot taken about 1934.

It had been 12 years since his last acting job when, at the age of 50, he was offered a part in Mori Dexter's *Little Shepherd of Kingdom Come* (1961). But before he could make his return to the screen he was stricken with cancer. He died on October 11, 1960, just as the film was to begin shooting.

LEFT Alan Curtis played Joan Crawford's husband in the 1937 drama, Mannequin. *In his short movie career, Curtis appeared in more than 50 motion pictures.*

Alan Curtis

Born July 24, 1909
Died February 2, 1953

Suit model turned screen heavy Alan Curtis had three great loves: fine clothes, pretty actresses, and foreign cars. Though none of them would kill him, the latter came close. In 1945, his English roadster crashed with a milk truck in Burbank, California. Curtis was lucky to survive with only some broken bones—but just eight years later he would die from complications following kidney surgery.

According to lore, Curtis (born Harry Ueberroth) was discovered while driving a taxi cab in his native Chicago. A passenger, admiring his strong jaw and broad shoulders, offered him a job posing for a suit ad. Curtis's modeling career took off from there. He was working in France when he caught the attention of an American film producer. After a screen test, he landed bit parts in a number of films, including RKO's *Winterset* (1936) starring Burgess Meredith. Despite his easy entree into Hollywood, Curtis was a realist about his talents. To a journalist who called him a fifth-rate actor, Curtis quipped back, "I'm not fifth rate, I'm second rate!"

He soon moved to MGM, where Joan Crawford convinced director Frank Borzage to give him a part in her upcoming film *Mannequin* (1937). Though Alan Curtis was most often cast as a villain or thug, he gave a sensitive portrayal of composer Franz Schubert in *New Wine* (1941), and starred in the war drama *Remember Pearl Harbor* (1942). He is best remembered for his 1944 portrayal of an innocent man framed for the murder of his wife in Universal's *The Phantom Lady* (1944). Encouraged by its success, the studio began grooming him for more sympathetic roles—but his car accident interrupted the upward swing of his career. Curtis sued the truck company and the driver for damages of $50,000, eventually settling out of court for an undisclosed sum. Following a lengthy recovery, he made a few minor films, then moved to New York to work in television.

In 1953, Curtis checked into St. Clare's Hospital in New York for kidney surgery, and while in recovery his heart suddenly stopped beating. His doctors cut into his chest and massaged his heart back to life. Technically, he had been dead for four minutes, and his revival was reported as a medical miracle. But he died less than a week later, at 43. He was survived by two brothers; among his ex-wives were actresses Ilona Massey and Priscilla Lawson.

Bobby Darin

Born May 14, 1936
Died December 20, 1973

RIGHT Bobby Darin and Sandra Dee were married in 1960. After their divorce, Darin worked on Senator Robert Kennedy's presidential campaign.

BELOW One great singer meets another: Bobby Darin was a guest on The Judy Garland Show *in November 1963.*

Velvet-voiced crooner Bobby Darin famously said that he planned to be a star by 21, a legend by 25, and an institution by 30. Though he was known for his egotism, Darin's drive was born of necessity as much as of arrogance. Childhood rheumatic fever had left him with a heart condition that was destined to cut his life short. With the clock ticking, he pursued his goals relentlessly. Though he didn't quite fulfill his wildly ambitious agenda, his charisma and talent made him a popular success as both a singer and an actor until his early death at the age of only 37.

Born Walden Robert Cassotto in a rough section of New York City's Bronx, Bobby Darin was a street-smart city boy with a cocky charm that would later become his trademark. His father, a small-time gangster, was long gone by the time he was born, and Darin was brought up by his grandmother and his much older "sister" Nina. It wasn't until Darin was 32 that he learned that Nina was his mother. Starting out his music career as a drummer in a school band, Darin performed in the Catskills as a teenager, and at the age of 20 he was awarded a record contract.

Like most of his Italian-American singer contemporaries (Dean Martin, Frankie Avalon, Fabian), "Cassotto" traded in his cumbersome surname. Sporting a new moniker derived from the faulty neon sign of a Chinese restaurant, "Bobby Darin" hit the big time in 1958 with his novelty single "Splish Splash"—the catchy, childlike ditty made the Top 40, with more than 100,000 sales. Against the advice of Dick Clark, who thought it would estrange his teen fan base, Darin recorded Kurt Weill's "Mac the Knife" in the following year. His bid for greater musical credibility paid off royally. A hit with young and old alike, his stylish and sophisticated interpretation became one of a handful of definitive versions of the song.

As the press began to contrast the enormity of his ego with his more human-scaled talents, Darin continued to push himself into new territories, making his credited film debut in *Pepe* (1960). Dazzled by the glitter of Hollywood, he married golden-haired teen starlet Sandra Dee of *Gidget* fame. Darin and Dee formed a partnership on-screen as well as off, appearing together in the bubblegum comedies *Come September*

(1961), *If a Man Answers* (1962), and *That Funny
Feeling* (1965). Their marriage, however, was a
darker saga. In his book *Dream Lovers* (1994), their
son, Dodd, paints Darin as an abusive, narcissistic
swinger, whose many infidelities fueled Sandra
Dee's devastating alcoholism.

Perhaps hoping to repeat his transition from
the lightweight "Splish Splash" to the more high-
brow "Mac the Knife," Bobby Darin sought out
increasingly challenging film roles. Playing a jazz
musician in John Cassavetes's *Too Late Blues* (1961)
and an incarcerated racist in *Pressure Point* (1962),
he proved he was capable of serious acting. His
film career peaked with his portrayal of a shell-
shocked soldier in *Captain Newman, M.D.* (1963),
which won him an Oscar® nomination for Best
Actor in a Supporting Role.

Vacillating between "art" and pop culture, Darin
sometimes gave the impression that he wanted to
be all things to all people. This was especially true
as the burgeoning counterculture threatened to
make his smooth, old-school stylings obsolete.
Divorced from Dee in 1967—and shattered by his
"sister's" confession that she was his mother—Darin

grew his hair long, sold his possessions, and moved to Big Sur. Re-emerging in 1970 as "Bob
Darin," he alienated Las Vegas by making anti-war speeches and playing folk ballads instead
of his hits. A few months later, however, he was back as the old Bobby Darin, promising in his
slippery fashion to satisfy hipper fans with shows at the Troubadour.

Darin's uneasy marriage of Las Vegas showmanship and counterculture sensibilities continued in two television specials, *The Darin Invasion* and *Mack is Back!*, but while shooting the
former, his heart condition worsened, causing him to collapse on stage. After successful open-
heart surgery, his health and career were flourishing. It was a trip to the dentist that sent him
on the road to an early death. As a heart patient, he was supposed to take antibiotics to prevent
harmful bacteria from infecting his bloodstream. Failing to do so—for reasons that would
remain mysterious—Darin was soon diagnosed with blood poisoning. For a year his health
deteriorated, and he finally died of heart failure on December 20, 1973, following surgery.

The ever-ambitious Darin has been climbing toward legend status ever since his death.

In 1990, he was inducted into the Rock
and Roll Hall of Fame, and a few years
later a four-CD set was enthusiastically
greeted with beaming reappraisals of
his virtuosic, wide-ranging output.
Finally, despite mixed reactions from
the critics, Kevin Spacey's biopic,
Beyond the Sea (2005), sparked a
major mainstream revival of interest
in Bobby Darin's life and work.

*ABOVE A scene from
That Funny Feeling
(1965). Bobby Darin
once said, "Conceit is
thinking you're great;
egotism is knowing it."*

*LEFT With Glenn Ford
(right) in an episode of
the television series,
Cade's County (1971).
Darin also appeared in
Wagon Train, Burke's
Law, and Ironside.*

Joan Davis

Born June 29, 1907
Died May 22, 1961

*ABOVE Joan Davis
and her daughter,
Beverly, ham it up
for the cameras. Davis
was known and loved
for her slapstick style
of comedy.*

Comedienne Joan Davis was a rarity among entertainers of her time: a savvy businesswoman who took control of her career and competed in a man's world. Known for her cracked voice, rubber face, and generally zany antics, she was one of the most popular stars of radio and early television—as well as acting in a string of hit movies—but success took its toll.

Born in St. Paul, Minnesota, Madonna Josephine Davis began her career as a child in vaudeville. In 1931 she married fellow vaudevillian Si Wills, and two years later they had a daughter. Mack Sennett gave Davis her first break in the movies, casting her in the comic short *Way Up Thar* (1935). For the next ten years, she worked steadily as a featured player in close to 50 films alongside Dick Powell, Shirley Temple, Abbott and Costello, and many others. But it was in radio that Joan Davis would become a household name. She took over Rudy Vallee's show when he enlisted in the Coast Guard, and in 1944 became the highest paid woman in radio, signing a four-year contract at a million dollars a year—only Bob Hope and Jack Benny out-earned her.

In the mid-1940s Davis had an affair with singer Eddie Cantor, also married, and appeared with him in two films. Romance blossomed on *Show Business* (1944) and died four years later on *If You Knew Suzie* (1948). Davis divorced Wills and created her own production company; in 1952 her show *I Married Joan* co-starring Jim Backus was picked up by NBC to compete with *I Love Lucy*. But as her career flourished, her mental health seemed to deteriorate.

Davis, who had always been rather moody, became notorious for her temper and insensitivity to others, provoking a few lawsuits. Jim Backus later recalled, "Joan's behavior was enough to make a psychiatrist hit the couch." Despite the continued success of *I Married Joan*, she retired in 1955, exhausted from the double duty of running her own production company and starring in a hit show. She had intended to make occasional film and theater appearances but, perhaps due to her reputation, she never worked again.

On May 21, 1961, Davis was at home in Palm Springs, when she experienced back pains. Her mother took her to the hospital, and she died early the next morning of a heart attack. Greater tragedy struck two years later, when the Palm Springs house burned, killing her mother, daughter, and two grandchildren.

Star Shot

Joan Davis's daughter, Beverly Wills, made regular guest appearances on *I Married Joan* playing the part of Joan's sister, despite an age difference of 27 years.

RIGHT In 1945, Bob Hope and Joan Davis were named the king and queen of comedy. Davis made a guest appearance on Hope's show in November 1956.

Star Shot

Marguerite de la Motte

Born June 22, 1902
Died March 10, 1950

Silent-era nymphette Marguerite de la Motte was born in Duluth, Minnesota, and later moved with her family to San Diego. As a child, she dreamed of being a ballet dancer. She reputedly studied with the great Anna Pavlova, and it was dancing that got her into the movies. De la Motte was in her mid-teens when screen idol Douglas Fairbanks spotted her in one of Grauman's lavish prologues at the Million Dollar Theater. Taken with her saucer eyes and auburn waves, he invited her to be his leading lady.

The diminutive de la Motte debuted with Fairbanks in *Arizona* in 1918, remaining by his side as he swashbuckled his way through *The Mark of Zorro* (1920), *The Three Musketeers* (1921), and *The Iron Mask* (1929) among others. One of the youngest leading ladies of her time, de la Motte claimed she got her education preparing for movie parts. Subjects of her starlet's curriculum included boating, surfing, knitting, and dancing a quadrille.

Fairbanks wasn't de la Motte's only leading man. In 1924 she married John Bowers, with whom she had starred in *Desire* and *Richard the Lionhearted* the previous year. Unfortunately, he was a heavy drinker, and as her career flourished, his was going down the tubes. They had already separated when, in 1936, Bowers committed suicide—his body washed up on the beach in Santa Monica. De la Motte remarried, but divorced her second husband, attorney Sidney H. Rivkin, four years later, fed up with his angry outbursts and tyrannical whims.

With the rise of talking pictures, de la Motte's career—like those of many other silent film stars—began to falter. After making just a handful of appearances in the 1930s and 1940s, she retired from the screen altogether, and took a decidedly unglamorous job as an inspector in a Southern California war plant. Later she moved to San Francisco, where she worked with the Red Cross. Though she hadn't acted for 10 years at the time of her death, she had more than 60 film credits to her name.

Marguerite de la Motte died in San Francisco on March 10, 1950, of a cerebral thrombosis following surgery. Coincidentally, it was the day after the funeral of famed showman Sid Grauman, who, according to a number of Hollywood stories, had been partly instrumental in the young actress's discovery 30-plus years earlier.

Lya De Putti

Born January 10, 1899
Died November 27, 1931

With her black bob and sultry saucer eyes, Lya De Putti was a classic vamp of the silent cinema. Arriving in Hollywood from Germany, she was celebrated as "the loveliest girl in Berlin," but with the advent of talking pictures, her European accent became a liability. By the time of her death in 1931, her type had been banished from the silver screen. Earlier that year, *The New York Times* declared, "The dark-haired, slithering siren of the screen has gone. A sweet young thing, usually blonde, has usurped her throne."

Born in Vecsés, Hungary, near Budapest, De Putti was the daughter of a count, and a relative of Germany's Prince von Bismarck. She married at a young age to Zoltan de Szepessy, a judge, and had two daughters, but soon abandoned her family for a career as a danseuse. While performing at the Winter Garden in Berlin, she was noticed by the German director Joe May, who cast her in *Das Indische Grabmal* (1921). After establishing herself on the German screen, she earned her place in movie history with her starring role opposite Emil Jannings in the ground-breaking international sensation, *Varieté* (1925).

A sexy tale of jealousy and murder set in a circus, *Varieté* was hailed by one reviewer as "the strongest and most inspiring drama that has ever been told by the evanescent shadows." Director Ewald André Dupont's symbolic imagery and cinematographer Karl Freund's kinetic camera made an enormous impression on Hollywood. De Putti was immediately contracted with Famous Players-Lasky, but she would never again have a comparable hit.

Lya De Putti's American films include D.W. Griffith's *The Sorrows of Satan* (1926), as well as *The Heart Thief* (1927) and *Buck Privates* (1928). When sound came in, she was no longer a hot commodity in Hollywood, and she accepted an offer to make a film in England. Apparently, she was more than happy to leave Hollywood. She told a London newspaper, "The place deadens you. There is no opera, no theater, no life … the people talk of nothing but movies."

In 1930, Lya De Putti moved to New York to work in theater. The following year, she was hospitalized when a chicken bone became stuck in her throat. It was surgically removed, but infection followed. After a second operation, she developed pleurisy and pneumonia, and despite the efforts of seven doctors, the 32-year-old actress soon died. A few months later, her ex-husband, Zoltan de Szepessy, shot himself in the head in a Budapest hotel. At the time of her death, De Putti's estate was so diminished by debt that her two daughters received only about $475 each.

BELOW Lya De Putti was a classic vamp of the 1920s. She appeared in over 30 motion pictures, her last role as Katie Fox in The Informer *(1931).*

Sandy Dennis

Born April 27, 1937
Died March 2, 1992

Sandy Dennis came to film through theater, and even after winning an Academy Award®, always saw herself as a stage actress first. Bohemian and down-to-earth, Dennis rejected the glamor of Hollywood and Broadway. For most of her career she lived in a Westport, Connecticut, farmhouse with an entourage of cats and dogs. Co-star Richard Burton described her as "one of the most genuine eccentrics I know of."

Born in Hastings, Nebraska, in 1937, Sandra Dale Dennis was inspired to become an actress when she saw Joanne Woodward and Kim Stanley in *A Young Lady of Property* on television. After a brief stint at college, she headed for the stages of New York City. Studying with Herbert Berghof and later with Lee Strasberg, Dennis developed her singular style, marked by stammering, neurotic speech patterns, and an air of fragile innocence.

She made her screen debut in 1961 with a supporting role in *Splendor in the Grass*, but it was on Broadway that she would become a star. She won two consecutive Tony® Awards for her performances with Jason Robards in *A Thousand Clowns* (1963) and Gene Hackman in *Any Wed- nesday* (1964). Returning to film in 1966, she appeared with Elizabeth Taylor, Richard Burton, and George Segal in the screen adaptation of Edward Albee's *Who's Afraid*

ABOVE Elizabeth Taylor (left), George Segal (seated), Richard Burton, and Sandy Dennis in Who's Afraid of Virginia Woolf? (1966).

of Virginia Woolf?, which follows two university faculty couples through a night of debauched melodrama. Her portrayal of the frail and simpering Honey won her an Oscar® for Best Actress in a Supporting Role. The following year she played a young New York school teacher in *Up the Down Staircase* (1967), and won the Moscow Film Festival award for best actress. Her performances in *Sweet November* (1968) and *The Out-of-Towners* (1970) were also well-received.

Despite the accolades, critics were not always kind. Pauline Kael famously noted that Dennis had "made an acting style of post-nasal drip." But her unique presence and disciplined artistry made her popular with directors until her death. Other film credits include Robert Altman's *Come Back to the Five and Dime, Jimmy Dean, Jimmy Dean* (1982), Woody Allen's *Another Woman* (1988), and Steven Spielberg's television movie *Something Evil* (1972).

In 1990, when Dennis returned to Nebraska to appear in *The Indian Runner* (1991), the first film directed by Sean Penn, she had already been diagnosed with ovarian cancer. *The Indian Runner* would be her last film. She died in her Connecticut home in 1992, after a two-and-a-half year battle with the disease. Memorial donations in her name went to an animal rescue fund.

Star Shot

Sandy Dennis was romantically involved with jazz musician Gerry Mulligan for many years (though she denied reports that they had married).

LEFT Famous drag queen Divine played two straight roles in his film career: as crime boss Hilly Blue in Trouble in Mind *(1985) and as Detective Langella in* Out of the Dark *(1989).*

Divine

Born October 19, 1945
Died March 7, 1988

BELOW Divine once said, "The last thing my parents wanted was a son who wears a cocktail dress that glitters, but they've come around to it."

Director John Waters described the screen persona of his friend and muse Divine as a fusion of Jayne Mansfield and Clarabelle the clown. Appearing in numerous Waters films, the 350-pound (159-kg) drag queen embodied the cult filmmaker's affectionate vision of America as a carnival of the grotesque. Though he enjoyed his image, Divine once said: "I am a character actor, and one of my characters happens to be a loud, vulgar woman."

Born Harris Glenn Milstead in the Baltimore, Maryland, suburb of Towson, he and his family moved to nearby Lutherville in the late 1950s. There Milstead befriended John Waters. The chubby, effeminate youth came of age in the Baltimore gay scene, and for several years ran a hair salon, a gift from his parents intended to keep him out of trouble. But in 1972, Milstead left his family without a forwarding address—and Divine was on his way to underground film stardom.

As a member of Waters's pot-and-amphetamine-fueled repertory group, The Dreamlanders, Divine burst into notoriety with his appearance in *Pink Flamingos* (1972). The trashy proto-punk fantasia opened at the Elgin Theater in New York, and ran for 50 weeks as word spread of the now infamous finale in which Divine eats dog doo fresh off the sidewalk. In 1981, Waters and the Dreamlanders went mainstream with the wacked-out suburban melodrama (of "Odorama" fame), *Polyester*.

Around the same time, Divine and his parents were reconciled. As they began to accept their son in drag, America began to accept Divine as a man. He played male roles in two Alan Rudolph films, and in *Hairspray* (1988)— his last collaboration with Waters—he really showed his range, portraying loving mother Edna Turnblad *and* racist television station owner Arvin Hodgepile.

For many years Divine had suffered from depression and sleep apnea, both conditions related to his obesity. But as his personal and professional life improved, he lost some weight and even quit his pot habit. Things were looking up when he was cast as Uncle Otto in the television series *Married With Children*. But on the first day of shooting, Divine failed to appear. His manager went to look for him at the Regency Hotel in Los Angeles, and found him dead in his bed, a faint smile on his face. The coroner found that he had died of an enlarged heart, but his manager said he preferred to think that Divine had died of happiness.

"You know, I'm not licked. A champ gets off the floor...."

RIGHT On location at the Lasky Ranch while shooting The Wheel of Life *(1930). During this period, Richard Dix was earning around $4,500 a week.*

Richard Dix

Born July 18, 1893
Died September 20, 1949

Popular with men and women alike, Richard Dix was one of the most successful stars of the silent screen. Best known for his westerns, the ruggedly handsome actor actually had a versatile career that began with light comedies and ended with mysteries and thrillers.

Richard Dix was born Ernest Carlton Brimmer in St. Paul, Minnesota. As a young man, Dix excelled in football and drama, but at his father's insistence he went to college intending to be a surgeon. Dix eventually dropped out and worked a desk job while studying acting at night. Soon he was playing in stock theater around the country. After serving in World War I, he went to Hollywood and landed his first major film role, playing twins in Goldwyn's *Not Guilty* (1921).

Richard Dix appeared in Cecil B. DeMille's *The Ten Commandments* (1923), and followed this up with a series of light comedies, among them *Womanhandled* (1925) and *The Quarterback* (1926). Dix also became known for his portrayals of Native Americans. In 1930 he was honored by the Kaw people, who inducted him into their tribe as a tribute to his "true characterizations of the Indian."

With his stage background, Dix had no trouble making the transition to sound, and he is best remembered for his Oscar®-nominated performance in *Cimarron* (1931), which won for Best Picture. As a newspaperman whose move to the Western frontier stirs up his thirst for adventure, Dix is at his manly best. Even as he drifted into B-grade movies, he could turn in a riveting performance—witness his portrayal of lunatic Captain Stone in *The Ghost Ship* (1943).

Dix went into semiretirement in 1946 due to previous coronary problems. In August 1949 he had a heart attack on board a ship after a vacation in France. He returned to the United States and started to travel home by train, but by the time he reached Chicago he was virtually pulseless. He was hospitalized for a month, then flown to Los Angeles. He died soon after of a chronic heart ailment in Hollywood Presbyterian Hospital on September 20, 1949, with his second wife, Virginia, by his side. His physician, Dr. George Berg, linked his illness to his acting, telling the press, "His courageous willingness to tackle physically taxing roles and his disdain for doubles doing his hard work for him took their toll." Conscious until the last moment, Dix fought for his life with all the vigor of the screen heroes he portrayed.

Robert Donat

Born March 18, 1905
Died June 9, 1958

*ABOVE Robert Donat
with Phyllis Calvert in
The Young Mr. Pitt
(1942). The film was
directed by Carol Reed
and also featured Robert
Morley and John Mills.*

Star Shot

**Robert Donat helped to
make Errol Flynn a star.
He turned down two roles
that would advance
Flynn's career: Captain
Blood and Robin Hood.**

*RIGHT Robert Donat
appeared as Benedick in
William Shakespeare's
play,* Much Ado About
Nothing, *performed at
the Aldwych Theatre in
London in 1946.*

*G*one with the Wind swept the Oscars® in 1939, but Clark Gable, in all his swaggering glory, was bested by a shy, sickly Brit who wasn't even there to pick up his statuette. Robert Donat was voted Best Actor for his life-spanning portrayal of a tender-hearted schoolmaster in *Goodbye Mr. Chips. The New York Times* called it an "incredibly fine characterization," noting, "Mr. Donat has wisely understated him, played him softly, doubled his poignance." His victory was all the more impressive given that after making one film in Hollywood he had declined further offers—chiefly because his chronic asthma made the hot, dry climate insufferable. Donat's ailments interfered with his career throughout his life, and he only made 20 films, but he is counted among England's finest actors.

Suave and slender, with a rare grace, Donat based his screen career on playing quintessentially English gentlemen. In fact, he was born Friedrich Robert Donath, the son of a Polish civil engineer in Manchester. An introverted, awkward boy, when he was 11 he took elocution lessons to correct his stammer and soften his thick Lancashire accent—years later he became known for his wonderful speaking voice. He made his stage debut in *Julius Caesar* at 16, and in 1930 he hit the stages of London.

Donat's first plays in the West End were flops, but he distinguished himself enough to receive—and turn down—an offer from Irving Thalberg. Instead he signed with Sir Alexander Korda, and had his first big success in *The Private Life of Henry VIII* (1933), the film that brought English cinema to the attention of the world. When Hollywood made him a second offer, Donat voyaged west to star in *The Count of Monte Cristo* (1934). Throughout his stay he was sick and depressed, and it was evident that his quiet, self-deprecating nature wasn't cut out for Tinseltown stardom, so Donat headed home. His next film was Alfred Hitchcock's future classic, *The 39 Steps* (1935), which made him popular on both sides of the Atlantic.

Although Donat wouldn't go to Hollywood, in 1937 he signed a four-picture deal with MGM to make films in England. The first was *Knight without Armour* (1937) with Marlene Dietrich. During shooting, Donat's asthma was so bad that Laurence Olivier was kept on standby in case he was unable

to complete the film. He got through it, and even as his sickness ate away at his confidence, his career approached its peak. Donat earned his first Oscar® nomination for his role in *The Citadel* (1938)—director King Vidor called him "the most helpful and cooperative star" he'd ever met. The following year he won for *Goodbye Mr. Chips*, beating not only Clark Gable, but also acting heavyweights Laurence Olivier and James Stewart.

Donat was suited to historical dramas, appearing as British Prime Minister William Pitt in *The Young Mr. Pitt* (1942) and Irish statesman Charles Stewart Parnell in *Captain Boycott* (1947). But it was almost ten years before he had a success comparable to *Goodbye Mr. Chips*, with *The Winslow Boy* (1948). His uniquely deft touch is on full display in this true story of an attorney trying to prove the innocence of a schoolboy accused of theft. The following year he made his directorial debut with the farcical *The Cure for Love* (released early in 1950), casting himself as a sergeant who returns to his village on leave and finds that he is braver in war than in love. Claims that he was, at 45, too old for the romantic lead were proved wrong when his leading lady, Renée Asherson, became his second wife (his first was Ella Annesley Voysey).

The 1950s saw the sad decline of Donat's career as his health deteriorated. During a stage production of Samuel Beckett's *Murder in the Cathedral*, he was so debilitated by his asthma that oxygen cylinders were kept in the wings. As it became more difficult to work, it also became more necessary, since he could no longer afford his medical bills. After a four-year absence from film, he accepted the role of "the Mandarin" in *The Inn of the Sixth Happiness* (1958). The true story of a missionary (played by Ingrid Bergman) in 1930s China, it would be his last film.

Donat worked hard, creating a poignant performance despite the awkwardness of appearing in "Chinese" makeup, but the effort destroyed him. He suffered a collapsed lung, and on May 18, a week after the film wrapped, he was rushed to a London hospital, critically ill. He died a few weeks later from a cerebral hemorrhage brought on by his asthma. On the last day of shooting, Ingrid Bergman had wept during their parting scene, knowing all too well that her gentle co-star's days were numbered. Donat's final words on screen were, "We shall not see each other again, I think. Farewell."

LEFT Robert Donat (right) shares a drink and a conversation with film producer Alexander Korda. Korda was married for a time to Merle Oberon.

BELOW In the title role of Goodbye Mr. Chips *(1939), Robert Donat reminisces about his long career as a classics teacher in an English boarding school.*

Diana Dors

Born October 23, 1931
Died May 4, 1984

Growing up in working-class Swindon, England, Diana Mary Fluck—as she was then known—dreamed of Hollywood stardom. Eventually she would be called the British Marilyn Monroe, quite cheerfully capitalizing on her cartoonish resemblance to the American one. But instead of a Hollywood star, she became a tabloid star. For decades, her turbulent personal life was one of the most popular soap operas in England.

Though her legacy would suggest otherwise, Diana Dors was, in fact, a capable actress. Studying at the London Academy of Music and Dramatic Arts, she was proclaimed the most promising drama student in her class. Her first motion picture appearance was in *The Shop at Sly Corner* (1947) with Oskar Homolka, and the following year she was cast in David Lean's *Oliver Twist*. But her name in lights presented a problem: what if the "L" fell off the marquee? She adopted her grandmother's name, but despite both her talent and the precautionary name change, her career would be built on sexuality. Over the next several years she strutted her stuff playing bad girls in mostly bad pictures.

In 1951, she married hot-headed scammer Dennis Hamilton. A master at generating hype, he spun tales for the press at every opportunity. Whether or not his handiwork helped, in 1956 Dors broke out of her B-movie rut with *Yield to the Night*, a thoughtful prison drama in which she plays a woman on death row. Its success brought her to Hollywood, where she made two films—*The Unholy Wife* (1957) and *I Married a Woman* (1958). She had an affair with co-star Rod Steiger, and got into enough trouble to prompt the tabloid headline, "Go home Diana." She did, but things weren't much better there. She left Hamilton when he pulled a gun on her, and he died of syphilis soon after. In 1959 she married actor Richard Dawson and they had two sons, Mark and Gary.

The mid-1960s brought a new style of glamor, epitomized by the slim and urbane Julie Christie. Buxom Dors was way out of vogue. As her career faded, her personal life remained in the spotlight. She divorced Dawson in 1966 and married again, this time to alcoholic actor Alan Lake, who eventually found God and converted Dors to Catholicism. In 1982, she was diagnosed with ovarian cancer when a malignant cyst burst. She died in May 1984, but the tabloid finale came five months later when, on the 16th anniversary of their meeting, Lake shot himself in the head in their son's bedroom.

ABOVE Diana Dors penned two separate autobiographies, For Adults Only *in 1978 and* Behind Closed Doors *in 1979.*

ABOVE RIGHT Diana Dors with her third husband, Alan Lake, in a scene from the 1970 London stage production of Three Months Gone.

Star Shot

Diana Dors is one of many influential people who feature on the cover of The Beatles' 1967 landmark album, *Sgt. Pepper's Lonely Hearts Club Band.*

Paul Douglas

Born April 11, 1907
Died September 11, 1959

ABOVE *Paul Douglas was to play a baseball team manager in an episode of* The Twilight Zone *written for him by Rod Serling, but he died before filming finished.*

Beefy radio announcer Paul Douglas made his Broadway debut at the age of 39. As the story goes, his friend Garson Kanin was struggling to cast the part of junk tycoon Harry Brock in the play *Born Yesterday*. He told his wife, actress Ruth Gordon, "What we need for this part is a big, loud-mouthed s.o.b.—like Paul Douglas." She said, "Well, why don't you get Paul Douglas?" The play ran for 1,024 performances, and Douglas and leading lady Judy Holliday garnered rave reviews.

As a child, the Philadelphia native relished the role of Shylock in a school production of *The Merchant of Venice*, but despite his passion for acting, the practical consideration of where his next meal was coming from took priority for the next 30 years. Orphaned young, he sold paint and worked at a train station, then went to Yale until he was drafted to play professional football with the Frankford (Philadelphia) Yellow Jackets. Later he became a sportscaster, and then one of the most successful announcers in radio, working as a straight man for Jack Benny as well as Burns and Allen. He also hosted Glenn Miller's last concert in 1944.

After his Broadway success, Douglas was Hollywood bound. He debuted in Joseph Manckiewicz's Oscar®-winning social satire, *A Letter to Three Wives* (1949), establishing his niche playing blustery but good-hearted big shots. In 1956 he reteamed with Judy Holliday in the boardroom farce *The Solid Gold Cadillac*. Praised for his deft comic touch, one critic noted Douglas's "uncanny ability to lose the laugh but win the scene." Other credits include *Angels in the Outfield* (1951), *Executive Suite* (1954), and *The Mating Game* (1959).

Famously ugly, Paul Douglas kidded, "Guys look at me and say, 'If that mug can get a girl it's a cinch for me.' Girls look at me and thank God for the guy they're with." Nonetheless, he was married five times. He wed his last wife, actress Jan Sterling, in 1950, and they remained together until his death.

In August 1959, Douglas was hospitalized for exhaustion, but his doctors found nothing wrong with him. A month later, he died of a heart attack in his Hollywood Hills home, collapsing on the way from his bed to the bathroom. His wife called the fire department, then gave him mouth-to-mouth resuscitation, but to no avail. He had been slated to appear in *The Apartment* (1960), which went on to win an Academy Award® for Best Picture. He would have been a perfect fit in Billy Wilder's poignant anti-corporate romantic comedy.

Star Shot

While touring North Carolina in 1955, Douglas was quoted as saying, "The South stinks. It's a land of sowbelly and segregation." Though he denied the comment, the tour was canceled.

Josh Ryan Evans

Born January 10, 1982
Died August 5, 2002

The 3 foot, 2 inch (1 m) tall soap star Josh Ryan Evans was born with achondroplasia, a type of dwarfism, and made a career of playing small children and babies. He attributed his success in part to his size. "If I was just another blond-haired, brown-eyed actor," he once told a reporter, "I'd be left unrecognized."

A native of Hayward, California, Evans traced his interest in acting to a childhood spent watching television and movies while recovering from a series of surgeries to replace his heart valves. As soon as he was well enough, the charming and intrepid youth started handing out business cards backstage at musicals. He was 12 when he landed his first part, playing a dancing baby in a Dreyers ice cream commercial, and soon after he made his film debut in *Baby Geniuses* (1999). Returning to television, he became a regular on *Passions*. His inventive characterization of a doll who is turned into a boy by a witch earned him a cult following and two Soap Opera Digest awards. Other small-screen credits include a child prodigy lawyer on *Ally McBeal* and Tom Thumb in the A&E miniseries *P.T. Barnum* (1999) starring Beau Bridges.

Josh Ryan Evans's biggest film role was in *How the Grinch Stole Christmas* (2000). Director Ron Howard initially cast him for a quick walk on, but was so delighted with Evans that he expanded the part. Evans portrays the pug-faced young Grinch in a series of flashbacks, giving a sympathetic view of how Jim Carrey's character came to be so infamously misanthropic. After filming, Evans, then a high school senior, told the *Los Angeles Times* that he was considering interning with Ron Howard, and perhaps going to film school. He died less than two years later at age 20 due to complications from a congenital heart condition, following a medical procedure at a San Diego hospital.

Passions co-star Juliet Mills remembered Evans as a "little fairy being who was already very close to the other world." Perhaps influenced by the occult themes of their show, the two had often spoken of spiritual matters. Six months after his death, she appeared in a televised séance on *Beyond with James Van Praagh*, allegedly making contact not only with Evans, but also with family friend Sir Laurence Olivier.

ABOVE Josh Ryan Evans with a fellow cast member, Jeffrey Tambor, on the set of How the Grinch Stole Christmas *(2000).*

Star Shot

In a morbid case of life imitating art, on the day of Evans's death, his character, Timmy, died in that day's episode of NBC's supernatural drama, *Passions*.

LEFT Josh Ryan Evans at the 2000 Soap Opera Digest awards. His size did not seem to bother him—he always said "Dream big!"

Myrna Fahey

Born March 12, 1933
Died May 6, 1973

A bright-eyed brunette with a distinctly Irish sparkle, Myrna Fahey made scores of television appearances throughout the 1960s. It was once reported that she played eight out of ten sheriff's daughters on television. Unfortunately, despite high visibility and decent residuals, that wasn't exactly what Myrna Fahey was aiming for when she left her Maine home after high school to try her luck in Hollywood. For much of her career she pushed for more interesting parts, with only limited success.

Directly descended from the *Mayflower*'s Captain Andrew Newcomb, Fahey's family had deep roots in Maine. Her move to California made her the first of her clan to venture west. After studying at the Pasadena Community Playhouse for less than a year, she landed an agent and began appearing in small television roles, most notably on *Matinee Theater*, a much respected live drama show. However, according to Fahey, it wasn't until she began taking classes with Sanford Meisner that she really began to master the art of acting. They appeared together in *The Story on Page One* (1960), written and directed by Clifford Odets.

The standout in Fahey's short filmography is B-movie king Roger Corman's *House of Usher* (1960), based on Edgar Allan Poe's classic horror story. Vincent Price stars as the deranged Roderick, who will stop at nothing to keep his sister Madeline (Fahey) from carrying on their cursed family line. Fahey told the *Los Angeles Examiner*, "It's some role.... I'm buried alive, go into a cataleptic fit, finally go mad." With the success of *House of Usher*, Fahey returned to the small screen, playing not a sheriff's daughter, but the lead in a CBS miniseries version of *Father of the Bride* (Elizabeth Taylor, to whom Fahey was often compared, had played the part in the 1950 film.) Roles in television's *Peyton Place* (1964) and *The Great American Beauty Contest* (1973) followed.

Fahey's personal life was not widely publicized. She never married, despite reports of her engagement to a banker in 1960. Her most notable beau was Joe DiMaggio. While dating him in 1964 she began receiving mysterious death threats. The FBI eventually determined that they were being sent by a mental patient who couldn't stand the thought of DiMaggio "two-timing" on his ex, the late Marilyn Monroe. Fahey died nine years later, at the age of 40, at St. John's Hospital, Santa Monica, California, after a long battle with cancer. Upon her death, her body was returned to her native Maine for burial in the family plot.

ABOVE *Myrna Fahey (center) at a beach party for MGM players. Fahey appeared in a number of television shows, including* Zorro, Perry Mason, Hawaiian Eye, *and* Batman.

Douglas Fairbanks

Born May 23, 1883
Died December 12, 1939

RIGHT Douglas Fairbanks (right) as D'Artagnan, who meets the man in the iron mask in the classic 1929 adventure film.

The film critic C. A. Le Jeune observed that Douglas Fairbanks's death "robbed the movies of a bit of themselves—a drop of the life-blood that made them gay, and great, and indomitable." With glinting eyes and a zesty grin, Fairbanks leaped, dashed, and somersaulted across the silver screen as if reveling in the sheer wonder of "pictures that move." His unflagging energy and eternal optimism held up offscreen as well, making him a role model for youth and a true pioneer in the business of cinema. The consummate man of action, Fairbanks embodied the naive optimism of a young nation on the rise.

Douglas Elton Ulman was born in Denver, Colorado, in 1883, the son of a prominent Jewish lawyer and a Catholic southern belle. Ruined by a bad investment in a silver mine, his father abandoned the family in 1888, and the boy took his mother's stately maiden name, Fairbanks. He first acted at the age of 12, playing an Italian paperboy, and later joined a local theater company without success. He went on to attend Harvard, but soon dropped out to travel in Europe. On his return he worked as a clerk on Wall Street until the lights of Broadway drew him back to the stage. He debuted in 1902, and had his first hit several years later in *Man of the Hour*. Even then, Fairbanks's destiny was uncertain. Marrying Anna Beth Sully in 1907, he went to work for her father's soap company. Fortunately for Fairbanks, the firm went bust a year later, and he returned to the stage. With his career on the rise, it was a happy time, and 1909 saw the birth of Douglas Jr.

By 1915, Fairbanks was a major theatrical star, attracting the interest of the nascent film industry. Mack Sennett and D. W. Griffith's Triangle Film Corporation offered him a three-year contract, and he was soon living the high life in California on his $2,000-a-week salary. Cranking out a movie a month, he had his first success with *His Picture in the Papers* (1916). Despite being a chain smoker, he had always kept himself fit, and his regular writer-director team of Anita Loos and John Emerson made Fairbanks's considerable athletic prowess integral to his on-screen persona. A dashing, ever-smiling hero who laughed in the face of danger, Fairbanks was hugely popular as America's young men headed off to war in Europe. A model of manhood, Fairbanks was made an

LEFT Handsome, debonair, courageous.... Such was Douglas Fairbanks's box office appeal that in 1930 he was paid $300,000 for starring in Reaching for the Moon.

honorary official of the Boy Scouts, and took the opportunity to preach his philosophies of self-denial, optimism, and rigorous exercise.

For all his high-minded morality, Douglas Fairbanks wasn't above a little extramarital activity, provided it was discreet. He fell in love with "America's Sweetheart," Mary Pickford, on a World War I Liberty Bond tour. She was a bigger star than he was, and also married, yet they managed to keep their affair secret for some time, often using work as an alibi. In 1919, they joined forces with D. W. Griffith and Charlie Chaplin to form United Artists. As the industry's greatest superpowers, the foursome now had unprecedented control over their work, from production to distribution. A year later, Fairbanks and Pickford—who were both

recently divorced from their first spouses—finally married, despite warnings that their images might not withstand the whiff of adultery. But fans were thrilled at the creation of Hollywood's first royal couple. Fairbanks—known for his snobbery—played the role to its fullest, making "Pickfair" their castle and entertaining European nobles alongside the local elite.

Now writing (as Elton Thomas) and producing his films, Douglas Fairbanks dominated the silent screen with a series of lavish adventure comedies. *The Mark of Zorro* (1920), *The Three Musketeers* (1921), and *The Black Pirate* (1926), among other films, made Fairbanks an enduring icon of swashbuckling virility. It wasn't until the sound era that the public got its wish to see Pickford and Fairbanks on screen together. By then their marriage was on the rocks— their portrayal of warring lovers in *The Taming of the Shrew* (1929) was a bittersweet reflection of reality. The same year saw Fairbanks reprise his role as D'Artagnan in *The Iron Mask*, and for the first and only time, cinema's liveliest action hero died on screen. After filming, his doctors warned him that his excessive exercise was a risk to his heart.

Fairbanks's on-screen death was all too symbolic, as the advent of sound heralded the end of his reign in Hollywood. His few films of the 1930s fared poorly, and in 1933 he and Pickford separated. They divorced in 1936, the same year he announced his retirement from the screen. He lived in Europe for a while, returning to Los Angeles with a new wife, Lady Sylvia Ashley. Their marriage was cut short in 1939 when Fairbanks died of a heart attack in their Santa Monica home. Sylvia Ashley apparently had a taste for Hollywood royalty, as she went on to marry Clark Gable in the later years of his career.

ABOVE United Artists is born. Mary Pickford, D. W. Griffith (wearing hat), Charlie Chaplin, and Douglas Fairbanks (right), photographed during a moment of motion picture history.

Last Words

"I've never felt better."

LEFT Don Q, Son of Zorro (1925) was the sequel to The Mark of Zorro *(1920). Douglas Fairbanks was the ultimate action hero of the silent era.*

Frances Farmer

Born September 19, 1913
Died August 1, 1970

Once dubbed "The Bad Girl of West Seattle," Frances Farmer was Hollywood's golden girl in the 1930s. After her triumphant performance in *Come and Get It* (1936), Louella Parsons predicted that the 23-year-old beauty would be greater than Garbo; the film's director, Howard Hawks, later raved that she "had more talent than anyone I ever worked with." It is a tragic loss to cinema that she never fulfilled her tremendous potential. Constitutionally incapable of playing the game of Hollywood stardom, Farmer stuck to her "bad girl" ways, drinking, swearing, and espousing leftist politics. Her punishment far exceeded her crimes, and Farmer's life descended into an Orwellian nightmare of Cold War psychiatry.

Growing up in left-leaning Seattle, Washington, Frances Farmer was steeped in politics from an early age. Her father was a lawyer with labor sympathies, while her mother, Lillian, was a rabid anti-Communist and patriot (she once bred a red, white, and blue chicken!). Frances was a bright, outspoken teenager, winning both praise and notoriety for an essay titled, "God Dies." She went on to study journalism and drama at the University of Washington, working her way through as a movie theater usherette. When a local communist newspaper sponsored a contest to send a student to the Soviet Union, Farmer won, setting off a public battle with her mother in the local press.

On her return from Russia, Frances Farmer moved to New York, hoping to join the Group Theater, whose revolutionary merging of art and politics she admired. Instead, she was offered a screen test with Paramount—a month later she went to Hollywood with a seven-year contract. Debuting in *Too Many Parents* (1936), she had her greatest film success that same year, displaying virtuosic range in her dual roles as mother and daughter in *Come and Get It* (1936). It premiered in Seattle, at the theater where she had once worked. "Remember me?" she taunted a minister who had denounced her in his church. "I'm the freak from West Seattle High." Back in Hollywood, she proved to be a reluctant starlet, refusing to grant interviews or parade about in glamorous outfits. Instead, she focused on her acting and devoted her spare time to political causes.

After taking a leave from her contract to perform in summer stock, Farmer was offered a dream role with the Group Theater, but her much-lauded turn as Lorna in Clifford Odets's *Golden Boy* (1937) left her disillusioned. Finding her theatrical heroes as petty and back-stabbing as the Hollywood elite, she later wrote, "the shock of having my faith in the theatrical ideology shaken was the first and heaviest blow leading to my smash-up." Back in Hollywood, she found that her association with the radical theater group had cemented her anti-American image. As punishment, she was relegated to B-grade movies. Once her great proponent, Louella Parsons now noted unsympathetically, "The highbrow Frances Farmer, who found Hollywood so beneath her just a few years ago, is playing, of all things, Calamity Jane."

Depressed and alienated, Farmer began drinking heavily and taking amphetamines to control her weight (it was later discovered that the drug could cause symptoms of schizophrenia).

ABOVE Frances Farmer married three times; her first husband was actor Leif Erickson, to whom she was married for six years.

LEFT Frances Farmer and Fred MacMurray play bickering lovers who work for rival newspapers in the 1937 Paramount drama, Exclusive. *Farmer also starred in* Ebb Tide *in that same year.*

According to some accounts, local authorities had it in for the "pinko" actress. Given her lawless nature, it was just a matter of time before they found an opportunity to nail her. In October 1942, she was pulled over for drunk driving on her way to a party. The incident snowballed, and in January 1943 she was hauled off to jail, kicking and screaming. Photographs taken at the time show her to be surly and disheveled, and hauntingly defiant. By the end of the decade, all traces of that rebel spirit would be stripped away.

Denied a lawyer's representation, Farmer was sentenced to 180 days at the screen actors' sanitarium in La Crescenta. There, with her mother's blessing, she received daily insulin shock treatment. Upon her release, Farmer returned to Seattle, intending to become a writer. A power struggle with her mother followed—for Lillian, the greatest evidence of her daughter's insanity was her rejection of a glamorous Hollywood career. With the assistance of the diabolical Dr. Donald Nicholson, who generally considered political radicals insane, Lillian had her daughter committed.

At Steilacoom, a notoriously abusive mental hospital, Farmer endured a barrage of brutal "treatments," astonishing the staff with her resilience in the face of electroshock therapy, hydrotherapy, and experimental drugs; she was also allegedly raped and tortured. In and out of the hospital for a number of years, she finally emerged in 1949, bland and broken—although no records are now in existence, it is generally believed that she underwent a lobotomy. She lived unobtrusively for another two decades, converting to Catholicism and even hosting an Indianapolis television show. Her death was traceable to the unspeakable injustices she had suffered. She died of throat cancer in 1970—probably the result of her hospital diet of toxic drugs.

ABOVE Frances Farmer in 1936. This was the year she made Come and Get It, *for which she was described as the "screen's outstanding find" of that year.*

RIGHT Frances Farmer in 1936. Will There Really Be a Morning? *is her own account of the horrors she endured while wrongfully held in a mental hospital.*

Marty Feldman

Born July 8, 1933
Died December 2, 1982

Marty Feldman's unconventional looks, cockney charm, and anti-establishment attitude made him an icon of 1970's slapstick. Small and wiry, with a shock of frizzy hair and bulging eyes—one of them disconcertingly wayward—he once told a reporter, "Physically, I am basically equipped to be a clown." His eyes might have been straightened with surgery, but Feldman, like his many fans, saw his idiosyncrasies as assets. He is best known as Gene Wilder's kooky sidekick Igor in Mel Brooks's 1974 horror spoof *Young Frankenstein*.

Born in a working-class Jewish neighborhood in London's East End, Feldman quit school at 15, aspiring to the serious undertakings of poetry and jazz, but his comic leanings proved irrepressible. In the early 1960s he began writing for British radio and television, and in 1967 he teamed up with future Monty Python members John Cleese and Graham Chapman to create *At Last, the 1948 Show*. Soon he had his own BBC comedy series, the short-lived but influential *Marty*—and then Hollywood called with a part in *Young Frankenstein* (1974).

His immediate success convinced Feldman and Lauretta (his wife since 1959) to move to Los Angeles, and he was soon co-starring in Gene Wilder's *The Adventure of Sherlock Holmes' Smarter Brother* (1975) and Mel Brooks's *Silent Movie* (1976). Both were hits, and with his box office appeal well-established, he was given the opportunity to direct and star in two of his own scripts. *The Last Remake of Beau Geste* (1977), in which he amusingly cast Michael York as his twin brother, received mixed reviews, but the religious farce *In God We Trust* (1980) bombed. *Variety* sarcastically noted that it was "a rare achievement—a comedy without laughs."

Disheartened by the downward turn his writing and directing career had taken, Feldman returned to acting, accepting a part in the pirate farce *Yellowbeard* (1983). On his second-to-last day of shooting, he suffered a massive coronary, possibly related to food or shellfish poisoning, and collapsed in his Mexico City hotel room. Medics were called, but they were unable to revive him. The day before, the 49-year-old actor had told reporter David Lewin in what would be his last interview, "Comics are acutely aware of the fear of death. These are our demons, and I am trying to exorcise them from myself."

ABOVE Marty Feldman as Igor ("Call me Eye-gore") in Young Frankenstein *(1974). Feldman is buried at Forest Lawn Cemetery near Buster Keaton.*

Star Shot

As a writer, Marty Feldman was influenced by James Thurber and Mark Twain. He once quipped, "The pen is mightier than the sword, and is considerably easier to write with."

RIGHT Mel Brooks believed that Feldman's diet of dairy foods and eggs, combined with his excessive coffee intake, contributed to his early death.

Betty Field

Born February 8, 1913
Died September 13, 1973

Splitting her time between stage and screen, Betty Field became known in Hollywood for her commitment to artistic integrity over stardom. In an era when actresses were typically pigeon-holed, Field resisted the tyranny of typecasting, appearing in diverse roles throughout her career. She chose her projects based on the material, rather than the size of either the part or the paycheck, and often favored scripts based on literature.

Born in Boston in 1913 (some sources say 1918), and shuttled around the Northeast after her parents' divorce, Fields decided young that she wanted to be an actress. She enrolled at the American Academy of Dramatic Arts in New York, and before her graduation in 1934 was cast in a London production of Gerald Miller's *She Loves Me Not*. By the end of the decade she had established herself on Broadway and made one of her most memorable film appearances, as the ill-fated rancher's wife in the Oscar®-nominated *Of Mice and Men* (1939), adapted from John Steinbeck's classic novel.

Field's unusual contract with Paramount allowed her to return to New York for half the year to work in theater, and in 1940 she took the lead in Elmer Rice's *Two on an Island*. Two years later she married the writer, embarking on an artistic union that would shape her career. For her virtuosic performance in his play *Dream Girl*, Fields won the New York Critics Circle Award for 1945–46—a particularly remarkable feat given that her character was on stage for less than three minutes each night. She and Rice had three children, and were divorced in 1955.

Though admirable, Field's commitment to the stage did result in a less stellar film legacy than her talent warranted. Her final leading role was Daisy Buchanan in the 1949 version of F. Scott Fitzgerald's *The Great Gatsby*. She went on to make memorable appearances in supporting roles in *Bus Stop* (1956), *Peyton Place* (1957), *BUtterfield 8* (1960), *Birdman of Alcatraz* (1962), *7 Women* (1966), and *Coogan's Bluff* (1968).

In 1973 John Schlesinger cast Field in his adaptation of Nathaniel West's *Day of the Locust* (1975). She was about to leave for Los Angeles to begin filming, when she suffered a cerebral hemorrhage. She died in Hyannis, Massachusetts, where she had been vacationing with her third husband, Raymond Olivare (her second marriage, to Edwin Lukas, had ended in divorce).

ABOVE Betty Field and MacDonald Carey gaze into each other's eyes in The Great Gatsby *(1949). Alan Ladd played the title role.*

Star Shot

After her death, Betty Field's part in *Day of the Locust* (1975) went to another actress with one foot on Broadway, the other in Hollywood— Geraldine Page.

Errol Flynn

Born June 20, 1909
Died October 14, 1959

By 1934, Douglas Fairbanks had made his last film, and America was looking for the next great swashbuckler. With his flashy swordsmanship, athletic body, and irresistible charm, Errol Flynn was a natural for the job. Rising to stardom in *Captain Blood* (1935), he quickly became cinema's lustiest rogue—on screen and off. Unlike the wholesome Fairbanks, Flynn was a dangerous, reckless character, with famous appetites for sex and liquor. For most of his career, these indulgences enhanced his rakish appeal, but they would also be his undoing.

Born in Hobart in the Australian state of Tasmania, Flynn always had a talent for trouble. Later in life, he would embellish his youthful escapades, creating his own mythology. Memorable childhood scenes included accidentally killing two platypuses en route to Europe for scientific study (his father was a distinguished zoologist) and losing his virginity to the family maid at the age of 12; unsurprisingly, he was expelled from nearly every school he attended. In his late teens, he moved to New Guinea, where he allegedly dabbled in a variety of shady enterprises, from diamond smuggling to slave trading. Accused of killing a man, he beat the rap with a self-defense plea. Errol Flynn's entrée into film came on a fluke, when an Australian producer happened to see his picture and cast him in the docudrama *In the Wake of the Bounty* (1933). A year later, with a bit of training under his belt, he sailed for England to pursue an acting career.

Flynn's success was rapid. After a brief stint with a repertory company, he landed a role in the low-budget British thriller, *Murder at Monte Carlo* (1934). Warner Bros.' London office took notice, and soon he was crossing the Atlantic to go to work in Hollywood. During the voyage, he met the French actress Lili Damita, who would later become the first of his three wives. Upon his arrival in Los Angeles, he was briefly relegated to minor roles, but when Robert Donat fortuitously dropped out of *Captain Blood* (1935), Damita helped secure the novice Flynn an audition. It was on his own merits that he beat out Clark Gable for the part.

Exploiting Flynn's natural swagger and cheerful arrogance, the film's director, Michael Curtiz, established a highly bankable rapport with Flynn. Over the next decade, they made some 12 films together, including *The Charge of the Light Brigade* (1936), the all-time classic *The Adventures of Robin Hood* (1938), *Dodge City* (1939), and *The Sea Hawk* (1940). *The Adventures of Robin Hood* (1938) saw him paired with Alan Hale, who was to become his regular sidekick, and Olivia de Havilland, his recurring screen love. According to Bette Davis, the strong-willed, classically trained de Havilland was the unrequited love of Flynn's life. Yet he wasn't one to sit around pining.

As Flynn's success grew, so did his bad-boy reputation, and stories of his drinking, brawling, and womanizing became commonplace (only

ABOVE A merry man until his dying day, Errol Flynn starred memorably in The Adventures of Robin Hood *(1938).*

BELOW Errol Flynn earned $500 per week for his work in the action-adventure film Captain Blood *(1935).*

LEFT Errol Flynn had two daughters with his sec-ond wife, Nora Eddington: Rory (left) and Deirdre. Flynn also had a daughter, Arnella, with Patrice Wymore, and a son, Sean, with Lili Damita.

Last Words

"I've had a hell of a lot of fun and I've enjoyed every minute of it."

later would his exploits with men be added to the reports). In 1942, his real-life adventuring caught up with him, when he was tried for the statutory rape of two young girls, Peggy Satterlee and Betty Hansen. Eligible for a 150-year sentence if found guilty, Flynn hired cutthroat Hollywood lawyer Jerry Giesler, who destroyed the girls' credibility and got his celebrity client acquitted.

After the Japanese attack on Pearl Harbor in 1941, Flynn became a U.S. citizen so that he could join the American forces, but he was deemed unfit for service due to heart trouble, recurrent malaria, and tuberculosis. It was a demoralizing blow to his ego, and becoming a war hero on the screen only emphasized his feelings of inadequacy. Nonetheless, he had a series of successes with director Raoul Walsh, including *Desperate Journey* (1942), *Uncertain Glory* (1944), and *Objective Burma!* (1945). Later claims that Errol Flynn was a Nazi sympathizer have been given little credence. His second wife, Nora Eddington, adamantly denied the charge, stating, "He hated authority, especially policemen." She debunked another myth about her famous ex-husband when she asserted that he was not, in fact, especially well-endowed.

Flynn once said, "My difficulty is trying to reconcile my gross habits with my net income." As the 1940s wore on, his statement was truer than ever. His taste for drinking spread to narcotics, and his preparation for roles suffered accordingly. He decamped to Europe in the early 1950s, and his investment in a never-completed production of *William Tell* virtually ruined him. In 1957, he returned to Hollywood and played a series of screen drunks, including his hero, John Barrymore (whose corpse he once stole as a practical joke!). He suffered a fatal heart attack in Vancouver at age 50, and was buried with six bottles of whiskey. His tell-all autobiography, *My Wicked, Wicked Ways*, was published a few months after his death.

RIGHT Errol Flynn once said, "I am the epitome of twentieth century cosmopolitanism, but I should have been born an explorer in the time of Magellan."

Clark Gable

Born February 1, 1901
Died November 16, 1960

It Happened One Night (1934) won Clark Gable an Oscar®, and *Gone with the Wind* (1939) made him a legend, but when the 59-year-old actor saw a rough cut of *The Misfits* (1961), he told the film's writer, Arthur Miller, "This is the best thing I did in my life." A truly melancholy piece of Americana, with Hollywood heavyweights playing broken souls, it was hardly a typical Gable vehicle. As an aging rodeo cowboy, the King of Hollywood looks worn and weathered—and in retrospect, the film itself seems to signal the demise of classic Hollywood cinema. It is eerily fitting, then, that John Huston's mournful masterpiece would be both Gable's and Marilyn Monroe's final film.

Gable was crowned "King of Hollywood" in MGM's commissary in 1938, but despite his innate charisma, stardom hadn't come to him easily. Born William Clark Gable in 1901, the self-described "slob from Ohio" quit school at 14 and took a job at a tire factory. He was interested in acting, and worked in a theater until his father took him to Oklahoma to drill for oil. In 1922, Gable ran off to join a theater troupe headed by Josephine Dillon. They later married, though she was 17 years his senior, and moved to Hollywood, where he began to get bit parts. Divorcing her in 1930, Gable returned to stage acting and married another older woman, the wealthy Maria "Ria" Langham.

He was performing on Broadway when Lionel Barrymore took an interest and set up a screen test for him. Studio executives all around town were famously unimpressed, making much of Gable's "floppy" ears. In fact, his ears were the least of his problems—the soon-to-be heartthrob had false teeth and bad breath, and was said to be "underendowed." But then again, as MGM soon realized, Gable's charm and swagger eclipsed everything else. In 1931, he was signed on, and made his first screen appearance with Joan Crawford in *Dance, Fool, Dance*—they would be lovers on and off for years.

Clark Gable's career-making role in *It Happened One Night* (1934), opposite Claudette Colbert, allegedly came as punishment. In 1933, Gable killed a pedestrian while driving under the influence of alcohol, and studio boss Louis B. Mayer bribed an underling to take the fall. Even after all the trouble he'd caused, the cocky star had the nerve to complain about the roles he was getting. To teach him a lesson, Mayer loaned him out to Columbia for what promised to be an inconsequential little picture. With Gable at his

ABOVE Gone with the Wind *(1939), with Clark Gable and Vivien Leigh, is featured on a 1990 U.S. Postal Service commemorative stamp.*

Star Shot

Clark Gable holds the dubious honor of being Adolf Hitler's favorite movie star. Hitler offered a generous reward to whoever could capture Gable and bring him to the Führer.

RIGHT With Claudette Colbert in Frank Capra's It Happened One Night *(1934). Gable's sense of comic timing in the film was highly praised.*

smart-alecky best, the film won five Oscars®, and went down in motion picture history as the first screwball comedy.

As much of a ladykiller off-screen as on, Gable counted many stars among his conquests, but he would only marry one: the kooky Carole Lombard. They first worked together on *No Man of Her Own* (1932), and in 1939—following Gable's divorce from Langham—they tied the knot. *Gone with the Wind* was released the same year, to frenzied enthusiasm. Though Gable was beaten out for the Oscar®, Rhett Butler became one of cinema's most indelible, and quotable, icons. Gable was riding high when tragedy struck.

On January 16, 1942, Lombard was killed in a plane crash on her way home from a war-bond tour. Despite Gable's infidelities—and Lombard's brash public remark that he was no great lay—their marriage had been a happy one in its way. Gable mourned her loss with quantities of liquor, then volunteered for the Air Corps. He came back in one piece, but by then the years of smoking and drinking had begun to wear on his famous sparkle. With a few exceptions, his remaining films were unmemorable—until *The Misfits*.

Shooting began on July 21, 1960, and continued on and off until November. By all accounts, it was a grueling affair. Despite the relentless heat, Clark Gable insisted on doing his own stunts—including being dragged through the dirt by a truck. Adding to the stress, Huston's gambling was jeopardizing the film's funding, and Monroe was late, forgetful, and generally disruptive. When they finally wrapped, Gable vented, "Christ, I'm glad this picture's finished. She near gave me a damn heart attack." Fateful words.

On November 6, he suffered a heart attack, and ten days later he succumbed to a second while recovering in a Hollywood hospital. Gable's only *legitimate* child, John Clark Gable, was

ABOVE Marilyn Monroe is comforted by Clark Gable in The Misfits *(1961). Gable considered the film his best work.*

born the following spring, to his fifth wife Kay (his fourth wife was Lady Sylvia Ashley, Douglas Fairbanks's widow). But in 1994 it was revealed that a one-night-stand in 1935 with Loretta Young had resulted in a daughter—to save their careers, Young had pretended the child was adopted. Clark Gable was laid to rest beside Lombard, returning in death to the days when he was King.

RIGHT Clark Gable once said of his acting ability, "I'm just a lucky slob who happened to be in the right place at the right time."

John Garfield

Born March 4, 1913
Died May 21, 1952

ABOVE John Garfield's daughter, Katherine, suffered an allergic attack at the age of six and died. Garfield never fully recovered from her death.

Star Shot

If John Garfield's politics were controversial, they didn't deter his fans. Ten thousand turned up for his memorial service, making it the most attended celebrity funeral in New York since Rudolph Valentino's.

RIGHT Lana Turner and John Garfield steamed up the screen with their passionate affair in The Postman Always Rings Twice *(1946), based on James M. Cain's novel.*

One of the most high-profile victims of McCarthyism in Hollywood, John Garfield left behind a biography worthy of the brooding rebel heroes he portrayed. He is heralded as the first method actor to hit the big screen, and influenced a long line of vulnerable tough guys, including Marlon Brando, James Dean, Robert De Niro, and Sean Penn.

The son of immigrant Russian Jews, Garfield—born Jacob Julius Garfinkle—grew up in the mean streets of New York. A predilection for fighting landed him in P.S. 45, a school for problem youths, where he began to channel his aggression into boxing and acting. Recognizing his talent, playwright Clifford Odets—a friend from the Bronx—drafted Garfield into the Group Theater, where the young man impressed the other members of the Group with his authentic street style. He was soon starring in seminal productions of Odets's *Waiting for Lefty* and *Awake and Sing*.

Garfield made his screen debut in 1938 in Michael Curtiz's *Four Daughters*. His smoldering performance earned him an Oscar® nomination for Best Actor in a Supporting Role. Working within the studio system for nearly a decade, he established himself as a new kind of screen hero: the urban macho with a soft side. On the heels of two of his greatest successes, *The Postman Always Rings Twice* (1946) and *Humoresque* (1946), Garfield started his own production company in 1947, looking to bring a political side to his work.

Two years later the pioneering actor had made arguably the most important films of his career. In *Body and Soul* (1947), which earned him his second Oscar® nomination, he stars as a slum kid who rises to boxing stardom by selling out to the mob; in *Force of Evil* (1948), a cult film noir favorite, he plays a corporate lawyer working in the numbers racket. Both films can be read as indictments of Capitalist America, but though he leaned to the left, he was never a communist.

Nonetheless, John Garfield was called to testify before the House Un-American Activities Committee in April 1951. He refused to either confess or name names, and was blacklisted. Soon after, he and his wife, Roberta, separated, and Garfield sunk into a deep depression. He died of a heart attack on May 21, 1952, in the Manhattan apartment of actress and dancer Iris Whitney. Though he'd had heart problems in the past, Garfield's daughter later maintained it was HUAC that killed him.

Peggy Ann Garner

Born February 3, 1932
Died October 16, 1984

At the height of her success, teen star Peggy Ann Garner raked in $1,500— and 1,300 pieces of fan mail—each week. Born in Canton, Ohio, in 1932, Garner was modeling and playing summer stock by the time she was six. Her overambitious stage mother, Virginia, soon moved her only child to Hollywood, and in 1938 she debuted in *Little Miss Thoroughbred*. Four years later, the bright-eyed blonde was signed on at Fox, where she would work, attend school, and eventually live in a little house that had once been home to Shirley Temple.

In 1945, MGM offered to buy out Garner's contract and star her in *National Velvet*. Fox refused to release her, and the part went to the young Elizabeth Taylor. Virginia was furious, but Fox had big plans for their starlet. She was cast as Francie Nolan in Elia Kazan's *A Tree Grows in Brooklyn* (1945), based on Betty Smith's best-selling novel. Garner's sensitive portrayal of a tenement girl who dreams of being a writer earned her an honorary Academy Award®. Nonetheless, three years later Fox failed to renew Garner's contract, and her Hollywood career was all but over.

Perhaps spurred by tensions about her uncertain future, Peggy Ann Garner made headlines in 1949 when she demanded that her father replace her mother as her legal guardian, due to Virginia's "extravagant mode of living." Taking her waning career into her own hands, the 17-year-old "has-been" moved to New York to study at the Actors Studio. Before long, she was up on the stage, appearing in *The Man* with Lillian Gish on Broadway, and in a touring production of *Bus Stop*. In 1951 she starred in her own television show, *Two Girls Named Smith*, and she would continue to make small-screen appearances until the late 1960s.

Nonetheless, like many one-time child stars, Garner struggled to sustain her career as an adult. She later explained, "Once you're out of circulation in Hollywood, it's hard to get back in." Family life also slowed her down. She was married three times, and had a daughter in 1957 by her second husband, actor Albert Salmi. During the 1960s she worked in real estate, and in the 1970s she became the first woman sales representative at Buick Hollywood. She died of pancreatic cancer at age 52, at the Motion Picture and Television Hospital in Woodland Hills, California—but not without making one last return to the screen, in Robert Altman's *A Wedding* (1978).

ABOVE One of Peggy Ann Garner's most memorable roles is that of young Jane Eyre in the 1944 film of that name. Joan Fontaine played the adult Jane.

Star Shot

Peggy Ann Garner's mother, Virginia, outlived her only daughter and only grandchild, Catherine Ann Salmi, who died of heart disease in 1995 at the age of 38. Virginia passed away six months later.

Gladys George

Born September 13, 1900
Died December 8, 1954

Gladys Anna Clare's slow rise to stardom dates back to 1900, the year of her birth in Patten, Maine. For her traveling thespian parents, it was a mere stop on the road. Little Gladys made her inevitable stage debut at the age of three and hit Broadway at 15, appearing with dancer Isadora Duncan in *The Betrothal*. Soon the precocious actress was spotted by Thomas H. Ince and signed on as a contract player. Unfortunately, she was badly burned by a grease fire, and when she recovered, her services were no longer desired.

Her real break didn't come until 1935, when she starred in *Personal Appearance* on Broadway. It was a big hit, and Gladys George was invited back to Hollywood for *Valiant Is the Word for Carrie* (1936). Memorable roles in *Madame X* (1937), *The Maltese Falcon* (1941), and *The Best Years of Our Lives* (1946) followed, but lead roles became scarce, and the actress had long since tired of playing "bad women."

George was vivacious, with an unpolished, natural warmth. Her large, otherworldly eyes gave her an aura of tragedy. It was that quality of pathos that made her portrayals of fallen women—from the defiantly redeemed to the hopelessly depraved—so effective. Her role as a prostitute who rises above her circumstances to care for two orphaned children in *Valiant Is the Word for Carrie* (1936) won her an Oscar® nomination for Best Actress.

Splashy headlines like "The Actress and The Bellhop" made Gladys George's multiple ill-fated marriages a public spectacle in the 1920s, 1930s, and 1940s. When the bellhop, her fourth and youngest husband, proved "indifferent" and "neglectful," the petite blonde divorced him, eventually moving into a modest duplex in Los Angeles' Echo Park area.

In December 1954 a neighbor found the one-time star unconscious in her apartment, and rushed her to Cedars of Lebanon Hospital. Gladys George died there three hours later. The early obituaries suggested a suicidal overdose of barbiturates. It was, perhaps, a believable fate for a has-been with a messy personal history and a long history of playing floozies and drunks—but the autopsy revealed no drugs in her system. George had been treated for throat cancer, but the cause of death, it was concluded, was a cerebral hemorrhage or stroke.

ABOVE Toward the end of her life, Gladys George guest starred in an episode of the highly rated television western series, Hopalong Cassidy.

Star Shot

Cast as a housewife in *I'm from Missouri* (1939), Gladys George gushed, "I find it stimulating to play a normal woman.... I'm pretty sure they don't know just how lucky they are."

RIGHT Gladys George (left) played Carrie in Valiant Is the Word for Carrie *(1936), with Charlene Wyatt (center) and Jackie Moran as the orphaned children she looks after.*

John Gilbert

Born July 10, 1899
Died January 9, 1936

Many a silent film star's career was ruined by the arrival of talkies. John Gilbert would go down in history as the poster boy for this unfortunate phenomenon. According to the mythology, his voice was nasal and high-pitched, and the dancerly pantomime that had made him the "perfect lover" was rendered ridiculous by the introduction of dialogue. Further, his alcoholic bad-boy persona off-screen was only tolerable in direct proportion to his box office draw, becoming an embarrassment as his appeal waned. All reasonable points, but what truly clinched his demise was a falling-out with studio boss Louis B. Mayer. With an enemy at the top, his downward spiral became inevitable.

John Gilbert was born John Cecil Pringle in Logan, Utah. The son of traveling actors, he was a de facto cast member in his parents' theater troupe from his infancy. His mother died when he was a teenager, and the young Gilbert was left to fend for himself. "Hungry enough to eat out of garbage cans," he pursued film acting, eventually landing his first lead role in *Princess of the Dark* (1917).

Over the next decade, Gilbert would become Hollywood's highest paid star, and his trademark pointy nose would define the word "handsome" for a generation. Gilbert classics include the bizarre circus tale *He Who Gets Slapped* (1924), Erich von Stroheim's typically decadent *The Merry Widow* (1925), and *Love* (1927), in which he plays Vronsky to Greta Garbo's Anna Karenina. His most enduring work, however, would be *The Big Parade* (1925). Directed by King Vidor, this profoundly humanistic tale of a soldier's disillusionment with war was the silent era's second most popular film after *Birth of a Nation* (1915).

As an actor, John Gilbert played lover to some of the screen's most enduring women, and in real life he was a notorious heartbreaker. Gilbert married and divorced four actresses, but his name is most famously linked with the exotic Swedish émigré, Greta Garbo. They first appeared together in *Flesh and the Devil* (1926), and news stories of their real-life romance made them a hot ticket at the box office. Despite studio grumblings, Garbo secured him his final prominent role, in *Queen Christina* (1933). In late 1935, Gilbert collapsed in his swimming pool; six weeks later, he succumbed to a heart attack. It was rumored that Marlene Dietrich was in bed with him when he died.

Leatrice Gilbert Fountain lost her father when she was only 12. Her sensitive and well-researched biography of her father, *Dark Star*, was published in 1985.

BELOW John Gilbert is said to have proposed to Greta Garbo (left) in 1927, but the actress was unwilling to commit to marriage.

Betty Grable

Born December 18, 1916
Died July 2, 1973

ABOVE Betty Grable in 1969. Grable and her second husband, Harry James, had two daughters, Victoria and Jessica.

In 1943, Grable married big-band leader Harry James after meeting him on the set of *Spring Time in the Rockies* (1942). Though they divorced, her crypt reads "Betty Grable James."

RIGHT With John Payne in The Dolly Sisters *(1945). During the 1940s, 20th Century Fox insured Betty Grable's legs for $1,000,000.*

It was once reported that one in 12 servicemen trekked off to war with a picture of Betty Grable tucked inside his duffel bag. In one of Hollywood's most famous photographs, Grable stood bare-legged in a white bathing suit, tossing her head over her shoulder to flash a "cheesecake" smile. More than three million copies of this picture were distributed, in small sizes for carrying close to the heart and larger ones to pin up in lockers and barracks. Many more were painted on bomber planes. The message was, "Follow me home, I'm what you're fighting for." For those GIs who did return home, there she was, up on the screen, the biggest star of her day.

Pushed by her over-ambitious mother, Ruth Elizabeth Grable took dancing lessons from a young age. In her teens, Grable and her mother left their home in St. Louis, Missouri, for Hollywood. Grable debuted at 14 with a minor role in *Let's Go Places* (1930), and later appeared in a memorable duet, "Let's K-nock K-nees," with Edward Everett Horton in the Ginger Rogers and Fred Astaire flick, *The Gay Divorcee* (1934). For the most part, her first decade in the business found her in routine musicals, with no future in sight. In 1937 she married former child-star Jackie Coogan; they divorced in 1940. That same year, Grable left Hollywood for Broadway, prompting Hollywood to finally take note.

Signed by 20th Century Fox, the unpretentious and pragmatic actress insisted, "I was just lucky." But the studio moguls were the lucky ones. During her peak years, Grable's pictures brought in over a hundred million dollars. Specializing in gala musicals like *Down Argentine Way* (1940), *Tin Pan Alley* (1940), and the post-war *Mother Wore Tights* (1947), Grable wasn't much of an actress, but even *The New York Times* critics jabbed gently, then moved on to the happy spectacle of her "shapely gams."

As popular sex symbology evolved in post-war America, Grable's career waned. She continued to work on Broadway and in nightclubs intermittently until her death from lung cancer at the age of 56. One of her final film performances, in *How to Marry a Millionaire* (1953), was trumped by newcomers Marilyn Monroe and Lauren Bacall, whose assets included bustier silhouettes— and some serious acting skills. Grable herself once commented cheerily, "Let's face it, very little acting goes into my work!" Perhaps even more compelling than those famous legs was her lighthearted, girl-next-door personality— she made audiences feel comfortable, and, in wartime, that was a luxury worth paying for.

Gloria Grahame

Born November 28, 1923
Died October 5, 1981

Reserved and sulky, with a rather wry soulfulness, Gloria Grahame made her mark as the prototypical film noir bad girl, but was distinctive in any part. She won an Academy Award® for her supporting role in *The Bad and the Beautiful* (1952). But unfortunately, even Oscar® gold couldn't save the sultry honey-blonde actress from the personal demons that plagued her career.

Born Gloria Grahame Hallward, the Los Angeles native was raised by her mother. Jean Hallward supported her family by teaching acting and producing plays at the Pasadena Playhouse. Gloria made her stage debut at nine, and went on to do theater in New York until she was discovered by an MGM talent agent. Finding "Hallward" too theatrical, Louis B. Mayer signed her on as Gloria Grahame.

Her first noteworthy role was the coquettish Violet in *It's a Wonderful Life* (1946), starring James Stewart and Donna Reed. Specializing in flirts and floozies with a sexy lisp and an undercurrent of pathos, Grahame was nominated for an Oscar® for her portrayal of a jaded dance hall girl in Edward Dmytryk's indictment of anti-Semitism, *Crossfire* (1947). Arguably her most affecting performance came in 1950, when she played opposite Humphrey Bogart in Nicholas Ray's heartbreaking Hollywood-set film noir, *In a Lonely Place* (1950).

Meanwhile, Grahame had become obsessed with her looks, viewing every tiny imperfection as a glaring flaw. In 1946 she had the first of numerous plastic surgeries, but no "fix" could dispel her gnawing insecurities. It didn't take long for word to get around that she was difficult to work with, and her needy, narcissistic behavior on the set of the musical *Oklahoma!* (1955) damaged her reputation irreparably.

By 1957 her career was in decline, and she had divorced three husbands—most notably director Nicholas Ray, who later claimed he only married her because she was pregnant. Grahame found her way back into the spotlight in 1960, when she scandalously wed Ray's son from a previous marriage, the 20-year-old Tony Ray.

After raising their two children, Gloria Grahame made a minor comeback in 1971, and continued to act professionally until her death. In the early 1970s, she was diagnosed with breast cancer—after treatment it went into remission, only to return in 1980. Just as she was about to open in a London production of *The Glass Menagerie*, she was rushed back to the United States. Grahame once told a reporter, "I dote on death scenes"—she played her last in New York City's St. Vincent's Hospital on October 5, 1981.

ABOVE During the 1960s, sultry Gloria Grahame appeared in the television shows Burke's Law, The Outer Limits, *and* The Fugitive.

Star Shot

On screen, Gloria Grahame most often hailed from the wrong side of the tracks, but she was in fact a descendant of the Plantagenet kings of England.

Gilda Gray

Born October 24, 1901
Died December 22, 1959

Dubbed "The Queen of the Shimmy Shakers" by Al Jolson, Polish immigrant Gilda Gray made her fame and fortune on a dance she purportedly invented as a teenager performing in a Wisconsin saloon. When a customer asked what she was doing, she said "shaking my chemise." Her accent rendered it "shimmy"—and an international dance sensation was born. In the 1920s, Gilda Gray epitomized the happy abandonment of inhibitions of the jazz age, but her glory days were numbered. She went out with drop-waist dresses and bathtub gin, returning to the public eye only as a has-been.

Born Marianna Michalska in Poland in 1901 (some sources say 1899), Gray was a victim of violent times. Her parents were killed in an uprising, and Gray was sent to an orphanage. She was later adopted and taken to the United States by her foster parents to escape a Russian pogrom in Krakow. Calling herself Mary Gray, she shimmied her way to the Ziegfeld Follies, co-starring with Will Rogers when she was 20. It was famed vaudeville singer Sophie Tucker who renamed her Gilda, inspired by her golden hair. (In another version of the story, the name Gilda came from a magazine article Sophie had read.)

Despite Gray's Eastern European stock, the shimmy was given an exotic spin. It was billed as a sacred dance, "similar to that done by South Sea maidens at love festivals," and her first major film role was in Jesse L. Lasky's *Aloma of the South Seas* (1926). She followed with *The Devil Dancer* (1927) and *Piccadilly* (1929). A small part in *Rose-Marie* (1936) was her last. Her only further dealings with Hollywood concerned a lawsuit against Columbia Pictures. Gray claimed that the Rita Hayworth vehicle *Gilda* (1946) was based on her life, and eventually settled out of court.

During her peak years Gilda Gray made millions, but in 1941, after losing a bundle in the stock market crash of 1929, she declared bankruptcy. "Well, I had three husbands," she commented later, "and you know, they're very expensive." They were, in chronological order, concert violinist John Gorecki; her manager, Gaillard "Gil" Boag; and Venezuelan diplomat Hector de Briceno (also known as Hector Briceno de Saa). Her only child was a son, Martin, from her first marriage. After years of estrangement, the two were reunited on *This Is Your Life* in 1954.

In 1959, Gray was living in obscurity in a modest Hollywood Boulevard apartment. On December 22, she suffered a heart attack while recovering from a bout of food poisoning at a neighbor's home. An ambulance was called, but efforts to save the one-time star were futile.

ABOVE The Shimmy Queen, Gilda Gray, in 1924. Her dancing skills were shown to great advantage in the film The Devil Dancer *(1927).*

Star Shot

Gilda Gray visited Poland in 1939. She had donated money to worthy causes in her homeland, and was awarded the Polish Legion of Honor Cross.

Mitzi Green

Born October 22, 1920
Died May 24, 1969

BELOW Mitzi Green with Jackie Coogan in Huckleberry Finn *(1931). Green's musical talents meant that she still had a career after child-stardom.*

Star Shot

Mitzi Green starred in a little-known but charming television sitcom, *So This is Hollywood* (1955). She played an aspiring stuntwoman named Queenie Dugan.

RIGHT Mitzi Green at eight years old. At 14, she was featured in the musical comedy Transatlantic Merry-Go-Round *(1934).*

The daughter of vaudevillians Joe Keno and Rosie Green, Mitzi Green grew up touring the country with the popular stars of her day. She made her first stage appearance at the age of only three, after a theater manager overheard her impersonating Sadie Burt in her mother's dressing room. A few years later the precocious young girl was headlining as Little Mitzi, the child mimic, and at age eight she made the transition to cinema, appearing in *The Marriage Playground* (1929) at Paramount.

The studio was so impressed with her talents that they signed her on for three years, making her their first child star with a long-term contract. She appeared in 15 films over the next six years, including *Paramount on Parade* (1930), *Huckleberry Finn* (1931), *Little Orphan Annie* (1932), and, most memorably, *Tom Sawyer* (1930), in which she played Becky to Jackie Coogan's Tom. At the age of 12 she was making $1,500 a week, but as she hit her teenage years, film roles became scarce. Unlike many child stars, however, Green continued to have a career after Hollywood.

Mitzi Green returned to vaudeville, breaking box office records at Chicago's State Lake Theatre, then studied acting in Ogunquit, Maine, with Florence Reed. Her efforts paid off when Rodgers and Hart gave the 16-year-old actress the lead in *Babes in Arms*; it became a smash hit on Broadway, and made *The Lady Is a Tramp* Green's trademark song. At 21 she was cast in the musical comedy *Let Freedom Ring*, and before rehearsals were over she had married her director, Joseph Pevney. They had four children, and remained together until her death.

A performer at heart, Green juggled the demands of career and family for two decades, impressing audiences at Ciro's and the Copacabana with her masterful impersonations of Ethel Barrymore, Sophie Tucker, Milton Berle, and others. For many years she was shy of returning to Hollywood as a "has-been," but in the 1950s she overcame her fears, appearing in *The Bloodhounds of Broadway* (1952), as well as an Abbott and Costello picture, *Lost in Alaska* (1952).

Green often spoke of retiring to spend more time with her family, and finally did so in 1961, after playing Rose—the mother of Gypsy Rose Lee—in a touring version of the Broadway show *Gypsy*. About seven years later she was stricken with cancer. She died at home in Huntington Beach, California, at the age of 48, after an eight-month illness.

Sigrid Gurie

Born   May 18, 1911
Died   August 14, 1969

When producer Samuel Goldwyn discovered Sigrid Gurie in 1938, he thought he had struck gold: a Norwegian Garbo. He wasn't alone in his quest to find a rival for MGM's empress of mystery—Paramount had signed Marlene Dietrich in 1930, banking on her throaty voice and beguiling accent to give Garbo a run for her money. Dubbing Gurie the "Siren of the Fjords," Goldwyn first cast her with Gary Cooper in *The Adventures of Marco Polo* (1938). The pair made Hollywood history in their roles as Chinese princess and Italian explorer—not for their acting, but for a record-breaking screen kiss that lasted for over four minutes.

Gurie went on to star opposite Charles Boyer, Basil Rathbone, and John Wayne, but Sam Goldwyn's great hopes for his starlet proved ill-founded. By the early 1940s, her career was already in decline, due in part to the scandal that erupted when the press got wind of her divorce proceedings. It was revealed in 1938 that "Miss" Gurie was in fact Mrs. Thomas H. Stewart of Cucamonga, California—worse, the exotic beauty was a native of Brooklyn, New York, and had passed herself off to Goldwyn as a veteran of the Norwegian Royal Theater.

The accent, however, was real. Gurie's father was a Norwegian engineer who was sent to the United States for work, and the family had spent only a few years in Brooklyn before moving back to Norway. She returned to the United States in 1934, after studying acting in London and Paris. Nonetheless, for the American public, the mystique was gone. Sigrid Gurie continued to appear in motion pictures until 1952, but never became a big-name star. Her credits include *Algiers* (1938), *Three Faces West* (1940), and *Enemy of Women* (1944).

After winning her divorce from Stewart in 1939, Sigrid Gurie remarried twice—once by long-distance telephone. Sometime after her retirement from the screen, she moved to San Miguel de Allende, a Mexican hideaway popular with foreigners. She died of an embolism in a Mexico City hospital on August 14, 1969. The "Siren of the Fjords" was 58, and all but forgotten.

Ironically, the not-Norwegian-enough actress had a twin brother who went down in Hollywood history as a great Norwegian hero. During World War II, Knut Haukelid led a raid on a heavy water plant in Nazi-occupied Telemark, Norway. The successful mission helped thwart German attempts to develop the A-bomb, and was dramatized on screen in *The Heroes of Telemark* (1948).

Joan Hackett

Born March 1, 1934
Died October 8, 1983

Feisty actress and feminist Joan Hackett never cared much for Hollywood. At 17, already a successful fashion model, she turned down a seven-year contract with 20th Century Fox. Though she came of age in the 1950s, her nonconformist style and complete indifference to the commercially driven whims of the entertainment industry made her a better fit in the decades that followed. She once said, "Some actresses will sacrifice anything to become a star. I just don't want the gold ring on the merry-go-round that much. All I want is for the merry-go-round to play my song."

BELOW Joan Hackett as Laura in Tennessee Williams's gut-wrenching masterpiece The Glass Menagerie, in 1966.

Some mistook Hackett's confidence for snobbery, but her upbringing was a modest one. She was born in East Harlem, New York, during the Depression. Her Irish father was a volatile drinker and one-time bootlegger. Her Italian mother was a free spirit, known to dive into the icy East River on a dare. Hackett described feeling disconnected from her family, and learning early on to look after herself. An uncommon beauty, she was offered modeling work and soon dropped out of her restrictive Catholic high school. Gracing the covers of national magazines, her face caught the attention of 20th Century Fox, but despite their generous offer, Hackett chose to remain in New York. She studied acting with Uta Hagen, Mary Welch, and Lee Strasberg, and in 1961 became a Broadway success, starring in *Call Me by My Rightful Name*. In 1965, Hackett married actor Richard Mulligan (they would divorce in 1973).

It wasn't until 1966 that she made her film debut, in an adaptation of Mary McCarthy's unsentimental novel of female friendship, *The Group*. She followed with one of her finest performances, as a lonesome frontier wife in *Will Penny* (1968). Other movie credits include *The Terminal Man* (1974) and Paul Simon's *One Trick Pony* (1980). After years of forging an uncompromising path through Hollywood, Hackett received an Oscar® nomination for her powerful portrayal of a bitter socialite in Neil Simon's *Only When I Laugh* (1981). Another story about the bonds between women, it won her a Golden Globe® Award for Best Actress in a Supporting Role.

Hackett died of ovarian cancer just a year later. Her self-determination had earned her a reputation for being difficult to work with, but her admirers celebrated her spirit of independence and perfectionism. On the unpaved road leading up to Hollywood's St. Victor's Church on the morning of Hackett's funeral, her friend Nancy Olson Livingston said wryly, "Leave it to Joan, taking us on the hard road, right to the last."

Star Shot

In life, the energetic and hard-working Hackett loved her rest. The epitaph on her gravestone in the Hollywood Forever Cemetery reads: "Go away—I'm asleep."

RIGHT In Ambush *(1949), Jean Hagen played an abused wife, Martha. She appeared with John Hodiak (left) and Robert Taylor.*

BELOW Jean Hagen, dressed as a man in a scene from Adam's Rib *(1949). Her character, Beryl, causes friction between Tom Ewell and Judy Holliday.*

Jean Hagen

Born August 3, 1923
Died August 29, 1977

Versatile red-head Jean Hagen is best known as Lina Lamont in *Singin' in the Rain* (1952). Her over-the-top portrayal of a silent film star whose grating voice keeps her out of the talkies earned Hagen an Oscar® nomination for Best Actress in a Supporting Role. Sadly, both the quality of the role and the attention were exceptions in her Hollywood career. A talented actress with theater training and artistic integrity, Hagen was too often relegated to stock roles in B-grade movies. Even while fighting for more diverse parts, she gave her all to every role, elevating mediocre material with what director John Huston described as a "wistful, down-to-earth quality rare on the screen."

Raised in Chicago and Indiana, Hagen—born Jean Shirley Verhagen—graduated from Northwestern University in 1945, then moved to New York to join one of her college friends, aspiring actress Patricia Neal. She was working as an usherette for a run of *Swan Song* at the Booth Theater when writer Ben Hecht offered her a small part in the play. A few years later director Anthony Mann spotted her in *The Traitor*, and in a matter of days she was signed to MGM and cast in *Ambush* and *Adam's Rib* (both released in 1949).

Jean Hagen worked steadily for five years, playing a steady parade of tarts and floozies and, alternatively, wives, in mostly unmemorable titles. Her first substantive role resulted in one of her finest performances, as the pitiable Doll Conovan in the film noir classic *The Asphalt Jungle* (1950)—critics, however, were generally too dazzled by Marilyn Monroe to notice. With *Singin' in the Rain* (1952) they noticed, but even an Oscar® nod wasn't enough to wake the studio up to her true potential. When her contract expired, Hagen moved into television, playing Danny Thomas's wife in his ABC series *Make Room for Daddy*.

The show was a hit, but Hagen grew restless playing the goodly matron, until even the bad girl typecasting of her MGM days looked appealing. She told one reporter, "I'd like to breathe harder than I do." To that end, in 1955 she took a role as a sex-crazed seductress in *The Big Knife*, and the following year she quit television to return to the big screen. After a string of disappointing roles, including some wives, she retired in 1964. In the early 1970s, Hagen was diagnosed with throat cancer. She died in 1977 at the Motion Picture Hospital at the age of 54.

Carrie Hamilton

Born   December 5, 1963
Died   January 20, 2002

As Carol Burnett wrapped up her CBS Special on November 26, 2001, she could barely get through her trademark song. "I'm so glad we've had this time together…." she sang, quavering with emotion. She was, no doubt, thinking about her daughter, Carrie Hamilton, who had been diagnosed with lung cancer in August. Burnett wanted to cancel the show, but Hamilton encouraged her to go on as planned. The tumors quickly spread to Hamilton's brain, and in January 2002, the 38-year-old actress/musician died of cancer-related pneumonia at Cedars-Sinai Medical Center in Los Angeles. Her mother and siblings were at her side.

Relations between mother and daughter hadn't always been close. In her teens Carrie got heavily into drugs in an attempt to escape her vicarious celebrity. "I was always Carol Burnett's daughter," she told *People* at 15. "When I got high, I wasn't anymore. I wanted my own image." Driven by memories of her alcoholic parents, both of whom died young, Burnett was determined to control her daughter's substance abuse, and soon checked her into rehab. Hamilton emerged a year later, clean and sober at 15—after a relapse at 17, she remained sober for the rest of her years. "I wanted to be a rock star," Hamilton said later, "and I couldn't do that if I was dead."

Hamilton enrolled at Pepperdine University in Malibu, where she studied music and acting. The flamboyant young actress's big break came in 1986 when she was cast in the television series *Fame*. She also sang and played keyboards in a heavy metal band, Big Business. She made her feature film debut in 1988 as aspiring punk rocker Wendy Reed in *Tokyo Pop*, a character whose outrageous outfits and party-girl bravado made Hamilton a natural for the part. Other films included *Checkered Flag* (1990) and *Cool World* (1992). She went on to star in the first touring production of the Broadway hit *Rent*, and made numerous television appearances. A short film she wrote and directed, *Lunchtime Thomas*, won the Women in Film Award at the 2001 Latino Film Festival.

Empowered by her recovery and her own artistic success, Hamilton came to embrace her identity as "Carol Burnett's daughter." In 1988, she and her mother traveled to Moscow to share their experiences and help introduce Alcoholics Anonymous to the Soviet Union. At the time of Hamilton's diagnosis, she was writing a play based on her mother's memoirs—*Hollywood Arms* opened in Chicago several months after Hamilton's death.

ABOVE Musician and actress Carrie Hamilton (left) is photographed with her famous mother, Carol Burnett (center), and her sister, Jodie, at the Broadway premiere of Moon Over Buffalo.

Jean Harlow

Born March 3, 1911
Died June 7, 1937

With her pale skin, creamy gowns and platinum hair, Jean Harlow looked like a goddess of light, yet her film persona was decidedly earthy. Before the Hayes Office rigidly laid down the law about sex in the movies, Harlow sauntered onto the screen with iced-up nipples and a sassy seductiveness that made wordplay on "harlot" inevitable. Like her followers, Marilyn Monroe and Madonna, the original blonde bombshell created an unmistakable image of irrepressible sexuality, defying the world to make it a point of shame.

In real life, however, Jean Harlow—born Harlean Carpenter—was a passive figure, living out her domineering mother's thwarted dreams of stardom. "Harlean" was derived from her mother's maiden name—"Jean Harlow"—and when the young starlet's budding career demanded a new moniker, the choice was obvious. Sweet-natured to the point of servility, Harlow rarely made her own decisions, and only after she'd started drinking heavily did she express anger. She did derive some pleasure from her creative talents, but sadly it wasn't enough to counter the multiple tragedies of her short life.

Born in Kansas City to "Mother Jean" (as she called herself) and a successful dentist, Harlow married a wealthy businessman and moved to Hollywood when she was just 16. Mother Jean soon followed, with a greedy new husband in tow, and began her campaign to make her daughter a star. It didn't take much. The teenager had only to stand outside the studio gates, and executives would hand her letters of introduction. Starting out as an extra girl, then graduating to bit parts, she was featured in Laurel and Hardy shorts and in Lubitsch's *The Love Parade* (1929), among other films.

Howard Hughes gave Harlow her break, casting her in *Hell's Angels* (1930). In one memorable scene, she brings the hero back to her place and inquires, "Would you be shocked if I put on something more comfortable?" In that moment, Harlow's screen image was born, along with an enduring catchphrase. After loaning her out for a handful of films, Hughes "sold" Harlow to MGM, and they soon had a hit with *Red-Headed Woman* (1932). As scandalous as it was successful, the film was banned in some countries, and prompted the Hayes Office to tighten its guidelines for the portrayal of adultery.

On July 2, 1932, Harlow married Irving Thalberg's right-hand man, Paul Bern. Rumors about the groom abounded—was he gay, impotent, a sadomasochist?

But nothing could prepare Hollywood, or Harlow, for his shocking death just two months later. Bern was found naked in a pool of blood in his home dressing room. To this day, there is some argument over whether it was murder or suicide. Harlow's most authoritative biographer, David Stenn, argues that Bern shot himself after a confrontation with an estranged common-law wife, and that poor Jean was in the house when it happened. Irrationally blaming herself, she began to drown her sorrows in liquor.

Amazingly, Harlow's career was unscathed. *Red Dust* opened six weeks later, and, as if fiction could atone for reality, Clark Gable—the antithesis of Bern in every way—stepped in as her most natural leading man. Their quick-witted sparring and overt sexuality made for wonderful screen chemistry, and they appeared together in five more films. In real life, however, she made another bad match, marrying the cinematographer Harold Rosson. When they divorced, she fell hard for William Powell, who toyed with her affections—and she drank more.

Professionally, however, she was beginning to be seen as an actress, and not just a sex symbol. She gave one of her best performances in George Cukor's sadly satiric *Dinner at Eight* (1933), holding her own with a formidable cast. The imposition of the puritanical Hayes Code in 1934 pushed her to keep developing her comic talents. A reviewer of *Wife vs. Secretary* (1936) noted appreciatively, "not one trace of the Harlow hot-cha remains. She plays the secretary for her mentality, not her physical beauty."

ABOVE Jean Harlow and an assistant on the set of Riff Raff *(1936). Harlow's co-star in the film was Spencer Tracy.*

BELOW Emulated by many, few have come close to the amazing phenomenon that was Jean Harlow.

In 1937, while filming *Saratoga*, the 26-year-old Harlow fell ill, and just 10 days later news of her death rocked Hollywood. Those who knew her suspected her drinking, but, while it didn't help matters, the real culprit was kidney disease brought on by an illness in her teen years. Tragically, with better care she might have lived. According to the reigning mythology, Mother Jean was a devout Christian Scientist, and wouldn't allow the ailing star to see a doctor. In fact, during her final illness Harlow had around-the-clock medical attention. Her case was, however, mishandled by one of her doctors, contributing to her painful, gruesome death from kidney failure.

Heartbroken and penitent—and shrewdly manipulated by Mother Jean—Powell spent $30,000 to have Harlow interred at the Great Mausoleum in Hollywood's Forest Lawn Cemetery. Needless to say, Mother Jean reserved herself a spot as well, and later joined Harlow in her final resting place.

Cassandra Harris

Born December 15, 1952
Died December 28, 1991

ABOVE Pierce Brosnan and Cassandra Harris. After Harris's death, Brosnan adopted her two children.

One of Hollywood's most devoted couples, Cassandra Harris and Pierce Brosnan were married in London in 1977. At the height of the hunky Irishman's *Remington Steele* fame, envious fans would chide Cassandra about her good fortune, but Brosnan told one reporter, "What they don't realize is that I'm the lucky one." But his luck took a turn for the worse in 1987 when his beloved wife was diagnosed with ovarian cancer. After a grueling four-year battle with the disease, she died in her room at the Kenneth Norris Jr. Cancer Hospital and Research Institute in Los Angeles. Her husband was by her side.

A native of Sydney, Australia, Cassandra Harris began acting as a child, appearing in numerous Shakespeare plays and in a television production of Arthur Miller's *The Crucible*. She was awarded an acting scholarship at 16, and at 19 her critically acclaimed performance in the film *Five Days* won her an invitation to perform in the British National Theatre. Relocating to London, Harris worked on stage and in television, and married film and record producer Dermot Harris (brother of actor Richard Harris). They had two children, and later divorced.

She first met Brosnan one day in 1970, when he was in London doing a play with director Franco Zeffirelli. Recalling that encounter years later she told a reporter, "I had no interest in him at all.... But we had much in common—acting, books, music—and once we started talking, we never stopped." Seven years later they married.

According to Brosnan, it was Cassandra who spearheaded their move to Los Angeles in 1981, encouraging him to take a gamble on his career. It paid off richly when he landed the lead in *Remington Steele*. That same year, Harris made her only major Hollywood film, appearing as Countess Lisl in *For Your Eyes Only* (1981), with Roger Moore as James Bond. She also became a regular on her husband's show, playing his ex-mistress, a con-artist named Felicia. Even before her diagnosis, however, she had stopped acting, devoting herself to raising her children, and to running their company, Kilkenny Productions.

Brosnan credits her for his own success both as a nurturing support for his career, and as a teacher. When he began *Remington Steele*, he had never done light comedy before, and she helped him find the right tone. After her death Brosnan told a reporter, "I do believe in an afterlife. I do believe that I'll see Cassie again."

Star Shot

After her split from Chaplin, Mildred Harris had a brief romance with the Prince of Wales, who later became King Edward VIII but would abdicate to marry Wallis Simpson.

BELOW *Mildred Harris appeared in over 120 films. Her final role was an uncredited one in* Having Wonderful Crime, *released in 1945.*

Mildred Harris

Born November 29, 1901
Died July 20, 1944

Silent film star Mildred Harris is most often remembered as the first wife of comedian Charlie Chaplin, but the 16-year-old bride was already a star in her own right when they married on October 23, 1918. The couple had one child, Norman Spencer, who was born with severe disabilities and died just three days after his birth—the inscription on his gravestone reads simply "Mousy."

In 1920 Harris demanded a divorce, charging that Chaplin was a political radical who "never did anything but think." She received a $300,000 settlement from the well-heeled Little Tramp, yet declared bankruptcy two years later, apparently due to expenses associated with several illnesses. In later years she stressed her independence from her ex-husband, pointing out that she had never appeared in any of his movies, and had dropped his name immediately after their divorce became final.

Born in Cheyenne, Wyoming, Harris got her start at age nine in the films of Thomas H. Ince, and came into prominence under the guidance of Lois Weber at Universal. At the time of her marriage to Chaplin, she had nearly 40 titles to her name, including early film versions of L. Frank Baum's Oz books and D. W. Griffith's *Intolerance* (1916). After many more silent movies, Harris went on to make a splash with the coming of sound, starring in *Melody of Love* (1928), Universal's first talkie, but her career dropped off soon after. In the 1930s she did a burlesque act in night-clubs around the United States, Canada, and Europe. Commenting on her impersonation of Garbo, the press liked to note that Greta was just a Stockholm beautician when Harris was queen of Hollywood.

Though her first marriage was the most historic, her second was longer lived. In 1925, two days after Chaplin married Lita Grey, Harris married Eldridge T. McGovern. The couple had a son, John, but divorced in 1929. Five years later, romance blossomed while she was performing in a musical revue. The show's producer, brewer and former professional football player William K. Fleckenstein, became her third husband.

In 1942 Harris decided to give Hollywood another go and registered for extra work through Central Casting. A press release announced, "Miss Harris is back in Hollywood, and bravely trying for a comeback from the bottom of the ladder." In 1944, after making a few film appearances, she went in for abdominal surgery, and died of pneumonia ten days later at Cedars of Lebanon Hospital in Los Angeles. She was 42 years old.

Laurence Harvey

Born October 1, 1928
Died November 25, 1973

LEFT *Laurence Harvey with his third wife, Pauline Stone. They had just one child, a daughter named Domino, born in the year of Harvey's death.*

During his last interview, cancer-ravaged Laurence Harvey recalled, "I was invariably typecast as affected, heartless, and narcissistic." By most accounts, including his own, he had more than a little in common with his screen persona. Tall, dark, and handsome, with a reptilian remoteness, Harvey was not an easy point of identification for audiences, though for some he held a caddish charm. At his best, he portrayed cold, barren souls to uncanny perfection.

Laurence Harvey was born Hirshke Skikne (his first name is usually reported as "Larushka," but his family has corrected that) in Lithuania, to Jewish parents. In the early 1930s, with war brewing on the horizon, his family moved to South Africa, and Harvey quickly learned English. A bright and adventuresome youth, he served in World War II as a teenager and later won a scholarship to study acting at London's Royal Academy of Dramatic Art. He went on to perform Shakespeare at the prestigious Old Vic theater, and appeared in a number of British-made B-grade films beginning with *House of Darkness* (1948).

In 1959, Laurence Harvey hit pay dirt with his portrayal of the ruthlessly ambitious antihero in *Room at the Top.* A classic of Britain's "angry young man" cinema, it earned him an Oscar® nomination and several offers from Hollywood. In 1960, he appeared in *The Alamo* and *BUtterfield 8,* and critic Hedda Hopper hailed him as "easily the most exciting and talented newcomer." For the most part, however, he failed to make good on his initial promise, and his performances were often ridiculed by the press. Harvey took it out on his leading ladies. Of Kim Novak, his co-star in *Of Human Bondage* (1964), he coolly remarked to *Time* magazine, "Kim is a very attractive girl, but why does she try to act?"

Harvey is best remembered today for his creepy characterization of the brainwashed political assassin in John Frankenheimer's surreal Cold War psycho-drama *The Manchurian Candidate* (1962). At the time of its release, however, it did little at the box office, and a year later it was pulled from distribution—not because of its foreshadowing of the Kennedy assassination, but due to a contract dispute with United Artists. By the mid-1960s, Harvey's career was in decline, and forays into writing and directing didn't help. He died of cancer in his London home in 1973; 15 years later, *The Manchurian Candidate* (1962) was rereleased to rave reviews.

Star Shot

Harvey was married three times. His first wife was British actress Margaret Leighton; the second was Joan Perry; and, finally, he married fashion model Pauline Stone just a year before his death.

RIGHT Laurence Harvey in 1959. In the 1960s, Harvey appeared as himself in some popular television shows, including What's My Line? *and* The Milton Berle Show.

Allison Hayes

Born March 6, 1930
Died February 27, 1977

B-movie queen Allison Hayes achieved cult status for her starring role in *The Attack of the 50-Foot Woman* (1958). Buxom to begin with, Allison Hayes is quite a spectacle at those proportions, but the movie also appeals as a female revenge fantasy—at one point the oversized (due to genetic meddling by an alien) woman squeezes her husband and his mistress to death. Never mind the bad writing and cheesy effects— the poster alone immortalized Hayes as an icon of feminine strength. Given the physically depleting illness she endured later in life, it's not a bad way to remember her.

Allison (then Mary Jane) Hayes was born on a military base in Charleston, West Virginia, and grew up in Washington, D.C. An accomplished pianist, she considered a career in music, but in 1949 the statuesque beauty was invited to represent D.C. in the Miss America Pageant. Her next big break reportedly came at a party she attended with an embassy secretary. On seeing her, Mrs. Earl Warren, wife of the Supreme Court Justice, remarked, "What a pretty girl. She ought to be in the movies." A talent scout happened to hear her, and Hayes was offered a screen test. (Another story says that Hayes moved to Hollywood at the urging of Carmel Myers.)

Changing her name to Allison, she signed with Universal in 1954, eventually leaving the studio to be a free agent. She hit her stride in the late 1950s, when she starred in a succession of shamelessly trashy horror flicks: *Zombies of Mora Tau* (1957), *The Undead* (1957), and *The Hypnotic Eye* (1960). In the early 1960s she worked in television, with regular roles on *Acapulco* and on *General Hospital*. Her last movie was *Tickle Me* (1965) with Elvis Presley. But her career came to an abrupt end in 1965, as a mysterious illness began to take over her life. Her symptoms included hair loss, difficulty walking, and an uncharacteristically surly manner.

After hundreds of inconclusive tests, Hayes took matters into her own hands. She came upon a small book called *Toxicology of Industrial Metals,* and realized she was suffering from blood poisoning. It was later determined that a calcium supplement she'd taken for many years had a high lead content. She was diagnosed with leukemia in 1976, and died in a La Jolla, California, hospital the following year, after a blood transfusion. Heroic to the end, Hayes successfully campaigned to ban the importation of the toxic calcium pills.

ABOVE Allison Hayes with Brett Halsey. Hayes had a flair for comedy, and was featured in the Dean Martin vehicle, Who's Been Sleeping in My Bed? *(1963).*

Star Shot

At the height of her "scream queen" fame in 1958, Allison Hayes modeled for Frederick's of Hollywood's sexy lingerie catalog and *Gent* magazine.

Susan Hayward

Born June 30, 1918
Died March 14, 1975

RIGHT Susan Hayward enjoys the company of Flight Lieutenant Carroll McColpin during a party thrown for war heroes in the 1940s.

Star Shot

On August 10, 1951, Susan Hayward left her mark in the forecourt of Grauman's Chinese Theatre in Los Angeles. Her footprints are the only ones set in gold dust.

Redheaded spitfire Susan Hayward received five Oscar® nominations, finally winning for her role as a convict on death row in *I Want to Live!* (1958). The motion picture's title, in all its exclamatory excess, could serve as Hayward's personal motto. Known for her tough-girl attitude and indomitable spirit, she was true to her nature to the last, battling terminal cancer with all her powers. After giving her six months to live, her doctor was astonished to see her continue to rally for two and a half years, as malignant tumors spread throughout her brain. "She was one of the great fighters," he told the press when she finally succumbed. "I've never seen anything like it."

Susan Hayward, born Edythe Marrener, was raised in Brooklyn, New York, in a Flatbush tenement. Her father worked at Coney Island, but Edythe preferred movies to carnival rides, and spent many an afternoon at the cinema, imagining herself up there on the screen.

The determination that would get her there was first put to the test when she was hit by a car at the age of seven. Her doctor predicted that she would never walk again, but after enduring months in a body cast, then struggling with braces, she was back on her feet.

Graduating from high school, she started drama classes, then signed up with a modeling agent. It was a spread in the *Saturday Evening Post* that got Edythe her big break. Her attractively feisty personality must have come through in the photos, because they inspired a call from David O. Selznick's office inviting her to audition for the role of the decade: Scarlett O'Hara, in *Gone with the Wind* (1939).

Needless to say, she didn't win the part— but she got an agent and changed her name to Susan Hayward. For the next ten years she was

ABOVE At the 1956 Cannes Film Festival, Susan Hayward picked up the award for Best Actress for her moving role in the film I'll Cry Tomorrow *(1955).*

passed from studio to studio, appearing mostly in B-grade movies. A classy exception was the foreign legion drama *Beau Geste* (1939), starring Gary Cooper, but it was in playing bitches and floozies in lesser films that she defined her screen personality. Her career took a turn with *Smash-Up: The Story of a Woman* (1947). In a variation on the star-is-born story, she plays an alcoholic singer who sacrifices her career for her husband's. It was the first of four films with related themes, including *I'll Cry Tomorrow* (1955), the story of entertainer Lillian Ross's triumphant battle with alcoholism; all four films would earn Hayward Oscar® nominations.

As she finally found her niche in gritty, painful melodramas about strong women with big problems, Hayward's life began to mirror the tone of her pictures. In 1944, she had married actor Jess Barker, only to leave him two months later, despite the fact that she was pregnant. They reunited, and the following year she gave birth to twin boys. As his career dwindled, hers flourished, causing tensions that would erupt violently in 1953, when Barker reportedly hit Hayward and shoved her into their swimming pool naked, prompting neighbors to call the police. They divorced the following year, but after an encounter with her ex-husband in 1955, Susan Hayward attempted suicide by trying to overdose on sleeping tablets.

With her 1957 marriage to attorney and former FBI agent Floyd Eaton Chalkley, she entered a happier chapter of her life, settling with him in Georgia. Her career, too, reached a new high, when she was cast in Robert Wise's *I Want to Live!* (1958). Originally titled *The Barbara Graham Story*, it's the harrowing true account of a woman sent to the gas chamber for a crime she may not have committed. Hayward's fiery yet poignant characterization of Graham won her an Academy Award®, prompting her frequent producer, Walter Wanger, to sigh in relief, "Thank God, now we can all relax."

ABOVE Susan Hayward shares a tender moment with Gregory Peck in The Snows of Kilimanjaro *(1952), based on a story by American writer Ernest Hemingway.*

Despite a few successes, Susan Hayward's screen output slowed over the course of the 1960s. When her husband died in 1966, she took some time off. She returned to the screen for a part in the trashy cult classic *Valley of the Dolls* (1967), but her best work was now behind her. Tragically, her worst work would return to haunt her.

Starring John Wayne as Genghis Khan and Susan Hayward as a Tartar princess, *The Conqueror* (1956) was, deservedly, a box-office flop, but its legacy in Hollywood is enormous. After Wayne's death from cancer in 1979, it was calculated that 91 of the 220 cast and crew members had been diagnosed with the disease, and about half of those had died. The reason was painfully obvious: *The Conqueror* was shot just 137 miles (220 km) from an atomic test site at Yucca Flat, Nevada. Hayward succumbed to brain tumors in 1975, before the truth came out—if she'd known she was the victim of the U.S. government's unconscionable failure to protect public health, chances are she would have kept on fighting.

LEFT Susan Hayward appeared in more than 60 movies. She once said, "I don't relax because I don't know how.... Life is too short to relax."

Wanda Hendrix

Born November 3, 1928
Died February 1, 1981

BELOW In Ride the Pink Horse *(1947), Wanda Hendrix starred with Robert Montgomery. In 1971, she was in an episode of* Bewitched *with his daughter, Elizabeth Montgomery.*

Wanda Hendrix arrived in Hollywood a tiny, doll-faced teenager, and almost instantly became a star. Two years later, in 1949, newspapers would announce the dark-haired beauty's fairy tale marriage to actor Audie Murphy, America's most decorated war hero. As an adult, her career fizzled, perhaps due in part to the sexist values of the times. While married to Murphy, Hendrix noted, "No matter what it is, I can't ever be better at anything than Audie is."

Born Dixie Wanda Hendrix in Jacksonville, Florida, Hendrix was the only child of parents who were often gone for work. She grew up largely on her own. "I longed for two things," she recalled. "First, a home. And next, I wanted to be important to somebody or something." At the age of six, she announced that she was going to be a screen star, "because everyone seemed to think stars were the most important people in the world." During her early teenage years, her drama coach brought her to the attention of a Hollywood talent scout. Before long, she and her mother had moved to Los Angeles, and Hendrix began earning more money each month than her parents would ever see in a lifetime.

Wanda Hendrix scored her first role in *Confidential Agent* (1945), and worked steadily for the next few years, growing into womanhood in *Nora Prentiss* (1947), *Miss Tatlock's Millions* (1948), and *Song of Surrender* (1949), among other films. She was not a great talent, but her screen presence had a certain vitality and soulfulness, which was particularly evident in *Ride the Pink Horse* (1947), a taut blackmail drama set against the colorful backdrop of a New Mexico fiesta. Hendrix appeared with Murphy only once, in 1950's *Sierra*. A year later their marriage would end in a stormy divorce, fueled by Murphy's war trauma symptoms and gambling.

Soon Hendrix's name was more often seen in the tabloids than on the screen, and she only made a handful of films after 1954. That year, she married James Stack (brother of actor Robert Stack), but that didn't work out either. Hendrix later confessed, "After two marriages failed I just withdrew into myself and didn't care whether I worked or not." She died of pneumonia in 1981, after a long illness. Despite her disappearance from screens, Wanda Hendrix left an indelible mark on moviegoers in the late 1940s.

LEFT Sonja Henie in Wintertime *(1943). Henie was not the only Olympian to pursue a Hollywood career: swimmer Johnny Weissmuller became the screen's most famous Tarzan.*

Sonja Henie

Born April 8, 1912
Died October 12, 1969

In Hollywood, the blonde, blue-eyed film star and Olympian Sonja Henie was known as the Esther Williams of ice skating. In her native Oslo, however, she is less fondly remembered as Hitler's favorite athlete. Rumored to be a fascist sympathizer, she was, in any case, a darker, more complex character than her wholesome, dimple-cheeked public image suggested. Shrewd, materialistic, and ambitious, she was also an innovative skater whose sense of showmanship redefined the sport for future generations.

At the age of eight (some sources say six), Henie got her first pair of skates as a Christmas gift. Already a dancer, she won her city's junior skating championship the following year. Studying ballet in London and skating seven hours a day, Henie perfected her signature dancer-like style, and in 1928 she won her first of three consecutive Olympic gold medals. The influence of her perpetual smile and graceful flourishes was great, bringing out the expressive side of what had previously been a more technical, athletic event.

In 1937, Henie went professional, and toured the United States with a glittery ice revue. On opening night at the Polar Palace, studio boss Darryl Zanuck was in the audience. He quickly offered Henie a contract with 20th Century Fox at $10,000 a picture—and once she'd secured herself star billing, they made a deal. Her first three motion pictures, *One in a Million* (1936), *Thin Ice* (1937), and *Happy Landing* (1938), were smash hits. With lavish production numbers showcasing her stellar skating and elaborate headdresses, the small matter of her acting skills was easily overlooked. By the early 1940s, however, audiences were losing interest, and Henie returned to the big business—one she practically invented—of the ice show spectacular.

A self-made millionaire, Henie also married money. Her first two husbands were wealthy Americans, and her third was Norwegian shipping magnate Niels Onstad. (Tyrone Power, who romanced her in her studio days, was the one who got away.) Influenced by Onstad, she began collecting modern art. In 1968, they presented Oslo with a $3.5 million glass and stone museum, intended to house the gems of their art collection, and also Henie's jewelry and medals. A year later, at age 57, she died of leukemia in an ambulance plane en route from Paris to Oslo. Despite her philanthropy, Henie's legacy is not widely celebrated in Norway.

ABOVE In Second Fiddle *(1939), Sonja Henie plays a skater who falls for Tyrone Power, a situation that reflected their real lives.*

Star Shot

Sonja Henie became the youngest ever Olympian when she competed in the 1924 Winter Olympics (then called the International Winter Sports Week) in Chamonix, France, at the age of 11.

RIGHT The glitz and glamor of the Jazz Age were captured in Francis Ford Coppola's The Cotton Club *(1984), starring Gregory Hines (center) as a nightclub hoofer.*

BELOW Gregory Hines with daughter Daria. Daria and Francis Ford Coppola's daughter, Sofia, played street kids in the film The Cotton Club *(1984).*

Gregory Hines

Born **February 14, 1946**
Died **August 9, 2003**

Once called the "Pied Piper of Tap," Gregory Hines almost single-handedly revived the percussive, old-school dance style for a new generation. He was a successful actor, and as an African-American, selected his roles carefully to resist racial stereotyping. Hines worked in film and television, but Broadway was the most natural outlet for his talents (he was also a choreographer and singer). In 1992 he won a Tony® for his energetic portrayal of jazz innovator Jelly Roll Morton in *Jelly's Last Jam*. Little more than a decade later, the lights of Broadway would dim in reverent memory of Gregory Hines.

Born in New York City on Valentine's Day, 1946, Hines was "hoofing" before he was even three. In the early 1950s, he and his older brother, Maurice Jr., began performing their tap act around the country, billed as the Hines Kids, and later (with the addition of their father on drums) as Hines, Hines, and Dad. He got his real education in the smoke and glitter of America's nightclubs, where he absorbed all he could from the old-timers. Among his heroes were Chuck Green, Buster Brown, and Sammy Davis, Jr., whose look he emulated as a teenager. In later years, Hines often paid homage to his roots.

In a 1986 *Playboy* interview, he recalled that the Hineses were often the first African-American act ever to perform at a particular club, "and that felt wonderful." At the same time, it also emphasized that in much of the country, segregation was the norm. His first real awareness of racism came on a hot day in Miami, Florida. As he headed for a drinking fountain he noticed that one was marked "white," the other "colored." "Who wants colored water?" he thought to himself, approaching the forbidden bubbler. Fortunately his companions pulled him away before he could drink, knowing all too well the hazards of even the most innocent transgression.

The boys appeared on Broadway and, with their father, went national on the Johnny Carson and Ed Sullivan shows. But for Hines, coming of age in the 1960s, tap began to look like an outdated art form. In 1973, he split up the group—already fraught with family tensions—and moved to Venice Beach, California, catching the last of the hippie years. He played in a jazz-rock band, experimented with drugs, joined consciousness-raising groups—and for years he didn't even own a pair of tap shoes. Having left behind his first wife and their daughter, he now hooked up with Pamela Koslow, a feminist activist and guidance counselor; they would marry in 1981.

By the late 1970s, Hines was struggling to make ends meet, and missing his daughter terribly. Though relations with his brother had always been stormy, when Maurice invited him to stay with him in New York, Gregory accepted. He landed a part in *The Last Minstrel Show*, and after struggling to get himself back in shape, went on to dance with his brother in *Eubie!*, earning his first Tony® nomination. Hines was hoofing again, but his hippie days hadn't been for naught. Having broken out of the family mold and experienced life differently, he returned to his art with a new freedom and expressiveness. In the years to come he would develop a distinctive style, both scrappy and virtuosic. His goal, he once said, was "to make it as real as possible, as natural as possible."

Hines's film career began in 1981, when he appeared in Mel Brooks's *History of the World: Part I*, and a few years later he was lauded for his "rare screen presence" in Frances Ford Coppola's *The Cotton Club* (1984). Casting the Hines brothers as a tap duo that breaks up when one of the boys goes solo, Coppola effectively exploited their personal conflicts. Perhaps some of that brotherly competition also came into play in Taylor Hackford's Cold-War dance drama *White Nights* (1985), which finds Hines in his element, play-ing off—and sometimes one-upping—ballet superstar Mikhail Baryshnikov. Later Hines became a familiar face on television, with a recurring role on *Will and Grace*. He scored an Emmy® nomination for his portrayal of legendary tapper Bill Robinson in the biopic *Bojangles* (2001). Though he often took non-dancing roles, Hines made it clear that acting was just a job—tap was his life.

Late in 2002, Hines was diagnosed with liver cancer. Performing a solo show in the spring, he was in top form, but the following August he died in an ambulance on the way to the hospital. At the time of his death, he was engaged to Negrita Jayde, who would have been his third wife. Hines's legacy lives on in everyone he inspired. Some, including tap icon Savion Glover, he mentored formally. Ever the advocate for the joys of tap, Hines finished off his live performances by inviting the audience up to the stage for a thumping free-for-all.

ABOVE During 1997, Gregory Hines had his own sitcom, The Gregory Hines Show. *A television favorite, he made a guest appear-ance on* Law and Order *in early 2003.*

LEFT Gregory Hines embraces his co-stars, Tonya Pinkins (center) and Keith David (right), backstage at the hit Broadway musical, Jelly's Last Jam.

John Hodiak

Born April 16, 1914
Died October 19, 1955

RIGHT Actors Ricardo Montalban (left), Clark Gable, and John Hodiak are taught Native American sign language by Chief Nipo Strongheart (far right) in preparation for Across the Wide Missouri *(1951).*

The news of John Hodiak's death spooked Hollywood. It was the third in a streak of sudden deaths, after Robert Francis (July 31) and James Dean (September 30).

BELOW In Trial *(1955), John Hodiak (right) plays prosecutor John Armstrong. Here he questions the witness, Angel (Rafael Campos).*

John Hodiak introduced himself to millions of moviegoers when he came up for air from the waste-filled sea in the opening scene of Hitchcock's *Lifeboat* (1944). The smudge belonged to a soon-to-be leading man who had made a name for himself in Hollywood without ever changing his name. The studio insisted "nothing is romantic about 'Hodiak,'" but he was adamant: "I like my name, it sounds like I look." Indeed, audiences, critics, and many leading ladies—including Anne Baxter, whom he married in 1946—found Hodiak very romantic.

He was born in Pittsburgh, Pennsylvania, the son of Ukrainian immigrants. Later, the family moved to Hamtramck, Michigan, where his father worked in an automobile factory. Performing in church plays as a child, Hodiak got a taste for acting. As a young man, he was shut out of the radio business because of improper diction, but he tried again with more success after an office job at General Motors gave him the opportunity to "correct" his speaking patterns. In 1942, an MGM talent scout singled him out, and he made a screen test with Canada Lee. Alfred Hitchcock discovered him by sheer luck while considering the actress for a part.

World War II-era audiences were looking for reassurance, and the square-jawed, dark-haired Hodiak was welcomed as a down-to-earth family man. His second film, *A Bell for Adano* (1945), set the tone for his good guy persona, casting him as an Army officer who tries to restore a Sicilian village to its pre-war innocence. But Hodiak also had a dark side, as evidenced in the film noir classic *Somewhere in the Night* (1946); in another military role, he plays a vet with amnesia, desperately seeking his lost identity. With his marriage to Anne Baxter, Hodiak's status as a top leading man seemed untouchable—that is, until Hollywood hunks Clark Gable and Robert Taylor came home from war. In 1951, Hodiak and Baxter welcomed their daughter Katrina into the world, but soon both his career and his marriage were on the rocks (he and Baxter would divorce in 1953). He left Los Angeles for a stint on Broadway, which he later called "the most wonderful experience of my life."

John Hodiak would return to Hollywood for a part in the race-themed courtroom drama *Trial* (1955) starring Glenn Ford, but while shaving on the morning of its nationwide release, he died instantly from a heart attack.

Judy Holliday

Born June 21, 1921
Died June 7, 1965

The moment she stepped onto the stage as ditzy Billie Dawn in *Born Yesterday*, Judy Holliday was pigeonholed as a dumb blonde. In fact, the brainy New Yorker graduated from high school at 16, and had an IQ of over 170. Early in her career she confided to *The Los Angeles Times*, "I live in fear of being typed by these roles. You have no idea what they do to you. I feel as if I had my brains in a vise." Yet even as a dumb blonde with an accordingly curvaceous figure, Holliday displayed comic genius in a handful of urban romantic comedies that were almost as smart as she was.

Born Judith Tuvim in New York City, she was descended from Russian Jews—"Holliday" is a loose translation of the Hebrew "Tuvium." After high school she worked at Orson Welles's Mercury Theater, then formed a nightclub act with some other young hopefuls, including Betty Comden and Adolf Green, who would eventually write *Bells Are Ringing* for Holliday. Exposure at Hollywood's Trocadero led to some small film roles, but her breakthrough was on the stage.

Jean Arthur was originally slated to play Billie Dawn in Garson Kanin's 1946 comedy *Born Yesterday*, but she fell ill just three days before opening night. Holliday was drafted, and almost instantly she was bringing down the house with her stupefied gaze and squeaky, off-kilter voice. Back in Hollywood, she played in *Adam's Rib* (1949), making a fan of Katharine Hepburn. Meanwhile, Harry Cohn—who referred to Holliday as "that fat Jewish broad"— was preparing to produce *Born Yesterday* (1950) at Columbia, but he wanted Lana Turner. Hepburn conspired to make sure the part went to its rightful owner, and Holliday won her first and only Oscar®.

Other hits followed, including *It Should Happen to You* (1954) and *The Solid Gold Cadillac* (1956), but her finest dumb blonde part was played before the anti-communist McCarran Committee, in 1951. Asked about some donations she'd made to suspect groups, the left-leaning actress gave the judge her best Billie Dawn stare and played brilliantly dumb.

In the early 1960s, Holliday was diagnosed with breast cancer and had a mastectomy, but the disease later spread to her throat. She died in her sleep at Mount Sinai Hospital, New York, in 1965, aged 43. In reference to her trial in the blacklisting days, Garson Kanin eulogized, "Her behavior under pressure was a poem of grace."

Star Shot

Judy Holliday was married to Columbia Records executive David Oppenheim from 1948 to 1957; they had one son. In the late 1950s she began a music career of her own, singing ballads.

BELOW The bubbles in Judy Holliday's bath are adjusted before shooting a scene from It Should Happen to You *(1954). Peter Lawford was her co-star in the film.*

ABOVE The team of Doris Day and Rock Hudson, pictured here in a scene from Lover Come Back *(1961), was a top box-office draw for a number of years in the early 1960s.*

RIGHT Rock Hudson and Marilyn Monroe in March 1962. A few months later, Monroe would be dead in suspicious circumstances.

Rock Hudson

Born November 17, 1925
Died October 2, 1985

With his hunky physique and toothpaste-commercial smile, Rock Hudson was a towering symbol of all-American manhood throughout the 1950s and into the 1960s. As times changed, his wholesome, manicured masculinity went out of vogue, but in 1985, Hudson gained a tragic new cultural relevance, when he revealed that he had AIDS. He became the first major star to give a face to the still mysterious illness, and indirectly exposed a long-guarded secret: he was gay. Ironically, what at one time would have destroyed his career now gave his films new vitality, reminding audiences that there was more to Rock Hudson than met the eye.

For all his brawn, Hudson—the "Beefcake Baron"—had a vulnerable, gentle nature, the product of a painful childhood. Born Roy Harold Scherer, Jr., in Winnetka, Illinois, he was five when his father abandoned the family. His mother remarried, and Roy took his stepfather's surname. An alcoholic ex-Marine, Wallace Fitzgerald beat both wife and stepson, inflicting lasting psychological damage. No doubt eager to leave home, Hudson served in the Navy, then moved to Los Angeles in 1946. There, to the sheer delight of housewives, the devastatingly handsome youth worked as a vacuum cleaner salesman and delivery man until he was discovered by Henry Willson, a savvy agent with an eye for studly talent (Tab Hunter was another of his finds).

Given the name Rock Hudson, after the Rock of Gibraltar and the Hudson River, he made his debut in *Fighter Squadron* (1948), then signed a contract with Universal. Fortunately for the inexperienced player, it was the only studio that still had a comprehensive training program, and he applied himself diligently to lessons in acting, elocution, and even sword-fighting. Still, his thespian skills were limited, and for five years he played uncomplicated machos in B-grade films. It was the German émigré Douglas Sirk, directing him in *Taza, Son of Cochise* (1954), who saw the actor's true potential.

Sirk once said of Hudson that he "seemed not too much to the eye, except very handsome. But the camera sees with its own eye. It sees things the human eye does not detect." What Sirk's camera perceived in Hudson was a firm, tranquil morality rising above the decadent hypocrisy of 1950s America. In a handful of sweeping, tear-stained melodramas—including *Magnificent Obsession* (1954), *All That Heaven Allows* (1955), and *Written on the Wind* (1956)—Hudson transcends good looks and good hygiene to convey purity of heart in a world gone bad. His new credibility as an actor earned him a part with Elizabeth Taylor and James Dean in the epic *Giant* (1956), and an Oscar® nomination followed.

Star Shot

During the making of his first film, *Fighter Squadron* (1948), Rock Hudson showed his lack of acting experience by needing 38 takes to get one line right.

With fans swooning for him all over the world, Hudson became one of Hollywood's most eligible bachelors. Privately he made no secret of either his homosexuality or his sexual appetite, while publicly he put on his best straight drag. The charade undoubtedly took its toll, yet behind closed doors it was a relatively liberated time for gays in Hollywood—provided you played by the studios' rules. The loyal, authority-respecting Hudson did just that. He even married Willson's secretary, Phyllis Gates, in 1955 to fend off a scandalous exposé. They divorced in 1958.

More effective than Hudson's real marriage in asserting his heterosexuality was his on-screen pairing with Doris Day. Though they only made a few films together—most memorably *Pillow Talk* (1959) and *Lover Come Back* (1961)—their names, forever linked, conjure up a blissful world of innocently sexy repartee and frothy pop romanticism. In retrospect, their films seem full of knowing winks to Hudson's double life (as documented in Mark Rappaport's 1992 film, *Rock Hudson's Home Movies*), but at the time, their surface sheen and peppy optimism left no room for anything dark or secret. As a grittier breed of screen heroes emerged, Rock Hudson was left behind to represent the naive and somewhat superficial values of a bygone era. He finished out his career on television, starring in *McMillan & Wife* during the early 1970s and later appearing on the campy nighttime soap *Dynasty*.

Diagnosed with HIV in 1984, Hudson at first maintained his familiar silence, fearful of blowing his cover. As he grew sick before the public eye (he was still appearing on *Dynasty*), rumors began to circulate, but the truth didn't come out until shortly before his death. Appearing at a press conference with Doris Day in July 1985, Hudson was alarmingly emaciated. Ten days later he went public with his illness, expressing the hope that his suffering might help raise awareness of the deadly disease. He died on October 2, a month shy of his 60th birthday. His sometime lover Marc Christian later charged that Hudson had put him at risk of infection, keeping his diagnosis secret as they continued to have sex; he sued for millions, eventually reaching a private settlement with the estate.

LEFT Rock Hudson met Elizabeth Taylor on the set of the high-profile ranch epic, Giant (1956), and they remained close friends until his death.

BELOW In Never Say Goodbye *(1956), Rock Hudson is unexpectedly reunited with his wife, played by Cornell Borchers, whom he believed was dead.*

Jim Hutton

Born May 31, 1934
Died June 2, 1979

Boyish and lanky, with an offbeat charm, Jim Hutton was often compared to James Stewart. Born Dana James Hutton in Binghamton, New York, in 1934, he studied journalism and drama in college, but was soon kicked out for his imaginative pranks. In 1955 he hit Greenwich Village, where he was, as he put it, "a beatnik before the word was invented." A few years later, with no prospects and an empty stomach, he joined the Army, enticed by the meal plan. Strangely enough, that's where the young actor got his big break.

While stationed in Germany on his tour of duty, Jim Hutton founded the American Community Theatre of Berlin, the city's first English-speaking theater. He was discovered there by the German-born Hollywood director Douglas Sirk, who was scouting locations for his next picture, *A Time to Love and a Time to Die* (1958). Sirk cast the thespian soldier as a neurotic Nazi who commits suicide, and in 1958, soon after Hutton's return to the United States, he was signed on at MGM.

Hutton's next feature was *The Subterraneans* (1960), based on the beat novel by Jack Kerouac. Thereafter he made his mark in a string of romantic romps and crackpot comedies, typified by his pairing with Paula Prentiss in the campy spring break classic *Where the Boys Are* (1960). Audience favorites, the tall pair—he was 6 foot, 5 inches (1.96 m) to her 5 foot, 10 inches (1.78 m)—made several more films together, among them *The Honeymoon Machine* (1961) and *Bachelor in Paradise* (1961).

In the latter 1960s, Jim Hutton branched into war and adventure films—including Sam Peckinpah's *Major Dundee* (1965), and *The Green Berets* and *Hellfighters* (both released in 1968) with John Wayne, but his career was decidedly in decline. Turning to television, in 1975 Hutton hit on the role that for many would define him: absent-minded sleuth Ellery Queen. Based on the classic detective novels, NBC's *Ellery Queen* ran for just one season, but has remained a cult favorite for mystery buffs.

ABOVE Jim Hutton and Paula Prentiss enjoy a game of volleyball. They made four films together, including The Horizontal Lieutenant *(1962).*

In 1979, Hutton was diagnosed with liver cancer and checked into the Los Angeles New Hospital for treatment. A month later, he invited some friends to the hospital to celebrate his 45th birthday, but he was too tired for the party. He took a nap instead—and never woke up. Hutton, once quoted as saying that marriage and a movie career were incompatible, was survived by his second ex-wife and three children.

Michael Jeter

Born August 26, 1952
Died March 30, 2003

Perhaps children adored *Sesame Street's* Other Mr. Noodle because he understood what every child needs to hear: it's okay not to be perfect. The Other Mr. Noodle was Michael Jeter, a self-described "odd and squirrelly-looking" actor, more familiar to adults as the befuddled Herman Stiles from the 1990s sitcom *Evening Shade*. Hailed as an "actor's actor" by *The Los Angeles Times* and much admired by contemporaries Robin Williams and Tom Hanks, Jeter played vulnerable misfits on stage and screen until his death at age 50.

"I know I am not what one normally would think of as fit for fantasy, and that is fine," Jeter remarked in a 1993 interview. In an industry where actors are pressured to maintain the illusion of perfection, Jeter was heroically honest about himself and his history. Accepting his 1990 Tony® Award, he said, "If you are out there tonight and you have a problem with alcohol and drugs, I stand as living proof that you can stop." In 1997, he disclosed that he was HIV-positive, helping to change the climate of fear surrounding AIDS in the entertainment industry. Some thought these frank admissions would hurt his career, but instead they earned him a deep respect.

In his youth, Jeter was not so comfortable with himself. Born in Lawrenceburg, Tennessee, to a conservative Southern Baptist family, he had a difficult time accepting that he was gay. While studying medicine at Memphis State University, he made two big discoveries—acting and drugs. In 1979, he debuted in Milos Forman's now classic film musical *Hair,* but his acting career would come to a halt in the mid-1980s when he began the long process of recovery from an addiction that had begun to ravage his body.

In 1989, he returned to acting, playing a dying bookkeeper in the Broadway musical *Grand Hotel,* a performance that earned him a Tony® Award. He was later cast opposite Burt Reynolds in the sitcom *Evening Shade,* a role that garnered Jeter an Emmy® in 1992. He also played in several feature films, portraying a down-and-out transvestite cabaret singer in *The Fisher King* (1991), a priest in *Sister Act 2: Back in the Habit* (1993), and a soulful death row inmate in *The Green Mile* (1999). Jeter's last film would be *The Polar Express* (2004). While still in production, he died unexpectedly from an epileptic seizure at his home in Los Angeles. Despite his HIV-positive status, a recent physical had found him in good health.

Star Shot

Even though Michael Jeter died before *The Polar Express* (2004) was completed, there was enough footage of the actor (which was later computer animated) to keep him in the movie.

BELOW In an attempt to raise awareness of the realities of living with HIV, Michael Jeter supported a number of AIDS charities.

Rita Johnson

Born August 13, 1913
Died October 31, 1965

Making her film debut in 1937, the year of Jean Harlow's death, Rita Johnson was touted as the platinum blonde's successor. Though she was the more versatile and talented actress of the two, Johnson never reached Harlow's dizzy heights of stardom. Appearing in more than 50 films, she gained a reputation for playing sophisticated, scheming mistresses, but in 1948 her career was cut short by a freak accident.

At high school in her hometown of Worcester, Massachusetts, Rita Johnson could never get a part in the school play. While she was studying piano at the New England Conservatory of Music, however, she landed a bit part in a Civic Repertory show featuring Rosalind Russell. This led to touring with a stock company, and eventually she settled in New York. There she branched into radio work—at one time she was the "voice of Jurgens lotion."

In 1937, Johnson was signed at MGM and given the lead role in *London by Night*. Over the next decade she demonstrated an impressive range, appearing in everything from light family fare to the darkest film noir. In 1940, she left MGM after a dispute over a part that she allegedly claimed "wasn't important enough." She moved to Columbia for 1941's charming death comedy *Here Comes Mr. Jordan* (remade in 1978 as *Heaven Can Wait*). Johnson is at her best in the dark classics *They Won't Believe Me* (1947) and *The Big Clock* (1948).

On the evening of September 6, 1948, actress Mary Ainslee went to pick Rita Johnson up for a party. Arriving at her apartment in the Chateau Marmont, she found Johnson dazed, with a huge lump on her head. Her friend tucked her into bed—and Johnson slipped into a coma. Three days later, surgeons performed a delicate and lengthy operation to remove a blood clot from her brain. Johnson remained comatose for two and half weeks, as police investigated the cause of the injury. At first they suspected assault, but eventually concluded that the culprit was Johnson's bulky, beauty salon-style hair dryer! Her maid confirmed that the dryer had slipped and hit her head at least once before.

Johnson recovered enough to go back to work, but she never regained her previous footing. She died in 1965 at Los Angeles's General Hospital after suffering a brain hemorrhage, probably due to the old head injury. One of her last roles was as a nurse in *Emergency Hospital* (1956).

BELOW Rita Johnson starred with George Murphy in the thriller London by Night *(1937), directed by Wilhelm Thiele.*

Carolyn Jones

Born April 28, 1929
Died August 3, 1983

Carolyn Jones didn't get star billing until, after years of playing "that blonde," she dyed her hair and cut it "wild." Her six minutes on screen as a sexy, dark-haired existentialist in *The Bachelor Party* (1957) won her an Academy Award® nomination. After that, Jones made it clear there was no going back: "Nobody—but nobody— is going to change my hairdo. I hated those blonde tramps I had to play." Known for having the "biggest blue eyes in the industry," Jones played memorable kooks and vamps, working steadily but always typecast in minor, eccentric roles. In 1964, she landed her dream role as television's least matronly mother, Morticia Addams of *The Addams Family*. Like Carolyn Jones, Morticia Addams couldn't care less how much fun blondes have.

Her dark-humored, oddball screen persona was the antithesis of the real Carolyn Jones. A bubbly, self-described "nouveau success," she enjoyed every single moment of being a star and relished the Hollywood high life. From 1953 to 1965, she was married to Aaron Spelling, who was on his way to becoming one of television's most successful writer/producers. She once gleefully told the press, "We make money and I want to spend it." After her divorce from Spelling, she was married to director Herbert S. Greene from 1968 to 1977.

Growing up in Amarillo, Texas, Carolyn Sue Baker, as she was then known, was a shy, lonely child desperate to overcome her self-consciousness. She found herself in high school drama and, upon graduation, promptly moved to California and squirmed her way (lying about her age) into a Pasadena Playhouse production of Tennessee Williams's *Summer and Smoke*. She quickly attracted the attention of talent scouts and made her film debut as a play-girl in *The Turning Point* (1952). She worked steadily for years, making small appearances in *The Big Heat* (1953), *The Seven Year Itch* (1955), and numerous other films before receiving her career-changing Oscar® nomination.

Hailed as an overnight success, Carolyn Jones quipped, "Seven years is my overnight." More prominent—though still typecast—roles followed in *Marjorie Morningstar* (1958), the Elvis vehicle *King Creole* (1958), and *Ice Palace* (1960). Her performances were consistently singled out by the critics, but it wasn't until the creation of the truly unforgettable Morticia Addams that this "saucer-eyed vamp" secured her place in entertainment history. Jones died in 1983 after a long struggle with colon cancer. She had recently married actor Peter Bailey-Britton, and was a regular in the daytime series *Capitol*. Living on in eternal syndication, her gothic, proto-punk fashions make her a cult favorite today.

Star Shot

Carolyn Jones married her third husband, actor Peter Bailey-Britton, while she was undergoing chemotherapy. She wore a lace and ribbon cap to hide her baldness.

Bobby Jordan

Born April 1, 1923
Died September 10, 1965

ABOVE Bobby Jordan (center, at front) with The Dead End Kids in a promotional shot for 1939's Hell's Kitchen. *The gritty drama was a huge box office hit.*

Star Shot

Not to be beaten to the punchline, Jordan once told a reporter, "I did all right for a while, but then I came to the dead end, if you'll pardon the pun."

RIGHT Bobby Jordan (bottom row, at right) was considered the best actor of the gang, and at one time received more fan mail than all the others put together.

Epitomizing the Hollywood cliché of the washed-up teen star, Bobby Jordan died of cirrhosis of the liver at 42, broke and all but forgotten. He had made his name in the 1930s as part of an ensemble of juvenile actors known as the "Dead End Kids." At the height of his career he lived in a swanky Beverly Hills mansion, supporting his entire family on his $1,500 a week paycheck.

Raised in Brooklyn, Bobby Jordan attended the New York Professional Children's School. In 1935, he and some classmates were cast in Sidney Kingsley's gritty urban street drama *Dead End*. A year later, the boys were all signed at MGM, and they reprised their Broadway roles as scrappy, streetwise adolescents in the 1937 motion picture version of Kingsley's play, starring alongside Humphrey Bogart. The boys were dubbed "The Dead End Kids," and a string of films followed. Most often they played delinquent types, as in the classic *Angels With Dirty Faces* (1938). In Hollywood's most glittery era, their films were part of a small minority that reflected the hard times outside the studio gates.

Reinventing themselves periodically—as The East Side Boys, then The Bowery Boys—they moved into comedy and adventure, enduring well into the 1940s. In 1943, Jordan enlisted in the infantry, returning to The Bowery Boys in 1946. In past efforts he often stood out as the troublemaker who sets the stories in motion, but Jordan now found himself eclipsed by some of the other "boys." He left the gang in 1947. Yet, despite some previous successes as a solo actor, he made only three more film appearances.

Married in 1946, Jordan and his wife, Lee, divorced in 1957, a year after his last screen role, and she took custody of their son. By now his childhood riches were gone—and Jordan was drinking heavily. He worked as a bartender, a salesman, and later an oil driller, to no avail. In 1958, he claimed bankruptcy when he was arrested for failure to pay alimony and child support.

In August 1965, Jordan collapsed at a friend's Los Angeles house and was admitted to the Sepulveda Veterans Administration Hospital for treatment of his ailing liver. He died there a few weeks later.

LEFT Diane Keaton and Richard Jordan in Interiors *(1978). In the same year, Jordan played Jean Valjean in a television movie of* Les Miserables.

Richard Jordan

Born July 19, 1938
Died August 30, 1993

When Richard Jordan became known to the world as the Irish immigrant-turned-tycoon in the captivating NBC miniseries *Captains and the Kings* (1976), he was ambivalent about his success. Though his edgy good looks, baritone voice, and hedonistic ways made him a perfect candidate for stardom, the Hollywood fantasy never appealed to him. Throughout his career, he pursued intellectual rigor and artistic fulfillment, rather than commercial success, playing memorable secondary roles in cinema, while earning critical acclaim in theater and television. Speaking with *The Los Angeles Times* about his decision to become an actor, he said, "If I'd wanted to make money, I could have become a lawyer like the rest of my family. I did it because, as preposterous as it sounds, I wanted to be an artist."

Born in New York, Robert Anson Jordan graduated from Harvard University and studied acting in Paris. Taking the stage name "Richard" to avoid confusion with another actor, Jordan spent eight years with Joseph Papp's New York Shakespeare Festival. For Jordan, it was "like learning Bach if you're going to be a pianist."

He made his film debut in 1970, appearing in *Lawman*, a stoic modern Western starring Burt Lancaster. Though his filmography is of mixed quality, he often collaborated with strong actors and directors, appearing with John Wayne and Katharine Hepburn in *Rooster Cogburn* (1975), and working with Woody Allen and David Lynch in *Interiors* (1978) and *Dune* (1984) respectively. He was particularly effective in Victor Nunez's *A Flash of Green* (1984), the subtle, character-driven story of a Florida real estate swindle.

Richard Jordan's most prominent work was in television. He was often cast as a villain or some other unsympathetic type. His best-loved performance, as Joseph Armagh in *Captains and the Kings* (1976), takes his character's ruthless drive and ambition to its breaking point, showing the devastating effects of power. It won him a Golden Globe® and made him a familiar face in quality television productions for years to come. Meanwhile, he continued to work in theater, winning an Obie® Award for a 1983 off-Broadway production of Vaclav Havel's play, *Protest*, and directing a well-received *Macbeth* for the 1990 Shakespeare Festival. Just three years later, at the age of 55, Jordan died of a brain tumor in his Los Angeles home. He made his last television appearance that same year, in another hit miniseries, *Gettysburg*.

Raul Julia

Born March 9, 1940
Died October 24, 1994

RIGHT Raul Julia with his two sons and a young fan. Children and parents alike loved him as Rafael in Sesame Street, *a role he played from 1971 to 1972.*

Raul Julia was inspired to become an actor when he saw Errol Flynn's *The Adventures of Robin Hood* (1938) as a child in San Juan, Puerto Rico. For a performer who would become defined by his passionate, robust personality and his commitment to social justice, it was an apt beginning. Julia is most widely remembered as Gomez, the love-struck patriarch of *The Addams Family* (1991) fame, but his credits ranged from Shakespeare to political biopics to musicals. The most successful Latino actor of his generation, Raul Julia resisted stereotyping throughout his career. At the same time, he embraced his heritage and sought out roles that expressed his sense of racial and political injustice.

Julia got his first taste of acting as a devil in a first-grade play, and by college he was doing a nightclub variety show. One evening, comedian Orson Bean was in the audience. Impressed with the energetic and soulfully handsome young performer, he encouraged Julia to study acting in New York. Julia emigrated to the United States in 1964, and made his Manhattan debut that same year, appearing in a Spanish-language production of Calderon's *Life is a Dream* at the Astor Place Playhouse. True to his populist ideals, he also did bilingual community performances as a member of Phoebe Brand's Theater in the Street.

In 1966, producer Joseph Papp cast Julia as Macduff in *Macbeth*, initiating a very long and fruitful relationship. Papp would be an encouraging mentor over the years, and Julia became a regular in his New York Shakespeare Festival productions—eventually he would serve on the board of directors. At first, however, the work was scarce. To support himself between plays, Julia taught Spanish, sold magazines, and for a while even had a day job at Papp's Public Theater, but by the early 1970s he was a full-time actor. The turning point was his 1971 run as Proteus in a boldly modern musical version of *Two Gentlemen of Verona*. It earned him the first of four Tony® nominations, and national attention.

BELOW In Tempest *(1982), based on the Shakespeare play, Raul Julia played Kalibanos. Molly Ringwald, in her first picture, was Miranda.*

Other landmark roles in his celebrated stage career include MacHeath in *Threepenny Opera* (1976), with Meryl Streep; Othello (1979) to Richard Dreyfuss's Iago; the Fellini-esque director in the musical *Nine* (1982); and Don Quixote in *Man of La Mancha* (1992). Papp once said of Julia, "He was always outrageous in his acting choices. He's larger than life all the time when he's on the stage." It's a testament to his enormous flexibility as an actor that on the screen

ABOVE Raul Julia
(right) with William
Hurt in a scene from
the groundbreaking
Kiss of the Spider
Woman (1985).

it was a more subdued approach that would first win him wide acclaim.

With his Broadway success, Julia started getting small film roles, most notably in *The Panic in Needle Park* (1971) and *Eyes of Laura Mars* (1978). His talents were better showcased as a suave waiter with big dreams in Frances Ford Coppola's quirky contemporary musical *One from the Heart* (1982), but the picture bombed. Even so, box office potential was a minor consideration for the idealistic actor.

Signing on to do a politically minded, gay-themed independent feature with South American director Hector Babenco, Julia waived his fee for a share of future profits, expecting little return. It was a shock to everyone involved when *Kiss of the Spider Woman* (1985) became a huge hit in the United States. As a macho, Marxist political prisoner and his flamboyantly gay cellmate, Julia and co-star William Hurt won rave reviews. It was Hurt who would also win an Oscar®, but *The New York Times* emphasized the symbiotic nature of their performances, stating, "If Mr. Hurt has never been so daringly extroverted on the screen before, Mr. Julia has never been so restrained. And they meet halfway in a manner that is electrifying."

Julia's film career took off, and in the late 1980s *Variety* ranked him the third busiest star, after Gene Hackman and Charlie Sheen. In the decade before his death, he appeared with Jane Fonda in *The Morning After* (1986), Harrison Ford in *Presumed Innocent* (1990), and Anjelica Huston in both *The Addams Family* (1991) and its sequel, *Addams Family Values* (1993). With success came the freedom to choose projects that reflected his politics. In *Romero* (1989), he starred as the assassinated Salvadoran archbishop; in the miniseries *The Burning Season*, shot shortly before his death, he played the murdered rainforest activist, Chico Mendes.

RIGHT Raul Julia with
Anjelica Huston in the
highly successful The
Addams Family (1991).
After his death, Julia's
body was taken back to
Puerto Rico for burial.

In 1994, Raul Julia was diagnosed with cancer, but he had reportedly been in good health when he suffered a stroke in October of that year. He was admitted to a Long Island hospital, and died there about a week later, after slipping into a coma. The following year he was awarded a posthumous Emmy® for his outstanding work in *The Burning Season*. His widow, dancer Merel Poloway, accepted the award on his behalf, saying, "I hope that you will always keep him in your heart, as I will always keep him in my heart."

Madeline Kahn

Born September 29, 1942
Died December 3, 1999

Madeline Kahn's cartoonish voice and brilliantly offbeat character-izations made her a darling of 1970s comedy and left an indel-ible impression on audiences throughout her prolific career. In contrast to her loopy screen persona, however, in real life the petite redhead was reserved, bookish, and somewhat proper. Yet, as she herself observed, this undercurrent of seriousness contributed to her distinctive comic style. Discussing the Mel Brooks films for which she is best remembered, she noted, they "relied on broad, gross, flat-out humor, and I am the antithesis of that…. I think that's why it was funny."

Born Madeline Gail Wolfson in Boston, Massachusetts, she moved to New York with her mother after her parents' divorce. She rarely saw her father, and later took her stepfather's name, Kahn, though that marriage didn't last either. A creative, introverted child, she spent much of her time alone, daydreaming, listening to music, and letting her imagination run free. Encouraged by her mother—a frustrated actress and opera singer—Kahn took singing and dancing lessons, and, despite her rather antisocial inclinations, performed in high-school dramatics. Winning a scholarship to Hofstra University, Long Island, she started out as a drama major, but graduated in speech therapy. After college, she found a job at a public school, but quickly became bored with it and returned to New York to pursue a career in acting.

At first, Kahn's trained singing voice was her greatest asset. She worked in musicals and operas, then debuted on Broadway in *New Faces of 1968*. As her stage success grew and she became a familiar face on talk shows, Kahn caught the eye of Hollywood director Peter Bog-danovich. Casting her as Ryan O'Neal's dowdy fiancée in *What's Up, Doc?* (1972), he show-

ABOVE A talented singer, Madeline Kahn performed at the 100th birthday tribute to legendary American composer Irving Berlin in 1988.

RIGHT Madeline Kahn with comedian and friend Bill Cosby in 1997. Always a favorite with audiences, Kahn won the People's Choice Award for Best Female Performer in 1984.

cased her comic ability, if not her sex appeal. Even so, she nearly upstaged Barbra Streisand. Reviewer Vincent Canby wrote, "Miss Kahn, who has a voice that sounds as if it had been filtered through a ceramic nose, just about takes off with the movie." The following year, Kahn won an Oscar® nomination for her supporting role as a carnival floozy in Bogdanovich's *Paper Moon* (1973), losing to her young co-star, Tatum O'Neal.

A chance meeting with Mel Brooks in a studio cafe-teria led to another fruitful partnership with a director. In her first Brooks film, the madcap western *Blazing Saddles* (1974), Kahn dazzled as the Marlene Dietrich-esque Lili Von Shtupp, gaining her second Oscar® nod in two years, again for Best Actress in a Supporting Role. Kahn became a staple in Brooks's zany, decade-defining comedies, mak-ing memorable appearances in the horror spoof *Young Frankenstein* (1974) and the Hitchcock parody *High*

Star Shot

Madeline Kahn's first film role was in a 15-minute short entitled *De Düva: The Dove* (1968), which parodied the films of Swedish director Ingmar Bergman.

Anxiety (1977), as well as the less well-received *History of the World: Part I* (1981). Mel Brooks once described her as "one of the most talented people that ever lived."

Yet despite her indisputable talent, all too often Kahn found herself working with good casts and/or directors in films that turned out to be turkeys. As she became less satisfied with her Hollywood career, she returned to stage work and branched into television. She was Tony® nominated for the musical *On the Twentieth Century* (1978) and the 1989 revival of *Born Yesterday*, before winning in 1993 for her brilliant turn as ditzy Jewish matron Gorgeous Teitelbaum in *The Sisters Rosensweig*. On the small screen, her Emmy® nomination for *Wanted: A Perfect Guy* (1986) was overshadowed by the failure of two series, *Oh Madeline* (1983–84) and *Mr. President* (1987–88).

Early in her career Kahn struggled equally with the highs and lows of fame. Insecure and uncomfortable with praise, she spent many years in therapy building up her self-confidence and learning to separate herself from her work. Though she had several long-term boyfriends, her parents' failed marriages—as well as her independent spirit—made her resistant to commitment. Later in life, however, she was more comfortable with herself, both personally and professionally. In the 1990s, she started seeing attorney John Hansbury, who would be her partner until her death, and after her Tony® win, her career picked up momentum. She appeared in Oliver Stone's *Nixon* (1995), supplied the voice of Gypsy Moth in the animated film *A Bug's Life* (1998), and became a regular on the television series *Cosby* from 1996 to 1999.

Speaking of her improving self-esteem, Kahn once told an interviewer, "I think I'm talented—I just hope someday I live to be old and talented." Sadly, this was not to be. In September 1998, she was diagnosed with ovarian cancer. Determined to get the most out of life, she went ahead with her role as an unhappy housewife in indie charmer *Judy Berlin* (1999), before checking into Mount Sinai Medical Center where she underwent aggressive treatment from August to November 1999. She and Hansbury were married in a private ceremony at her Park Avenue apartment on October 10, and Kahn died less than two months later.

Kay Kendall

Born May 21, 1926
Died September 6, 1959

In the mid-1950s, British actress Kay Kendall was hailed as "the new Carole Lombard," for the simple reason that she was both beautiful *and* funny. In retrospect, however, the comparison seems eerily prophetic. Like her predecessor, she would marry a prominent actor—and die tragically young, in her thirties. Despite her short career, Kendall shines in a handful of roles that capture her spontaneity, sophistication, and warmth.

Born Kay Justine Kendall McCarthy, in Withernsea, England, Kendall hailed from a family of entertainers—her parents were a dancing team and her grandmother, Marie Kendall, was a music hall legend. At the age of 12, she joined the chorus line at the London Palladium—remarkably, the leggy brunette was already tall enough to qualify. Later, she and her sister, Kim, formed a music hall act, and by the mid-1940s, Kendall was making small appearances in mostly forgettable films. She had her first lead in the musical *London Town* (1946), and was romantically involved with its director, Wesley Ruggles.

The film bombed spectacularly, and Kendall left to study acting in Italy and Germany, then worked in theater for a while. Returning to film with a contract at Rank in 1950, she eventually found a role to showcase her talents in the delightful car-race comedy *Genevieve* (1953). She won her stardom playing the drunk trumpeter at a Brighton restaurant in a scene that would come to exemplify her high-brow clowning.

Struggling to find suitable vehicles for their new star, Rank loaned Kendall out to MGM for *The Constant Husband* (1955), and—contrary to the title of the film—she was soon having a dramatic affair with her married leading man, Rex Harrison. In 1957, he learned from Kendall's doctor that she was dying of leukemia. He promptly divorced his wife, Lilli Palmer, and married Kendall, who would remain ignorant of her true condition until her death.

That same year, Kendall played a showgirl in George Cukor's *Les Girls* (1957), earning a Golden Globe® and international stardom for her sparkling performance. She worked with Harrison again on *The Reluctant Debutante* (1958), but the onset of illness disrupted shooting on what would be her final film, *Once More, with Feeling* (released in 1960). Though the film was completed, Rank sued her for breach of contract shortly before she died.

Barbara La Marr

Born July 28, 1896
Died January 30, 1926

BELOW Barbara La Marr in The Shooting of Dan McGrew *(1924). She once famously said, "I like my men like I like my roses: by the dozen."*

Journalist Adela Rogers St. Johns rated silent actress Barbara La Marr as "the most beautiful of all women who have ever appeared before the camera." But life wasn't easy for the petite, raven-haired starlet, and she turned to drugs and alcohol to quell the pain. She once told St. Johns, "It would have been better if I was a lot uglier."

Touted as a Southern belle from Richmond, Virginia, La Marr was more likely born in Yakima, Washington. As a baby, she was adopted by a journalist and his wife. Reatha Watson, as she was then called, joined a theater company at the age of only six, eventually touring the country's stages. Mrs. Watson took her talented daughter to Hollywood when she was 13, apparently leaving her on her own. Before long, Reatha was arrested when a club where she was dancing was raided. Deeming her "too beautiful to be alone in a big city," the judge sent her home. The story resurfaced years later, and La Marr was dubbed, "The Too Beautiful Girl."

But first the precocious teen embarked on a string of cursed marriages. At 16 she wed ranch hand Jack Lytell, who promptly died. At 17 she married lawyer Lawrence Converse, who turned out to be married with children; he died during surgery before bigamy charges could be brought against him. Husbands three, four, and five were dancer Phil Ainsworth, vaudevillian Ben Deeley, and actor Jack Dougherty. Disillusioned with love, La Marr—now a rising star—adopted a baby boy in 1923. There was speculation that he was actually her illegitimate son.

Love left Barbara La Marr broken, but success also contributed to her undoing. Her breakout year was 1920, when she wrote five stories for the screen and debuted in *Harriet and the Piper*. Then Douglas Fairbanks chose her for the coveted role of Milady in *The Three Musketeers* (1921); she went on to star opposite screen luminaries Ramon Novarro and John Gilbert. However, in 1923, while shooting *Souls for Sale*, she was given morphine for a sprained ankle. Already a drinker, the troubled party girl became addicted to the drug. By 1925, she was also suffering from tuberculosis. In October of that year, La Marr collapsed on the set of *The Girl from Montmartre* (1926)—it would be her last film.

La Marr retreated to Altadena, California, dying there a few months later. Though the official cause of death was anorexia, drug abuse and tuberculosis no doubt contributed to her demise. La Marr's son was adopted by her close friend, actress ZaSu Pitts.

Veronica Lake

Born November 14, 1922
Died July 7, 1973

In her earthy 1969 autobiography, Veronica Lake recalls the Mother Superior at her Catholic high school telling her, "Someday, Constance Keane, you'll be a nun ... but you must learn to control that rebellious nature of yours." Connie promised to do so—and proceeded to become a Hollywood sex goddess, earning a damning reputation for her unprofessional behavior, promiscuity, and debauchery before drinking herself to death at the age of 50. She was no nun, certainly, but one can't help suspecting that the winsome, deadpan charm and startling lack of pretense found in Lake's best performances reveal more about the woman behind the famous hair than the cold facts of her troubled life ever could.

Born Constance Ockleman in Brooklyn, New York, in 1922 (some sources say 1919), she adopted her stepfather's name—Keane— after her seafaring father was killed in a ship explosion. The family relocated to Canada, then Miami, Florida, where Connie attended high school. She had always been difficult, but now her mother, also named Constance, began to notice a delusional streak. She took Connie to a psychiatrist, who diagnosed the 15-year-old girl with schizophrenia. She resisted treatment, so Constance let it go, and began pushing her beautiful daughter to become an actress.

A year later, the busty bombshell was crowned Miss Florida (the title was revoked when it was discovered she was underage), and the Keanes moved to Hollywood. By 1939, she was getting bit parts—she had also become a regular at Ciro's, partying late into the night. Musical director Busby Berkeley first took note of her hair—she was playing a schoolgirl in *Forty Little Mothers* (1940), and her silky blonde tresses kept falling over one eye. But it was producer Arthur Hornblow, Jr. who made the "peek-a-boo" her trademark hairstyle, and gave her a tantalizing name to go with it.

"Veronica Lake" debuted in *I Wanted Wings* (1941), and over the next few years her popularity soared. Soldiers taped her sultry photos to their barrack walls, while their stateside girlfriends emulated her cascading, sideswept waves—until the government intervened. Apparently the lady factory workers were getting their peek-a-boos caught in the machinery. Lake was compelled to restyle her hair for her appearance as a nurse in *So Proudly We Hail* (1943). Her performance was hailed by critics, proving that she was an actress, and not, in the words of one reporter, just "a sullen voice and a head of yellow hair."

Today Veronica Lake is most fondly remembered as the bittersweet actress-turned-tramp in Preston Sturges's big-hearted Hollywood satire, *Sullivan's Travels* (1941), and for a handful of classic dark films in which she starred with Alan Ladd. Measuring 5 feet, 1 inch (1.55 m) in height, Lake was first paired with Ladd on *This Gun for Hire* (1942) because she was just about the only leading lady in town who wasn't taller than the 5 foot, 4 inch (1.63 m) actor. They followed up with *The Glass Key* (1942), *The Blue Dahlia* (1946), and other pictures.

Lake's poor reputation dated back to her *I Wanted Wings* days, when clashes on set prompted her to go AWOL for three days. As her fame grew, Lake found herself mentally incapable of dealing with the pressure, and she began to drink more, often in private. Paranoid and thin-skinned, she lashed out at her co-stars, making instant enemies. By 1950, she was considered unhirable. Not surprisingly, her personal life, too, spun out of control.

Lake had married art director John S. Detlie in 1940. They had a daughter one year later, just a month after shooting wrapped on *Sullivan's Travels*. While pregnant with their second child, she tripped on a cable. The baby was born premature and didn't survive—neither did the marriage. She would marry three more times, and had many lovers (among them, Milton Berle and Aristotle Onassis). With her second husband, the heavy-drinking and heavy-spending Hungarian director André de Toth, she had two children; the couple declared bankruptcy in 1951 and divorced the following year. Lake packed her bags for New York.

ABOVE Veronica Lake's hands are tied by a crew member in preparation for a scene in the classic film This Gun for Hire *(1942). Director Frank Tuttle is on the right.*

Lake worked in television, film, and theater on and off for the next 20 years, often exploiting her dubious status as a fallen sex symbol, even as she quietly mocked the title—she preferred "sex zombie." At one point, she had fallen into obscurity, only to resurface in 1962 working as a bartender at the low-rent Martha Washington Hotel. It was there that she met her "deepest love," Andy Elickson, a seaman like her father. Dashing her fantasy of "getting married and tossing away the bottle," he succumbed to the ravages of alcoholism a few years later. Lake followed suit in 1973, dying of acute hepatitis while staying with friends in Burlington, Vermont. Her final motion picture was the unwatchable *Flesh Feast* (1970), a perversely apt representation of the tragedy her life had become.

LEFT In London in 1969. Veronica Lake was married four times: to John S. Detlie in 1940, André de Toth in 1944, Joseph A. McCarthy in 1955, and Robert Carleton-Munro in 1972.

Elissa Landi

Born December 6, 1904
Died October 21, 1948

A true Renaissance woman, the Venice-born actress and novelist Elissa Landi was something of an anomaly in 1930s Hollywood. Despising gossip and small talk, she steered clear of the industry hot spots. Her introversion earned her the sobriquet "the loneliest woman in Hollywood," but Landi saw it rather differently. Without any of Garbo's world-weary theatrics, the often outspoken actress explained, "I adore solitude." It gave her time to pursue her many passionate interests, including gardening, horseback riding—and, above all, writing.

The daughter of a count and reputedly descended from an Austrian empress, Landi was presented to American audiences as a European aristocrat. Count Carlo Zanardi-Landi was in fact her stepfather, but he raised her as his child, giving her the finest European education. Her youthful accomplishments are staggering—she published her first novel at 19! It was her writing that brought her to the stage when she joined a repertory company to gather material for a book she was writing. A year later, she was playing lead roles on the British stage.

Landi debuted on the screen with a bit part in *London* (1926), and went on to star in a handful of European films. She hit Broadway at the invitation of director Rouben Mamoulian, and appeared in *A Farewell to Arms*. She then moved on to Hollywood to play the incomparable Charles Farrell's love interest in the unmemorable *Body and Soul* (1931). She worked steadily throughout the 1930s, but despite her talent and a good initial effort from the studio publicity department, audiences never developed a taste for her. Today she is best remembered as the Christian maid in *The Sign of the Cross* (1932) and as Robert Donat's leading lady in the adventure film, *The Count of Monte Cristo* (1934).

As Landi's acting career petered out, her writing flourished—she published five novels between 1938

ABOVE In The Sign of the Cross *(1932), Elissa Landi starred alongside many fine actors, among them Ronald Colman and Warner Baxter.*

and 1942. In 1943, she married author Curtiss Kenny Thomas and retired from the screen. They moved to Kingston, New York, where she continued to write, and raised their daughter. Just four years later, she was diagnosed with cancer. Landi died in a Kingston hospital at the age of 43 after a nine-month illness—her husband had hidden the truth from her, so she never knew she had terminal cancer. Though her books are out of print and her movies are rarely shown, Landi remains an intriguing Hollywood figure, notable for her intellect and independence.

Michael Landon

Born October 31, 1936
Died July 1, 1991

When Michael Landon appeared on *The Tonight Show* to talk to Johnny Carson about his battle with cancer, the show achieved its second-highest ratings ever. Critics were not always kind to the righteous, shaggy-haired actor, director, and writer, but America loved him. A major force in television for three decades, Landon distinguished himself by not only entertaining audiences, but also nourishing their spirits with his sincere and uplifting family dramas.

Landon once said, "I created family relationships where people stay together because they communicate." His own childhood lacked such bonds. Born Eugene Maurice Orowitz in Forest Hills, New York, he grew up a Jewish-Catholic outsider in mostly Protestant Collingswood, New Jersey. His parents' turbulent marriage made his home life so unstable that he continued to wet his bed into his teens, as documented in his autobiographical television movie *The Loneliest Runner* (1976). In high school he found refuge in athletics and became a national javelin champion, winning a scholarship to UCLA. Already wearing his hair long, he didn't fit in with the crew-cutted jocks, so he soon dropped out and took up acting.

He made his credited film debut in the schlock favorite *I Was a Teenage Werewolf* (1957), and moved to television for a lead role in *Bonanza*. Running from 1959 to 1973, it was the most popular television program in the United States in the mid-1960s. By then, Landon was writing and directing episodes, developing his trademark themes of old-fashioned family values. When it ended, he created *Little House on the Prairie* (1974–1983), based on Laura Ingalls Wilder's series of books about frontier life. Like his next show, *Highway to Heaven* (1984–1989), *Little House on the Prairie* was often pooh-poohed for being preachy and saccharine—but it was a hit with audiences.

To some, Landon was a hypocrite whose real personality fell short of his wholesome image. At one time Landon was addicted to tranquilizers, and though he kicked that habit, he remained a heavy drinker and smoker (undoubtedly factors in his illness). In Landon's professional life, he was controlling and temperamental, and with two failed marriages, his personal life was equally fraught—yet his final marriage, to makeup artist Cindy Clerico, was a happy one. In April 1991, he was diagnosed with pancreatic cancer, which soon spread to his liver. Whatever his failings, it was fitting that Landon's wife and all of his nine children were at his ranch with him when he died.

LEFT Michael Landon with his Little House on the Prairie *family. From left, Melissa Gilbert, Karen Grassle, Melissa Sue Anderson, and Lindsay Greenbush.*

Star Shot

Actress Melissa Gilbert, who played Michael Landon's daughter in *Little House on the Prairie*, named her second son after Landon. Landon's son took Gilbert to her 1981 senior prom.

BELOW A high school javelin champ, Michael Landon suffered an arm injury that effectively ended his university javelin career.

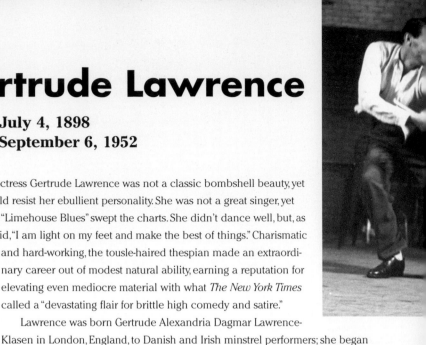

Gertrude Lawrence

Born July 4, 1898
Died September 6, 1952

Theater actress Gertrude Lawrence was not a classic bombshell beauty, yet few could resist her ebullient personality. She was not a great singer, yet her 1924 hit "Limehouse Blues" swept the charts. She didn't dance well, but, as she once said, "I am light on my feet and make the best of things." Charismatic and hard-working, the tousle-haired thespian made an extraordinary career out of modest natural ability, earning a reputation for elevating even mediocre material with what *The New York Times* called a "devastating flair for brittle high comedy and satire."

Lawrence was born Gertrude Alexandria Dagmar Lawrence-Klasen in London, England, to Danish and Irish minstrel performers; she began her career at the age of four selling programs in the theater lobby. She made her stage debut in a pantomime version of *Babes in the Woods* when she was ten. During her early teens, she was a chorus member of the Liverpool Repertory Company where she met Noel Coward, who became her lifelong friend. Coward later made his name as a prolific playwright and performer. His first hit song, "Parisian Pierrot," was first sung by Lawrence in his 1923 revue, *London Calling*.

In her 1945 autobiography, *A Star Danced*, Lawrence charts a classic rags-to-riches story, remembering the childhood thrill of fleeing from creditors with her family's scant belongings piled atop a grocer's cart. While the poverty of her youth may have been overstated, Lawrence achieved her status as an actress through sheer toil and determination, without any sense of entitlement. At 13, she earned a scholarship to London's Conti Dancing Academy, and by 1920, she was a radiant and sophisticated star of the London stage.

Lawrence made her Broadway debut co-starring with Beatrice Lillie in *Andre Charlot's Revue of 1924*, seducing New Yorkers with her signature song "Limehouse Blues" and prompting critic Percy Hammond to write "every man in town is, or will be, in love with her."

ABOVE Gertrude Lawrence (left) and Jane Wyman in The Glass Menagerie *(1950). Preferring theater, Lawrence appeared in only nine films.*

RIGHT When Gertrude Lawrence married Richard Aldrich, Noel Coward (left) sent her a telegram saying, "Dear Mrs A Hooray. You are finally de-flowered."

Among her many admirers were composers George and Ira Gershwin, Cole Porter, Kurt Weill, and Richard Rodgers and Oscar Hammerstein, who supplied some of the most powerful material of her career. In 1926, Lawrence starred on Broadway in George Gershwin's *Oh, Kay!*, for which she received rave reviews, one critic calling her "an actress of genius." Her distinctive rendition of the song "Someone To Watch Over Me" was hugely

popular and consolidated both Lawrence's and Gershwin's reputations. She became even more famous when she paired up with Noel Coward in his hit musical comedy, *Private Lives*, which played in London in 1930 and on Broadway in 1931. Lawrence appeared again with Coward in *Tonight at 8:30* (1936). Other notable Broadway appearances include *Susan and God* (1937) and *Lady in*

LEFT *Rehearsing for Tonight at 8:30. Noel Coward (right) directs Graham Payn and Gertrude Lawrence in the hit Broadway show.*

BELOW *Gertrude Lawrence's final performance as Anna in the Broadway musical* The King and I *was only three weeks before her death.*

the Dark (1944), based on the book by Moss Hart and written for her by an impressive duo: Kurt Weill composed the music and Ira Gershwin wrote the lyrics.

Her first film was *The Battle of Paris* (1929), a musical co-starring Charles Ruggles, and she soon became a familiar face in British cinema, featuring in such films as *Aren't We All?* (1932); *No Funny Business* (1933), with Laurence Olivier; *Mimi* (1935), with dashing Douglas Fairbanks, Jr., (with whom she had an affair); *Rembrandt* (1936), with Charles Laughton; and *Men Are Not Gods* (1936), which also starred Miriam Hopkins. Lawrence played in only one Hollywood film, as Amanda Wingfield, the indomitable mother and fading Southern belle, in Tennessee Williams's *The Glass Menagerie* (1950). The reviews were mixed, but movies, in any case, were not her passion. She was totally absorbed in the rich life of the theater, "the place where one learns the art of acting and fulfills the dreams of the actor."

In the last few years of World War II, Gertrude Lawrence toured extensively with the USO, entertaining the Allied troops in Europe and the Pacific with her unique interpretations of the most popular songs of the time.

Gertrude Lawrence, or Gertie, as she was known to her friends and family, was married twice: to Francis Gordon-Howley, with whom she had a daughter, Pamela; and to theater owner and producer, Richard Aldrich. That marriage lasted until her death.

Gertrude Lawrence died in a New York City hospital at the age of 54, due to complications from liver cancer. Not far away, her name still lit up Broadway, announcing her final starring role in Rodgers and Hammerstein's *The King and I*. Asked by Lawrence to turn the story into a musical for her, they created such memorable tunes as "Getting to Know You" and "Shall We Dance?". Lawrence dazzled audiences until the very end, refusing a medical treatment that would have kept her from working. She was reportedly buried in the pink satin gown she wore in the musical.

Vivien Leigh

Born November 5, 1913
Died July 7, 1967

BELOW Vivien Leigh as Karen Stone in The Roman Spring of Mrs. Stone *(1961). As a young actress, Leigh took her then husband's middle name as her professional surname.*

Nearly everything in Vivien Leigh's career was overshadowed by her performance as Scarlett O'Hara in the legendary film, *Gone with the Wind* (1939). She made nine films after that, but she is still best remembered as the determined Southern belle fighting for survival in the Civil War-era American South. Her personal life was nearly as legendary, and much more notorious, than her professional. Her marriage to stage icon Laurence Olivier was gossiped about incessantly, and reports of infidelity, alcoholism, and the onset of Leigh's mental illness kept them in the public eye until their divorce and Leigh's later, untimely death.

She was born Vivian Mary Hartley in 1913 (some sources say 1911), within sight of Mount Everest in Darjeeling, India. When she was five, she was sent to London and enrolled in a convent, where future actress Maureen O'Sullivan was a fellow classmate. Leigh studied briefly at London's Royal Academy of Dramatic Art before making her film debut in 1935's *Things Are Looking Up*. She also fell in love with and married an attorney, Herbert Leigh Holman, in December 1932, at the age of 19; they had a daughter, Suzanne, two years later. A few forgettable movies followed, until her first important film role, starring opposite Laurence Olivier in *Fire Over England* (1937). Despite her marriage to Holman and Olivier's to Jill Esmond, the two began a well-publicized affair. Vivien Leigh fought for roles opposite Olivier in William Wyler's *Wuthering Heights* (1939) and Alfred Hitchcock's *Rebecca* (1940), but was considered too unknown in America and lost out respectively to Merle Oberon and Joan Fontaine. She and Olivier did appear again together in *21 Days Together* (1940), as well as in numerous stage productions. Vivien Leigh also appeared with Conrad Veidt in *Dark Journey* (1937), opposite Rex Harrison in *Storm in a Teacup* (1937) and 1938's *Sidewalks of London* (also released as *St. Martin's Lane*), and with Lionel Barrymore and Maureen O'Sullivan in *A Yank At Oxford* (1938).

Meanwhile, in the United States, David O. Selznick was mired in two-year-long search for a star to play the lead female role in his production of *Gone with the Wind*. Leigh loved the character of Scarlett when she read Margaret Mitchell's novel, and was determined to land the role. She arranged a meeting with Selznick through his brother, Myron, who was also Olivier's agent. It reportedly took place on the backlot of the Selznick Studio on the first day of shooting, when Myron introduced Leigh to his brother by shouting, "Meet Scarlett O'Hara." Leigh did a screen test for then-director George Cukor that

evening, and two weeks later she had the part. Many grumbled at the audacity of casting a Briton for this most Southern of roles, but the casting was perfect; Leigh transformed herself into a smoldering Southern beauty, imperfect and calculating, but captivating nonetheless. The film was nominated for ten Academy Awards®, and Leigh won the Oscar® for Best Actress. The role brought her fame and fortune, and the following year she received something else she desired, a divorce from Holman. Five days later, she and Olivier were married. She won a coveted role opposite Robert Taylor in MGM's *Waterloo Bridge* (1940), was reunited on screen with Olivier in Alexander Korda's *That Hamilton Woman* (1941), and was Cleopatra to Claude Rains's Julius Caesar in the film adaptation of George Bernard Shaw's *Caesar and Cleopatra* (1945).

LEFT Electrifying performances from Vivien Leigh and Marlon Brando ensured the success of A Streetcar Named Desire (1951).

BELOW With Charlton Heston (left) and Laurence Olivier. Even after their divorce in 1960, Leigh kept Olivier's photo beside her bed.

When Leigh was cast as Blanche DuBois in Tennessee Williams's *A Streetcar Named Desire* (1951), she reprised the role that she had played in Olivier's earlier London stage production. This was an entirely different type of Southern lady, and Leigh was again perfectly cast, delivering a powerful performance opposite Marlon Brando's memorable Stanley Kowalski. For the second time in her career, Leigh had personified one of the great female heroines of film, and just as before, she won an Oscar® for her efforts. She also was awarded the British Academy Award, and Best Actress honors from the Venice Film Festival and the New York Critics Association.

She was, however, quite ill by this time. She had contracted tuberculosis in 1945, and was physically frail thereafter. She also struggled with mental illness much of her life, although reports differ as to the exact diagnosis, ranging from manic depression and bipolar disorder to full-blown schizophrenia. She had also suffered a miscarriage in 1944 during the filming of *Caesar and Cleopatra*. In 1953, she had a nervous breakdown during the shooting of *Elephant Walk* (1954) and was replaced by Elizabeth Taylor. Leigh was hospitalized and administered both psychiatric drugs and electroshock therapy. She later suffered a second miscarriage, and her worsening tuberculosis weakened her physically. She was exhibiting increasingly bizarre behavior, and Olivier divorced her in 1960. Despite the difficulty of her later life, she appeared in three more pictures, *The Deep Blue Sea* (1955), opposite a young Warren Beatty in *The Roman Spring of Mrs. Stone* (1961), and in Stanley Kramer's *Ship of Fools* (1965). She died alone in her Eaton Square flat in London from tuberculosis at the age of just 53.

BELOW As enduring screen heroine, Scarlett O'Hara. Vivien Leigh once said, "People who are very beautiful make their own laws."

RIGHT Peter Lorre with first wife, Celia Lovsky. Lovsky is said to have brought Lorre to the attention of director Fritz Lang, which led to his casting in M *(1931).*

Peter Lorre

Born June 26, 1904
Died March 23, 1964

BELOW Peter Lorre in Crime and Punishment *(1935). His performance as the tortured murderer seeking redemption is one of the most powerful of his career.*

Known as "The Walking Overcoat," Peter Lorre was diminutive, barely 5 feet, 5 inches (1.6 m) tall, with a moon-shaped face, gapped teeth, bulging eyes, and a naturally melancholy expression. His appearance, combined with a distinctive Austro-Hungarian accent, made him perfect for the odd, often sinister, character roles he gained fame playing. He broke onto the international film scene with a mesmerizing performance as the child murderer in Fritz Lang's masterpiece, *M* (1931), and added color to classics *The Maltese Falcon* (1941) and *Casablanca* (1942). "Whatever I do, I'll always be the grimacing villain who pushes helpless people down the stairs," he once said. "In my first movie I murdered children.... I've bettered myself in the meantime: I'm murdering adults now." He aged poorly, and despite reliably solid performances, his later films were often forgettable.

He was born László Löewenstein in Rózsahegy, Hungary, and from the age of four was raised near Vienna. He was born into affluence, the son of businessman Alois Löewenstein, and there was little to suggest the career that lay ahead. He left home and worked as a bank clerk in 1922, until it was found that he was playing hooky from the bank, having a friend punch his time card for him. He took his subsequent discharge as a sign that it was time to pursue his true love, the stage, and he set off for Breslau, Germany, where he landed a position with director Leo Mittler's ensemble. His first major role came in Galsworthy's *Society* in Zurich, and he continued working in stage productions, including appearances at the Schauspielhaus in Zurich and the Kammerspiele in Vienna. He appeared in bit parts in two films before being cast in Lang's *M* (1931). Lorre's fearful, pathetic, psychopathic child-killer, Hans Beckert, simultaneously engenders disgust, sympathy, and fascination as he is slowly hunted by both the forces of law and the underworld. It was a spectacular performance, and it made Lorre an international star. He appeared in several more German productions, but fled to Paris, and then London, as the Germans came to power in 1933. In London, he was cast by Hitchcock in *The Man Who Knew Too Much* (1934), despite the fact that he had little command of the English language. Legend has it that he bluffed his way through the meeting with Hitchcock by smiling, laughing, and nodding his head whenever Hitchcock spoke. He

then learned much of his part phonetically. If the story is true, it didn't seem to bother Hitchcock much, because he later cast Lorre in *Secret Agent* (1936).

Lorre arrived in Hollywood, playing the mad Dr. Gogol in *Mad Love* (1935), and Raskolnikov in Josef von Sternberg's film adaptation of Dostoyevsky's *Crime and Punishment* (1935). He later said that Raskolnikov was his favorite role of his career. He took on the role of Japanese detective/judo-expert in a series of eight *Mr. Moto* films, of which *Thank You, Mr. Moto* (1937) is generally considered the best. In the 1940s, he

was teamed with bulky Sydney Greenstreet in eight Warner Bros. dramas, including John Huston's 1941 classic *The Maltese Falcon*, the iconic *Casablanca* (1942), *The Mask of Dimitrios* (1944), *Three Strangers* (1946), and *The Verdict* (1946). He was able to show his comic talents by parodying his typically disturbed on-screen persona in pictures like *Arsenic and Old Lace* (1944) and *My Favorite Brunette* (1947). In 1951, Lorre returned to Germany and wrote, directed, and starred in the underappreciated *The Lost One* (1951). It was then back to Hollywood for an appearance in John Huston's *Beat the Devil* (1953). He also made several television appearances in the 1950s and 1960s, including a turn as the very first James Bond villain, Le Chiffre, in a 1954 television pilot of *Casino Royale*. He had gained weight later in life, giving him a puffy, worn-out appearance. He had also suffered from hypertension since the mid-1950s. Despite his physical health, he continued playing character roles in films of uneven quality; standouts include appearances in Rouben Mamoulian's *Silk Stockings* (1957), as a clown in *The Big Circus* (1959), in Roger Corman's *Tales of Terror* (1962) with Vincent Price, and with Price and Boris Karloff in *The Raven* (1963) and *The Comedy of Terrors* (1964).

Lorre was married three times, first to Celia Lovsky, who became an actress in film and television after their 1945 divorce. His second marriage, to actress Kaaren Verne, also ended in divorce. A third marriage, to Annemarie Brenning, produced a daughter, Catharine. Lorre and Brenning separated in October 1962. A divorce hearing was scheduled for March 23, 1964, but Lorre did not make it. He suffered a stroke and died at 12:00 P.M. that afternoon at the age of 59. He was cremated and his ashes were placed in an urn at the Hollywood Forever Cemetery. His final film, the Jerry Lewis vehicle *The Patsy* (1964), was released posthumously.

ABOVE *The film noir classic* The Maltese Falcon *(1941) featured Humphrey Bogart (far left), Sydney Greenstreet (seated), Peter Lorre, and Mary Astor.*

Star Shot

The cartoon character Ren, from the animated television series *Ren and Stimpy*, was inspired by Peter Lorre, according to the cartoon's creator, John Kricfalusi.

LEFT *Peter Lorre with Sophia Loren in 1957. Lorre was in demand as a radio actor, his famous voice the star of many thrillers.*

Diana Lynn

Born October 7, 1926
Died December 18, 1971

RIGHT My Friend Irma (1949) featured, from left, Jerry Lewis, Marie Wilson, Diana Lynn, and Dean Martin. Later in her career, Lynn made guest appearances in the television shows Burke's Law *and* The Virginians.

Diana Lynn spent most of her short film career excelling in sassy, smart-mouthed, precocious kid-sister roles on the Paramount lot. She delivered wisecrack lines with aplomb and generated a devoted fan following in the 1940s, but never rose above light comedies and B-grade pictures, and retired from film in her early thirties.

She was born Dolores Loehr in Los Angeles on October 7, 1926. Her mother, a well-known piano teacher, started her on the instrument at a young age, and Lynn gave her first piano recital at the age of six. She played accompaniment to a child violinist auditioning for a role in *They Shall Have Music* (1939). The violinist didn't get the part, but Diana Lynn was signed to a role. Her big break came when she was cast as Ginger Rogers's roommate in Billy Wilder's *The Major and the Minor* (1942). She won favorable notices for her performance, and was cast as Betty Hutton's caustic kid sister in Preston Sturges's minor masterpiece, *The Miracle of Morgan's Creek* (1944). Similar roles followed in *And the Angels Sing* (1944) with Hutton and Fred MacMurray, and in *Henry Aldrich Plays Cupid* (1944). She became a star after *Our Hearts Were Young and Gay* (1944) with friend Gail Russell. A sequel, *Our Hearts Were Growing Up* (1946), didn't fare as well at the box office. Her other films include *Every Girl Should Be Married* (1948), *My Friend Irma Goes West* (1950), *Bedtime for Bonzo* (1951) opposite an anonymous chimpanzee and Ronald Reagan, *Meet Me at the Fair* (1953), *You're Never Too Young* (1955), and *The Kentuckian* (1955).

After retiring from motion pictures, Diana Lynn appeared occasionally on the stage, winning critical acclaim in London and Los Angeles in *The Moon is Blue*, and on Broadway in *Mary, Mary*. Her first marriage, to architect John C. Lindsay, ended in divorce. Her second marriage, to Mortimer W. Hall, treasurer of the *New York Post* and son of *Post* publisher Dorothy Schiff, lasted until her death and produced four children, including actress Daisy Hall.

After a 15-year absence from the silver screen, she agreed to return in Universal's *Play It As It Lays* (1972), but on December 9, 1971, she suffered a brain hemorrhage. She was admitted to Mt. Sinai Hospital, and died nine days later from a stroke at the age of 45. She was buried at the Episcopal Church of the Heavenly Rest in Manhattan, New York.

LEFT A promotional shot of Diana Lynn taken in 1955. A talented pianist, Lynn once recorded George Gershwin's famous "Rhapsody in Blue."

Hattie McDaniel

Born June 10, 1895
Died October 26, 1952

The contentious debate over whether Hattie McDaniel blazed a new trail for African-American actors or merely perpetuated the racist caricature of the black mammy has at times overshadowed the remarkable comic timing that made her a star in the first place. She was born in Wichita, Kansas, in 1895, the youngest of 13 children and the daughter of a freed slave. By the time she was 15, McDaniel had appeared on stage in vaudeville and nightclubs. By 1931, she'd arrived in Hollywood, but unable to land a role in films, was forced to work as a maid.

Her big break came with *The Little Colonel* (1935), starring Shirley Temple, and she also appeared in *Alice Adams* (1935) and *Show Boat* (1936). She played maids in each, but her maids were something new: assertive, forthright, and bombastic. David O. Selznick cast her in *Gone with the Wind* (1939), and her vibrant, humanizing performance as Scarlett O'Hara's maid won her the Academy Award® for Actress in a Supporting Role, the first ever awarded to an African-American actor. Indeed it is her most famous role. However, she was never able to escape "mammy" roles, and never again matched the success she had with *Gone with the Wind*. In addition, some in the black community condemned her for the portrayal. The NAACP charged that McDaniel had "degraded herself and her race." McDaniel responded that she'd rather play a maid and earn $700 a week than be one and earn $7, but in private, the charges stung. She had little choice; even after the Oscar®, producers and studios were reluctant to cast her in more varied roles. Although she appeared in over 80 films after *Gone with the Wind*, her later roles became progressively more caricatured and stereotypical.

McDaniel led a troubled personal life. In 1941, a false pregnancy and dwindling opportunities in pictures led to a period of severe depression. She eventually turned her attention to radio in the late 1940s, starring in the hit broadcast, *Beulah*. However, in 1951, she was diagnosed with breast cancer, and died on October 26, 1952. McDaniel's last wish, to be buried alongside her well-known peers in the Hollywood Cemetery, was denied because of the facility's "whites-only" policy. In 1999, the Cemetery dedicated a memorial to McDaniel seeking to redress the prior discrimination.

BELOW With Vivien Leigh in Gone with the Wind *(1939). In 1946, Hattie McDaniel appeared in Walt Disney's wonderful musical,* Song of the South.

Lawrence McKeen

Born September 1, 1924
Died April 2, 1933

Lawrence "Sunny" McKeen became a major star at the age of two, appeared in 45 shorts before turning seven, and was dead by age eight, the victim of a rare blood disease. He is mostly forgotten today, but in the late 1920s, "Sunny" McKeen was a sensation: he was awarded the key to Philadelphia by the Mayor; he frolicked on the White House lawn with President Calvin Coolidge; he played ball with New York Yankees legend Babe Ruth; he appeared in numerous print ads; and even had a candy bar named after him. He was born Lawrence David McKeen, Jr., the son of film director Lawrence McKeen, Sr. His break came in 1926 when he was chosen to take the role of Baby Snookums in the Stern Brothers Comedy Company's serial, *The Newlyweds*. The serial was based on the comic strip of the same name written by George McManus, who would later go on to even greater success with the comic strip *Bringing Up Father*.

The Newlyweds ran in national papers for 12 years, ironically outlasting McKeen himself. The strip detailed the exploits of a beautiful wife, her homely husband, and their mischievous toddler, Baby Snookums, who had, at all times, a perfectly pointed cowlick on the top of his otherwise bald head. In 1926, Stern Brothers and Universal produced the first of what would be 39 shorts in the series, *The Newlyweds' Neighbors*. The film was a hit, and Snookums quickly took center stage in the series in pictures such as *Snookums' Tooth* (1926), *Snookums Disappears* (1927), and *Fishing Snookums* (1927). He appeared in six *Newlyweds* shorts in 1926, 19 in 1927, eight in 1928, and six more in 1929. During this time, he appeared with numerous actors and actresses playing the roles of his parents, including Ethlyne Clair, Syd Saylor, Derelys Perdue, Jack Egan, Joe Dooley, and Robert Young.

After the demise of *The Newlyweds* shorts, "Sunny" McKeen left the Baby Snookums persona behind in several shorts for Universal directed by Harold Beaudine, including *Baby Talks* (1929), *Christmas Cheer* (1929), *His Bachelor Daddies* (1930), and *Brother For Sale* (1930). He also appeared in 1930's *She's a He*, in which he's dressed up as a girl throughout in order to receive an aunt's inheritance. In 1933, McKeen contracted sepsis, a rare blood disease caused by an overwhelming infection of the bloodstream by bacteria. He passed away from the disease on April 2, 1933, at the age of eight. He is buried in Forest Lawn Memorial Park in Glendale, California.

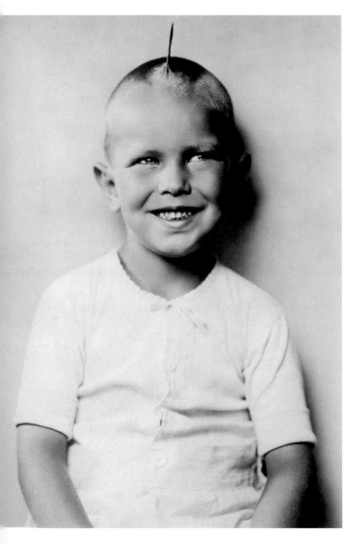

ABOVE Lawrence McKeen in his Baby Snookums attire, flashing his cheeky grin. Poor storage conditions led to the destruction of The Newlyweds *films.*

Nina Mae McKinney

Born June 12, 1912
Died May 3, 1967

Nina Mae McKinney was Hollywood's first glamorous African-American star, and one of the most beautiful women of her time. A vivacious, multi-talented chorus girl when discovered at 16 by King Vidor, she emerged a full-blown star after her very first film. But the lack of leading roles for black actresses in Hollywood and McKinney's own difficult temperament kept her from reaching such heights again, and she ended her days in near obscurity.

She was born Nannie Mayme McKinney in Lancaster, South Carolina, in 1912 (sometimes reported as 1913). A natural performer, she left school at 15 to join the chorus of the Broadway musical *Blackbirds* (1928), starring Bill "Bojangles" Robinson. Her spirited performance caught the eye of director King Vidor, who cast her in his next picture, *Hallelujah* (1929), the first talking picture with an all-black cast. She was captivating in the role of the seductress "Chick."

Irving Thalberg commented that McKinney was "one of the greatest discoveries of the age," and it wasn't long before she was signed to a five-year deal with MGM Studios, the first African-American actress the studio ever signed.

However, Nina Mae McKinney found very few suitable follow-up roles. She eschewed the stereotypical comic "mammy" roles and appeared in only two more Hollywood pictures, *Safe in Hell* (1931) and *Reckless* (1935), before departing for Europe. There, she appeared in British productions, including *Kentucky Minstrels* (1934); *Sanders of the River* (1935), starring opposite Paul Robeson; and *The Devil's Daughter* (1939). McKinney also routinely performed cabaret in European nightclubs, billed as "The Black Garbo," and made appearances on both British stage and television. Offscreen, McKinney led a turbulent, unhappy private life. She was married for a time to a jazz musician, Jimmy Monroe.

She attempted a Hollywood comeback in the late 1940s, appearing in Elia Kazan's *Pinky* (1949), but bit parts in other films, including non-speaking roles as servants, did nothing to revive her career. McKinney spent her last years in obscurity, watching as a handful of glamorous African-American actresses like Dorothy Dandridge and Lena Horne rose to prominence in Hollywood. She suffered a heart attack and died on May 3, 1967, five weeks before her 55th birthday. Her passing went unnoticed by the press. However, in recent years, McKinney's talents have found greater appreciation, and in 1978 she was inducted into the Black Filmmakers Hall of Fame.

ABOVE Nina Mae McKinney with a friend in 1933. The Hollywood system could not cope with a sexy African-American female star, so she never achieved the fame she deserved.

Star Shot

To celebrate Lancaster County's 200th birthday, a mural was commissioned featuring five famous Lancaster natives. Nina Mae McKinney is the only woman depicted on the Wall of Fame.

LEFT Nina Mae McKinney appeared as Chick in Hallelujah *(1929). McKinney is often credited as being the first African-American woman to appear on British television.*

Steve McQueen

Born March 24, 1930
Died November 7, 1980

Star Shot

McQueen was invited to dinner at the home of director Roman Polanski and actress Sharon Tate the night Tate was brutally murdered by the Charles Manson Family. Luckily he canceled the appointment.

Since Steve McQueen's death in 1980, he has slowly transcended mere superstar status and become one of a few genuine silver screen icons—alongside Monroe, Dean, and Wayne. He was born to play the rebellious anti-hero, and became a star doing so in motion pictures like *The Magnificent Seven* (1960), *The Great Escape* (1963), and *Bullitt* (1968). Above all, he was the paragon of cool; it was his style and attitude, more than his acting, that reverberated with the public. His clean-cut, American look has continued to inspire designers and marketers alike: in the 1990s the Gap based an ad campaign on his image; designer Jean-Charles de Castelbajac dedicated a show to him in 2001; Ford Motor Company modeled its 2001 Mustang on the car McQueen drove in *Bullitt*, and digitally superimposed McQueen into commercials for its Puma and Mustang models; Gotham Games even made it possible to be McQueen as he attempts to break out of the Stalag Luft III prison camp in their 2003 video game *The Great Escape*. Not bad for an actor whose last film was released a quarter century ago. Despite his enormous popularity, by nearly all accounts, McQueen was not a pleasant person—moody and withdrawn, quick to anger, difficult to work with, and notoriously tight-fisted with cash. His first wife, Neile Adams, recounted abusive behavior, chronic unfaithfulness, and prodigious drug use. Yet despite his imperfections, McQueen remains a screen idol, and is perhaps the perfect screen representation of the social rebelliousness of the 1960s, when he appeared in his greatest films.

ABOVE Steve McQueen with Ali MacGraw in 1974. Around this time, McQueen was earning about $1.5 million per film, plus a percentage of the earnings.

He was born in Indianapolis, Indiana, in 1930. His father abandoned the family six months later, and his mother, an alcoholic, eventually left McQueen in the care of relatives in Slater, Missouri, where by all accounts he found trouble early and often. "I didn't exactly grow up like in *Father Knows Best*," he once said of his childhood. He was later shipped off to a reform school in Chino, California, and then spent the late 1940s working odd jobs, including in the oil fields in Texas and as a lumberjack in Canada. He joined the Marines in 1947, but went A.W.O.L. for two weeks and was punished with more than a month in the brig. After his discharge, he made his way to Greenwich Village and again worked odd jobs, including as a bartender and television repairman. By 1952 he had turned his attention to acting, and was learning the craft at the Neighborhood Playhouse, studying under Uta Hagen

RIGHT Steve McQueen (center) with two of his co-stars from the war adventure film The Great Escape *(1963), James Garner (left) and James Coburn.*

and briefly at the Actors Studio. He made his stage debut in a walk-on role in a Second Avenue Yiddish theater, then made his Broadway debut replacing Ben Gazzara in *Hatful of Rain* in 1955. In 1956, he made his film debut with a bit part in *Somebody Up There Likes Me* (1956). He landed the lead in the low-budget sci-fi film, *The Blob* (1958); became well-known playing bounty hunter Josh Randall on television's *Wanted: Dead or Alive*; and appeared in John Sturges's *Never So Few* (1959).

LEFT The Cincinnati Kid, played by Steve McQueen, deals cards to Joan Blondell in the 1965 film. The movie also featured Edward G. Robinson.

He got his big break when Sturges cast him in the role of Yul Brynner's second-in-command in *The Magnificent Seven* (1960). The picture was a hit, and McQueen emerged a star. He was memorable as a disturbed soldier in *Hell Is For Heroes* (1962). He appeared again for Sturges, this time as Captain Virgil Hilts in *The Great Escape* (1963). McQueen was able to act out his love for motorcycles on screen, performing many motorcycle stunts himself, and the film made McQueen perhaps the most popular male star of the decade.

BELOW "In my own mind, I'm not sure that acting is something for a grown man to be doing." McQueen knew that his bankability was based on more than his acting skills.

He followed with several dramas and romances, including with Natalie Wood in *Love With The Proper Stranger* (1963), with Tuesday Weld in *Soldier in the Rain* (1963) and *The Cincinnati Kid* (1965), and with Lee Remick in *Baby the Rain Must Fall* (1965). He was nominated for an Academy Award® for his performance as a seaman in *The Sand Pebbles* (1966), losing to Paul Scofield for *A Man For All Seasons*. He appeared in two classics in 1968, *Bullitt* and *The Thomas Crown Affair*, cementing his superstar status. Sam Peckinpah directed him twice in 1972, in *Junior Bonner* and opposite Ali MacGraw in *The Getaway*. He and MacGraw married in 1973, divorcing five years later. His later films were somewhat uneven, including *Papillon* (1973), *The Towering Inferno* (1974), and *An Enemy of the People* (1978). By then he was suffering from depression, had gained weight, and grown a beard. In 1979, he was diagnosed with mesothelioma, a form of lung cancer. He married model Barbara Minty in January 1980, and made two more pictures, *Tom Horn* (1980) and *The Hunter* (1980). McQueen pursued unorthodox treatment for his cancer, but died of the disease at an unlicensed clinic in Mexico on November 7, 1980, at the age of 50. He was cremated, and his ashes were scattered over the Pacific Ocean.

ABOVE *Silvana Mangano appeared opposite some of the world's great leading men, including Kirk Douglas, Yves Montand, and Anthony Quinn.*

Silvana Mangano

Born April 21, 1930
Died December 16, 1989

Silvana Mangano was one of the great beauties of the cinema and an international star at 19. But she cared little for stardom, and by the time of her death in 1989, she had been overshadowed by fellow Italian sirens Sophia Loren and Gina Lollobrigida, and by her husband, producer Dino De Laurentiis.

She was born in Rome, Italy, in 1930 to a Spanish-Sicilian father and English mother. At 16, she took the top prize at the 1947 Miss Rome beauty contest, and went on to work as a model. Her first important movie role was in *This Wine of Love* (1946), but her big break came with Giuseppe de Santis's *Bitter Rice* (1949). The film was a leading example of the post-war Italian neo-realist movement, and Mangano's performance as a peasant girl offered a captivating combination of innocence and earthy sensuality that made her a worldwide sensation. She also caught the attention of the film's backer, Dino De Laurentiis, and they married within the year.

Mangano went on to work with some of the greatest directors in cinema: with Vittorio De Sica in *Gold of Naples* (1954); Luchino Visconti in *Death in Venice* (1971), *Ludwig* (1972), and *Conversation Piece* (1974); and Pier Paolo Pasolini in *Oedipus Rex* (1967), *Teorama* (1968), and *The Decameron* (1971). But from the start, she seemed bored by her film career. She once told an interviewer for the *Los Angeles Times* that she disliked being a film star. "What does she want to do instead?" the interviewer asked Mangano's interpreter. After a lengthy discussion, the interpreter replied, "She says, her youthful ambition was to be a ballet dancer. She never achieved it, so she will be forever unhappy." Silvana just nodded.

She had four children with De Laurentiis: three daughters, including producer Raffaella De Laurentiis, and a son, Federico, who was killed in a plane crash in Alaska in 1981. Mangano retreated from the public eye after her son's death, and she and De Laurentiis separated in 1983. She was coaxed out of retirement by her daughter, Raffaella, for David Lynch's sci-fi epic, *Dune* (1984). By the time she filed for divorce from De Laurentiis in 1988, she had known for some time that she suffered from lung cancer. In the fall of 1989, she underwent surgery to remove the tumor in her lungs, but suffered a heart attack during the procedure. She slipped into a coma and died several days later in her Madrid hospital at the age of 59.

Star Shot

Federico Fellini wanted to cast Silvana Mangano opposite Marcello Mastroianni in *La Dolce Vita* (1960), but Dino De Laurentiis blocked the move, reportedly jealous that Mangano and Fellini had been childhood sweethearts.

RIGHT *Dino De Laurentiis and Silvana Mangano with three of their four children. De Laurentiis controlled every aspect of Mangano's career.*

Marilyn Maxwell

Born August 3, 1921
Died March 20, 1972

Marilyn Maxwell's persona—that of the blonde bombshell with curves in all the right places—at times overshadowed the many wonderful performances she gave during her nearly 30-year career. She was assuredly a beauty, but she was also a multi-talented entertainer, and repeatedly held her own in scenes with some of the biggest names in Hollywood.

She was born Marvel Marilyn Maxwell in Clarinda, Iowa, and was a song-and-dance girl from the start: dancing with a child ballet group at the age of three, touring the Midwest with her piano-playing mother at the age of ten, and performing as a big-band singer with Amos Ostat's band at 16. She went on to vocalist gigs with both the Buddy Rogers and Ted Weems Orchestras before being discovered and brought to Hollywood by an MGM talent scout in 1942. After a six-month stint studying acting at the Pasadena Playhouse, Maxwell was ready for her film debut: the Robert Taylor vehicle *Stand By For Action* (1942). She followed that with seven films in 1943 alone, including *Salute to the Marines*, *Dr. Gillespie's Criminal Case*, and *Swing Fever*. She appeared with Van Johnson and Lionel Barrymore in several of the Dr. Gillespie pictures, including *Three Men in White* (1944); with Kirk Douglas in *Champion* (1949); with Clark Gable in *Key to the City* (1950); and with Bob Hope in *The Lemon Drop Kid* (1951).

ABOVE Marilyn Maxwell and Bob Hope talk to reporters in 1951. A popular personality, Maxwell appeared in an episode of I Love Lucy *in October 1970.*

Maxwell was alternately cast as a sultry "blonde menace" or as a good-natured comic siren. Throughout her career, she struggled, with mixed results, to establish herself as a legitimate songstress in musicals. She put her singing and dancing talents to good use during numerous USO tours with Bob Hope during World War II and the Korean War, and at one time had her own radio show on the Armed Forces Radio Service. She also made numerous television appearances in the 1950s and 1960s, including on *The Colgate Comedy Hour*, *Bus Stop*, and *The Bob Hope Show*. She was married three times, but all three marriages ended in divorce. On March 20, 1972, Maxwell was found dead in the bedroom of her Beverly Hills home by her 16-year-old son, Matthew Davis. She had been undergoing treatment for high blood pressure and pulmonary disease for some time, and had suffered a heart attack during the night.

Carmen Miranda

Born February 9, 1909
Died August 5, 1955

BELOW The earrings, bangles, beads, and, of course, the headdress: all unmistakable trademarks of the amazing Carmen Miranda.

She was "The Brazilian Bombshell," the lady in the tutti-frutti hat that captured the imagination of the world before her untimely death. Carmen Miranda became a legend in only a dozen Hollywood films. The image of her frantically dancing, her Baiana-style costume swirling, tropical fruit exploding from her impossibly high headgear, has become classic. She became one of the highest paid women entertainers in Hollywood in the 1940s, and has been impersonated by Bob Hope, Milton Berle, Jerry Lewis, Mickey Rooney, Bette Midler, Bugs Bunny, and countless unknown drag queens worldwide. Yet she is more than just a camp icon—she is a legendary figure of twentieth-century entertainment.

She was born Maria do Carmo Miranda da Cunha, not in Brazil, but in Marco de Canavezes, Portugal. Her family moved to Rio de Janeiro in 1910, where her father worked as a fruit wholesaler. She had several hit records in Brazil, and appeared in films there, including *Banana da Terra* (1939), which introduced the Afro-Brazilian Baiana-style costume she used throughout the rest of her career. She had become Brazil's biggest pop star when Broadway producer Lee Schubert brought her to New York in May 1939 to appear on Broadway with Abbott and Costello in *The Streets of Paris*. Upon her arrival in New York, waiting journalists asked her if she knew English. Reportedly, she replied, "I know twenty words in English. I say money, money, money, and I say hot dog! I say yes, no and I say money, money, money and I say turkey sandwich and I say grape juice." During her performance, she wore six-inch heels and a crown of fruit, and her frenetic dancing and undeniable stage presence made her an star. She followed with a now legendary engagement at the Waldorf-Astoria, then was quickly signed by Fox, and put to work in a string of "banana republic" musicals, beginning with *Down Argentine Way* (1940). It was a hit in America, but many in Brazil hated it, and Argentina briefly

banned the film until certain edits were completed. She returned to Brazil for a triumphant homecoming and musical extravaganza, but was met with rejection by many Brazilians because of her alleged Americanization. Miranda left Brazil in October 1940 and never returned to perform there. Back in Hollywood, she appeared in *That Night in Rio* (1941), *Week-End in Havana* (1941), and *Springtime in the Rockies* (1942). She then was cast in the Busby Berkeley-directed camp classic, *The Gang's All Here* (1943), in which she sings "The Lady with the Tutti-Frutti Hat."

Miranda was reportedly the ninth-highest paid woman in the United States in 1945, earning over $200,000. For a brief spell, Miranda became the personification of Brazilian culture to the entire world, even as some in her adopted homeland continued to criticize her for playing what they complained was a stereotype, an idea of what Americans thought Brazilians were like. Still, she loved the connection with Brazil, and once replied, "Look at me and tell me if I don't have Brazil in every curve of my body."

However, all was not well with Miranda. She reportedly suffered from depression in the 1940s, and rumors of drug use became more frequent, including one story that she kept a stash

of cocaine hidden in a secret compartment in one of her platform shoes. She began to rely on pharmaceutical drugs as well. She also underwent two cosmetic surgery operations on her nose in the 1940s, one of which reportedly detrimentally affected her health for the rest of her life. In 1947, she married American producer David Sebastian, and the marriage would last until her death, although there were reports that it was not a happy union. The year before, she had left Fox, but her later freelancing films were not as well received as her earlier ones, including *Copacabana* (1947); *A Date With Judy* (1948), with Elizabeth Taylor and Wallace Beery; and what would become her final film, the Martin and Lewis vehicle *Scared Stiff* (1953). This led to a complete nervous breakdown in 1953. She returned to Brazil to recuperate for 14 months. In April 1955, ready to resume her career, she returned to the United States for a four-week engagement in Las Vegas, then in July, a two-week engagement at Havana's Tropicana Club. On August 4, she taped a performance for *The Jimmy Durante Show*, then went back to her Beverly Hills home to celebrate with family. She went to bed, but some time after midnight she suffered a heart attack and died. Upon word of her death, Brazil declared a day of national mourning, and in 1978, the country memorialized her by dedicating a museum to her legacy, the Carmen Miranda Museum in Rio de Janeiro.

Maria Montez

Born June 6, 1912
Died September 7, 1951

Maria Montez was "The Queen of Technicolor," a Dominican beauty who appeared in numerous B-grade pictures in the 1940s featuring action-packed adventure and exotic locales. She was born Maria Africa Antonia Gracia Vidal de Santo Silas in Barahona in the Dominican Republic, in 1912 (some sources say 1917 or 1918). Her father, Ysidoro Gracia, was a diplomat, and her mother, Teresa Vidal de Santo Silas, was the daughter of a Spanish noblewoman and a Dutch political refugee. One of ten children, Montez was educated in Spain.

Star Shot

Five years after Montez's death, Jean-Pierre Aumont married actress Marisa Pavan, the twin sister of actress Pier Angeli, who died of a barbiturate overdose at the age of 39.

By all accounts, auburn-haired Montez was ambitious, beautiful, and had a sense of destiny from the start. A brief marriage at the age of 20 to Irish banker William McFeeters ended in divorce. When her father died, Montez made her way to New York for what turned out to be a brief stop on the road to Hollywood stardom. After a brief modeling career, she began appearing on the New York stage. Universal Pictures signed her. Reportedly, the name "Montez" was a tribute to famous Spanish dancer Lola Montez.

She made her screen debut in *Boss of Bullion City* (1940), and followed with parts in *The Invisible Woman* (1940), *That Night in Rio* (1941), *South of Tahiti* (1941), and *Moonlight in Hawaii* (1941). Campy by today's standards, many of her films featured fantastic costumes, musical extravaganzas, and brilliant Technicolor. Other pictures include *Bombay Clipper* (1942), *Mystery of Marie Roget* (1942), *Arabian Nights* (1942), *White Savage* (1943), *Ali Baba and the Forty Thieves* (1944), *Gypsy Wildcat* (1944), *Cobra Woman* (1944), *Tangier* (1946), and *Pirates of Monterey* (1947).

BELOW Maria Montez is quoted as having said, "When I see myself on the screen, I am so beautiful, I jump for joy."

Montez met actor Jean-Pierre Aumont in October 1942, and they married the following July. Their only child, daughter Tina Marquand (born Maria Christina Aumont), was born on February 14, 1946. After *Pirates of Monterey*, Montez's contract with Universal was not renewed. Montez and Aumont then co-starred in the ill-fated production *Siren Of Atlantis* (1949). After moving to France, Aumont's brother, Francois Villiers, directed the pair in *Hans le marin* (1948). Next came several motion pictures in Italy. In the summer of 1951, Montez's agent, Louis Schurr, proposed that Montez return to Hollywood to revive her career. Montez accepted, but it was not to be. On September 7, 1951, Montez's body was discovered in the bathtub of her Paris home. She had either suffered a heart attack while taking a bath, or lost consciousness and drowned. She was buried in the Cimetiére du Montparnasse in Paris, France.

Cleo Moore

Born October 31, 1928
Died October 25, 1973

Cleo Moore was a curvaceous canary blonde who specialized in "bad girl" roles in B-pictures. She had, according to nearly every article printed about her, an absolutely stunning 37-22-36 hourglass figure, and at her peak in the 1950s was a rival of Monroe and Mansfield. Despite her on-screen charm, she never rose above B-picture status, and by the age of 30 had retired from films.

Cleo Moore was born on Halloween in Baton Rouge, Louisiana. Most sources list her birth year as 1928, but a few list it as early as 1923. In 1944, she married Palmer Long, the son of Huey P. Long, who had served as the Governor of Louisiana and as a U.S. Senator before being assassinated in the Louisiana Capital House in 1935. The marriage lasted only six weeks.

The young actress moved to California in 1946 and worked as a model before making her motion picture debut in Columbia Pictures' *Congo Bill* (1948). She followed with *This Side of the Law* (1950) at Warner Bros. RKO signed her and she made six movies for them between 1950 and 1952, often appearing in "shady lady" roles, including *Dynamite Pass* (1950), *Rio Grande Patrol* (1950), *Hunt the Man Down* (1950), *Gambling House* (1951), *On Dangerous Ground* (1952), and *The Pace That Thrills* (1952). She had more prominent *femme fatale* roles in actor-director Hugo Haas's productions, including *Strange Fascination* (1952), *One Girl's Confession* (1953), *Bait* (1954), *The Other Woman* (1954), and *Hold Back Tomorrow* (1955).

Moore was a natural at publicity. In 1954 she made national headlines when she kissed Chicago television personality Jack Eigen for more than five minutes on air, purportedly to combat censorship of kissing on television. Eigen was fired by his network, but told the press that it had been worth it. In 1955, Moore announced that she was running for Governor of Louisiana. Several months went by before anyone realized that at age 26, Moore was four years too young to meet the State's age requirement for governors, which was then 30. She dropped out of the race, stating that she'd run after she turned 30, but she never did. In 1957, Moore, unhappy with her collaboration with Haas, retired from pictures for good. In 1961, she married builder Herbert Heftler, and went on to find some success in the real estate industry. On October 25, 1973, Moore suffered a coronary arrest and died, six days shy of her 45th birthday.

ABOVE Cleo Moore (left) with fellow blonde bombshell Jayne Mansfield. Mansfield would also die an early death, in a 1967 car accident at the age of just 34.

Frank Morgan

Born June 1, 1890
Died September 18, 1949

"I am Oz, the Great and Powerful." These are the words for which Frank Morgan is best remembered. The actor who brought to life L. Frank Baum's Wizard in *The Wizard of Oz* (1939) was born Francis Philip Wuppermann on June 1, 1890, the 11th child of a well-to-do immigrant family. He did not turn immediately to acting, but after a stint at a university and several odd jobs, eventually followed his older brother, Ralph, onto the stage in 1913.

His stage career culminated a decade later with his role as the Duke in *The Firebrand*. In 1913, he met Alma Muller, the socialite, and they wed secretly the following year. They stayed together until Morgan's death. He began his film career in silent pictures, including *The Suspect* (1916) and *The Girl Philippa* (1916). However, it was in the sound era that he began to make his mark. In 1934, he revisited his stage role of the Duke in the film *The Affairs of Cellini*, based loosely on *The Firebrand*. The role garnered Morgan his first Academy Award® nomination, for Best Actor, which went instead to Clark Gable for *It Happened One Night* (1934). He signed with MGM in 1933, and eventually became one of a handful of actors reportedly given a "lifetime contract" with the studio. He also helped reorganize the Screen Actors Guild after the studios' 1933 attempt to cap actors' salaries.

His success playing comic roles led him to land the title role in *The Wizard of Oz*. Initially a box-office disappointment, the film would become the beloved classic it is today only after its 1949 re-release and subsequent annual television airings. Morgan was nominated for his second Academy Award®, for Best Actor in a Supporting Role, for his performance in *Tortilla Flat* (1942), but again lost out, this time to Van Heflin for *Johnny Eager* (1942).

Despite struggling with an alcohol problem his entire adult life, Frank Morgan was remarkably prolific, appearing in 64 credited roles between 1933 and 1949 in films such as *The Great Ziegfeld* (1936), Frank Borzage's *The Mortal Storm* (1940), and Ernst Lubitsch's *The Shop Around the Corner* (1940). Morgan died in his sleep of natural causes in his home in Beverly Hills on September 18, 1949. He was 59.

Star Shot

Frank Morgan was not the first choice to play the Wizard in *The Wizard of Oz* (1939); MGM originally wanted W. C. Fields or Ed Wynn.

LEFT Frank Morgan (at right)
appeared with Steffi Duna and
Charles Collins in the charming
musical Dancing Pirate *(1936).*

Janet Munro

Born September 28, 1934
Died December 6, 1972

ABOVE In 1963, Janet Munro married British actor Ian Hendry. They had two children, Sally and Corrie, and were divorced a year before her death.

Sprightly, freckle-faced Janet Munro arrived in America already on top. Discovered by Walt Disney himself while casting in Munro's native England, Munro became, at age 23, the first actress ever signed to a long-term contract with the studio. The Hollywood establishment quickly crowned her Disney's brightest young star, and the public adored her vibrant portrayals of plucky, winsome ingénues.

Munro was born in the seaside resort town of Blackpool, England. Her Scottish father, Alex Munro, had run away from home at the age of nine to join a circus, and eventually became a top variety comedian in Britain. Her English mother also performed in variety, and Janet had her first walk-on role at the age of two. Munro's mother died five years later, and soon thereafter World War II broke out. Her father was named head of British Royal Air Force entertainment, and Munro grew up enduring arduous entertainment tours of troop camps. Dressed in kilts, she belted out Scottish songs, danced, and acted as her father's straight-man in his act. By her early twenties, Janet Munro had appeared in several films and television programs, and in 1958, she was named "Miss Television" in England. She followed that with her successful audition for Disney.

Disney capitalized on Munro's youthful appearance by repeatedly casting her younger than her age. She appeared as a young Irish lass opposite Sean Connery in *Darby O'Gill and the Little People* (1959), as a young Swiss miss in *Third Man on the Mountain* (1959), and as the teenaged Bertie in *Swiss Family Robinson* (1960). Her last notable film role followed a year later with the sci-fi thriller *The Day the Earth Caught Fire* (1961). Like many other young stars, Munro found it difficult to make the transition to adult roles, and although she appeared in over a dozen film and television movies before her death, never regained the celebrity of her early career.

With her career in decline during her early thirties, Munro slid into alcoholism. Three months after her 38th birthday, Munro collapsed at her London home, and died en route to the hospital. Some reports stated that she had choked to death while drinking tea. The official cause of death was listed as acute myocarditis, and chronic ischemic heart disease.

Jules Munshin

Born February 22, 1915
Died February 19, 1970

Zany song-and-dance man Jules Munshin is best remembered as a World War II sailor making the most of a 24-hour pass in New York City with buddies Frank Sinatra and Gene Kelly in 1949's *On the Town*. But Munshin's career spanned vaudeville, Broadway, film, and television, and despite a short filmography, he worked with a remarkable list of film legends, including Audrey Hepburn, Judy Garland, Fred Astaire, Maurice Chevalier, Ann Miller, Cyd Charisse, Esther Williams, and Dean Martin, not to mention Sinatra and Kelly.

ABOVE Broadway's Call Me Mister (1946) shot Jules Munshin (seated) to stardom, putting him firmly on the road to Hollywood.

He had a face for comedy, with expressive, hang-dog eyes, and got his start telling jokes, singing, and dancing in the Catskill Resorts in upstate New York. He moved on to vaudeville, and also sang, at one time performing as the vocalist for the George Olson band. He made his stage debut in 1942 in *The Army Play by Play*, and followed by touring in a production of *About Face*, and roles in *Make Mine Manhattan* and *Pack Up Your Troubles*. Munshin became a star in 1946 and won the Donaldson Award for his performance in *Call Me Mister*, about soldiers returning to civilian life.

Hollywood beckoned, and Munshin made his film debut in *Easter Parade* (1948). Munshin had a small role in the Judy Garland musical, as the head waiter in a scene with Fred Astaire, but he made the most of it. He pitched an idea for a gag to the producers: he would make a salad in front of Astaire, but entirely in pantomime—no salad, no bowl, no utensils. After three months of rehearsing, Munshin was hilarious in the three-minute scene. He was then cast in the Busby Berkeley-directed *Take Me Out to the Ballgame* (1949) with Sinatra, Kelly, and Esther Williams. With Sinatra and Kelly's film *On the Town* (1949), Munshin reached a new level of stardom.

Star Shot

The opening number in Jules Munshin's musical film *On the Town* (1949), "New York, New York," was actually filmed on location in that city.

After the success of *On the Town*, he returned to the stage and was quite choosy about film roles. He appeared with Audrey Hepburn in *Monte Carlo Baby* (1951), with Fred Astaire and Cyd Charisse in *Silk Stockings* (1957), and with Maurice Chevalier in *Monkeys, Go Home* (1967). His Broadway roles included *The Gay Life*, *Barefoot in the Park*, and *The Front Page*. His last picture was *Mastermind* (released in 1976). He was rehearsing for an American Palace Theater production of *Duet For Solo Voice* in New York when he had a heart attack and died three days before his 55th birthday.

RIGHT The Manhattan skyline behind them, Frank Sinatra (left), Jules Munshin (center), and Gene Kelly take in the sights in On the Town (1949).

Barbara Nichols

Born December 30, 1929
Died October 5, 1976

Barbara Nichols was a plain-talking, curvaceous comedienne with a distinctive scratchy voice and a knack for playing dumb blondes and sexy floozies. Often compared to blonde bombshell extraordinaire Marilyn Monroe, Nichols saw herself more as a personality than as an actress. "I've never even looked upon myself as an actress," she once told an interviewer. "Monroe's a natural comedienne, but she can't act. I don't care if I never play *The Brothers Karamazov*."

She was born Barbara Marie Nickerauer in Queens, New York, on December 30, 1929. She won several beauty contests in her early twenties, being crowned Miss Long Island Duckling, Miss Loew's Paradise, and Miss Loew's Valencia. She worked as a model and a chorus girl at the Latin Quarter before making her Broadway debut playing Valeria, a baby-voiced chorus girl in a production of *Pal Joey* in 1954. That performance brought television offers, including a stint on *Sid Caesar Presents*. In 1956, she received her first major film role, appearing as the innocent stripper in *Miracle in the Rain* (1956).

The following year was very good for Nichols. She appeared as Rita, a nightclub girl, in *Sweet Smell of Success* (1957) with Burt Lancaster and Tony Curtis. The role offered only nine minutes of screen time, but Nichols made the most of them, and received critical and audience acclaim for her performance.

She was upgraded to a major role in the movie version of *Pal Joey* (1957), with Frank Sinatra and Rita Hayworth. She also appeared in *The Pajama Game* (1957), with Doris Day. Other films include Raoul Walsh's *The King and Four Queens* (1956), with Clark Gable; Walsh's World War II picture, *The Naked and the Dead* (1958); *Who Was That Lady?* (1960), with Tony Curtis, Dean Martin, and Janet Leigh; and *The Disorderly Orderly* (1964), with Jerry Lewis. Her final film was *Won Ton Ton, the Dog Who Saved Hollywood* (1976), with Milton Berle, Bruce Dern, and Madeline Kahn. In the late 1950s, she had turned to television, and made numerous guest appearances on hit shows like *The Jack Benny Program, Dragnet, The Beverly Hillbillies, Batman, Adam-12, Green Acres*, and *The Twilight Zone*.

Nichols suffered from liver disease in her late forties, and in the summer of 1976 she fell into a coma. She recovered consciousness for several days in September, but suffered a relapse and eventually succumbed on October 5, 1976, at the age of 46.

ABOVE Barbara Nichols was never given a leading role, but her wisecracking style meant that she stole many of the scenes she was in.

Mabel Normand

Born November 16, 1892
Died February 22, 1930

Mabel Normand was the "Queen of Comedy," the first—and perhaps the best—comedienne of silent film. She was in over 200 films, ran her own production company, and was the only woman ever to direct Charlie Chaplin. But scandal, drug addiction, and disease eventually destroyed her career.

She was most likely born in 1892, as stated by her family, or 1893, as listed in the 1900 U.S. Census. She was petite, barely 5 feet (1.5 m) tall, and radiantly beautiful, with large brown eyes perfect for the screen. In 1910, she made her film debut in bit parts for D. W. Griffith's Biograph films, then switched to Vitagraph, before returning to Biograph at the urging of comic actor Mack Sennett, with whom she had a long romance. When Sennett established his new studio, Keystone, in Hollywood in 1912, Normand went with him.

Charlie Chaplin arrived at Keystone in 1913, and Normand and Chaplin began appearing in a series of one- and two-reelers together. They also starred, with Marie Dressler, in *Tillie's Punctured Romance* (1914), the first feature-length comedy. Mabel Normand later appeared with Roscoe "Fatty" Arbuckle in a series of "Fatty and Mabel" comedies. In 1916, she created the Mabel Normand Feature Film Company, and produced several comedies, including her greatest success, *Mickey* (1918). She appeared in *Molly O'* (1921), the same year that Fatty Arbuckle was accused of the rape and murder of model Virginia Rappe. Although he was later acquitted of all charges, the scandal destroyed his career and devastated Normand.

Then on February 7, 1922, Mabel was the last known person to see the director William Desmond Taylor before he was murdered. Although she was exonerated by the facts and never charged, the scandal took a toll on her both personally and professionally. Normand appeared in *Suzanna* (1923) and *The Extra Girl* (1923), before scandal struck once again. Her chauffeur shot and injured oil millionaire Courtland Dines with a gun registered to Normand. Although, again, she was not implicated, this second shooting scandal proved too much. She appeared in a few Hal Roach shorts in 1926, but her career was over.

That year, she married actor Lew Cody, possibly as a party gag. In 1928, she was diagnosed with tuberculosis. Years of drinking and drug use had taken their toll, and she was admitted to Pottenger Sanitarium in Monrovia, California, on September 11, 1929, where she died five months later.

ABOVE Mabel Normand (left), Roscoe "Fatty" Arbuckle, and Araminta "Minty" Durfee in an early Mack Sennett comedy. Normand was one of the major reasons for the success of Sennett's studio, Keystone.

Last Words

"I wonder who killed poor Bill Taylor? … I sigh and surrender."

LEFT In The Extra Girl (1923), Mabel Normand plays a girl who dreams of Hollywood stardom, but fails to achieve it. Normand herself achieved stardom, but couldn't hold on to it.

Cathy O'Donnell

Born July 6, 1925
Died April 11, 1970

Star Shot

In *Ben-Hur* (1959),
Cathy O'Donnell played
her final role, that
of Charlton Heston's
sister, Tirzah.

Cathy O'Donnell began and ended her brief career in two of the greatest movies ever made, but mostly languished in low-budget B-grade pictures in the years between. A delicate, brown-haired beauty, O'Donnell was born Ann Steely on July 6, 1925 (some sources say 1923) in Siluria, Alabama. Her father operated the town's sole movie theater, and young O'Donnell spent most Friday nights of her childhood watching pictures there. After high school, she enrolled in Oklahoma City University's drama department, but after only a year left school and headed for the bright lights of Hollywood.

Just days after her arrival, she was spotted at the counter of Schwab's Drug Store by agent Ben Medford. He took her to meet Sam Goldwyn, who liked her so much that he offered her a contract without seeing her screen test. She adopted the name "Peters" and was sent off to study drama at New York's American Academy of Dramatic Arts. After several months touring with a road company in *Life With Father* (1945), O'Donnell was spotted by director William Wyler, who cast her in *The Best Years of Our Lives* (1946). She received critical acclaim for her role as the girlfriend of Harold Russell, a genuine veteran who had lost both hands in combat, and the film was a sensation, winning seven Academy Awards®, including Best Picture.

O'Donnell's next few pictures were unspectacular, although *They Live By Night* (1949) and *Side Street* (1950) both featured the pairing of O'Donnell with Farley Granger. Off-screen, O'Donnell found romance with William Wyler's older brother, Robert, and on April 11, 1948, they eloped to Las Vegas and quietly married. Sam Goldwyn, who had been nurturing a "Hollywood romance" between O'Donnell and Granger in the press, was so incensed that he ripped up O'Donnell's contract.

Cathy O'Donnell appeared in mostly low-budget clinkers in the latter part of her career, although a few notable films stand out, including William Wyler's *Detective Story* (1951), and *The Man from Laramie* (1955), co-starring James Stewart. Her last motion picture role would be in Wyler's *Ben-Hur* (1959), which won the Academy Award® for Best Picture that year. After retiring from film, O'Donnell appeared on several television programs in the late 1950s. In the mid-1960s, she was diagnosed with cancer, and she died of a cerebral hemorrhage caused by the cancer on April 11, 1970, in Los Angeles. Robert Wyler, 19 years her senior, died only nine months later after suffering a heart attack.

ABOVE Cathy O'Donnell starred with Farley Granger in They Live By Night *(1949). Never much of a glamor girl, O'Donnell was the personification of the girl next door.*

Heather O'Rourke

Born December 27, 1975
Died February 1, 1988

Heather O'Rourke became famous for a single line in her first feature film: "They're heeere!" Her childish, simple delivery in the Steven Spielberg-penned *Poltergeist* (1982) creeped out millions and helped spawn two sequels. Tragically, the three films would be the only features of O'Rourke's career. She died at the age of 12 due to cardiopulmonary arrest caused by a severe bowel obstruction, the result of a congenital birth defect.

She was born in San Diego, California, on December 27, 1975. At the age of only three, she won a local "Little Miss" contest, and showed natural ability as a singer and dancer. The following year, she became an advertising model for Mattel Toys, then appeared in commercials for McDonalds and the Long John Silvers restaurant. At the age of five, O'Rourke and her mother were having lunch at the MGM commissary; her older sister, Tammy, was a child dancer in the MGM musical, *Pennies From Heaven* (1981). Steven Spielberg happened to walk by and invited Heather to an interview. She responded that she was not allowed to talk to strangers. Charmed, Spielberg set up the meeting. At the interview, it was O'Rourke's thin, but chilling scream that won her the role of Carol Anne Freeling in *Poltergeist*.

Following her breakout success, O'Rourke became a regular on *Happy Days* during the 1982 season. She also appeared in several other television series, including *Fantasy Island*, *Webster*, and *Still the Beaver*. Two television movies followed: the spy adventure film, *Massarati and the Brain* (1982), and with 1980s teen idols River Phoenix and Molly Ringwald in *Surviving* (1985). Next came the *Poltergeist* sequel, *Poltergeist II: The Other Side* (1986), in which O'Rourke's familiar tagline mutated into "They're baaack!" *Poltergeist III* (1988) followed two years later.

Heather O'Rourke began to show signs of the congenital birth defect that would take her life during the production of *Poltergeist III*. On January 31, 1988, she was suffering from flu-like symptoms. The following morning, O'Rourke collapsed in her home. She was airlifted to the Children's Hospital and Health Center in San Diego and resuscitated. It was determined that she was suffering from an acute intestinal stenosis, or bowel obstruction, that had later burst, causing an infection that spread throughout her body. Although she underwent surgery, she suffered from septic shock, which triggered a cardiopulmonary arrest. She died at 2:43 P.M. on February 1, 1988. A body double was subsequently used in a few scenes of *Poltergeist III*, and the ending was reshot to exclude O'Rourke's character.

ABOVE Craig T. Nelson holds Heather O'Rourke in Poltergeist *(1982). O'Rourke once said, "I never watch horror movies as a rule."*

Helen Parrish

Born March 12, 1924
Died February 22, 1959

Helen Parrish was a wistful, charming child star who successfully bridged the gap to adult roles and enjoyed a 30-year career that spanned silent films, talkies, radio, and television. There is some conflicting information regarding her birth, but nearly all sources note her birth year as between 1922 and 1924. Helen Parrish was born in Columbus, Georgia, and taken to Hollywood at the age of three by her parents. She happened to accompany her mother and older sister to the Central Casting office one day to register the sister. No registrations were being taken that day, but the younger Parrish was such a hit with the casting office that three weeks later she was making her film debut beside slugger Babe Ruth in *Babe Comes Home* (1927). A new star had accidentally been born.

She followed with a continuing role in the *"Our Gang"* comedies, and also appeared in the *Smithy* serials. Fox signed the young actress to a contract, and she appeared with William "Hopalong Cassidy" Boyd in *His First Command* (1929), one of the early talking pictures. She then appeared in bit roles in several important films, including *The Big Trail* (1930), with John Wayne; *Cimarron* (1931), with Irene Dunne; and *The Public Enemy* (1931), with James Cagney and Jean Harlow. She took a few years off during the notorious "awkward age" for teens, and returned in the Deanna Durbin vehicle, *Mad About Music* (1938). Universal Studios signed her, and she completed the successful transition to adult roles with appearances in lightweight fare and westerns such as *Three Smart Girls Grow Up* (1939) and *First Love* (1939), both with Durbin; *I'm Nobody's Sweetheart Now* (1940); *Too Many Blondes* (1941); *They All Kissed the Bride* (1942), with Joan Crawford; *X Marks the Spot* (1942); and *The Wolf Hunters* (1949).

She moved to television in the late 1940s, and starred in her own variety show, *The Hour Glass*, and the program *Panorama Pacific*. Her career was briefly overshadowed in the mid-1950s by an ugly divorce proceeding against her husband, screenwriter Charles Lang, Jr. The scandalous nature of the charges made headlines and included testimony about Parrish's alleged adulterous affair with band leader Muzzy Marcellino, and allegations of abuse by Lang. Parrish was granted a divorce, but lost custody of her two children. In 1956, she married producer John Guedel. In 1958, Parrish discovered that she had cancer. She fought the illness for several months, but succumbed to the disease on February 22, 1959, at the Hollywood Presbyterian Hospital. She is buried at the Hollywood Forever Cemetery.

ABOVE Like all child actors, Helen Parrish (bottom left) attended school at the studio. She was working on Seed *(1931) at the time this photograph was taken.*

☆ Star Shot

The year 1959 was a bad one for graduates of the "Our Gang" comedies. In addition to Helen Parrish's death, Carl "Alfalfa" Switzer was shot to death on January 21, and Don "Fats" Law died on February 5.

RIGHT Helen Parrish with Robert Stack in First Love *(1939). Parrish is possibly best remembered as the thorn in Deanna Durbin's side.*

Luana Patten

Born July 6, 1938
Died May 1, 1996

L uana Patten was a sensation at the age of eight, retired by 14, a star again at 18, and retired for good at 30. Her film career began when Walt Disney spotted the six-year-old model on the cover of *Women's Home Companion* and signed her for his first motion picture with live actors, *Song of the South* (1946). The Long Beach native played "Ginny" opposite the young Bobby Driscoll. They were the first actors given a long-term contract with Disney. Patten was again paired with Driscoll in the Disney films *Melody Time* (1948) and the technicolor *So Dear to My Heart* (1949). She was also featured in *Fun and Fancy Free* (1947), and was "loaned" to MGM for *Little Mister Jim* (1946). The child actor was talkative during interviews, telling one reporter, "I brush what teeth I have often." She worked with Disney for five years before she was released. At 14, she left the business, in part because of a dearth of roles for children in the so-called awkward phase, and enrolled in Woodrow Wilson High School in Long Beach.

Wasting no time after her 1956 graduation, Luana Patten returned to the silver screen, appearing in Universal's *Rock, Pretty Baby* (1956). Not long afterward, Patten was tapped for Disney's *Johnny Tremain*

ABOVE Luana Patten and George Peppard in Home From The Hill *(1960). Patten also appeared on the television shows* Dragnet 1967 *and* Adam-12.

(1957). The contemporary accounts of Patten's teenaged "comeback" describe her tiny waist and long, blonde ponytail, and compare her with a young Kathryn Grayson or Wanda Hendrix. Patten's contract with Universal-International also yielded starring roles in *Joe Dakota* (1957) and *The Restless Years* (1958). By December 1959, Patten had a four-year, two-picture-a-year contract with MGM; she featured in the MGM films *Home From The Hill* (1960), directed by Vincente Minnelli, and in *Go Naked in the World* (1961).

In 1960, she married John Smith, who acted in the television western *Laramie*. The two actors met in May 1959 when they were tied back-to-back for a scene in television's *Cimarron City*. They vowed never to be apart for more than two weeks, but the marriage lasted only two-and-a-half years. Patten then traveled in Europe and appeared in Disney's 1966 technicolor production, *Follow Me, Boys!*. She later appeared in pioneer-theme television shows such as *Rawhide*, *Wagon Train*, and *Bonanza*. She retired in the early 1970s to the San Fernando Valley, and died on May 1, 1996, at the age of 57, from respiratory failure after a long bout with cancer.

Alice Pearce

Born October 16, 1917
Died March 3, 1966

"Being beautiful has never been one of my problems," Alice Pearce once told an interviewer. She was a diminutive woman, with wide eyes, a toothy grin, and a hideaway chin. But Pearce capitalized on her unusual appearance, becoming an accomplished comedienne and one of the finest character actors of her time. Two years before her death, she found fame as nosy neighbor Gladys Kravitz on television's *Bewitched*.

Although Pearce typically played ill-mannered and unattractive characters, she was in fact brought up the child of privilege. Her father, a banker, was sent to manage his bank's affairs in Europe when Pearce was a year and a half old. She was raised in Antwerp, Rome, Paris, and Brussels, before returning to her native New York for boarding school at 15. By then, she was fluent in French, Italian, and German, as well as English. She majored in drama at Sarah Lawrence College, and after graduation decided on a career in theater, much to the dismay of her parents. She made her stage debut in Broadway's *New Faces of 1943* (1943), and followed that with *On the Town* (1944). When Gene Kelly brought the musical to the screen in 1949's *On the Town*, Pearce reprised her role. She then made a foray into television, hosting her own 15 minute variety show on ABC called *The Alice Pearce Show*. Other movie appearances include *How to be Very, Very Popular* (1955), *My Six Loves* (1963), Billy Wilder's *Kiss Me, Stupid* (1964), *Dear Heart* (1964), *The Disorderly Orderly* (1964), *Dear Brigitte* (with James Stewart, 1965), and *The Glass Bottom Boat* (with Doris Day, 1966), her last film. She continued working on stage as well, appearing in numerous productions, including *Look, Ma, I'm Dancing*; *Gentlemen Prefer Blondes*; *Fallen Angels*; and *Bells Are Ringing*. She was awarded the Outer Circle Critics Award for best supporting actress in *Angels*.

In the fall of 1964, while working on *Bewitched*, Pearce discovered that she had incurable ovarian cancer. Soon after, she met and fell in love with the director Paul Davis, and they married within the year (Pearce's first husband, songwriter John Rox, had died in 1957). She continued with her role on *Bewitched* for nearly two years, but finally died at her home in Hollywood on March 3, 1966 at the age of 48. Alice Pearce was awarded an Emmy® posthumously for *Bewitched* a few months after her death.

ABOVE In Bewitched, *Gladys Kravitz (Alice Pearce) often saw witchcraft being performed, but her husband, Abner (George Tobias), thought she was just "crazy."*

LEFT Alice Pearce was the only member of the original stage production of On the Town *to also appear in the 1949 motion picture.*

Anthony Perkins

Born April 4, 1932
Died September 12, 1992

Star Shot

Perkins's widow, Berry Berenson, was killed when her plane was deliberately crashed into the north tower of New York's World Trade Center by hijackers on September 11, 2001.

When one thinks of Anthony Perkins, one invariably also thinks of Norman Bates, the mother-obsessed, homicidal innkeeper in Alfred Hitchcock's *Psycho* (1960). Rarely in the history of film has an actor become so closely associated with a role in the minds of the public, and rarely has one role been such a mixed blessing for an actor. Although the Bates role ensured that Perkins continued working throughout his life, he was forever typecast as a neurotic, time and again playing lost souls, psychotics, and deranged killers.

He was born in New York City, the son of stage and occasional film actor James Ripley Osgood Perkins and Jane Esselstyn Rane. His father was frequently away on tour with stage productions or in Hollywood, and then died of a heart attack when Perkins was only five. Perkins thus grew very close to his mother, who by his own account was extremely controlling of her son. He later said his suffocating relationship with his mother helped him to understand the psyche of Norman Bates. By his teens, Perkins and his mother had left Manhattan for Brookline, Massachusetts, and he began his acting career at the age of 14 working in summer stock. Perkins attended the prestigious private school, Buckingham, Browne & Nichols, in Cambridge, Massachusetts, and matriculated to Rollins College in Florida. He made his film debut as the awkward boyfriend of Jean Simmons in George Cukor's *The Actress* (1953). After that, Perkins transferred to Columbia University to continue his studies, but was quickly signed by Elia Kazan to

ABOVE Joan Fontaine and Anthony Perkins in the 1954 production of Tea and Sympathy. *Critic Brooks Atkinson said that Perkins gave a "mature performance."*

RIGHT Before his marriage, Anthony Perkins was rumored to have had affairs with actor Alan Helms and dancer Rudolf Nureyev.

make his Broadway debut in *Tea and Sympathy*. Perkins played a "mother's boy" struggling to come to terms with his homosexuality, a role that struck close to home, as Perkins was himself coming to grips with his own homosexuality. He caught the eye of William Wyler, who cast him as Gary Cooper's son in *Friendly Persuasion* (1956). The performance garnered Perkins his first and only Oscar® nomination, for Best Actor in a Supporting Role. A rumored romance with actor Tab Hunter during this period was kept well under wraps. He began working regularly, including as Jack Palance's son in the western *The Lonely Man* (1957), as a baseball player suffering a nervous breakdown in *Fear Strikes Out* (1957), with Sophia Loren in *Desire Under the Elms* (1958), and with Gregory Peck, Ava Gardner, and Fred Astaire in *On the Beach* (1959). The studios weren't sure what to make of Perkins in these early years, touting him as "a young Jimmy Dean," but casting him in roles that accentuated his adolescent shyness, and at times his sexual ambiguity, which undercut his leading man prospects and hinted at the character roles he would become famous playing.

Perkins's memorable performance in *Psycho* helped make the film one of the most successful horror films of all time, and made Norman Bates an iconic screen villain. He left Hollywood for Europe in 1960. Perkins appeared opposite Ingrid Bergman in *Goodbye Again* (1961), for which he won the best actor award at the Cannes Film Festival, then in two films for Claude Chabrol, *The Champagne Murders* (1967) and *Ten Days Wonder* (1971), and as Joseph K. in Orson Welles's *The Trial* (1962). Back in Hollywood, he appeared in Mike Nichols's *Catch-22* (1970), John Huston's *The Life and Times of Judge Roy Bean* (1972), Sidney Lumet's

ABOVE A versatile actor, Anthony Perkins's talents were often overlooked because of his convincing performance as the unbalanced Norman Bates in Psycho *(1960).*

Murder on the Orient Express (1974), and Ken Russell's *Crimes of Passion* (1984). He co-wrote the screenplay for *The Last of Sheila* (1973), and directed the film *Lucky Stiff* (1988). Perkins reprised the role of Norman Bates in three sequels, *Psycho II* (1983), *Psycho III* (1986), which he also directed, and a television movie, *Psycho IV: The Beginning* (1990).

Perkins reportedly underwent aversion therapy to rid him of his homosexuality in 1971, and two years later married fashion photographer Berry Berenson, sister of actress Marisa Berenson, and granddaughter of French fashion designer Elsa Shiaparelli. They had two sons, actor Osgood "Oz" Perkins and artist Elvis Perkins. Anthony Perkins was arrested in London in 1984 for possession of a small amount of marijuana and LSD, and again in 1989 for possession of marijuana, but was released both times after paying small fines. In 1990, Perkins was hospitalized for a case of Bell's Palsy, a temporary facial paralysis. Unbeknownst to him, someone took a sample of his blood and had it tested for the HIV virus. On March 27, 1990, the *National Enquirer* ran a front-page story stating that Perkins had AIDS. Perkins considered suing, but a second test verified that he was indeed suffering from AIDS. He died two-and-a-half years later, at the age of 60, at his home in Los Angeles from complications of AIDS. His death and his hidden homosexuality added to the sensationalized nature of his public persona, and helped to overshadow what was a long and versatile stage, film, and television career.

RIGHT Anthony Perkins with his photographer wife, Berry Berenson. They met in New York while he was filming Play It As It Lays *(1972).*

Susan Peters

Born July 3, 1921
Died October 23, 1952

In 1944, Susan Peters was MGM's most luminous rising star. Talented, dark-haired, and beautiful, Peters was born Suzanne Carnahan in Spokane, Washington, in 1921. Her father was killed in an automobile accident in 1928, and she and her mother soon settled in Hollywood, where Peters was discovered by a Warner Bros. scout while performing in a school play at Hollywood High a few weeks shy of graduation.

She auditioned for a role in the 1942 Ronald Reagan film *Kings Row*, but lost to Betty Field. Her first prominent role came in 1942's *Tish*, during which she fell in love with her co-star, Richard Quine. They married the following year. Peters's performance in *Tish* caught the attention of director Mervyn LeRoy, who cast her in *Random Harvest* (1942), starring Ronald Colman and Greer Garson. The performance garnered Peters an Academy Award® nomination for Best Actress in a Supporting Role. She followed with *Song of Russia* (1944), featuring Robert Taylor, and *Keep Your Powder Dry* (1945), starring Lana Turner.

ABOVE On the strength of her performances in the motion pictures Assignment in Brittany *and* Young Ideas *(both released in 1943), Susan Peters was named "Star of Tomorrow."*

On New Year's Day, 1945, Peters, on a duck-hunting trip with friends, was handling a .22-caliber rifle when the trigger accidentally discharged. The bullet severed Peters's spine, and she never walked again. Her feature film career ended after one final performance, *The Sign of the Ram* (1948), in which she played a wheelchair-bound murderess. Peters and Quine had adopted a son in 1946, but the marriage ended in divorce in 1948. Susan Peters then turned to the stage, touring the country in productions of *The Glass Menagerie* and *The Barretts of Wimpole Street*. In 1951, she appeared in *Miss Susan*, a daytime television soap, playing the role of a paraplegic attorney. However, it was cancelled after one season and Peters became reclusive, sinking further into depression. She died on October 23, 1952, officially from chronic kidney infection and bronchial pneumonia, but starvation was a significant contributing factor. Her physician, Dr. Ray Manchester, stated that he believed that Peters had simply "lost the will to live."

Star Shot

Richard Quine was a successful producer and director after Peters's death, and was involved in *Bell, Book and Candle* (1958) and *The World of Suzie Wong* (1960). He died from a self-inflicted gunshot wound in 1989.

RIGHT After the accident that crippled her, MGM paid Susan Peters's hospital bills and kept her on a retainer for a time; however, she made The Sign of the Ram *(1948) with Columbia Pictures.*

Jack Pickford

Born August 18, 1896
Died January 3, 1933

ABOVE The wedding of Jack Pickford and Marilyn Miller in 1922. Douglas Fairbanks is at bottom left, Mary Pickford is beside Miller, and Charlie Chaplin is behind and to the left of the bride.

While living, Jack Pickford was perhaps most famous for the women in his life: his sister, Mary Pickford, and the three actresses he married. In his career, Pickford enjoyed early success, but he was unlucky in marriage and in health. Born John Charles Smith in Toronto, Canada, Pickford became a U.S. citizen on July 13, 1920. His brief film career began in 1909, when Mary arranged that he be signed by Biograph Studios. When Mary signed a million-dollar contract with First National, she stipulated that Jack also be given a contract. Pickford went on to work for the Goldwyn Company, United Artists, First National Pictures, MGM, and the old FBO studios, and for a brief spell in the early 1920s produced his own pictures under the Jack Pickford Company. He was in 33 films after 1916, including *Great Expectations* (1917), *Tom Sawyer* (1917), *The Man Who Had Everything* (1920), *Garrison's Finish* (1923), *Waking Up the Town* (1925), and *Gang War* (1928), his final role.

Yet Pickford's personal life was troubled. His first marriage, to film star Olive Thomas, ended when she accidentally overdosed on mercury bichloride tablets (used to treat venereal disease) during their honeymoon. Rumors persisted that she had committed suicide, or that Pickford had given her the medication to combat the syphilis he had passed on to her. His next two marriages ended in divorce. Pickford was known as a hard-partying playboy, and soon the papers dedicated more ink to reporting his love life than his work.

In the years preceding his death, Pickford's health worsened, in large part due to his carousing lifestyle and use of illicit substances. In July 1928, he had a heart attack. In March 1931, he was in a serious car accident. In July 1932, he left for southern France for health reasons, but suffered a nervous breakdown there and was hospitalized on October 14, 1932. He never left the hospital, falling into a coma on January 3, 1933, and dying a few hours later. The direct cause of death was cited as multiple neuritis, affecting the brain center, but syphilis and years of drug and alcohol abuse were contributing factors. He was 36.

Last Words

"I've lived more than most men and I'm tired—so tired!"

RIGHT Dick Powell (left) on the set of The Singing Marine *(1937). Powell used his considerable vocal abilities to great advantage in this musical comedy.*

Dick Powell

Born November 14, 1904
Died January 2, 1963

Star Shot

Dick Powell starred in a radio serial, *Richard Diamond, Private Detective*, written and directed by Blake Edwards.

BELOW In 1940, Dick Powell and his wife, Joan Blondell, co-starred in the comedy, I Want a Divorce. *In real life, the couple had two children and divorced in 1944.*

Dick Powell's death from stomach cancer on January 2, 1963, has become infamous due to its purported cause, and has in some ways overshadowed his long career as an actor, director, and producer. In 1956, Powell produced and directed the Howard Hughes-backed adventure epic *The Conqueror*, about the life of Genghis Khan. The film was shot in the Escalante Desert near the town of St. George, Utah. Three years before, the government had conducted numerous above-ground atomic bomb tests at Yucca Flats, Nevada, just upwind of St. George. The cast and crew spent about 13 weeks exposed to lingering radiation. To make matters worse, Hughes reportedly had 60 tons (61 tonnes) of radioactive dirt shipped back to Hollywood for retakes. As many as 91 of the 220 people working on the film had contracted cancer by the 1980s, and 46 had died from the disease, including Powell, John Wayne, Susan Hayward, Agnes Moorehead, and Thomas Gomez. Actor Pedro Armendáriz committed suicide by gunshot in 1963 after learning that he had terminal cancer. Howard Hughes reportedly felt so guilty about the incident that he spent millions purchasing every available print of the film, and refused to allow it to be shown, until Paramount finally bought back the rights to the movie in 1974.

It was a sad end to a long and versatile career. He was born Richard Ewing Powell in Mountain View, Arkansas, in 1904, and started as a singer in the Charles Davis Band before being signed to a seven-year contract with Warner Bros. after appearing in its production of *Blessed Event* in 1932. He sang and danced his way through numerous musicals for Warner Bros., often paired with actress Joan Blondell, whom he would marry in 1936. Highlights of this period include *Gold Diggers of 1933* (1933), Frank Borzage's *Flirtation Walk* (1934), and Busby Berkeley's *Gold Diggers of 1935* (1935). He moved to Paramount for a memorable turn in Preston Sturges's *Christmas in July* (1940), then did several more musicals before reinventing himself by playing Philip Marlowe in *Murder, My Sweet* (1944). More straight roles followed in the 1940s, including in *Cornered* (1945), *Rogues' Regiment* (1948), and *The Reformer and the Redhead* (1950). He married his co-star of the latter, June Allyson, after his 1944 divorce from Blondell. In the 1950s, he moved behind the camera, producing and directing several films, including the above-mentioned *The Conqueror* (1956), *The Enemy Below* (1957), and *The Hunters* (1958). He also worked in television beginning in the 1950s, and starred in his own show, *The Dick Powell Show*, from 1961 until his death in 1963.

Gilda Radner

Born June 28, 1946
Died May 20, 1989

Star Shot

In 1994, Gene Wilder co-founded "Gilda's Club," an organization that brings people suffering from cancer, and their families, together to support one another.

Gilda Radner was a comic genius, and found the perfect outlet for her talents with her fellow "Not Ready for Prime Time Players" on NBC's *Saturday Night Live* in the 1970s. She was born in Detroit, Michigan, to Russian-born parents Herman Radner, a hotel businessman, and Henrietta (Dworkin) Radner, a legal secretary. Gilda was named after the title character in the Rita Hayworth film of 1946. Her father died when she was 14 (some sources say 12), leading the young Radner to develop her comedic talents to cope.

She graduated from high school in 1964 and enrolled at the University of Michigan, but dropped out after six years without a diploma. She moved to Toronto and landed the role of Gilmer McCormick in *Godspell* in 1972. She then joined Toronto's Second City troupe, which at the time included Dan Aykroyd and Eugene Levy. She arrived in New York for a role on *The National Lampoon Show*, then got her big break when producer Lorne Michaels hired her to be an original cast member on *Saturday Night Live*.

She quickly became a household name, as did fellow original cast members Dan Aykroyd, Chevy Chase, and Bill Murray. She stuck with the show for five seasons, opting not to play Olive Oyl opposite Robin Williams in Robert Altman's *Popeye* (1980) because the location shooting would have conflicted with the show. Her comedy album, *Gilda Radner, Live From New York* was a hit in 1979, and the following year she appeared in a film version of the show, *Gilda Live* (1980), directed by Mike Nichols.

She wed guitarist G. E. Smith on March 26, 1980, and they celebrated their wedding with a hot dog feast from a New York pushcart. She had appeared in bit roles in *The Last Detail* (1973) and *Blazing Saddles* (1974), but her first significant role came in the farce *First Family* (1980), with Bob Newhart and Madeline Kahn. Then, in 1982, she met and fell in love with comedian Gene Wilder on the set of the film *Hanky Panky* (1982). She divorced Smith, and married Wilder two years later in the south of France. She appeared again with Wilder in *The Woman in Red* (1984), then with Walter Matthau in *Movers and Shakers* (1985). While she was filming *Haunted Honeymoon* (1986) with Wilder, Radner had a miscarriage. That year, she was diagnosed with ovarian cancer. After a three-year battle, Radner died on May 20, 1989, at the Cedars-Sinai Medical Center. She was only 42 years old.

ABOVE Gilda Radner and Gene Wilder in 1986. Radner's autobiography, published in 1989, was called It's Always Something.

Charles Ray

Born March 15, 1891
Died November 23, 1943

Charles Ray was born in Jacksonville, Illinois, in 1891 and began his acting career at the old Mason Opera House in Los Angeles. He left the stage and entered pictures in 1915, beginning as an extra at Thomas H. Ince's studios in Santa Monica. As an innocent deserter of the Confederate Army, he became a star in the leading role in 1915's *The Coward*. Ray began specializing in "country boy in the big city roles," appearing in hits like *The Clodhopper* (1917), *The Sheriff's Son* (1919), and *The Egg Crate Wallop* (1919) with Colleen Moore. These roles shot him to stardom and he became one of the highest paid actors in Hollywood, at one point earning over $11,000 a week.

It has been suggested that Ray's ego made him difficult to work with. Whether true or not, Ray left Ince behind in 1921 and formed his own production company, Charles Ray Productions. He produced and starred in several pictures released successfully through United Artists, including *The Old Swimmin' Hole* (1921) and *A Tailor-Made Man* (1922). However, in 1923, Ray invested nearly his entire fortune, reportedly $600,000, in one movie, *The Courtship of Myles Standish* (1923). When the film flopped, Ray lost everything. His production company folded, and Ray declared bankruptcy that year. He would return to the screen in various productions, but his star had faded. He wasn't able to revive the popularity he had enjoyed in the early days.

Charles Ray worked sporadically through the transition to sound, including a stint under contract with MGM in the 1930s, but he wasn't able to make a full-fledged comeback. He tried his hand at writing, publishing a novel and a book of short stories, with little success. His first

ABOVE Charles Ray and Joan Crawford starred in Paris *(1926), set in the seedy under-world of the French capital. Ray appeared in over 150 films.*

wife, Clara Grant Ray, divorced him in 1934. A subsequent marriage to Frenchwoman Yvonne Guerin ended with her death in 1942. By the early 1940s, Ray appeared only in bit roles, often uncredited. In 1943, he developed an infection from an impacted tooth, which then spread to his throat. He entered Cedars of Lebanon hospital, and died from the infection five weeks later on November 23, 1943, at the age of 52. It was a surprising end to the life and career of a man who had once been one of the most popular stars in the world. He is buried in an unmarked grave at Forest Lawn Memorial Park in Glendale, California.

Robert Reed

Born October 19, 1932
Died May 12, 1992

RIGHT Robert Reed with The Brady Bunch co-stars Ann B. Davis (left) and Florence Henderson. Reed's character, Mike Brady, ranked 14th in a June 2004 TV Guide list of the "50 greatest television dads."

Star Shot

Robert Reed's fellow students at London's Royal Academy of Dramatic Art included Diana Rigg, Albert Finney, and Peter O'Toole.

In the end, Robert Reed is most often remembered for the role he enjoyed playing the least—that of Mike Brady, the clean-cut patriarch of television's *The Brady Bunch.* "I don't particularly want it on my tombstone," he once said. But the show's sugary, nostalgic take on middle-class family life struck a chord with the American public. *The Brady Bunch* ran for five seasons, became a cult classic in syndication, and spawned three spin-off shows, a number of television movies, stage performances, and two feature films. Reed's acting career included appearances on stage and in film, yet he is primarily remembered for his work in television.

Robert Reed was born John Robert Rietz in Highland Park, Illinois, and grew up in Muskogee, Oklahoma. He studied drama at Northwestern University in Illinois, and the Royal Academy of Dramatic Art in London. In 1957, he married Marilyn Rosenberg, and his only child, daughter Karen, was born soon thereafter, but the marriage ended in divorce after only one year. Reed's breakthrough role came in 1961 with the critically acclaimed television series, *The Defenders,* opposite E. G. Marshall. He followed that with both the CBS detective series *Mannix* (1967), opposite Mike Connors, and *The Brady Bunch* (1969).

After *The Brady Bunch* was cancelled in 1974, Robert Reed acted in the short-lived series *Nurse* (1981), as well as numerous television movies. He was nominated for Emmy Awards® three times, for his sensitive portrayal of a transsexual doctor on the television series *Medical Center* in 1975, and for his appearances in two television miniseries: *Rich Man Poor Man* (1976) and *Roots* (1977). Reed also starred on Broadway in *Barefoot in the Park,* *Avanti,* and *Doubles,* and toured in *The Owl and the Pussycat* and *California Suite.* His appearances on the big screen include roles in Otto Preminger's *Hurry Sundown* (1967) and Robert Wise's *Star!* (1968).

Reed was intensely private about his personal life, and upon his death in 1992 at the age of 59, the press reported only that Reed had suffered from colon cancer. Several days later, however, it was reported that Reed had been infected with the AIDS virus, and that an HIV infection had hastened his death. Questions about Reed's sexual orientation were deflected by family members, who stated that the public should focus on the fact that if "Dad Brady" could contract AIDS, anyone could.

LEFT In The Defenders *(1961), Robert Reed and E. G. Marshall played a father and son legal team that tackled controversial issues such as civil rights and abortion.*

Christopher Reeve

Born September 25, 1952
Died October 10, 2004

ABOVE Christopher Reeve with his wife, Dana, a few months before his death. Reeve once said, "Your body is not who you are. The mind and spirit transcend the body."

RIGHT Christopher Reeve as Superman. Reeve made guest appearances on the Superman television spin-off, Smallville, about the young Clark Kent.

Christopher Reeve became a household name portraying Superman on the big screen, but he will be best remembered as a tireless advocate for the disabled after a riding accident left him paralyzed from the neck down in 1995. He advocated the expansion of embryonic stem cell research, toured extensively to lobby for health insurance reform, and established the Christopher and Dana Reeve Paralysis Foundation, which has disbursed millions of dollars for research and to needy individuals. He also continued to act in and direct films until his death.

Born in New York City, the son of professor and poet Franklin Reeve and journalist Barbara Johnson, he began acting at the age of 15 in an apprentice program at the Williamstown Theater Festival, and continued on to Cornell University and The Juilliard School. In 1976, he made his Broadway debut opposite Katharine Hepburn in *A Matter of Gravity.* That year he auditioned for the part that would make him a star, the dual roles of Clark Kent and the "Man of Steel" in 1978's *Superman.* He beat out over 200 other actors for the part, and reprised the role three more times in sequels. Determined not to be typecast, he appeared as a psychopathic homosexual in *Deathtrap* (1982), in the period-piece *The Bostonians* (1984), in Merchant-Ivory's *The Remains of the Day* (1993), and in John Carpenter's remake of *Village of the Damned* (1995). Other films include *Somewhere in Time* (1980), *Monsignor* (1982), and *The Aviator* (1985). He also appeared on television in the 1970's soap *Love of Life*, the miniseries *Anna Karenina* (1985) and *Black Fox* (1995), and a remake of *Rear Window* (1998). He began directing after his injury, making television movies *In The Gloaming* (1997) and *The Brooke Ellison Story* (2004), his last project.

In May 1995, Christopher Reeve was participating in competitive horseback riding trials in Culpepper, Virginia, when his horse shied from a fence. Reeve was pitched forward and landed on his forehead, breaking his top two vertebrae and injuring his spinal cord. He turned his recovery process into a national crusade, embracing innovative therapies and working as an advocate for disability rights, despite the toll it took on his health. After nine years, many hospitalizations, and different treatments, Reeve developed an infection brought about by a pressure wound, which led to cardiac failure. At his side were his first partner, Gae Exton, his wife, Dana Reeve, and his two oldest children. He was 52. Dana later said that she believed Reeve actually died from an allergic reaction to medication, but "there was no autopsy so we don't know for sure."

Lee Remick

Born December 14, 1935
Died July 2, 1991

ABOVE *Lee Remick and James Stewart in 1975. Only two months before her early death, Remick unveiled her star on the Hollywood Walk of Fame.*

L ee Remick got her start in ballet and ended her career possessing an impressive roster of motion picture and television credits. She was born in Quincy, Massachusetts, on December 14, 1935. Her father was successful businessman Francis Edwin Remick and her mother was stage actress Margaret Waldo. Lee Remick studied classical ballet for ten years, then turned to modeling and acting in her teens. At the age of 16, she made her Broadway debut in *Be Your Age,* but the play flopped. Other stage work included *Annie Get Your Gun*, *Oklahoma*, *Showboat*, *Paint Your Wagon*, and *The Seven Year Itch*. She moved on to live television, appearing on *Studio One*, *Kraft Theatre*, and *American Inventory*.

After only one semester at Barnard College, Remick quit, wanting to act. She went to Hollywood at the age of 18 at the behest of director Elia Kazan, who had seen her on *Robert Montgomery Presents*. Kazan cast her as the sexy drum majorette, Betty Lou Fleckum, in *A Face In The Crowd* (1957). That year, Remick married television producer and director William Colleran, with whom she had two children. The marriage ended in divorce in 1968.

Remick's impressive cache of films were mostly very high caliber, including *The Long Hot Summer* (1958), Otto Preminger's *Anatomy of a Murder* (1959) with James Stewart, *Wild River* (1960), *Sanctuary* (1961), *Experiment In Terror* (1962), and *Sometimes a Great Notion* (1971) with Henry Fonda and Paul Newman. Her powerful performance as alcoholic Kirsten Arnesen in *Days of Wine and Roses* (1962) opposite Jack Lemmon garnered her an Academy Award® nomination. In 1964, Remick appeared in the Broadway musical *Anyone Can Whistle*, and followed with *Wait Until Dark*, which earned her a Tony® award nomination. She appeared in the films *No Way To Treat A Lady* (1968) with Rod Steiger and *Loot* (1970), before settling in London with second husband, William Rory "Kip" Gowans, then an assistant director in the English film industry. Later appearances include the television movie *Hustling* (1975), the play *Bus Stop* (1976), and the classic film *The Omen* (1976), with Gregory Peck.

During the 1989 filming in France of the television movie *Dark Holiday* (1989), Remick discovered that she had advanced kidney cancer, which had spread to the lungs. She died on July 2, 1991, at the age of 55.

John Ritter

Born September 17, 1948
Died September 11, 2003

John Ritter was born Jonathan Southworth Ritter at the same hospital in Burbank where he would later die. He was the youngest son of country-western singer and actor Tex Ritter and actress Dorothy Fay. Tex had hoped his son would become a lawyer, and John considered a career in politics before deciding on acting. He graduated from Hollywood High School, where he was, in his own words, "both the class clown and the student body president." He majored in drama at the University of Southern California, and studied acting with famed coach Stella Adler.

He made his motion picture debut in Disney's *The Barefoot Executive* (1971) with Kurt Russell and Raffles the Chimp. The chimp got a bigger part than Ritter. He moved quickly to the small screen, where he made numerous guest appearances on shows such as *M.A.S.H., Hawaii Five-O, The Mary Tyler Moore Show,* and *Kojak,* before landing his first steady role playing a minister on *The Waltons.* A very different role followed, as Jack Tripper, the girl-crazy "closeted heterosexual," on the ABC sit-com *Three's Company.* The show ran from 1977 to 1984, regularly finished in the top ten shows, and brought a new level of risqué humor and sexual innuendo to prime time television. It also made huge stars out of both Ritter and his co-star, Suzanne Somers. Ritter delighted audiences with his razor-sharp sense of comedic timing, patented pratfalls, and liquid-spewing double takes. He received an Emmy®, Golden Globe®, and People's Choice Award for the part.

ABOVE John Ritter (right) shares a laugh with Carrie Fisher and Ringo Starr. Ritter was a great admirer of The Beatles, and appeared on the television special Ringo *in 1978.*

After *Three's Company,* Ritter appeared in several other series, including the short-lived spin-off *Three's A Crowd, Hooperman,* and the animated *Fish Police,* each of which lasted only one season, and *Hearts Afire,* which ran from 1992 to 1995. John Ritter had strong roles in several made-for-television films, including *Unnatural Causes* (1986), for which he was nominated for a Best Actor Golden Globe® award, *The Dreamer of Oz* (1990), *Stephen King's It* (1990), and *Gramps* (1995) with Andy Griffith. He also received several Emmy® nominations for his role as the voice of Clifford on the animated series *Clifford The Big Red Dog.* Later guest appearances were well received critically, including turns on *Ally McBeal, Felicity, Buffy the Vampire Slayer,* and *Scrubs.*

RIGHT John Ritter with his mother, Dorothy Fay. She was the official greeter at Nashville's Grand Ole Opry, an important country-western music venue.

His film career was spotty. He appeared in mostly forgettable films like *Americathon* (1979), *Skin Deep* (1989), and *Stay Tuned* (1992), although the 1990 comedy *Problem Child* was a surprise hit. Later roles found him playing against type in independents, most notably as the gay store employee in Billy Bob Thornton's *Sling Blade* (1996). Other such films include *Tadpole* (2002), the

2003 Sundance entrant *Manhood*, and the post-humously released *Bad Santa* (2003), again starring Thornton. Other films include the sequel *Problem Child 2* (1991), *The Bride of Chucky* (1998), and *Panic* (2000) with Donald Sutherland and William H. Macy. Ritter also starred in over 50 plays during his career, and won critical acclaim in his Broadway debut, Neil Simon's *The Dinner Party*.

Ritter was married to Nancy Morgan from 1977 to 1996, and they had three children, actor Jason Ritter, who stars in the CBS drama, *Joan of Arcadia*; and daughters Carly and Tyler. When John Ritter strode onto the set of his hit television series *8 Simple Rules for Dating My Teenage Daughter* on September 11, 2003, things couldn't have been going better for him. It was his youngest daughter Stella's fifth birthday, and the day before his wedding anniversary to second wife, actress Amy Yasbeck, whom he'd met on the set of *Problem Child*. His own 55th birthday was in a week. And Ritter had finally found success again on prime time television after several failed sitcoms and an up-and-down career in film. Henry Winkler, Ritter's old friend and fellow actor, was guest appearing on the show that week, and around 4:15 P.M., Ritter told Winkler that he wasn't feeling well—he felt sick and had chest pains. He was rushed across the road to the Providence St. Joseph Medical Center in Burbank, where his condition quickly worsened. Doctors discovered a rare heart disorder called aorta dissection in Ritter's heart. The disease leads to a catastrophic failure of the aorta, the artery that carries blood to the brain and other major organs in the body. It is a deadly disease with a high mortality rate, it strikes quickly, and, unfortunately, its symptoms are the same as those of a heart attack so it is difficult to diagnose quickly. Ritter was rushed into surgery, but it was too late, and he died in the operating room just after 10 P.M. It was a sudden and unexpected end to a 30-year career that had made John Ritter one of the most beloved entertainers of his time.

LEFT John Ritter with his wife, Amy Yasbeck, in 1999. In 1967, when he was 18 years old, Ritter was a contestant on the television show, The Dating Game.

BELOW The cast of Three's Company, clockwise from left: Don Knotts, Richard Kline, Suzanne Somers, Ann Wedgeworth, John Ritter, and Joyce DeWitt.

Ruth Roland

Born August 26, 1892
Died September 22, 1937

Ruth Roland was the "Queen of the Thriller Serials," and one of the biggest stars of silent film from its beginnings through its maturity into an art form in the 1920s. She appeared in almost 200 shorts, features, and serials, often in action thrillers or westerns, and was voted one of the top ten western stars every year between 1911 and 1915, a feat usually reserved for men. She was also a shrewd businesswoman, and after briefly running her own production company, Roland retired from film in the 1930s a very wealthy woman.

She was born into a showbiz family; her mother was a professional singer and her father was a theater manager. She made her acting debut onstage at the tender age of three. In 1900, her parents divorced and not long afterward, her mother died and Roland went to live with an aunt in Los Angeles, California. By her teens, she was performing a vaudeville act there, and was discovered by a director for Kalem Pictures (later bought by Vitagraph). She made her feature debut in *The Old Soldier's Story* (1909) and acted in a handful of shorts over the next two years. By 1911 she had made an impact with audiences, particularly in westerns, and the following year she appeared in over 40 films. Highlights from her Kalem years include *Strong Arm Nellie* (1912), *A Mountain Tragedy* (1912), *The Kidnapped Conductor* (1912), *Sherlock Bonehead* (1914), and *The Peach at the Beach* (1914).

Roland moved to Long Beach-based Balboa Films in 1915, and appeared in several more comedy shorts, including *The Apartment House Mystery* (1915), *The Disappearance of Henry Warrington* (1915), and *The Sultana* (1916). She also appeared in her first serial, *Who Pays?* (1915), written and co-starring future director Henry King. The serial was a big hit, and Roland followed it up with several more at Balboa, including *The Red Circle* (1915) and *Hands Up!* (1918). In 1919, she established the Ruth Roland Serial Company, and created the hit serials *The Adventures of Ruth* (1919), *White Eagle* (1922), and *The Timber Queen* (1922). Roland became an action adventure superstar, although in reality she rarely did her own stunts, unlike fellow serial standouts Pearl White and Helen Holmes. After 1925, she rarely appeared in films, although she did try her hand at talking pictures in 1930's *Reno*, with disappointing box-office results. Her last film was 1935's *From Nine to Nine*. Her second marriage was to actor and renowned drama teacher Ben Bard, founder of the Ben Bard Drama School. Roland died in 1937 from cancer, and is buried in the Forest Lawn Memorial Park cemetery in Glendale, California.

ABOVE Ruth Roland pictured in 1920. For her first film role, in The Old Soldier's Story *(1909), Roland was paid the princely sum of $25 per week.*

Sabu

Born January 27, 1924
Died December 2, 1963

S abu was Hollywood's first real Indian film star, and became widely known as "Sabu the Elephant Boy" after the title role in his first film, *Elephant Boy* (1937). He was born Sabu Dastagir in the Karapur Jungle, near the town of Mysore, India. His mother died shortly after his birth, and his father died when Sabu was only seven. Sabu was working as a stable boy at the court of the Maharaja of Mysore when he was discovered by the British director Robert Flaherty and the producer Alexander Korda, who were on a scouting mission in India for their next picture, *Elephant Boy*. Sabu was subsequently cast in the leading role, and emerged from the film a star at the age of 12.

Appearances in *The Thief of Bagdad* (1940), *Arabian Nights* (1942), and as Mowgli in *The Jungle Book* (1942) cemented his reputation as a player in exotic adventure films. The latter two films also represented the pinnacle of Sabu's brief Hollywood career. He became an American citizen in 1944 and enlisted in the U.S. Air Force during World War II, becoming a gunner on B-24 bombers in the South Pacific and winning the Distinguished Flying Cross in combat.

After his service in the war, Sabu appeared in several pictures, including *Black Narcissus* (1947), *The End of the River* (1947), *Song of India* (1949), and *Hello, Elephant* (1952), but his star had faded and he soon retired from the screen. He married his co-star in *Song of India*, Marilyn Cooper, in 1948. They had two children and stayed together until Sabu's death. A nasty paternity suit filed in 1949 by his ex-fiancée, Brenda Marian Julien, dragged Sabu's name through the tabloids for several years. Sabu settled with Julien in 1953 and agreed to support the child, although he never admitted paternity. Another suit against Sabu, brought in 1952 claiming arson of his own home, further sullied Sabu's reputation. By the early 1960s, Sabu was operating a small furniture shop in Van Nuys. He attempted a comeback in 1963, including *Rampage* (1963) and *A Tiger Walks* (released posthumously in 1964), but died suddenly of a heart attack on December 2, 1963 at the age of 39.

RIGHT Sabu as the prince in Black Narcissus *(1947). Sabu's son, Paul, is a musician; his daughter, Jasmine, was an actress. She died in 2001.*

Star Shot

Sabu reportedly was known for walking his pet elephant down Winnetka Avenue in Chatsworth, California, leading neighbors to demand zoning restrictions prohibiting large animals on residential property.

Zachary Scott

Born February 24, 1914
Died October 3, 1965

Zachary Scott perfected the portrayal of suave, charming scoundrels in numerous B-grade pictures and westerns during the 1940s and 1950s, but never made the transition to more complex, leading-man roles. He was born in Austin, Texas, the son of a prominent surgeon. He initially pursued medicine at the University of Texas, but realized after a year that he was better suited for theater. In 1934, he took a job as a cabin boy on a freighter bound for Britain, determined to become an actor on the London stage. He joined the English Repertory Company, and received his first important role in *The Outsider* at the Theater Royal in Bath. He returned to the United States and married actress Elaine Anderson in 1935. By 1940, Scott was making inroads into the New York theater scene, with performances on Broadway in *Circle of Chalk*, *The Damask Cheek*, and *The Rock*.

Jack Warner spotted Scott during a production of *Those Endearing Young Charms*, and gave him the title role in *The Mask of Dimitrios* (1944). Scott's stock rose with his next two pictures: Michael Curtiz's *Mildred Pierce* (1945) with Joan Crawford, and Jean Renoir's *The Southerner* (1945). He gives the performance of his career in the latter, as the patriarch of a family of destitute sharecroppers. He seemed destined for a spectacular career, but it is generally believed that Warner Bros. didn't promote Scott well, and he spent his later years languishing in films not quite worthy of his talents. Other movies include *Cass Timberlane* (1947) with Spencer Tracy and Lana Turner, *Flamingo Road* (1949) once

ABOVE Zachary Scott and Patricia Morison in the play The Four Poster *(1963). After his death, the Zachary Scott Theatre Center in Austin, Texas, was established in honor of his memory.*

again with Crawford and Curtiz, and the western *South of St. Louis* (1949). In 1951, he left Warner Bros. to freelance, but worthy roles seemed to dry up. He divorced Anderson in 1950, and she married legendary novelist John Steinbeck that same year. Scott also suffered injuries in a freak boating accident with fellow actor John Emery in December 1949 near Topanga Canyon, California. Scott's injuries reportedly had a detrimental effect on his acting career.

He rebounded a bit with his second marriage, to stage actress Ruth Ford, in 1952, and an appearance that same year with Joan Bennett in a Chicago stage production of *Bell, Book and Candle*. However, by the late 1950s, Scott's career had waned, and he increasingly turned his attention to television, including appearances on *Your Show of Shows, Alfred Hitchcock Presents*, and *The New Breed*. In 1965, he discovered that he was suffering from a malignant brain tumor and began radiation treatment in New York. He underwent brain surgery that autumn, but the procedure was unsuccessful. He was flown to his mother's home in Austin, Texas, where he died on October 3, 1965, at the age of 51.

Dorothy Sebastian

Born April 26, 1903
Died April 8, 1957

In the 1920s and early 1930s, Dorothy Sebastian was a huge star of silent movies, a well-regarded actress and brilliant physical comedienne, and had appeared alongside several of the greatest names of the cinema. She was also known for two of the men in her life: Buster Keaton, with whom she had a long affair, and William Boyd, who gained fame playing "Hopalong" Cassidy on film and television.

Dorothy Sebastian began her career on Broadway as a showgirl in *George White's Scandals*, then came to Hollywood in 1924 and made her film debut in *Sackcloth and Scarlet* (1925), a now-lost film by the husband-wife production team of Rex Ingram and Alice Terry. In 1928, she appeared with Greta Garbo and John Gilbert in *A Woman of Affairs* (1928), and with Joan Crawford and Anita Page in *Our Dancing Daughters* (1928). The following year, Sebastian starred in Buster Keaton's last silent film, *Spite Marriage* (1929). She would also appear in his first talking picture, 1930's *Free and Easy*. Off-screen, Sebastian and Keaton shared a long romance, beginning in 1929 and possibly lasting until 1935, despite marriages for both during this period. Other notable films include with Garbo again in *The Single Standard* (1929), with Crawford and Page again in *Our Blushing Brides* (1930), an uncredited part in George Cukor's classic *The Women* (1939), and with screen cowboy Roy Rogers in *Rough Riders' Round-Up* (1939). After an absence from film for several years, she returned to make her final film, *The Miracle of Bells*, in 1948.

In 1929, Dorothy Sebastian met William "Bill" Boyd on the set of the Pathé production, *His First Command* (1929), and they married in Las Vegas in 1931. William "Bill" Boyd should not be confused with stage and silent film actor William H. Boyd. William "Bill" Boyd found fame and fortune portraying Bill "Hopalong" Cassidy in over 60 films in the 1930s and 1940s, and on a television series that began in 1949. It was a stormy marriage, however, and they divorced in 1935. A second marriage, to Miami Beach businessman Herman Shapiro in 1947, lasted until her death.

Dorothy Sebastian made headlines in 1937 when she was arrested and subsequently sued by a San Diego hotel for refusing to pay a $50 hotel bill. She was not only acquitted of all charges, but even won a countersuit against the hotel and was awarded $10,000. By 1957, Sebastian was seriously ill with cancer, and she eventually succumbed to the disease on April 8, 1957 at the Motion Picture Country House and Hospital, where she had been living for five months.

ABOVE
Personality-driven images such as this one, where she reads a book on how to fly a plane, made Dorothy Sebastian popular with audiences.

Star Shot

Before making her film debut, Dorothy Sebastian was a member of the Ziegfeld Follies. In her screen career, she featured in 62 movies.

LEFT Dorothy Sebastian with long-time lover Buster Keaton in Spite Marriage *(1929). Keaton wanted the film to be a talkie, but MGM released it with only music and sound effects.*

Peter Sellers

Born September 8, 1925
Died July 24, 1980

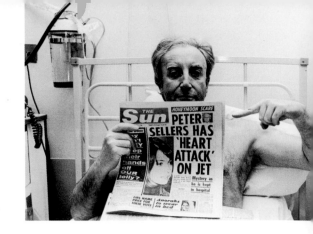

Was Peter Sellers a heartless, self-destructive madman, or an imperfect comedic genius who brought laughter and inspiration to legions of fans? The fascination with Peter Sellers has continued even a quarter century after his death. Several biographies and a recent biopic, HBO's *The Life and Death of Peter Sellers* (2004), have purported to uncover the dark side of Sellers's personality, asserting that he was mad, that he lost his grasp on reality toward the end, that he physically and psychologically abused his wives and children. Even his champions admit that Sellers was a complex, imperfect man. Perhaps he was, as he himself once said, "a man with no personality of his own," truly alive only when inhabiting those compelling, oddball characters he created onscreen. And to some extent, it's those characters (Inspector Clouseau, Chauncey Gardner, Dr. Strangelove) that have grown legendary by transcending their creator and entering into the pantheon of cinematic icons.

He was born Richard Henry Sellars (sic) in Southsea, Hampshire, England, in 1925, the son of show business parents. Their first son, Peter, had died in infancy the year before, and from the very beginning, little Richard Henry was known as Peter. Sellers's mother was dominant and overbearing, and the two had an unhealthy, overly close relationship. He discovered his talent for comedy performing at camp concerts while serving with the Royal Air Force. He toured the Middle East as a member of the Ralph Readers "Gang Show," then returned home and began performing at London's Windmill Theatre. He worked on several radio shows, then got his big break in 1949, when he teamed up with fellow veterans Harry Secombe, Spike Milligan, and Michael Bentine for BBC Radio's *The Goon Show*. Their new style of fast-paced, irreverent humor was a huge hit all over England, and they became household names overnight. Sellers made his motion picture debut with Secombe and Milligan in *Penny Points to Paradise* (1951), and then Bentine joined them for *Down Among the Z Men* (1952), but neither picture was as successful as the radio show.

Sellers won a supporting role in the classic British comedy, *The Ladykillers* (1955) with Alec Guinness, then appeared regularly in character roles in films like *The Smallest Show on Earth* (1957), *Up the Creek* (1958), and *tom thumb* (1958). He then played three roles in *The Mouse That Roared* (1959), including one in drag; appeared in fellow ex-Goon Milligan's short film, *The Running, Jumping and Standing Still Film* (1959), which earned critical acclaim at international festivals; and stole several scenes in *I'm*

All Right Jack (1959). He did his Indian imper-sonation in *The Millionairess* (1960) with Sophia Loren. Later, Sellers would assert that he and Loren had had an affair during production of the film. Loren, however, has remained silent on the issue. In any case, his infatuation with Loren destroyed his first marriage to Anne Howe.

Sellers tried his hand at directing himself in *Mr. Topaze* (1961), but it was not well received. However, he was impressive in a supporting role in Stanley Kubrick's 1962 picture, *Lolita*. Then, Peter Ustinov backed out of the role of Inspector Clouseau in Blake Edwards's *The Pink Panther* (1963). Sellers got the part and became an inter-national superstar. He followed with a tour-de-force performance in three roles, Group Captain Lionel Mandrake, U.S. President Merkin Muffley,

ABOVE Peter Sellers with his beautiful wife, Britt Ekland, in 1967. A few years earlier, in April 1964, Sellers became the first man to appear on the cover of Playboy *magazine.*

and Nazi sympathizer Dr. Strangelove in Stanley Kubrick's black comedy masterpiece, *Dr. Strangelove: or How I Stopped Worrying and Learned to Love the Bomb* (1964). He was nomi-nated for an Academy Award®, but lost to Rex Harrison for *My Fair Lady* (1964). He followed with another turn as Clouseau in the sequel *A Shot in the Dark* (1964), and his legend was assured. He appeared in two more *Panther* sequels, *The Return of the Pink Panther* (1975), and *Revenge of the Pink Panther* (1978), as well as the posthumously released *Trail of the Pink Panther* (1982), which was made up of outtakes from earlier films. The latter sequels lacked inspiration, but made Sellers rich. After *A Shot in the Dark* (1964), Sellers appeared in several films of varying quality, including Woody Allen's film debut, *What's New, Pussycat?* (1965); the Bond spoof *Casino Royale* (1967); and *I Love You, Alice B. Toklas!* (1968). In 1979, he gave per-haps his best performance as Chance the gardener in Hal Ashby's *Being There*. He was nomi-nated for his second Oscar® for Best Actor, but again lost out, this time to Dustin Hoffman for *Kramer vs. Kramer* (1979). His last film was the flop *The Fiendish Plot of Dr. Fu Manchu* (1980).

Sellers married four times. His second wife was Swedish actress Britt Ekland, and his fourth wife was actress Lynne Frederick. The first three marriages ended in divorce, and the last in separa-tion at the time of Sellers's death. Sellers had suffered from a heart condition for the last 16 years of his life. On April 5, 1964, he had a heart attack and had to bow out of Billy Wilder's *Kiss Me Stupid* (1964) after production had begun. He suffered another heart attack in 1977, and then on July 23, 1980, he suffered a third. Peter Sellers was rushed to Middlesex Hospital in London, but died at 12:26 A.M. on July 24.

Star Shot

Peter Sellers's fourth wife, Lynne Frederick, sued the producers of *Trail of the Pink Panther* (1982), saying that the film insulted her husband's memory. She won and was awarded $1,475,000 in damages.

LEFT The Goons in 1951. From left, Harry Secombe, Michael Bentine, Peter Sellers, and Spike Milligan. Among the characters made famous by Sellers were Bluebottle and Major Dennis Bloodnok.

Robert Shaw

Born August 9, 1927
Died August 28, 1978

Robert Shaw once proclaimed that he was the "highest paid, oldest unknown actor in the world." That was just after *A Man for All Seasons* (1966), and although he had been nominated for an Oscar® for Best Actor in a Supporting Role for his portrayal of King Henry VIII, it was his co-star, Paul Scofield, who won the Best Actor category and got all the attention. Robert Shaw would, of course, later gain the fame he so desired as a cantankerous shark hunter in Steven Spielberg's horror masterpiece *Jaws* (1975). But tragically, his film career would be cut short at the peak of that fame by his untimely death.

He was born on August 9, 1927 in Westhoughton, Lancashire, England, and raised in Cornwall and the Orkney Islands in Scotland. His father, a prominent surgeon who struggled with alcoholism, committed suicide when Shaw was 12 years of age. Shaw turned his attention to writing and acting. He studied at the Royal Academy of Dramatic Art, and made his West End debut in 1951 supporting Alec Guinness in *Hamlet*. He made his movie debut with a bit part in Guinness's *The Lavender Hill Mob* (1951), then appeared in the classic British war drama *The Dam Busters* (1954). Shaw gained notoriety with a short stint on British television's *The Buccaneers*, then presented his first play, *Off the Mainland*. He also published his first novel, *The Hiding Place*. He went back to theater for *The Long and the Short and the Tall*, then made his Broadway debut in 1961's *The Caretaker*. He married actress Mary Ure in 1963, and the marriage lasted until her death in 1975.

BELOW Robert Shaw in Jaws (1975). Shaw had an alcohol problem and once said, "I drink too much. Will you tell me one great actor who doesn't drink?"

Shaw began specializing as nasty villains, playing an assassin battling Sean Connery in *From Russia with Love* (1963), and Nazi Colonel Hessler in *Battle of the Bulge* (1965). Then came *A Man for All Seasons* and the resulting Oscar® nomination, which led to turns as a glowering Irish gangster in Best Picture winner, *The Sting* (1973), a wicked Sheriff of Nottingham opposite Connery's Robin Hood in *Robin and Marian* (1976), an anti-terrorist agent in *Black Sunday* (1977), and of course, the role of "Quint" in *Jaws*. In addition, the film *Situation Hopeless… But Not Serious* (1965) was based on Shaw's novel *The Hiding Place*, and his fourth novel, *The Man in the Glass Booth*, was filmed in 1975, although Shaw requested his name be removed from the credits.

Robert Shaw struggled with alcoholism all his life, which seriously affected his health, and on August 28, 1978, at the age of 51, he suffered a massive heart attack and died at the home he shared with his third wife and ten children in Tourmakeady, Ireland.

Ann Sheridan

Born February 21, 1915
Died January 21, 1967

A nn Sheridan was known as "The Oomph Girl." A glamorous, vivacious redhead, she projected a likable toughness in over 80 films during a career that spanned three decades. She was born Clara Lou Sheridan in Denton, Texas, and studied to be a teacher, but chose acting after winning a Paramount beauty contest. The first prize was a screen test. She arrived in Hollywood in 1932, and appeared along with the other winners of the contest in *Search for Beauty* (1934). Paramount quickly signed her to a contract, in part because she could ride a horse, and she made her film debut in a bit part in *Bolero* (1934) with George Raft and Carole Lombard. She acted in 14 more films as Clara Lou before changing her name to Ann Sheridan in 1935. Paramount let her go that same year, and in 1936 she was signed to a long-term contract with Warner Bros. She also married actor Edward Norris that year, the first of her three husbands. Warners publicized her as the million dollar "Oomph Girl" and quickly made her a star.

ABOVE Like Betty Grable, Ann Sheridan was a popular pin-up girl. In 1939, she was named Max Factor's "Girl of the Year."

She appeared in *Black Legion* (1937) with Humphrey Bogart, *The Great O'Malley* (1937), and *San Quentin* (1937), before landing her breakout role opposite James Cagney in *Angels with Dirty Faces* (1938). Sheridan then appeared in *Dodge City* (1939) with Errol Flynn, *Castle on the Hudson* (1940), and *Torrid Zone* (1940) again with James Cagney. In 1941, she went on strike for six months in an ill-fated attempt for better working conditions and higher pay. She was soon back, appearing opposite Ronald Reagan in *Kings Row* (1942). In 1942, Sheridan wed actor George Brent, but the marriage lasted less than a year. She appeared with Cary Grant in *I Was A Male War Bride* (1949), but by the 1950s, her film career was winding down. Her last film was *Woman and the Hunter* (1957). She also appeared on stage in shows such as *Kind Sir* and *Odd Man In*, both with Scott McKay. McKay's wife sued for divorce, naming Sheridan as co-respondent. Sheridan married McKay in 1966 and the marriage lasted until her death.

Star Shot

As a $75 per week player, Ann Sheridan claimed to be able to perform skills such as whistling through her fingers and "bulldogging a steer."

Sheridan moved to television, first in the soap opera *Another World*, and then in *Pistols and Petticoats*. By that time, her health was in serious decline. After the production's Christmas vacation, Sheridan returned to the set in January 1967 noticeably weak and frail. Ten days after calling the studio to let them know she could not come to work, Sheridan died of cancer at the age of 51.

LEFT Warner Bros. boss Jack Warner dines with two of his star actresses, Bette Davis (left) and Ann Sheridan, in 1945.

Last Words

"I'm all right."

Milton Sills

Born January 12, 1882
Died September 15, 1930

Milton Sills was the first, and perhaps the only, professor of philosophy ever to become a matinee idol. He was a handsome leading man in the 1920s, and a reliable box office draw until his sudden death. Sills was born into affluence in Chicago on January 12, 1882. His father, Milton Henry Sills, was a mineral dealer, and his mother, Josephine Antoinette Troost Sills, was from a wealthy banking family. Despite unimpressive grades in high school, he made his way into the University of Chicago and stayed on after graduation, first as a researcher and then a professor of psychology and philosophy. In 1905, actor Donald Robertson convinced the young professor that he should try his hand at acting, and it wasn't long before Sills was performing for Robertson's stock company in Chicago, the Donald Robertson Players. He made his stage debut in New Palestine, Ohio, in a small part in *Dora Thorne*. By 1908, Sills had made his way to New York and he quickly found success there, making his Broadway debut in February 1909 in *This Woman and This Man*. He went on to appear in over a dozen productions in the next few years, including *Diplomacy* (1910), *The Rack* (1911), *The Governor's Lady* (1912), *The Man Inside* (1913), and *Panthena* (1914). He married actress Gladys Edith Wynne in England in 1910.

ABOVE Milton Sills with his first wife, Gladys Edith Wynne. Sills was one of the 36 founders of the Academy of Motion Picture Arts and Sciences.

Producer William A. Brady offered Sills $350 a week to appear onscreen in his production of *The Pit* in 1914, and for the next two years Milton Sills appeared both onstage and in films. He came to Hollywood to appear in *The Honor System* in 1917, and quickly became a star. His star status was cemented with a leading role in *The Sea Hawk* (1924). That same year, he signed with First National, and appeared in nearly two dozen films before his final picture, *The Sea Wolf*, in 1930. Notable films include *Men of Steel* (1926), *The Silent Lover* (1926), *The Hawk's Nest* (1928), and Alexander Korda's *Love and the Devil* (1929). He co-starred with actress Doris Kenyon in numerous films, and the two married in 1926 following Sills's divorce from Wynne. Sills smoothly made the transition to sound, and his career seemed secure when he died suddenly of a heart attack while playing tennis at his Brentwood Heights home on September 15, 1930, at the age of 48. Ironically, the last words he spoke onscreen, in the posthumously released *The Sea Wolf* (1930), were, "I'm dying, but I never weakened."

Anita Stewart

Born February 7, 1895
Died May 4, 1961

Mostly forgotten today, silent film star Anita Stewart appeared in over 100 motion pictures and was one of the most radiant stars of the silver screen for nearly two decades. She was a contemporary of Norma and Constance Talmadge, with whom she had gone to high school, as well as Mary Pickford, Marguerite Clark, and Clara Kimball Young. At one time she is said to have received over 100 fan letters a day. With the advent of sound, however, she retired from pictures and spent the last three decades of her life out of the public eye.

Star Shot

In the early days of her career, Anita Stewart went by the name Anna Stewart and is credited as such in five films.

Sources conflict as to the year of her birth, ranging between 1895 and 1902. Her death certificate lists the last, but 1895 is the more reliable figure, as she was listed on the 1900 U.S. Census as a five-year-old. She was born and raised in Brooklyn, New York, and graduated from Erasmus High School. She studied for a musical career, but her brother-in-law, Ralph Ince, was a director at Vitagraph Pictures, and he convinced Stewart to try her hand at acting. She followed her older sister, Lucille, to New York and appeared in several films before her first major role in *The Wood Violet* (1912), directed by Ince and written especially for her. She did several more films with Ince, including the very successful serial *The Goddess* (1915). Other Vitagraph pictures include *The Daring of Diana* (1916) and *The Girl Philippa* (1916). In late 1917, Stewart broke her contract and signed with then fledgling producer Louis B. Mayer. Vitagraph sued, and received an injunction against both Stewart and Mayer. The suit was eventually resolved, and Stewart moved to First National and appeared in *Virtuous Wives* (1918) with William Boyd, *A Midnight Romance* (1919) with Jack Holt, and *Mary Regan* (1919), the latter two pictures being directed by Lois Weber, one of the first silent-era women directors.

A self-imposed retirement in 1922 lasted four years, and she returned in the Fox production *Rustling for Cupid* (1926). She retired from acting for good in 1928, without ever having appeared in a feature-length talking picture (although she appears in the 1932 short, *The Hollywood Handicap*). Her first marriage, to actor Rudolph Cameron, ended in divorce. Her second marriage, to millionaire businessman George Peabody Converse, also ended in divorce. She retired to a modest home in Beverly Hills that she shared with her sister, Lucille. On May 4, 1961, Stewart's body was discovered in her bedroom by her sister. The press reported that she had died from a heart attack, and her sister confirmed the story, but Stewart's death certificate lists the cause of death as "probably suicide" from an overdose of barbiturates. The exact nature of Stewart's death remains contested.

Lilyan Tashman

Born October 23, 1896
Died March 21, 1934

Known as "the best dressed woman of the screen," glamorous Lilyan Tashman excelled at playing ultra-sophisticated vamps in featured roles. "I'd far rather play the vamp role than the heroines," she once told an interviewer. "Men prefer charm to sweetness any day … and charm is the vamp's big stock in trade. It is a quality she simply must possess, if she is to lure the conventional hubby away from his peaceful fireside."

She was born in Brooklyn, New York, the youngest of seven sisters. Many sources list her birth year as 1899, although it was more likely closer to 1896, as listed in the 1900 New York Census. A popular story says that she was discovered one day while having tea at New York's Café de Paris. A man approached her table and said, "Mr. Ziegfeld would like to see you." She thought it was a practical joke, and responded, "If Mr. Ziegfeld wants to see me, tell him to come over to my table." Moments later, Flo Ziegfeld was standing at her side. He cast her in his Ziegfeld Follies in 1918, and she stuck with it for two years, working with future stars Marion Davies, Ina Claire, Eddie Cantor, and Billy Dove. (In reality, Tashman probably auditioned for Ziegfeld like many other young actresses at the time.) It was during this period that she met and fell in love with actor Edmund Lowe, and they married in 1925.

She left the Follies for the stage, and appeared in several memorable performances, including as a showgirl in *The Garden of Weeds* and *Gold Diggers*.

ABOVE Lilyan Tashman remains unmoved by the sweet nothings whispered in her ear by Richard "Skeets" Gallagher in Up Pops the Devil *(1931).*

Tashman made her screen debut in *Experience* (1921), then appeared in several small roles in films like *Head Over Heels* (1922) and *Manhandled* (1924) before director James Cruze picked her to reprise her role in Paramount's production of *The Garden of Weeds* (1924). She appeared with her husband, Lowe, the following year in *Ports of Call* (1925). She would go on to appear in 67 films, including *Bulldog Drummond* (1929), *Murder by the Clock* (1931), *The Road to Reno* (1931), *The Wiser Sex* (1932), and *Too Much Harmony* (1933) with Bing Crosby.

In 1933, she finally won her first important starring role, in *Wine, Women and Song*, and the film premiered at a Broadway theater on March 27, 1933, but Tashman was too sick to attend. She became ill from cancer during the production of *Frankie and Johnnie* (1936) in early 1934. When shooting ended, she had surgery to remove a brain tumor, but died in the hospital at the age of 37. *Frankie and Johnnie* was released two years later in 1936.

Estelle Taylor

Born May 20, 1894
Died April 15, 1958

E stelle Taylor was considered one of the most beautiful women of silent movies, gained notoriety with her marriage to boxing legend Jack Dempsey, and success-fully made the transition to sound films. During her 25-year career, she appeared in several important films, including Cecil B. DeMille's *The Ten Commandments* (1923).

She was born in Wilmington, Delaware, on May 20. Although most sources list her birth year as 1899, it's likely closer to 1894, as listed on her death certificate and the 1900 New York Census. Her father abandoned the family when Taylor was still a baby, and she was raised by her mother and grandmother. Both strenuously objected to her choice of an acting career, but she managed to get herself enrolled at Sargent's Dramatic School in New York. She was a hit in her New York stage debut, *Come On, Charlie*, and was quickly hired by Famous Players-Lasky as a double for Dorothy Dalton. She then made her screen debut in *The Golden Shower* (1919) for Vitagraph, and followed with the female lead in *The Adventurer* (1920) for Fox. Another leading turn in *While New York Sleeps* (1920) cemented her arrival.

In 1925, she gained even greater fame when she married former heavyweight champion Jack Dempsey. They appeared together in *Manhattan Madness* (1925), and on Broadway in *The Big Fight*. It was apparent from the start, however, that they weren't a good match. Lurid details of their contentious separation and divorce dominated headlines in 1931. It was widely reported that Taylor's dedication to her acting career led to the dissolution of the marriage. Taylor appeared in over 40 pictures, often playing the vamp or other woman, a part she excelled at. Highlights of her career include *Don Juan* (1926) with Warner Oland and John Barrymore, a

cameo in King Vidor's *Show People* (1928) with Marion Davies, Tod Browning's *Where East is East* (1929) with Lon Chaney, Vidor's *Street Scene* (1931), and *Cimarron* (1931). Her last film was Jean Renoir's *The Southerner* (1945).

After she retired from the silver screen, Taylor turned her attention to another great love—animal wel-fare. She was a strong advocate for the humane treatment of pets, and the founder and president of the California Pet Owners' Protective League. In late 1957, Taylor was diagnosed with cancer. She suc-cumbed to the disease on April 15, 1958, at her home in Los Angeles, and was buried at the Hollywood Forever Cemetery.

ABOVE Estelle Taylor in 1926. Her portrayal of Lucrezia Borgia in Don Juan (1926) is the role for which she is best remembered.

Star Shot

Estelle Taylor was the last person to see actress Lupe Velez alive. Velez committed suicide on December 13, 1944.

LEFT Director Wesley Ruggles takes film tests of actors Estelle Taylor (left), Richard Dix, and Irene Dunne, in prep-aration for shooting Cimarron (1931).

Robert Taylor

Born August 5, 1911
Died June 8, 1969

Robert Taylor was "The Man With the Perfect Profile," MGM's "New King" after Clark Gable left the studio, and for a dozen or so years, "Mr. Barbara Stanwyck." He was strikingly handsome, which helped him break into Hollywood in the early years. His good looks might also have made it difficult for critics to take him seriously, although complaints of Taylor's limited range as an actor were common. Regardless, he enjoyed enormous popularity with audiences throughout his career.

He was born Spangler Arlington Brugh on August 5, 1911, in Filley, Nebraska. His mother struggled with poor health all her life. Taylor's father, Spangler Andrew Brugh, was the manager of a grain elevator. When doctors could not cure his wife, Brugh enrolled in a medical program at the American School of Osteopathy, graduating in 1916. The family then moved to Beatrice, Nebraska, the next year, and Brugh practiced osteopathy and searched for a cure to alleviate his wife's illness. Taylor initially aspired to a career in music, beginning piano lessons at the age of ten, and cello lessons at 14. He studied the latter at Doane College in Crete, Nebraska, performing with the Doane Symphony Orchestra, and in the Doane String Quartet. He made his stage debut in December 1929 in a Doane College production. After two years, Taylor followed his cello professor to Pomona College in Claremont, California. It was there that he solidified his aspirations for a career in theater, and during a production of *Journey's End* in December 1932, was discovered by an MGM talent scout and offered a screen test. The studio signed him soon thereafter, and changed his name to Robert Taylor. He was loaned out to Fox for his first credited role in *Handy Andy* (1934), a Will Rogers comedy, then placed in a number of B-grade movies like *A Wicked Woman* (1934) and *Times Square Lady* (1935). His big break came with two films in 1935: *Broadway Melody of 1936* (1935) and the stirring melodrama *Magnificent Obsession* (1935). Both films raised his profile, but it was the latter that made him a star.

Taylor soon became a solid romantic lead, appearing opposite Janet Gaynor in *Small Town Girl* (1936), Barbara Stanwyck in *His Brother's Wife* (1936), Joan Crawford in *The Gorgeous Hussy* (1936), Greta Garbo in *Camille* (1936), Jean Harlow in her last full performance in *Personal Property* (1937), and with Stanwyck again in *This is My Affair* (1937). Zeppo Marx introduced Taylor to Stanwyck before *His Brother's Wife*, and by the end of shooting, the two were engaged in a discreet romance. They were married in 1939, although rumors circulated that both Taylor and Stanwyck were gay and that the marriage was for publicity purposes only. They divorced in 1951.

Other memorable motion pictures include *Broadway Melody of 1938* (1937) and *A Yank at Oxford* (1938), with Maureen O'Sullivan and Vivien Leigh. Taylor battled Franchot Tone and Robert Young for the love of Margaret Sullavan in Frank Borzage's *Three Comrades* (1938), and appeared with Hedy Lamarr in *Lady of the Tropics* (1939). There were reports of an affair between Taylor and Lana Turner during the filming of *Johnny Eager* (1942), causing a brief break with Stanwyck. In 1943, Taylor entered the Navy and served for two years. After his discharge, his roles got darker, and he played the mentally disturbed husband of Katharine Hepburn in Vincente Minnelli's *Undercurrent* (1946), a neurotic in *The High Wall* (1947), and a homicidal communist opposite Elizabeth Taylor in *Conspirator* (1949). Taylor made waves when he enthusiastically listed the names of fellow actors whom he believed to be communists while testifying before the House Committee on Un-American Activities in 1947. In 1950, he gave perhaps his best performance as a Native American in the period piece *Devil's Doorway*, then appeared as Marcus Vinicius in the hugely successful *Quo Vadis* (1951). In 1954, he married German-born actress Ursula Thiess.

ABOVE Franchot Tone (left) with his wife, Joan Crawford (second from left), at a nightclub with Barbara Stanwyck and Robert Taylor in 1940.

Although MGM kept his contract for 25 years, Robert Taylor's movie roles generally declined in quality during the 1950s. Some of the more memorable later pictures include *Ivanhoe* (1952), Nicholas Ray's *Party Girl* (1958), and *The Night Walker* (1964) with ex-wife Stanwyck. He also starred in his own television series, *The Detectives Starring Robert Taylor*, for several seasons beginning in 1959. In 1968, he went to Europe and made several unimportant films, one of which, *Hot Line* (1968), would be the last of his career. That year, after the removal of one of his lungs due to coccidiomycosis, Taylor discovered that he was suffering from lung cancer. He struggled with the disease for ten months, finally succumbing on June 8, 1969, at Saint John's Hospital in Santa Monica. California governor Ronald Reagan delivered the eulogy at Taylor's funeral. He is buried at Forest Lawn Memorial Park located in Glendale, California.

Star Shot

To prepare for his role in *Billy the Kid* (1941), Robert Taylor, who was right-handed, practiced drawing a gun with his left hand.

LEFT Robert Taylor played the title role in Ivanhoe *(1952), opposite Elizabeth Taylor. The film was based on the classic novel by Sir Walter Scott.*

Irving Thalberg

Born May 30, 1899
Died September 14, 1936

Star Shot

American novelist F. Scott Fitzgerald based the character of Monroe Stahr, hero of *The Last Tycoon*, on Irving Thalberg.

I rving Thalberg was Hollywood's "boy wonder," the "miracle man of the pic industry," and quite possibly, the most brilliant producer in Hollywood history. His name is legendary in the motion picture world. He was born in Brooklyn, New York, the son of a German Jewish lace importer. He was born with cyanosis and a congenital heart defect, and doctors said it was unlikely that he would live beyond 30 years of age. Knowing his time was short, he eschewed college and at 19 took a job as Carl Laemmle's personal assistant at Universal. He was promoted to general manager of the Studio at 20, and quickly made a name for himself by humbling Erich von Stroheim during the production of *Foolish Wives* (1922). Thalberg actually dismissed von Stroheim from *Merry-Go-Round* (1923) the following year. A sharp eye for talent led him to promote Lon Chaney in *The Hunchback of Notre Dame* (1923).

Louis B. Mayer lured him to his company in 1923, and he became production chief of MGM when it was formed by the merger of Mayer, Metro, and Goldwyn. There, Irving Thalberg battled von Stroheim again, demanding that *Greed* (1924) be cut down from its original massive length. He made MGM a first-rate studio, overseeing the production of numerous classics, including *Ben-Hur* (1925), *The Merry Widow* (1925), *The Big Parade* (1925), *The Crowd* (1928), *The Broadway Melody* (1929), *Anna Christie* (1930), and *Freaks* (1932). In 1927, Thalberg married Norma Shearer, and until his death, the two were one of Hollywood's great power couples. Thalberg is credited with guiding Shearer's career to six Oscar® nominations, including a Best Actress win in 1929, although Shearer's talent as an actress obviously also played a part.

Thalberg suffered from poor health his whole life, and in 1932 he had a heart attack. While recuperating in Europe, Mayer replaced him at MGM. Although his duties were reduced upon his return, he continued overseeing several film classics, including *The Barretts of Wimpole Street* (1934), *Mutiny on the Bounty* (1935), *A Night at the Opera* (1935),

and *Romeo and Juliet* (1936). Thalberg never took a screen credit on his productions, and it was only on *The Good Earth*, released posthumously in 1937, that his name appears onscreen. On Labor Day, 1936, Thalberg contracted a cold that quickly developed into a bad case of pneumonia. Weakened by his heart condition, he died from the pneumonia on the morning of September 14 at the age of 37. The following day, MGM suspended all activities for 24 hours in tribute. The entire motion picture industry ceased activity for five minutes at the start of Thalberg's funeral. The following year, the Academy of Motion Picture Arts and Sciences introduced the Irving Thalberg Award, which honors high achievement in production.

Tom Tyler

Born August 9, 1903
Died May 1, 1954

O ver his 30-year motion picture career, Tom Tyler found fame as a cowboy in silent westerns, portrayed the first comic book superhero of film, and finished his career in bit roles.

He was born Vincent Markowski in Port Henry, New York. Ironically, it was his rugged, athletic physique that gave him an entry into film. A former boxer and champion weightlifter (he reportedly held the world's weightlifting championship for 14 years), Tom Tyler found work as an extra in the early 1920s, including in *Ben-Hur* (1925), starring Ramon Novarro and Francis X. Bushman. He was signed to FBO Studios (the predecessor of RKO) and put to work in low-budget, silent westerns. His first starring role came in *Let's Go Gallagher* (1925), and he would make over 30 more films with FBO, many co-starring Frankie Darro as his diminutive sidekick. In 1929, Tyler moved to Syndicate Pictures, where he made his first talking film, the serial *The Phantom of the West* (1931). He worked with a speech coach to hide his slight Lithuanian accent, and successfully made the transition to talking pictures.

More westerns followed for several studios, including Syndicate, Universal, Monogram, and Reliable. Highlights include *The Cherokee Kid* (1927), *West of Cheyenne* (1931), and the serial *Battling with Buffalo Bill* (1931). In 1939, he portrayed John Wayne's adversary in John Ford's *Stagecoach*. By the late 1930s, starring roles were beginning to dry up for him. He appeared in minor roles in *Gone with the Wind* (1939), John Ford's *The Grapes of Wrath* (1940), and George Stevens's *The Talk of the Town* (1942). In 1941, Tyler's career was reborn when he portrayed Captain Marvel in the Republic Pictures' serial, *Adventures of Captain Marvel* (1941). Marvel was the very first comic superhero portrayed on the screen, and Tyler was again a star. He followed with another superhero role in the Republic serial, *The Phantom* (1943). He also portrayed "Stony Brooke" in 12 of Republic's *Three Mesquiteers* westerns.

Things turned bad for Tyler when he developed, in the early 1940s, a severe rheumatoid arthritis condition, making it difficult for him to act; it eventually crippled him. In addition, changing tastes limited the prospects of low-budget westerns. Tyler appeared in minor parts, often as "baddies," in the late 1940s and early 1950s, including John Ford's classic *Red River* (1948). In 1953, he moved to Hamtramck, Michigan, to live with his sister, and died there of a heart attack the following year at the age of 50.

BELOW Tom Tyler appears as the menacing mummy in the 1940 cult classic, The Mummy's Hand. He made over 200 films, but because he worked for only the smaller studios, Tyler never made much money.

*RIGHT In his youth,
Robert Urich was a tal-
ented football player.
He is pictured here on
the field at Florida State
University in 1965.*

Robert Urich

Born December 19, 1946
Died April 16, 2002

RIGHT In his youth, Robert Urich was a talented football player. He is pictured here on the field at Florida State University in 1965.

Robert Urich is best known for portraying the suave, sophisticated private investigator of television's *Spenser: For Hire* (1985), but he was a ubiquitous presence on American television from the early 1970s until his death in 2002, holding the record for having starred in 15 television series, more than any other actor.

Urich was born the son of Slovakian immigrants in Toronto, Ohio, a small steel mill town. He was raised a strict Catholic, and at one time considered becoming a priest. The ruggedly built, 6-foot, 2-inch (2 m) Urich was a natural athlete, good enough to win a four-year football scholarship to attend Florida State University. Any aspirations for a professional career in football were dispelled when an injury sidelined him during his senior year. Urich then hosted his own weekly television program at Florida State, and graduated with a bachelor's degree in radio and television communications. He then earned a master of arts degree in broadcast research and management from Michigan State University. Urich soon moved to Chicago and worked briefly as a television weatherman, and as an account executive for WGN radio. While at WGN, he was hired to play a young soldier for one night during a Jewish bond drive, and immediately fell in love with acting. He also lost his job at WGN when the company enforced its policy against moonlighting. Community theater soon followed, and then Urich got his big break when he was cast as Burt Reynolds's younger brother in a stage production of *The Rainmaker*. After the production, Reynolds persuaded Urich to move to Hollywood and pursue acting.

Urich made his television debut in September 1973 in the short-lived sitcom, *Bob & Carol & Ted & Alice*, then made his film debut the same year, playing bad cop Mike Grimes in *Magnum Force* (1973), the sequel to *Dirty Harry* (1971). Urich would not return to the big screen for nearly a decade, finding fame and fortune on television. In 1975, he landed the role of Officer Jim Sweet on ABC's popular *S.W.A.T.*, and appeared in 34 episodes from February 1975 through June 1976. In 1977, he appeared as tennis instructor Peter Campbell on ABC's *Soap*, but the character was unfortunately short-lived. He then appeared

LEFT In 1997, Robert Urich hosted a television series, Vital Signs, *that showed reenactments of real-life medical conditions, the patients who suffered them, and the doctors who treated them.*

opposite Lisa Hartman in *Tabitha* (1977), before receiving the role that would make him a star, as private detective Dan Tanna in *Vega$* (1978). The show ran for three seasons, and Urich became a household name. He appeared in several made-for-television movies, and the pictures *Endangered Species* (1982) and *The Ice Pirates* (1984), before being cast as another private investigator, this time in the Boston-based series, *Spenser: For Hire* (1985). The series was based on Robert B. Parker's popular mystery novels, and ran for three seasons. The role brought Urich even greater fame, and he would later reprise it in several television movies in the 1990s, including *Spenser: Ceremony* (1993), *Spenser: Pale Kings and Princes* (1994), *Spenser: The Judas Goat* (1994), and *Spenser: A Savage Place* (1995).

In 1996, he was diagnosed with synovial cell sarcoma, a rare form of cancer that attacks the joints. The cancer was initially discovered in his groin, but after undergoing chemotherapy, radiation treatment, and two surgeries, the cancer went into remission. Robert Urich continued working on television during much of his treatment, telling Amy Arched, "I had chemo at 8 A.M. and at 5 P.M. I was doing stand-up before a live audience. And I underwent major surgery on a Wednesday and was at work a few days after, with blood trickling down my leg." In 2000, Urich sued Castle Rock Television, claiming that they had cancelled his series *The Lazarus Man* (1996) and refused to pay him because he had cancer. The two parties settled out of court.

ABOVE Robert Urich (center) with Phil Morris and Joan Severance in Love Boat: The Next Wave. Urich played Captain Jim Kennedy from 1998 to 1999.

Other feature films include *Turk 182!* (1985), *The Angel of Pennsylvania Avenue* (1996), and *Clover Bend* (2001). Some of his other television credits include *It Had to be You* (1993) with Faye Dunaway, *Love Boat: The Next Wave* (1998), *Aftermath* (2001), and *Emeril* (2001). His final television movie, *Night of the Wolf* (2002), aired on Animal Planet the night before his death. Urich married twice: in 1968 to actress Barbara Rucker (they divorced in 1974), and in 1975 to actress Heather Menzies, who played Louisa von Trapp in *The Sound of Music* (1965). The couple established the Heather and Robert Urich Foundation for Sarcoma Research at the University of Michigan Comprehensive Cancer Center. Urich was also the recipient of the Gilda Radner Courage Award from the Roswell Park Cancer Institute, and was named the American Cancer Society national spokesman in 1998. In 2002, the cancer returned, and in early April he was hospitalized at the Los Robles Regional Medical Center in Thousand Oaks, California. He died there on April 16, 2002, at the age of 55. His funeral at St. Charles Borromeo Catholic Church in North Hollywood was attended by nearly 1,000 mourners.

LEFT Robert Urich at the Family Film Awards in 1996. Urich and Heather Menzies had three children: Ryan, Emily, and Allison. Menzies is a survivor of ovarian cancer.

Rudolph Valentino

Born May 6, 1895
Died August 23, 1926

Rudolph Valentino became a twentieth-century icon in spite of the fact that his career lasted little more than seven years. His exotic looks, smoldering and hypnotic glances, and unusual combination of machismo and androgyny ushered changing images of masculinity to the screen, much to the delight of swooning female audiences, and the contempt of some men, who questioned his sexuality and attacked his "prettiness." One famous article published in the *Chicago Tribune* a few weeks before his death characterized Valentino as a "pink powder puff" and a "painted pansy." Rumors of his sexual attraction to men, including a purported affair with fellow screen legend Ramon Novarro, have done little to affect his immortalization as Hollywood's first male sex symbol.

He was born Rodolfo Alfonzo Raffaelo Pierre Filibert Guglielmi di Valentina d'Antonguolla in Castellaneta, Italy, in 1895, the middle child of a veterinarian father and French schoolteacher mother. He did poorly at an agricultural school, later moving to Paris, where he learned to dance and party among the gay and bohemian subcultures. When the money ran out, he returned home to Castellaneta, then set sail for New York on December 9, 1913, his second-class fare paid by his mother. He was a gardener and a busboy before finding work as a taxi-dancer at Maxim's Restaurant. Rumors have persisted that he also worked as a gigolo. He also found himself enmeshed in several society scandals, and decided to head further west. He toured with a production of the musical *The Masked Marvel*, and continued on to San Francisco when the production folded in Utah. Soon he was living in Los Angeles, searching for work as an extra. Early pictures include *Alimony* (1917), *A Society Sensation* (1918), and *The Married Virgin* (1918).

On November 5, 1919, he married actress Jean Acker, but the marriage reportedly lasted only six hours, and Valentino was barred from the bedroom on their wedding night. Acker later stated that it had been a terrible mistake, and their divorce was finalized in 1922. It has been widely reported that Acker was a lesbian, and was the long-time lover of actress Alla Nazimova. Meanwhile, Valentino was finding work in bit roles as heavies, but not in romantic leads. It was screenwriter June Mathis who saw Valentino in 1919's *Eyes of Youth* and realized

that he would be perfect for the role of hero Julio Desnoyers in Metro's *The Four Horsemen of the Apocalypse* (1921). She convinced Metro to give him the role, and it made Valentino an overnight sensation. Alla Nazimova then reportedly chose Valentino to play her love interest in *Camille* (1921). He followed with the romance, *The Sheik* (1921), then played a matador in *Blood and Sand* (1922). Both were tremendously well-received by audiences.

During the shooting of *Camille*, Nazimova introduced Valentino to her friend (and purported lover) Natacha Rambova (born Winifred Shaughnessy). Valentino and Rambova hit it off, and in May 1922, they eloped to Mexicali, Mexico, not realizing that Valentino's divorce from Acker had not yet been finalized. Valentino was arrested for bigamy upon his return to Los Angeles, and spent several hours in prison. The charges were later dismissed, and the couple legally married in March 1923. Much has been written about the domineering Rambova, and rumors that theirs was a "lavender marriage." It is clear that Rambova took control of Valentino's career, alienating his relationship with studio executives, and making his onscreen image more effeminate in such box-office bombs as *Monsieur Beaucaire* (1924), *A Sainted Devil* (1924), and *Cobra* (1925). Rambova left him, and he began dating Pola Negri, possibly in an attempt to reassert his romantic image.

Valentino did better with *The Eagle* (1925), then was in the throes of a full-fledged comeback with *The Son of the Sheik* (1926), when on August 16, 1926, he collapsed and was admitted to New York's Polyclinic Hospital. He underwent surgery for a perforated gastric ulcer, but died a week later from peritonitis and septicemia. His death at the age of 31 sparked a national frenzy of mourning, and thousands turned out for ceremonies in New York and Los Angeles to pay tribute to the star. Newspapers reported several suicides purportedly inspired by Valentino's death, and legend has it that to this day, a mysterious "lady in black" shows up every year on the anniversary of Valentino's death at his grave at Hollywood Forever Cemetery.

It has been often speculated that the advent of sound would have brought an early demise to Valentino's career if he had lived, given his thick Italian accent and an acting style that might have been better suited to the exaggerated pantomime of silent cinema. Instead, he died at the peak of his fame, still beautiful, and it's that iconic image of him that has kept his legend alive for the more than three-quarters of a century since his death.

Star Shot

Because he died in debt, screenwriter June Mathis "lent" Valentino a space in her family crypt. His remains are still there, along with those of Mathis.

LEFT In one of his first films, Alimony *(1917), Rudolph Valentino earned only $5 per day. The "Latin lover" went on to become Hollywood's greatest star of the 1920s.*

Conrad Veidt

Born January 22, 1893
Died April 3, 1943

During a career that spanned four decades, Conrad Veidt was the man the world loved to hate. A talented character actor, adept at playing suave, sinister villains, Veidt is perhaps best remembered as the chilling Nazi, Colonel Strasser, in *Casablanca* (1942). He also received worldwide acclaim as Cesare the sleepwalker in the German expressionist masterpiece, *The Cabinet of Dr. Caligari* (1920). In addition to these two classics, Veidt appeared in over 100 films produced in Germany, England, France, and Hollywood.

He was born in Potsdam, near Berlin, Germany, in 1893, and was one of a group of actors trained by influential director and producer Max Reinhardt. Veidt's first acting role was on stage in the Reinhardt production of *The Sea Battle* (1917). He began appearing in films, specializing in demoniacal, tormented characters. By the end of 1926, he had performed in over 70 German films, including *Dr. Caligari*, and was well-known around the world. When John Barrymore invited him to come to the United States to play Louis XI in Barrymore's *The Beloved Rogue* (1927), Veidt jumped at the chance. He stayed in Hollywood for several more films, including *A Man's Past* (1927) and *The Man Who Laughs* (1928), but decided to return to Germany with the advent of sound pictures there. When the Nazis came to power, Veidt, who was of Jewish descent, fled to Austria, then settled in England. He became a British subject in 1938. Films during this period include *Rome Express* (1932), *I Was a Spy* (1933), *The Wandering Jew* (1933), and *Dark Journey* (1937) with Vivien Leigh. In 1940, he made an impression as Jaffar in Alexander Korda's *The Thief of Bagdad* (1940), the only color picture Veidt appeared in. That same year, Veidt returned to Hollywood, where he found great success playing more villainous roles, often Nazis, in *Escape* (1940), opposite Norma Shearer; *Nazi Agent* (1942); and, of course, *Casablanca* (1942). His final role was in *Above Suspicion* (1943), opposite Joan Crawford.

On April 3, 1943, Veidt was playing a game of golf with MGM producer Arthur Field at the Riviera Country Club in Hollywood. As he reached the eighth hole, Veidt paused, gasped, and collapsed to the ground. His personal physician, Dr. Joseph Bergman, happened to be playing on the same course, and was quickly called to his side. But it was too late; Conrad Veidt had suffered a massive heart attack, and Bergman pronounced him dead at the scene. He was 50 years old.

ABOVE Conrad Veidt and Mary Philbin in The Man Who Laughs *(1928). The film was based on the novel by great French writer Victor Hugo.*

RIGHT Conrad Veidt starred as the evil Jaffar in The Thief of Bagdad *(1940). Veidt married three times, and had one child, a daughter named Viola, born in 1925.*

Vera-Ellen

Born February 16, 1921
Died August 30, 1981

Vera-Ellen was known as the "female Fred Astaire," a one-name, hyphenated, dancing sensation in the 1940s and 1950s. She was equally adept at tap, toe, acrobatic, and dramatic dancing, and graced the dance floor with Gene Kelly, Fred Astaire, Danny Kaye, and others.

She was born Vera-Ellen Westmeyer Rohe in Cincinnati, Ohio. The year of her birth is contested as either 1921 or 1926. The hyphen in her name was the result of a dream her mother had in which she saw the name "Vera-Ellen" shining brightly in lights on a marquee. Vera-Ellen was a frail youngster, and her parents enrolled her in dance school in order to build up her body. She showed exceptional ability as a dancer, and in her mid-teens she left for New York to pursue a dancing career. She worked as a member of the renowned Rockettes troupe before making her Broadway debut in the 1939 musical, *Very Warm in May*. She also performed in *Higher and Higher*, Cole Porter's *Panama Hattie*, and *By Jupiter* opposite Ray Bolger, before catching the eye of Samuel Goldwyn in 1943. Goldwyn brought her to Hollywood and teamed her with Danny Kaye in *Wonder Man* (1945). She then danced with Gene Kelly in *Words and Music* (1948), making an impression in the spectacular "Slaughter on Tenth Avenue" number. Other films included *On the Town* (1949), with Gene Kelly and Frank Sinatra; *Three Little Words* (1950) and *The Belle of New York* (1952), both with Fred Astaire; and *Call Me Madam* (1953), with Donald O'Connor. In 1954 she made the classic *White Christmas*, which co-starred Bing Crosby, and in 1957 she appeared in her last motion picture, *Let's Be Happy*.

Vera-Ellen struggled with anorexia nervosa her entire life, and it led to premature aging and other serious health problems, including crippling arthritis, which led to her early retirement. Her personal life was also troubled. Her first marriage, to dancing partner Robert Hightower in 1945, ended in divorce. Her second, to millionaire Victor Rothschild in 1954, also ended in divorce, shortly after the death of their only child at the age of three months. In her later years, she became something of a recluse, rarely leaving her Hollywood Hills home, although she did continue to attend dancing classes until her death. By 1981, Vera-Ellen was struggling with cancer. She succumbed to the disease on August 30, 1981, at UCLA Medical Center. Most obituaries listed her age as 55, but the earlier birth year would have made her 60.

ABOVE Bing Crosby, Rosemary Clooney, Vera-Ellen, and Danny Kaye sing and dance in the classic musical White Christmas, *released in 1954.*

Star Shot

The dance sequences for Vera-Ellen in *Carnival in Costa Rica* (1947) were choreographed by famed Russian dancer-choreographer Léonide Massine.

Bobby Vernon

Born March 9, 1897
Died June 28, 1939

In the early part of the twentieth century, Bobby Vernon was a reliably popular star of slapstick short films, but the advent of talking pictures brought an end to his acting career. Today his memory stays alive in large part due to his many film appearances opposite screen legend Gloria Swanson while both were under contract at Keystone.

Vernon was born Sylvion de Jardin on March 9, 1897, in Chicago, Illinois. His parents were famous acting couple Harry Burns and Dorothy Vernon, each a veteran of both the stage and screen. The family moved to San Francisco when Bobby was young, and he was exposed to the theater from an early age. He made his stage debut at the age of 11 while working as a call boy for the comedy team Kolb and Dill. When Max Dill broke his leg during the production run of *The Rollicking Girl*, Vernon was brought on as a substitute. He moved to Long Beach in 1913 and made his film debut in Universal's Joker

ABOVE Bobby Vernon (right, in uniform) in Back from the Front *(1920). Vernon was popular with both audiences and critics.*

Comedies, including *The Tramp Dentists* (1913), *Mike and Jake Among the Cannibals* (1913), *The Joy Riders* (1913), and with Lon Chaney in *Almost an Actress* (1913). Hal Roach directed him in *The Hungry Actors* (1915), and Roscoe "Fatty" Arbuckle directed him in *Fatty and the Broadway Stars* (1915). The latter was the first film Vernon did after moving over to Mack Sennett's Keystone Film Company. Sennett paired Vernon with Gloria Swanson in a series of romantic comedies, partly because both were diminutive in stature—Vernon was only 5 feet, 2 inches (1.57 m) and Swanson was 4 feet, 11½ inches (1.5 m). They first appeared together in *The Danger Girl* (1916), and appeared in nine more comedies altogether, most notably in *Teddy at the Throttle* (1917), which co-starred both Wallace Beery (Swanson's first husband—there would be six) and Teddy, an enormous Great Dane.

Vernon joined the Navy during World War I, then returned to Hollywood to pick up his film career, signing with the Al Christie Film Company, where he went on to make dozens of comedy shorts between 1918 and 1929. During that time, he married and fathered a daughter named Barbara Vernon. Although he appeared in several talking pictures in 1932, the transition didn't go well, and he retired from acting later that year. In 1934 he went to work as a writer and comedy supervisor at Paramount Pictures, and was involved in several W. C. Fields and Bing Crosby films. He died at the age of 42 from a heart attack.

Star Shot

When the Hollywood Chamber of Commerce finally installed a star for Bobby Vernon on the "Walk of Fame" in 1961, it misspelled his first name as "Bobbie."

RIGHT Bobby Vernon and Claire Seymour in the Al Christie comedy Pearls and a Peach *(1921). Bobby Vernon appeared in more than 130 shorts and films.*

Deborah Walley

Born August 12, 1943
Died May 10, 2001

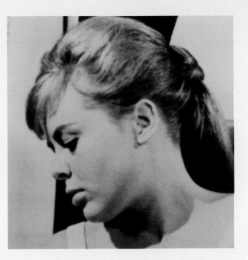

Deborah Walley became famous playing Gidget, and her petite size—just 5 feet, 2 inches (1.57 m) tall—and perky disposition made the spunky redhead perfect for the "boy-meets-girl" bikini-beach pictures of the early 1960s that featured big hairdos, small swimsuits, and lots of sand. Walley was a versatile actress, and after her Hollywood career ended, appeared often on the stage, became an accomplished producer and author, and founded two children's theater production companies.

She was born in Connecticut to ice-skating stars and choreographers Nathan and Edith Walley. She began her show business career ice skating at the age of three, but turned to acting by her teens, studying at New York's Academy of Dramatic Arts. By age 14 she was performing in summer stock productions, making her stage debut in a production of *Charley's Aunt*. She secured an agent, John Harvey, who secured her a toothpaste commercial and the part of an orphan on the television movie *Route 66* in 1960. Columbia executive Joyce Selznick spotted her in an off-Broadway production of Chekhov's *Three Sisters* and awarded her the starring role in Columbia's sequel to *Gidget* (1959), *Gidget Goes Hawaiian* (1961). The original "Gidget," Sandra Dee, had inconveniently married actor and singer Bobby Darin. Walley was named Photoplay Magazine's Most Popular Actress in 1961.

The following year, Walley appeared in Disney's *Bon Voyage!* (1962). The same year, she married actor John Ashley, but the marriage ended in divorce in 1966. Other movies include *Summer Magic* (1963), *The Young Lovers* (1964), the classic *Beach Blanket Bingo* (1965), *Ski Party* (1965) with Frankie Avalon, *Spinout* (1966) with Elvis Presley, *The Ghost in the Invisible Bikini* (1966), and *It's a Bikini World* (1967). Her last feature film was 1974's *Benji*. Other work included a co-starring role as Eve Arden's daughter in television's *The Mothers-In-Law*, which ran from 1967 to 1969. Walley also acted in a number of off-Broadway shows and for one season with New York's Shakespeare Repertory Company. Other guest appearances in television shows included *Gomer Pyle, U.S.M.C.*, and *The Virginian*.

In 1991, Walley moved to Sedona, Arizona, and co-founded the Sedona Children's Theater. She also co-founded the Swiftwind Theater Company to train Native Americans in film acting and production. In 1989, she wrote and produced an award-winning short film, *The Vision of Seeks-to-Hunt-Great* (1989), about a boy tracking a mountain lion. She also wrote a popular children's book, *Grandfather's Good Medicine*. On May 10, 2001, Walley died of esophageal cancer at her home in Sedona, Arizona, at the age of 57.

ABOVE Although Deborah Walley welcomed the role of Gidget, she also said that accepting it meant "that part of my dream of being a serious actress was over."

Star Shot

As well as performing in live-action films, Deborah Walley also provided the voices for a number of Disney characters, including three of the creatures in 1989's *Chip 'n' Dale Rescue Rangers*.

Star Shot

Pearl White's second husband mysteriously disappeared just weeks after their divorce in 1921, and later turned up in a sanitarium. In 1928, his pockets reportedly full of clippings about White, he shot himself.

Pearl White

Born March 4, 1889
Died August 4, 1938

BELOW Pearl White epitomized the feisty, daredevil heroine of the silent serials. Sheer adventure, along with death-defying stunts, ensured the lasting popularity of the serials.

Pearl White was an enthusiastic, daring, and generous star of early serials, legendary for never using a stunt double, for never visiting Hollywood, and for retiring to Paris with a small fortune. She was born in a pine shack in Green Ridge, Missouri. Her mother died during White's delivery, and her father raised her and her eight siblings. When White was seven, she made her stage debut in her hometown, filling in for a sick "Little Eva" in a traveling production of *Uncle Tom's Cabin*. She reportedly joined a circus at the age of 13 as a trapeze apprentice, but left when she injured herself in a fall. As a teen, she worked with stock companies in Springfield, Missouri, and Memphis, Tennessee, then landed her first film job with New York's Powers Company, making $5 a day to work in one-reelers. She moved on to Philadelphia's Lubin Company, but soon returned to New York, then signed a long-term contract with Pathé, reportedly earning $1,750 a week. She had already appeared in over 150 shorts and serials when she starred in Pathé's *The Perils of Pauline* (1914). The serial was a huge smash, and White became a star. There were 20 *Pauline* episodes, each a stand-alone story complete with murderous villains, hard-charging adventures, and exciting cliffhanger endings. The Hearst papers even ran novelized newspaper versions of Pauline's adventures.

The stunts were dangerous, but White considered them part of her job. In one famous stunt gone wrong, the anchor to a gas balloon was mistakenly released during filming. White soared to over 4,000 feet (1,200 m) above Manhattan before landing, and she once fell down a flight of stairs during a fight scene. She moved to Fox in 1919, and appeared in *The White Moll* (1920), *The Tiger's Club* (1920), *The Thief* (1920), *The Mountain Woman* (1921), *Any Wife* (1922), *Without Fear* (1922), and her last serial, *Plunder* (1923), with Pathé. In December 1922, White sailed for France, where she made her final film, *Terreur* (also known as *The Perils of Paris*, released in 1924). She then retired from films. She had married twice, first to actor Victor Sutherland, and then to Major Wallace McCutcheon, but each marriage ended in divorce. On August 4, 1938, White died of a liver ailment, probably cirrhosis of the liver brought on by years of heavy drinking, after a three-week illness in the American Hospital in Neuilly-sur-Seine, France. She was buried in the Passy Cemetery in Paris.

Warren William

Born December 2, 1894
Died September 24, 1948

LEFT Warren William (seated) played Julius Caesar in Cecil B. DeMille's Cleopatra *(1934). Claudette Colbert (center) was the Egyptian queen.*

Warren William was often known, unfortunately, as "The Poor Man's John Barrymore." His striking resemblance to Barrymore helped break him into film, but couldn't help him achieve A-list, leading-man status. William had abandoned a career in journalism for what would be a steady but unremarkable career in films. He appeared in few important pictures, including Cecil B.

Star Shot

Warren William was an amateur inventor, and once obtained a patent for a leaf-sucking vacuum cleaner for lawns.

DeMille's *Cleopatra* (1934), but otherwise languished in "district attorney" roles in B-grade mysteries and adventure films for the rest of his career.

Born Warren William Krech in Aitkin, Minnesota, he initially followed in the footsteps of his newspaper publisher father before serving in the Army during World War I. After his discharge, he got his start in theater touring camps with an Army troupe production of *Under Cover*. Back home, he joined a road company production of *I Love You*, and when it folded, landed with a stock company in Erie, Pennsylvania. His Broadway debut came in 1924's *The Wonderful Visit*, and he went on to appear in more than a dozen productions, including *Expressing Willie*, *The Blue Peter*, *Twelve Miles Out*, and *Let Us Be Gay*. In a review of *The Blue Peter*, critic Alexander Woolcott wrote that William "has a Barrymore accent… [and] looks the very image of the young Drew." It was enough to get him noticed and on his way. After appearing in small roles in a few silents in the 1920s, he made his talking film debut with two Warner Bros. productions in October 1931, *Expensive Women* and the lost film *Honor of the Family*. He went on to appear in over 60 pictures, most memorably as Julius Caesar opposite Claudette Colbert in *Cleopatra*, as well as with Ginger Rogers and Joan Blondell in *Gold Diggers of 1933* (1933), the melodrama *Madame X* (1937), with Blondell and Henry Fonda in *Wild Geese Calling* (1941), and with Claude Rains and Bela Lugosi in *The Wolf Man* (1941). He also appeared in *The Lone Wolf* mystery-adventure series, beginning in 1939, including with Rita Hayworth in *The Lone Wolf Spy Hunt* (1939). He also co-starred with Bette Davis in several of her early films, including *The Dark Horse* (1932) and *Satan Met a Lady* (1936), based on the novel by Dashiell Hammett. His last motion picture was the George Sanders-Angela Lansbury drama, *The Private Affairs of Bel Ami* (1947).

In late 1947, Warren William was stricken with multiple myeloma, a rare blood disease that affects the plasma cells. After a ten-month battle, he finally succumbed to the disease on September 24, 1948, at the age of 53.

ABOVE Warren William played Perry Mason, Erle Stanley Gardner's famous lawyer, in four films, beginning with The Case of the Howling Dog *(1934), which co-starred Mary Astor.*

Grant Williams

Born August 18, 1930
Died July 28, 1985

Grant Williams is best remembered today for playing the title role in the 1957 science fiction classic film, *The Incredible Shrinking Man.* The actor was born John Grant Williams in New York City on August 18, 1930 (some sources state 1931). His father was from Glasgow, Scotland, and reportedly was a war hero in the English Army during World War I. His great aunt was legendary Scottish opera star Mary Garden. Williams's acting career began when he won a role in a straw-hat theater in Garrison, New York at the age of 12 years. He attended high school in Glasgow for two years before returning to New York to attend Queens College. Before graduating, Williams dropped out of college to join the

ABOVE As Grant Williams becomes smaller and smaller in The Incredible Shrinking Man *(1957), the perils he faces become more and more daunting.*

U.S. Air Force in 1952, serving during the Korean Conflict at B-29 bases in Korea and Okinawa, Japan. After his discharge, he returned to the stage, performing in summer stock and touring with road companies. He finished his undergraduate degree at New York University, then studied with famed acting teacher Lee Strasberg in New York.

Williams broke into show business through live television, beginning in 1954 with appearances on *Kraft Television Theater,* and continuing with appearances on *Studio One, Soldiers of Fortune,* and *Lux Video Theater.* A talent agent spotted him and signed him, leading to a contract with Universal. He made his big screen debut as a thug in *Red Sundown* (1956), then in quick succession appeared in five Universal productions in two years, most memorably with Rock Hudson and Lauren Bacall in Douglas Sirk's *Written on the Wind* (1956). Then came his starring role in *The Incredible Shrinking Man* (1957), in which he played a man who shrinks after exposure to a radioactive cloud. The movie had great special effects and has become a cult classic. His subsequent films were generally genre and B-grade pictures, including *The Monolith Monsters* (1957), *The Leech Woman* (1960), and *The Doomsday Machine* (1972). He also appeared on the television detective series *Hawaiian Eye* for three seasons beginning in 1960. His final film was 1972's campy horror flick, *The Brain of Blood.*

Star Shot

Grant Williams was an accomplished pianist and singer, and sang with the New York Opera for a few seasons.

In the 1970s, Grant Williams retired from the screen, announcing that he had "outgrown acting," and established his own drama school. In June 1985, he was admitted to the Veterans Administration Hospital in West Los Angeles for peritonitis, an infection in the abdominal area. He developed blood poisoning (septicemia) from the condition and died at the hospital on July 28. Williams's body is buried at the Los Angeles National Cemetery.

Marie Wilson

Born August 19, 1916
Died November 23, 1972

Marie Wilson found fame portraying clueless stenographer Irma Peterson on radio and then television in the 1950s series, *My Friend Irma*. On screen, she was the perfect picture of wide-eyed innocence, her perpetually bewildered expression punctuated by a high-pitched squeal of a voice and a famously voluptuous figure. And she seemed to have no qualms about presenting herself as more of a sex symbol than as a serious actress. Columnist Darr Smith once asked her if it bothered her that everyone stared at her chest. "Why, no, honey," she replied, "why if people didn't stare, I'd think I'd lost something."

She was born Katherine Elizabeth Wilson in Anaheim, California, in 1916. Legend has it that she was working as a salesgirl in a Hollywood five-and-dime when she was spotted by a talent scout for Warner Bros. and given a contract. Wilson made her motion picture debut in bit parts, appearing as an extra in RKO's *Down to Their Last Yacht* (1934); as Mary Quite Contrary in the Laurel and Hardy classic *Babes in Toyland* (1934); and in the musicals *Ladies Crave Excitement* (1935) with Ann Sothern, William Keighley's *Stars Over Broadway* (1935), and *Broadway Hostess* (1935). Warner Bros. then made a major stardom push, putting her in light-hearted comedies and musicals such as *Boy Meets Girl* (1938) with James Cagney, *Broadway Musketeers* (1938) with Ann Sheridan, and *Fools For Scandal* (1938) with Carole Lombard and Ralph Bellamy. After that, she often appeared in B-grade films, such as *Rookies on Parade* (1941), *Harvard, Here I Come!* (1941), and *She's in the Army* (1942).

In 1942, she became a major celebrity after opening in Ken Murray's *Blackouts of 1942* at the El Capitan Theater in Hollywood. In seven years, she never missed a performance. She did a few more mostly forgettable films, and then struck gold when given the title role in the CBS radio show *My Friend Irma* in 1947. It's been reported that creator Cy Howard based the title character on Wilson. The role made her a national sensation, and it was a top-rated radio program for several years. She followed with an equally popular television series with the same name, which ran from 1952 to 1954, and two Paramount films, *My Friend Irma* (1949) and *My Friend Irma Goes West* (1950). She appeared in a few more films, her last being *Mr. Hobbs Takes a Vacation* (1962). She also made a couple of appearances on television before being diagnosed with cancer in 1967. She battled the disease for five years, finally succumbing on November 23, 1972, at her home in the Hollywood Hills.

ABOVE Jerry Lewis with Marie Wilson in My Friend Irma (1949). This was the first film to feature the Dean Martin–Jerry Lewis comedy partnership.

Star Shot

In 1957, Marie Wilson and her husband, Robert Fallon, adopted a baby girl, then were sued by the birth mother, who decided that she didn't want to give her up. To protect the child, Wilson and Fallon agreed to return the baby.

LEFT Known for her fabulous figure as well as her bubbly personality, Marie Wilson always maintained a strict exercise regime.

Anna May Wong

Born January 3, 1905
Died February 2, 1961

ABOVE *Anna May Wong (center) with Marlene Dietrich (left) and controversial film-maker Leni Riefenstahl in Berlin in 1928.*

RIGHT *Anna May Wong wanted to play main-stream roles, and quickly tired of racism. "Why is it," she asked, "that the screen Chinese is always a villain?"*

Anna May Wong was Hollywood's first Asian-American star, though the institutionalized racism of the time often relegated her to playing caricatured "Oriental" villains and temptresses in support of heavily made-up Caucasians starring in Asian roles. It's a testament to Wong's prodigious talent and irrepressible screen presence that she reached the cinematic heights that she did.

She was born Wong Liu Tsong on January 3 in Los Angeles. Her birth year is disputed in several sources, ranging from 1902 to 1907, but most say 1905. She was raised above a laundry operated by her parents. She got her start in film as an extra in *The Red Lantern* (1919), then landed her first real role playing Lon Chaney's wife in *Bits of Life* (1921). Wong appeared in an early technicolor picture, *The Toll of the Sea* (1922), but it was her portrayal of a skimpily clad slave girl opposite Douglas Fairbanks in *The Thief of Bagdad* (1924) that made her a star. Wong's popularity soared with her appearances in a string of so-called "Oriental mysteries" in the 1920s, including *Mr. Wu* (1927), *Streets of Shanghai* (1927), *Chinatown Charlie* (1928), and *The Crimson City* (1928) in support of an "Orientalized" Myrna Loy. Frustrated with the stereotyped roles she was being offered, she left for Europe in 1929. There, she won critical acclaim for her appearance opposite Laurence Olivier in a stage production of *A Circle of Chalk*, and appeared in her final silent, E. A. Dupont's *Piccadilly* (1929). She returned to the States to appear on Broadway in *On the Spot*, and reached the pinnacle of her film career holding her own against Marlene Dietrich in Josef von Sternberg's *Shanghai Express* (1932).

She lobbied for the starring Asian role in MGM's *The Good Earth* (1937), and turned down the studio's offered supporting role of the villainess Lotus when the lead was given to the German actress, Luise Rainer. She portrayed a sympathetic character in *Daughters of Shanghai* (1937), but found worthy roles increasingly difficult to find as World War II approached. She announced her retirement from film in 1942, and spent her later years living quietly in her Santa Monica home. She did, however, occasionally make television appearances on shows such as *Climax!* and *The Barbara Stanwyck Show*. She returned to the screen in a minor role with Lana Turner in *Portrait in Black* (1960), and was preparing for the role of the mother in *The Flower Drum Song* (1961), when she suffered a heart attack in her sleep and died on February 2, 1961.

Diana Wynyard

Born January 16, 1906
Died May 13, 1964

Diana Wynyard was a London stage actress who occasionally brought her skills to the silver screen. At the height of her career, Wynyard's repertoire included Shakespearean classics, works of Ibsen and Chekhov, and light comedy. She was a woman with gentle features, and contemporary critics considered her acting "the most beautiful in London." Although she would become an Academy Award®-nominated actress, she ultimately spurned a Hollywood career for her beloved London stage.

She was born Dorothy Isobel Cox in London, England, on January 16, 1906, the daughter of an English businessman. She was raised in England and educated in private schools. She made her stage debut in 1925 in a small role in *The Grand Duchess* at London's Globe Theatre. Wynyard then toured the country with a traveling stock company, and went on to work with the Liverpool Repertory Company. She made her West End debut in Walter Hackett's *Sorry You've Been Troubled*, and followed with a nine-month run of *Petticoat Influence*. She also appeared in *Lean Harvest* with Leslie Banks, *Wild Decembers*, *Design for Living,* and *Marching Song*.

In November 1932, she arrived in New York to appear on Broadway in *The Devil Passes*. She was quickly signed by MGM and made her motion picture debut as Princess Natasha in *Rasputin and the Empress* (1932), starring Ethel, Lionel, and John Barrymore. Wynyard then portrayed Jane Maryott in Noel Coward's *Cavalcade* (1933). She was nominated for an Academy Award® for Best Actress, and the film received nods for Outstanding Production, Art Direction, and Directing for Frank Lloyd. Only Wynyard didn't win; the Oscar® was awarded to Katharine Hepburn for *Morning Glory* (1933), her first nomination and first win.

Wynyard appeared in only 14 more films, including with John Barrymore again in *Reunion in Vienna* (1933), in the British National Films' production of *Gaslight* (1940), with Sir John Gielgud in *The Prime Minister* (1941), and in Alexander Korda's *An Ideal Husband* (1947). Her last film was Robert Rossen's *Island in the Sun* (1957), with a notable cast including James Mason, Joan Fontaine, Harry Belafonte, and Dorothy Dandridge. Wynyard also continued performing on the London stage, including in numerous Shakespearean productions. In 1953, she was named a Commander of the Order of the British Empire for her dramatic achievements.

Wynyard's second marriage was to noted film director Carol Reed in 1943, but the marriage ended in divorce in 1947. In 1964, she was rehearsing for a role opposite Sir Michael Redgrave in Henrik Ibsen's *The Master Builder*, but before it opened, Wynyard fell ill due to a kidney problem and entered a London hospital. She died on May 13, 1964, at the age of 58.

ABOVE In 1940, Diana Wynyard starred in Gaslight. *In 1944, MGM bought the rights to the story, and tried to have all prints of the earlier film destroyed. Luckily for cinematic history, MGM did not succeed in this quest.*

Predator

Tragic accident—or foul play by an unseen assailant? The mysterious deaths of some of Hollywood's most famous personalities rival the world's greatest whodunits. From William Desmond Taylor, the actor/director found shot in the back in 1922, to Lana Clarkson, the blonde-haired beauty fatally shot in 2003, Hollywood history is peppered with true-life tales of baffling deaths.

Perhaps the strangest death of all is that of Marilyn Monroe. The inexplicable delay in calling the police, the discrepancy between the autopsy finding and the evidence at the scene, and an alleged missing diary have piqued the public's curiosity for more than 40 years, and conspiracy theories—including the involvement of the Mafia—have never died. Mobster boss Lucky Luciano has been mentioned in association with the puzzling deaths of singer and actor Mario Lanza and glamorous actress Thelma Todd, while the Hong Kong underworld is rumored to have been involved in Bruce Lee's untimely exit from this life.

Whether rudimentary forensic techniques, poor police work, or unreliable witnesses are to blame, the deaths of some of Hollywood's most beloved members will never be fully explained. The memory of these stars will remain forever tainted by the gossip and innuendo surrounding their controversial deaths.

Lana Clarkson

Born April 5, 1962
Died February 3, 2003

ABOVE A few years before her death, Lana Clarkson set up her own production company, Living Doll Productions, hoping to steer her career in new directions.

Lana Clarkson was a fan of Marilyn Monroe, and her home was filled with Marilyn memorabilia. Ironically, Clarkson was born in the same year that Monroe died.

Tall, blonde, blue-eyed, and athletic, Lana Clarkson was the quintessential California girl. From a very early age Clarkson aspired to a show business career, and in her late teens she began to win small parts in popular television programs such as *Happy Days*, *Laverne and Shirley*, and *Fantasy Island*. Soon Clarkson was traveling the world as a fashion model, returning to Hollywood in 1980 for her first speaking role in a film: *Fast Times at Ridgemont High* (released in 1982), starring Sean Penn.

In 1983, Clarkson appeared in *Scarface* with Al Pacino and then *Deathstalker*, where she caught the attention of the director Roger Corman. He cast her as the lead in *Barbarian Queen* (1985), an action film for which Lana Clarkson, already an accomplished horsewoman, learned sword fighting and performed her own stunts. Similar roles followed: *Amazon Women on the Moon* (1987) and *Barbarian Queen 2: The Empress Strikes Back* (1989).

Clarkson was a hard worker, and when major film and television roles were not forthcoming in the 1990s, she kept herself employed doing commercials and bit parts, as well as trying her hand at stand-up comedy. She also devoted a great deal of her time to charitable causes. After she broke both her wrists in an accident in late 2001, she explored new creative possibilities, studying the crafts of producing and scriptwriting.

On February 3, 2003, Clarkson was working as a hostess at the House of Blues, a famous nightclub on Sunset Strip in Hollywood. At around 2:00 A.M., someone noticed her leaving the club with 62-year-old record producer Phil Spector. For several decades, Spector had been a virtual recluse and was considered eccentric and unpredictable. At the peak of his career in the 1960s and early 1970s, he revolutionized the music industry with his trademark "wall of sound," working with artists such as The Righteous Brothers, Tina Turner, and The Beatles.

A few hours after the couple left the nightclub, Spector's chauffeur claims that he heard a gunshot that seemed to come from the house, and phoned the police. (Spector claims that *he* phoned the police.) They found Clarkson's body in the foyer of Spector's Alhambra mansion—dead from a gunshot wound to the head. Spector was released on $1,000,000 bail, and although he insists that Clarkson committed suicide, on September 27, 2004, he was indicted on murder charges. If convicted, Spector could face life imprisonment.

RIGHT In Vice Girls *(1996), Lana Clarkson played an undercover police officer trying to catch a crazed killer who was murdering runaway girls.*

Albert Dekker

Born December 20, 1905
Died May 5, 1968

Although Albert Dekker was an attractive, well-regarded character actor with an impressive list of credits in film, theater, and television, he never achieved celebrity status—that is, not until his bizarre and perplexing death.

Born in Brooklyn, New York, Albert Dekker attended Bowdoin College in Maine where he studied psychology and was a member of the drama society. After graduation, he met theater luminary Alfred Lunt, who became his mentor. One of Dekker's early parts was in Eugene O'Neill's play *Marco Millions* (1928).

Dekker had had ten successful years on Broadway when he landed his first film role in *The Great Garrick* (1937). Over the next 30 years he would feature in close to 80 films. He was often cast as the bad guy, and his most infamous character was the crazy scientist in *Dr. Cyclops* (1940).

From 1944 to 1946, Albert Dekker served a term in the California state legislature. An outspoken Democrat, he was targeted in the McCarthy "witch hunt" and was unable to work in Hollywood for some years. After a brief return to Broadway, he made a screen comeback in 1959, appearing in several films, including *Suddenly, Last Summer*.

In 1968, at age 62, the future was looking bright for Dekker, both professionally and personally. He had just finished filming *The Wild Bunch* and was engaged to marry model Geraldine Saunders. When Dekker failed to keep a date with her on Friday, May 3, 1968, Saunders became increasingly concerned. On Sunday, May 5, she entered Dekker's apartment, accompanied by the building's manager. They forced open the locked bathroom door, and Saunders allegedly fainted at the grotesque sight. Dekker's naked body was kneeling in the bathtub, a noose around his neck hanging from the shower curtain rod. His lower extremities were purple; he had a hypodermic needle in each arm, a scarf around his eyes, and he was handcuffed and gagged with a device similar to a horse's bit. Obscenities were written in red lipstick on his chest, abdomen, and buttocks. Cameras and cash had been taken from the apartment.

Dekker's friends confirmed that he had shown no signs of depression or suicidal behavior. Speculation that he was killed by a male prostitute was soon refuted. The building manager (who soon disappeared) was also suspected. The county coroner postulated that Dekker could have died from "autoerotic asphyxiation," in which the oxygen supply to the brain is cut off, creating an intense orgasm. Finally, the cause of death was ruled as "accidental asphyxia."

ABOVE Albert Dekker's first film after his departure from politics was The Killers *(1946), starring Burt Lancaster (right) and produced by Mark Hellinger (center).*

RIGHT Serenade (1959), co-starring Zsa Zsa Gabor (right), was one of only two films Lanza made after his move to Italy. Lanza's wife, Betty, is on the left.

Lanza's wife, Betty, died as a result of substance abuse in early 1960. Their son, Marc, died in 1991 at age 37 from congenital heart disease, and in 1997, 48-year-old daughter Colleen was hit by a car and killed.

Mario Lanza

Born January 31, 1921
Died October 7, 1959

Mario Lanza (originally Alfredo Arnold Cocozza) was born and raised in the Italian neighborhood of South Philadelphia. Around the time he won a scholarship to the prestigious Berkshire Music Center in Massachusetts, Cocozza changed his name to Mario Lanza, the masculine version of his mother's name, Maria Lanza.

In 1943, Mario Lanza served in the Special Services unit of the U.S. Army, performing in the musical productions *On the Beam* and *Winged Victory*. His career took off after film mogul Louis B. Mayer saw him perform at the Hollywood Bowl in 1947 and signed him to MGM. He co-starred with Kathryn Grayson in *That Midnight Kiss* (1949) and *The Toast of New Orleans* (1950). By the time he played the title role in *The Great Caruso* in 1951, Lanza was a superstar. He was adored by legions of fans, and because he had successfully bridged the gap between classical and popular musical tastes, he sold millions of records.

However, Lanza was alienating people in Hollywood with his unprofessional behavior. He abused alcohol, prescription drugs, and especially food, alternating between huge eating binges and dangerous fad diets. At one point the 5-foot, 8-inch (1.7-m) tall Lanza weighed close to 300 pounds (136 kg). Because of his obesity (and perhaps differences with the director), only his voice was used in the 1954 film *The Student Prince*.

MGM did not renew his contract and, in 1957, Lanza moved to Italy with his wife and children. For the next two years he was chronically unwell, suffering from phlebitis, high blood pressure, and stress. He suffered a minor heart attack in April 1959 and another that August. In October 1959, Lanza admitted himself to a hospital in an attempt to lose weight. When his chauffeur came to see him on October 7, he allegedly found Lanza unconscious, with an empty IV tube pumping air into his veins—the cause of death was stated as a heart attack.

It has been rumored that not long before he died, Lanza had angered mobster boss Lucky Luciano by failing to turn up for the rehearsal of a concert in Naples that Luciano had organized. However, family and friends deny any possibility of Mafia involvement. Lanza's son Damon emphatically stated that there was "absolutely no proof of them [Lanza and Luciano] even meeting, ever," and that his father died of a heart attack after a long history of heart trouble.

BELOW Mario Lanza, whose musical hero was Enrico Caruso, made the cover of Time *magazine in June 1951.*

Bruce Lee

Born November 27, 1940
Died July 20, 1973

Star Shot

Bruce Lee made his film debut in *Golden Gate Girl* (1941) in San Francisco when he was only three months old. He played the part of a baby girl.

Chinese–American actor and director Bruce Lee (Lee Jun-Fan) was born in San Francisco, but spent most of his childhood in Hong Kong, where he acted in a number of films.

Lee took up dancing and *kung fu* as a way of channeling his restless adolescent energy. He returned to the United States in the late 1950s to study philosophy at the University of Washington. The intense and ambitious Lee also set up a martial arts school in Seattle. He married Linda Emery in 1964, and their son, Brandon, was born the following year.

While competing in a martial arts contest in Long Beach, California, in 1964, Lee impressed a group of television producers with his dancer's grace and natural theatrical ability (in another version of this story, hair stylist Jay Sebring filmed Lee at the tournament and gave the tape to producer William Dozier, who was impressed by Lee's talents). He was cast in the role of Kato in *The Green Hornet*, which ran for 26 episodes. Guest appearances on other television programs followed, but when he missed out on the coveted lead role in the *Kung Fu* series, Lee returned to Hong Kong with his family, which now included daughter Shannon.

Lee made a succession of action films in Hong Kong between 1971 and 1973: *The Big Boss* (1971), *Fist of Fury* (1972), and *Way of the Dragon* (1972). *Enter the Dragon* (1973), which had funding from Warner Bros., seemed certain to bring Lee the Hollywood stardom he so craved. But the frenetic pace was beginning to take its toll: Lee was tired, thin, and irritable. In May 1973, while filming *Game of Death*, he suffered a mild seizure.

On July 20, 1973, Lee and producer Raymond Chow were working at the home of Betty Ting Pei, Lee's *Game of Death* co-star. Chow left, and the others were to have joined him later that evening for dinner. But Lee had a headache, and Ting Pei gave him Equagesic, an analgesic containing meprobamate and aspirin. Lee went to sleep and never woke up. Ting Pei contacted Chow, and a doctor was summoned. Lee was rushed to Queen Elizabeth Hospital and was pronounced dead on arrival. An autopsy showed the cause of death to be a cerebral edema, probably due to a severe reaction to the Equagesic. Several weeks later an inquest was conducted, and the verdict was "death by misadventure."

Lee's death aroused much furor and speculation. Some believed he was murdered by the Hong Kong mafia, or possibly by some malicious Chinese martial arts masters. Others said that Lee's house had unfavorable *feng shui*, causing bad things to happen, and yet another belief was that his family was cursed. Brandon Lee's untimely death during filming of *The Crow* in 1993 supported that theory.

BELOW Kung fu *was virtually unknown in the West until* Enter the Dragon (1973) *was released in the United States. Sadly, Bruce Lee died within weeks of the film's release.*

Marilyn Monroe

Born June 1, 1926
Died August 5, 1962

Norma Jean Mortenson's life began just as grimly as it ended. She never knew her father, and her mother, Gladys, was frequently admitted to psychiatric institutions. Young Norma Jean spent most of her Los Angeles childhood being shuffled between foster homes, orphanages, and relatives. Little wonder, then, that the little girl found solace in books, movies, and fantasy.

When she was 15 she met 21-year-old Jim Dougherty, and married him in 1942 to avoid another foster home. Dougherty joined the Merchant Marines, and he was sent overseas in 1944. While working at the Radioplane factory, Norma Jean had her picture taken by an Army photographer. The camera captured her radiant sexual energy, and it wasn't long before Norma Jean was modeling for magazines.

The year 1946 would prove to be a watershed time in her life. She divorced her husband, dyed her hair blonde, signed a contract with 20th Century Fox, and changed her name: the phenomenon known as Marilyn Monroe was born.

From 1946 to 1952, Monroe appeared in 18 films; she had her first starring role in *Don't Bother to Knock* in 1952. *Niagara*, *Gentlemen Prefer Blondes*, and *How to Marry a Millionaire* (all 1953) cemented Monroe's status as a star.

In January 1954, Monroe wed baseball legend Joe DiMaggio, who did not support his wife's career plans. When the marriage ended less than a year later, Monroe threw herself into her movies: *There's No Business Like Show Business* (1954) was soon followed by *The Seven Year Itch* (1955). Ignoring contractual obligations, Monroe then took off to New York to study at the Actors Studio. She returned to Hollywood to star in *Bus Stop* (1956), arguably her finest performance. Monroe was eager to get back to New York and playwright Arthur Miller, and they married soon after his Reno divorce came through.

ABOVE With Eli Wallach. Just months before her tragic death, Marilyn Monroe sang a famously sultry "Happy Birthday" to President Kennedy at Madison Square Garden.

Monroe's unreliability caused disruptions on the sets of *The Prince and the Showgirl* (1957), *Some Like It Hot* (1959), and *Let's Make Love* (1960). By the time *The Misfits* was released in 1961, she had become increasingly dependent on sleeping pills and alcohol. Monroe and Miller were ill-suited from the start, and their marriage could not withstand two miscarriages, infidelities, work pressures, and Monroe's deteriorating emotional health.

RIGHT Marilyn Monroe's last movie, The Misfits *(1961), written for her by Arthur Miller (right), was also the last film for screen veteran Clark Gable.*

Something's Got to Give (1962) was well over budget, largely due to Monroe's frequent absences from the set. Monroe was fired, and then rehired, but never completed the film: she was pronounced dead in her Brentwood home during the early hours of Sunday, August 5, 1962.

Late on that Saturday night, Eunice Murray, Monroe's housekeeper, saw Monroe through her bedroom window and felt

LEFT Marilyn Monroe had a power over some men. Having divorced Monroe, Joe DiMaggio never remarried, and after her death he put red roses on her grave every week for 20 years.

that something was wrong. She phoned Monroe's psychiatrist, Dr. Ralph Greenson. When Greenson realized that Monroe was unconscious, he summoned Dr. Hyman Engelberg, who pronounced Monroe dead. Publicity manager Arthur Jacobs was also notified and came to the house, but it was more than four hours before the police were alerted.

Sergeant Jack Clemmons of the LAPD found Monroe's naked body lying face down on her bed, covered by a sheet. He observed that she was in a "soldier's position," with her hands by her side (although some reports state that one of her arms was outstretched, reaching for the phone). There were between eight and 15 empty or partially empty pill bottles on her bedside table, including an empty bottle of sleeping pills. The coroner determined that Monroe's death was a probable suicide by ingestion of the sedatives chloral hydrate and Nembutal.

Monroe certainly had a history of depression and suicide attempts. She may have felt abandoned by both President John Kennedy and Senator Robert Kennedy; she was thought to have been intimately involved with both men. But the suicide verdict has been disputed for a number of reasons. Joe DiMaggio, Jr., spoke to her on the phone that evening and found her to be in good spirits. And how would she have swallowed all those pills if there was no drinking glass in the room? Furthermore, the position of her body at death was not consistent with suicide, and her stomach was empty, with no traces of Nembutal crystals or pill casings. Drugs were found in her blood and liver, but there were no injection marks on her body.

So then how did the drugs get into Monroe's body? One theory is that Mrs. Murray (acting on Dr. Greenson's instructions) may have given Monroe a chloral hydrate enema to help her sleep, and that the drug reacted to the Nembutal she had taken earlier that day. However, Greenson and Murray never admitted to this procedure.

BELOW The legend lives on: in 1999, People magazine voted Marilyn Monroe the sexiest woman of the twentieth century.

Many people believe that Monroe was killed by the Kennedys. If it became public knowledge that either John or Robert was having an affair with Marilyn Monroe, it would ruin their careers. In addition, Monroe was alleged to have been privy to political information, which she is thought to have recorded in a diary. This diary (along with records of telephone calls) conveniently disappeared from Monroe's house; there is doubt about the diary's existence.

More recent theories propose that Monroe's death was engineered by someone who wanted to make it look like it was the Kennedys' doing. The FBI had been keeping a file on Monroe for years, and President Kennedy and J. Edgar Hoover were known enemies. The Mafia had a motive because of Robert Kennedy's crusade against organized crime, and some members of the CIA were unhappy with the president's handling of the Cuban missile crisis. The Los Angeles County District Attorney conducted an investigation in 1982 but could find no proof of foul play.

William Desmond Taylor

Born April 26, 1872
Died February 1, 1922

William Cunningham Deane-Tanner was born in Carlow, Ireland, in 1872 (some sources give the year as 1877), and in 1890 he came to the United States to seek his fortune. He got some small roles in Broadway plays and married Ethel May Harrison in 1901. Her wealthy father set him up in an antique shop in New York, but seven years later Deane-Tanner walked out on his family and business. He headed west, not telling anyone where he was going, and changed his name to William Desmond Taylor.

Taylor arrived in Hollywood in 1912 and was offered some minor parts before starring in *Captain Alvarez* (1914). It soon became apparent that he had a flair for directing, and among his films were the popular screen adaptations *Tom Sawyer* (1917), *Anne of Green Gables*

ABOVE After William Desmond Taylor's murder, the careers of Mabel Normand and Mary Miles Minter steadily declined, and they lapsed into obscurity.

(1919), and *Huckleberry Finn* (1920). During the course of his career he would work with screen stars Mabel Normand, Mary Pickford, and Douglas Fairbanks. In 1917 he was elected president of the Motion Picture Directors' Association, and in 1922 he became the head of his own production unit at Paramount Studio. Taylor had a penchant for starlets, and they in turn were drawn to his influence, sophistication, and magnetic charm.

At 7:30 A.M. on February 2, 1922, Taylor's butler, Henry Peavey, arrived at work to discover his employer's body lying in his West Lake Park bungalow apartment. The police confirmed that Taylor's death was caused by a single .38-caliber bullet wound in his back. Neighbors reported that they thought they had heard a gunshot between 7:45 and 8:15 P.M. the previous evening, and saw a person wearing a cap and overcoat leaving Taylor's apartment.

Over the years, various theories have evolved as to who may have killed Taylor. Keystone Cops star Mabel Normand was the last person to see Taylor alive (not long before the gunshot was heard). She was allegedly a cocaine addict, and could have been jealous over Taylor's relationship with young actress Mary Miles Minter, who was also among the suspects. Minter's passionate letters were found in Taylor's bedroom, and strands of her blonde hair were on his coat. Many people have laid the blame for the murder on Charlotte Shelby, Minter's controlling mother, who was known to carry a .38-caliber shotgun and was possibly in love with Taylor herself. Another key suspect was Taylor's former valet, Edward Sands, who had previously stolen large amounts of cash and jewelry. Drug dealers were also implicated because of Taylor's long-running crusade to rid the film industry of narcotics.

The case was never solved. When the police arrived, they found a number of people wandering around the house, so the crime scene was compromised and evidence was difficult to gather. Another theory is that moralists, who wanted to cover up the scandalous goings-on in Hollywood, were able to put a stop to the investigation.

Thelma Todd

Born July 29, 1905
Died December 16, 1935

ABOVE Johnny Weissmuller, Olympic swimmer and the movie world's most famous Tarzan, shares a joke with Thelma Todd at the beach in March 1935.

The glamorous actress who would become known as "The Ice Cream Blonde" had qualified as a teacher before winning the "Miss Massachusetts" crown in 1925. She was spotted by Hollywood talent scouts, signed a contract with Paramount in 1927, and in eight years would appear in over 100 films.

Todd's career began at an exciting time, just as the silent era was about to end and the "talkies" were in their infancy. After being cast in a number of short features, her first full-length role was in *Fascinating Youth* (1927). Later that year she co-starred with Gary Cooper in *Nevada*. Although she acted in a wide variety of genres, she was best known and loved as a comedienne, playing alongside Laurel and Hardy in *The Devil's Brother* in 1933 and *The Bohemian Girl* (released after her death in 1936), and with the Marx Brothers in *Monkey Business* (1931) and *Horse Feathers* (1932).

With producer Roland West, Todd decided to cash in on her famous name, and opened Thelma Todd's Sidewalk Café, a beachside restaurant/nightclub in Pacific Palisades. As well as a celebrity clientele, the restaurant attracted a somewhat criminal element. One night Todd patronized another nightclub, the famous Trocadero on Sunset Boulevard. Her chauffeur drove her home at around 3:00 A.M., and later reported that she was rather subdued.

The next morning her maid discovered Todd's body in the garage, about 300 feet (92 m) up the hill from her apartment. Todd was elegantly dressed in an evening gown and mink coat. Her body was slouched on the front seat of her Lincoln convertible. There was coagulated blood on her face and clothing, and her skin had spots of blood on it. The autopsy confirmed that her blood contained 75 percent carbon monoxide saturation and there was 0.13 percent alcohol in her brain tissue. There were no signs of struggle, and her death was ruled as suicide by carbon monoxide poisoning. Although most reports indicate that Todd was not a depressive person, she had been experiencing emotional and financial difficulties. However, some people believed that she was murdered, and there were plenty of unofficial suspects: ex-husband Pasquale DiCicco, with whom she argued that night at the Trocadero; Roland West, who was supposedly trying to end their relationship; and organized crime leader Lucky Luciano, who was trying to persuade Todd to turn part of her restaurant into an illegal casino.

Star Shot

In 1931, Thelma Todd starred in the drama *Corsair* with Chester Morris. She used the professional name Alison Loyd for this role.

LEFT As well as The Bohemian Girl, *two other Thelma Todd films,* All-American Toothache *and* Hot Money, *were released in 1936, the year after her death.*

Natalie Wood

Born July 20, 1938
Died November 29, 1981

A wistful, dark-eyed beauty, Natalie Wood was at her best playing characters suffering heartbreak and loss. She had certainly experienced her fair share of real-life emotional trauma. Her parents Maria and Nikolai Zakharenko were immigrants who had fled Russia and settled in San Francisco. Maria has been described as obsessive and overbearing to the point of being "close to certifiable"; Nikolai found solace in the bottle.

In early 1943, four-year-old Natasha (as she was then known) was hired as an extra in *Happy Land*, shot in nearby Santa Rosa. A frustrated actress herself, Maria was convinced that Natasha had the makings of a child star, so she packed up the family and moved to Los Angeles. Her dreams remained unfulfilled until 1946, when her daughter was cast alongside Orson Welles and Claudette Colbert in *Tomorrow Is Forever*. More roles soon followed: *The Ghost and Mrs. Muir* and the Christmas classic, *Miracle on 34th Street* (both in 1947).

The film that would mark her rite of passage, both personally and professionally, was *Rebel Without a Cause* in 1955. Wood was awarded her first Oscar® nomination for Best Actress in a Supporting Role for her part in this story of tormented, misunderstood teenagers. *Rebel*'s stellar cast included James Dean, Sal Mineo, and Nick Adams, all three of whom, like Wood, would meet with tragic and untimely ends. Wood embarked on a brief affair with the film's director, Nicholas Ray, who was more than 25 years her senior. At age 18, she married handsome actor Robert Wagner.

Wood's career reached its peak in the early 1960s, with a variety of strong and interesting roles. She received a Best Actress nomination for *Splendor in the Grass* (1961), a high-quality melodrama with sexual under-

currents, helped along by the chemistry between Wood and Warren Beatty. In the musicals *West Side Story* (1961) and *Gypsy* (1962), she displayed her versatility (although her voice was dubbed in *West Side Story*). Wood's sensitive performance in *Love with the Proper Stranger* (1963) with Steve McQueen scored another Oscar® nomination. Unfortunately, fame had an adverse effect on her marriage, and the Wagners divorced in 1962.

Wood's films of the mid- to late 1960s include *Inside Daisy Clover* and *The Great Race* (both in 1965), *This Property Is Condemned* (1966), and *Bob and Carol and Ted and Alice* (1969). She married British scriptwriter and producer Richard Gregson in 1969, and the short-lived union produced a daughter, Natasha.

After divorcing Gregson, she remarried Robert Wagner in 1972, and their daughter Courtney was born two years later. Wood devoted most of the next decade to motherhood. There were a few television parts, including *From Here to Eternity* (1979), for which she won a Golden Globe®.

On Thanksgiving weekend of 1981, Wood, Wagner, and their guest Christopher Walken (Wood's co-star in the sci-fi thriller *Brainstorm*, which was eventually released in 1983) were aboard Wagner's 55-foot (17-m) yacht, the *Splendour*. Skippered by Dennis Davern, the boat left Marina del Rey on November 27 and was heading to Catalina Island. Despite the luxurious surroundings and picture-perfect setting, the atmosphere was tense. Known for her jealousy and insecurity, Wood was feeling resentful because her husband had been spending a lot of time with his *Hart to Hart* co-star Stefanie Powers. And although Wood and Walken may not have been having an actual affair, it was certainly a flirtation. The copious amounts of alcohol consumed on the weekend added fuel to the fire.

The situation came to a head late on Saturday afternoon when the group took the dinghy and went ashore for dinner. At the restaurant there was a lot of drinking and arguing, which continued back aboard the *Splendour*. Close to midnight, Wood left the others, presumably to get ready for bed. About 30 minutes later, Davern discovered that the dinghy was missing, and when Wagner checked the master stateroom, Wood was not there. The police and Coast Guard were called, and after a night-long search, they found Wood's body at 7:44 A.M. on Sunday, November 29. She was lying in the water face down, dressed in a nightgown, socks, and waterlogged down jacket; the dinghy was 200 yards (180 m) away.

The police postulated that Wood was planning to get into the dinghy, possibly to take it ashore—a strange thing to do for someone who was a poor swimmer and terrified of dark water, but in her inebriated state, her judgment would have been seriously impaired. The theory is that while she was untying the dinghy, she slipped, hit her head, then fell into the water and drowned.

To add to the mystery surrounding her death, a woman on a boat that was anchored some 100 yards (90 m) from the *Splendour* reported that about 12:00 A.M. she heard a female voice calling for help, and a male voice respond that he would come and get her. In spite of the fact that the Los Angeles County Coroner said that there was room for further investigation, the death was ruled as accidental.

In 2004, a television biopic, *The Mystery of Natalie Wood,* made by her sister Lana, as well as a new biography were released, showing that there is still great interest in the life and death of this star who passed away so sadly and so alone.

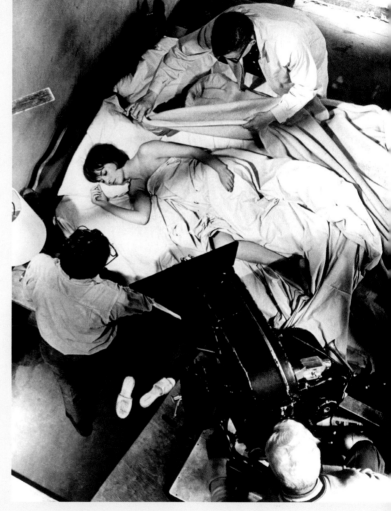

ABOVE Inside Daisy Clover *(1965) showed that unhappiness was an integral part of fame, a theme that resonated throughout Natalie Wood's short life.*

Dial M for Murder

With the slash of a knife or a shot from a gun, the flame of life was prematurely snuffed out for a number of Hollywood's actors and actresses. Others were subjected to unspeakable acts of violence, suffering a slow and agonizing slide toward death's door.

Sometimes it is the ones we love who do us the most harm. Susan Cabot found this out the hard way when her beloved son Timothy bashed her to death with a weight-lifting bar. Dominique Dunne literally died at the hands of her boyfriend John Sweeney—in a jealous rage, he strangled the life out of her. And Phil Hartman had no idea that his wife's drug addiction and alcoholism would see her turn from a wannabe actress into his cold-blooded murderer.

The extravagant Hollywood lifestyles of Sal Mineo and Ramon Novarro may have cost them their lives. Rumors that both crimes were money-, drug-, or sex-related continue to this day. And Sharon Tate's dream Hollywood life was only beginning when she was callously murdered by members of Charles Manson's "Family." In a cruel twist of fate, Haing S. Ngor survived the horrors of the Khmer Rouge in Cambodia, only to be shot outside his Los Angeles home, while Errol Flynn's son Sean gave up a promising film career to become a freelance photojournalist, only to be murdered in Cambodia.

Susan Cabot

Born July 9, 1927
Died December 10, 1986

ABOVE In 1959, Susan Cabot had a brief but tempestuous affair with handsome young King Hussein of Jordan.

Star Shot

Before she became a film star, Susan Cabot illustrated children's books in New York.

Like her contemporary Marilyn Monroe, Susan Cabot spent most of her childhood in foster homes, and married at age 17, hoping for happiness. She moved from Boston to New York, where she worked as a nightclub singer and a film and television extra.

Cabot was spotted by a Columbia director, and in 1950 was cast in *On the Isle of Samoa.* Later that year she signed a contract with Universal International, which cast her in a number of westerns: *Tomahawk* (1951) with Van Heflin; *The Battle at Apache Pass* (1952) with Jeff Chandler; *Duel at Silver Creek* (1952), *Gunsmoke* (1953), and *Ride Clear of Diablo* (1954) with Audie Murphy; and *Fort Massacre* (1958) with Joel McCrea. She made guest appearances in the television series *Have Gun Will Travel* in 1958 and 1959. Cabot also starred in *The Flame of Araby* (1951) and *Son of Ali Baba* (1952). Her first marriage, to Martin Sacker, ended in 1951.

Intending to start a Broadway career, Cabot opted out of her Universal contract, but was enticed back to Hollywood by Roger Corman, king of B-grade movies. Cabot played villainous vamps in low-budget flicks such as *Carnival Rock, Sorority Girl*, and *The Viking Women and the Sea Serpent* (all 1957); and *Machine-Gun Kelly* (1958). In 1959 she starred in what would be her best-known (and last) film, Corman's sci-fi cult classic, *The Wasp Woman.*

Cabot then devoted her energies to art and music. Her son, Timothy, was born in 1963 (father unknown), and in 1968 she married Michael Roman—the relationship lasted 15 years. She would probably have faded into obscurity had it not been for the events of December 10, 1986. While she was asleep, her son bludgeoned her to death with a weight-lifting bar.

Timothy was a dwarf, and had been taking growth hormones and steroids, which can have behavioral side effects. Cabot is believed to have been self-medicating with the hormones, exacerbating her already paranoid tendencies. It seemed that Cabot and her son had an unhealthy codependent relationship, and Timothy probably snapped after years of maternal suffocation, combined with the effects of the drugs. There was no proof that the murder was premeditated, and Timothy was charged with involuntary manslaughter and put on probation for three years.

RIGHT Susan Cabot's real name was Harriet Shapiro. She chose her professional name when she began taking acting classes in her teenage years.

Dominique Dunne

Born November 23, 1959
Died November 4, 1982

Star Shot

The bruises on Dominique Dunne's face during an appearance on *Hill Street Blues* are real—her boyfriend, John Sweeney, had beaten her up the day before.

Dominique Ellen Dunne grew up in a wealthy, talented, and sophisticated milieu. Her father, Dominick Dunne, was a versatile producer/writer and member of the Hollywood "A list"; her mother, Ellen "Lenny" Griffin Dunne, was a socialite. Two older brothers, Griffin and Alex, completed the family. But it was not all perfect—Dominick's drinking and drug abuse contributed to the breakdown of the marriage, and Lenny was stricken with multiple sclerosis.

After high school, Dominique spent a year learning art and Italian in Florence, and then returned to the United States to study drama at Colorado State University. However, she never completed her degree, and opted instead to try her luck as an actress. She soon landed guest roles in television movies and in popular television shows of the early 1980s such as *Lou Grant, Hart to Hart, Fame, CHiPs,* and *Hill Street Blues*. She is best known for her portrayal of Dana Freeling in Steven Spielberg's *Poltergeist* (1982).

When she was 22, Dominique fell in love with 25-year-old John Sweeney, a chef at the exclusive Ma Maison restaurant in Los Angeles. In just a matter of weeks they set up house together in West Hollywood, and Sweeney soon began to display his jealous and obsessive nature. During their year-long relationship, Sweeney was dangerously violent on a number of occasions and, fearing for her life, Dominique finally asked him to leave.

On October 30, 1982, while Dominique was preparing for her role in the sci-fi mini-series *V* with co-star David Packer, Sweeney turned up, pleading to be taken back. When she refused, Sweeney dragged her outside and strangled her. The ambulance arrived, and Dominique was rushed to Cedars-Sinai Hospital, where she remained unconscious and died five days later.

Dominick Dunne and his wheelchair-bound ex-wife were present throughout the entire murder trial in September 1983, and they were incensed when Sweeney was convicted only of involuntary manslaughter. The outcome could have been much different had Sweeney's former girlfriend and victim been allowed to testify, but the jury was denied the knowledge of Sweeney's prior history of domestic violence. Sweeney received a six-year sentence and was out of prison in just two-and-a-half years.

After Sweeney's release in 1986, he became head chef at The Chronicle in Santa Monica. Dominique's family and friends handed out notices to people in and around the restaurant that read: "The hands that prepared your food strangled Dominique Dunne on October 30, 1982." Sweeney lost his job, changed his name to John Maura, and left California. Dominick Dunne continues to devote his life to exposing the corruption of the criminal justice system.

ABOVE Only five months after the release of Poltergeist *(1982), Dominique Dunne (far left) was savagely murdered by her exboyfriend. Heather O'Rourke (far right) also died early—succumbing to cardiopulmonary arrest in 1988 at the age of 12.*

Sean Flynn

Born May 31, 1941
Died April 6, 1970?

RIGHT Sean Flynn was the obvious choice to star in Son of Captain Blood *(1962). Back in 1935, his father, Errol Flynn, had swash-buckled his way across the screen as the star of* Captain Blood.

Notorious screen idol Errol Flynn met exotic French actress Lili Damita on a ship traveling from England to America. It was a love-hate relationship from the start, and although Flynn was ill-suited to marriage—let alone fatherhood—he and Damita wed, and son Sean was born in 1941. (Errol Flynn married two more times and had three daughters.)

Errol Flynn and Lili Damita divorced in 1942, the same year that Errol was charged with statutory rape. Sean had very little contact with his father during his childhood, but he inherited his stunning looks and charisma. Errol Flynn once remarked that "Sean looks like me but better." Sean also inherited his father's lust for adventure: before he became an actor, Errol spent time in New Guinea as a gold prospector, slave trader, and diamond smuggler.

As a teenager, Sean made a brief television appearance on *The Errol Flynn Theatre* in 1957. He had just commenced his studies at Duke University in North Carolina when Errol died suddenly of a heart attack in 1959. Sean then decided that he was not cut out for an academic life, and would follow his father's path to Hollywood.

Sean's first screen role was in the teenage romance *Where the Boys Are* (1960). He then starred in the swashbuckling adventures *Son of Captain Blood* (1962) and *Sign of Zorro* (1963). For the next three years, he was cast mainly in B-grade films, but his restless spirit yearned for more exciting challenges. He spent some time in Kenya in 1965, and made his last film, *Singapore, Singapore,* in 1967.

Sean became a freelance photojournalist, and arrived in Vietnam in 1968 at the very height of the conflict. He was an expert at jungle survival and would go on treks with the Special Forces and Long Range Reconnaissance Patrols into the most remote areas of the country. His photographs display both a gritty realism and an acute sensitivity, and they capture the essence of the horrors of war.

On April 6, 1970, Sean Flynn and his friend Dana Stone rented motorbikes and left Phnom Penh to cover American fighting in Cambodia. Sean was on assignment with *Time* magazine and Stone was working for CBS. They were stopped at a checkpoint in eastern Cambodia and captured by the Viet Cong, never to be seen again. Both men may have been executed in 1971.

Although he was declared legally dead in 1984, Sean's mother, Lili Damita, never gave up hoping for his safe return. She died in 1994 at the age of 92 years.

Star Shot

The life of Errol Flynn's adventurous son was immortalized in the song "Sean Flynn," which appeared on The Clash's 1982 album *Combat Rock*.

Phil Hartman

Born September 24, 1948
Died May 28, 1998

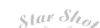

Comedian turned actor Phil Hartman was at the peak of his career when he was shot by his wife, Brynn Hartman, at the family home in Encino, California, on May 28, 1998. Hartman came to prominence during the 1980s as part of the famous Los Angeles-based comedy group the Groundlings. He also featured in the television show *Saturday Night Live* for eight seasons.

In the decade before his death, everything had gone right for Hartman. He had become the regular voice of Lionel Hutz and Troy McClure on the animated television show *The Simpsons*, had a starring role in the television comedy *NewsRadio,* and his movie career was blossoming with roles in modern comedy favorites such as *Three Amigos!* (1986), *Coneheads* (1993), *So I Married an Axe Murderer* (1993), and *Sgt. Bilko* (1996). It seemed as if everything in his life was on track for success and happiness, but this did not account for the problems that he and his third wife, Brynn, were experiencing.

Prone to violent outbursts, Hartman's wife was battling both cocaine and alcohol addictions, as well as a dependence on antidepressant medication. There was often talk of Brynn attending a rehab clinic for her addictions, and of Phil and Brynn undergoing family counseling. One night, after a long session of drinking with a female friend, Brynn returned to the couple's home—which Hartman had nicknamed the Ponderosa—and shot her husband in the head a number of times while he was sleeping. She rushed out of the house, leaving behind the couple's two children—Sean, 9, and Birgen, 6. The motive for the shooting is unknown, but there are rumors that Hartman, tired of dealing with her addictions, threatened earlier in the day to leave his wife for good.

Later, in a highly distressed condition, Brynn returned to the house with a friend, grabbed a second gun, locked herself in the main bedroom with her dead husband, and shortly afterward committed suicide with a single shot to the head. One police officer at the scene of the crime told the *Los Angeles Times* with brutal simplicity that the killing of Hartman was "an execution." A lifetime lover of the beach and of surfing, Phil Hartman's ashes were scattered around picturesque Catalina Island, just off the Californian coast.

ABOVE Pictured here with his wife, Brynn, in happier times, Phil Hartman won an Emmy Award® in 1988 for Outstanding Writing for Saturday Night Live.

LEFT Phil Hartman's unique sense of comic timing came to the fore in movies such as Jingle All The Way *(1996), which starred Arnold Schwarzenegger.*

Last Words

"Oh God! No! Help!
Someone help!"

Sal Mineo

Born January 10, 1939
Died February 12, 1976

If ever Hollywood made a star-crossed movie it has to be *Rebel Without a Cause* (1955). Four untimely deaths were to follow the movie's success. James Dean died in a car accident at the age of only 24. Nick Adams overdosed at age 36. Natalie Wood drowned when she was 43, and Sal Mineo was stabbed to death when he was only 37. Of all the deaths, Mineo's was perhaps one of the strangest and most mysterious.

Mineo was born in East Harlem, New York City and grew up in the Bronx; his parents were Sicilian, and his father was a self-employed casket maker. When he was in the fourth grade at Catholic school, Mineo played the part of Jesus Christ in a school play. Around the same time he joined a street gang, and was arrested at the age of 10 for stealing. Given a choice between juvenile detention or drama school, he quickly chose the latter and soon discovered that he had a talent for acting. He appeared in a number of Broadway plays, including *The King and I* with Yul Brynner and Gertrude Lawrence.

When he was only 15, Mineo arrived in Hollywood, and a year later he made his film debut in *Six Bridges to Cross* (1955). It was his role as Plato in *Rebel Without a Cause* (1955) that gave him instant stardom as well as the first of two Oscar® nominations (he remains one of the youngest people ever to

ABOVE With Jill Haworth in Exodus (1960). Sal Mineo's character, Dov Landau, joins the fight for a Jewish homeland at the end of World War II.

be nominated for an Oscar®). This led to subsequent roles in a range of movies including *Giant, Somebody Up There Likes Me*, and *Crime in the Streets* (all in 1956); *The Gene Krupa Story* (1959); *Exodus* (1960); *The Longest Day* (1962); and *Cheyenne Autumn* (1964). For his role in *Exodus*, Mineo was again nominated for an Academy Award® and lost, but won that year's Golden Globe® for Best Supporting Actor. Much to his disappointment, he missed out on a role in the 1962 epic *Lawrence of Arabia*.

During the filming of *Exodus*, Mineo had a relationship with his co-star, 15-year-old Jill Haworth. Although the romance was short-lived, they sustained a friendship. It turned out that Mineo preferred homosexual encounters—he was the first major actor to admit to being gay. He luxuriated in the Hollywood lifestyle and quickly gained a reputation as a beautiful young man interested in sexual masochism and drugs.

In 1969, Mineo made his directorial debut in the Los Angeles theater production of *Fortune and Men's Eyes*, a play that dealt with the theme of homosexuality in prison and that contained a

RIGHT Sal Mineo had the opportunity to demonstrate his own talents as a drummer when he played the title role in The Gene Krupa Story *(1959).*

Sal Mineo

violent rape scene. Despite its limited audience, the play was reasonably successful, but it did not do as well when it later moved to New York.

By the early 1970s, Mineo's good looks and box office appeal were fading. He was practically broke and was forced to earn his living by accepting minor television roles and playing one of the apes in *Escape from the Planet of the Apes* (1971). However, early in 1976, his career prospects were starting to improve. Mineo had starred in the San Francisco production of *P.S. Your Cat Is Dead* the previous autumn, and was in rehearsal for the play's Los Angeles season. His performance had received favorable reviews and he was optimistic about the future. He was also planning to produce and direct his first movie. But, as is often the case, just as the wheel of fortune looked as though it was turning for the better, fate had other plans.

On February 12, 1976, Mineo was returning from rehearsal to his apartment in West Hollywood when he was stabbed in the heart by an unknown attacker. Several people living nearby heard the actor's plea for help. Roy Evans, a neighbor, found him on the ground, his shirt saturated with blood, and gave him mouth-to-mouth resuscitation. Although an ambulance was called, it was too late. Sal Mineo was declared dead at 9:55 P.M.; the medical examiner pronounced the death as homicide caused by a single stab wound to the heart. The manner in which Mineo died seems sadly ironic, considering that in his heyday he was given the nickname "The Switchblade Kid" because in several of his films he played the part of a knife-wielding juvenile delinquent.

At the time, no one knew for certain who the murderer was. Witnesses came forward and described the assailant as either a blond-haired man or a Mexican. Was the murder a homosexual crime? Was it drug related? It was common knowledge that Mineo had been a regular cocaine user, and the autopsy also revealed a number of needle marks on his buttocks and other areas of the body.

The following year a woman claimed that Lionel Raymond Williams, an African-American with a criminal record, had boasted that he had killed the actor. Although he didn't fit any of the eyewitness accounts, Williams was brought to trial on January 9, 1979, pleaded not guilty to first-degree murder, and was convicted of second-degree murder. He was released from prison in the 1990s. There are still doubts about his involvement, however, as he never revealed a motive and always denied that he'd committed the crime.

LEFT After Rebel Without a Cause *(1955), Sal Mineo, pictured here with James Dean, played similar roles in* Crime in the Streets *(1956) and* The Young Don't Cry *(1957).*

BELOW It is rumored that ex-Beatle John Lennon, who would himself become a murder victim in 1980, once posted a reward to catch Sal Mineo's killer.

Haing S. Ngor

Born March 22, 1940
Died February 25, 1996

BELOW His success as an actor did not stop Haing S. Ngor from helping others. He is pictured here assisting a refugee in a Thailand border camp in 1988.

H aing S. Ngor was a most extraordinary and resilient man. He grew up in a Cambodian farming community, and despite a background of poverty, graduated from medical school with a degree in obstetrics and gynecology.

In 1975, Ngor became one of millions of Cambodians who would suffer at the hands of the Khmer Rouge communist guerrilla regime. Artists, intellectuals, and professionals were the main victims of Pol Pot's atrocities. Eventually Ngor was sent to a prison camp where he was tortured; most of his family were killed. The most devastating blow of all was the loss of his wife, who, denied medical care, died in childbirth. When the Khmer Rouge was overthrown in 1979, Ngor and one of his few remaining relatives, his niece Ngim, escaped into Thailand.

A year later he was living in Los Angeles.

In 1982, a casting director met Ngor at a wedding, and thought that he would be suitable for a role in Warner Bros.' upcoming film *The Killing Fields* (1984), based on actual events that took place in Cambodia during the 1970s (in another version of the story, a casting director saw Ngor in a friend's wedding photos and thought he would be suitable for the role). Ngor played the part of Dith Pran, the personal assistant to *New York Times* correspondent Sydney Schanberg. He had never acted before, but Ngor's own memories and experiences gave his performance great depth and emotional truth. Ngor found the role painful but cathartic, and won the 1984 Academy Award® for Best Actor in a Supporting Role. He hoped that his 1987 autobiography, *Haing Ngor: A Cambodian Odyssey*, would bring more awareness of the genocide that took place in his country.

During the next decade, Ngor appeared in a number of films including *The Iron Triangle* (1989), Oliver Stone's *Heaven and Earth* (1993), and *My Life* (1993) with Michael Keaton and Nicole Kidman, in which he played a psychic healer. Ngor also found roles in television programs such as *China Beach*, *Miami Vice*, and *Highway to Heaven*. With the proceeds of his film and television work, he set up a foundation to help rebuild his ravaged homeland and to assist Cambodian refugees in the United States.

On February 25, 1996, Ngor's body was discovered lying in the carport of his Los Angeles apartment building. He had died from two .38-caliber bullet wounds. Although it was initially thought that the killing was politically motivated, three members of a Chinatown street gang were arrested and subsequently tried and convicted of first-degree murder.

Even in death, Haing S. Ngor continues to be of service to the world. In addition to its other work, Ngor's foundation strives to promote conflict resolution and "combat the proliferation of youth violence, gang activity, and drug use."

Haing S. Ngor's 1984 Oscar® was the first to go to an Asian performer since Miyoshi Umeki *(Sayonara)* in 1957, and the first to go to a non-professional since Harold Russell *(The Best Years of Our Lives)* in 1946.

Ramon Novarro

Born February 6, 1899
Died October 30, 1968

K nown as "The Latin Lover," Ramon Novarro was born Ramón
Gil Samaniego in Durango, Mexico. His father was a dentist,
and Novarro, one of 13 children, enjoyed a comfortable lifestyle
until the family was forced out of their homeland by the Mexican
Revolution in 1910. They traveled to the United States, and Ramon
eventually settled in Los Angeles in 1914. He took jobs as a stage
manager and bit player for a theater company.

Returning to Los Angeles after a short trip to New York, where
he worked as an usher for the New York Philharmonic Orchestra,
Novarro decided to pursue his long-held dream of being a film
actor. He auditioned with every casting director in town, receiving
one rejection after another. Persistence paid off, however, and in
1917 he was an extra in Cecil B. DeMille's *The Little American*. His
first major role was as the villain in *The Prisoner of Zenda* (1922).

The public couldn't get enough of him. He starred in many
other successful films such as *Scaramouche* (1923), *Thy Name is
Woman* (1924), and *The Arab* (1924), but his most memorable role was in the expensive epic
Ben-Hur (1925). The "talkies" replaced silent films in the early 1930s, and Novarro was still in
demand; his Latino accent enhanced his sex appeal. On-screen lovers included stars such
as Greta Garbo, Myrna Loy, and Lupe Velez, but off-screen Novarro gravitated toward men.

A devout Catholic, Novarro struggled with guilt over his sexual orientation.
Novarro's career began spiraling downward as he entered his forties,
and he all but faded from the movie scene. In the 1960s he had a comeback of sorts, making guest appearances on television series such as
Dr. Kildare, *Rawhide*, and *Bonanza*. Although somewhat ravaged by
age and alcohol, Novarro was still handsome and debonair, and was
financially secure due to astute investments. Sadly, he often felt empty
and isolated, and resorted to male prostitutes to ease his loneliness.
On the night of October 30, 1968, Novarro invited two hustlers, brothers
Paul and Tom Ferguson, to his home. When Novarro refused their
violent demands for money, Paul Ferguson tied his hands and
feet with electrical cord and mercilessly beat and tortured
him, leaving him to choke on his own blood.

The police found the actor's body covered in welts
and bruises, his house ransacked. Although their
investigation showed that Tom Ferguson was on the
phone at the time of Novarro's beating and death,
the following year both brothers were convicted
of first-degree murder and were given a life sentence.
Tom was out in six years and Paul nine; Paul's violent streak
later led to a jail term for the rape of a Missouri woman.

*ABOVE Ramon Novarro
starred opposite Norma
Shearer in* The Student
Prince in Old Heidelberg
*(1927), a film that
cemented his reputation
as a Latin lover.*

Star Shot

**Having once considered
entering a religious order,
Ramon Novarro's very last
performance was that of a
priest in an episode of *The
High Chaparral* in 1968.**

*LEFT His definitive
portrayal of Ben-Hur in
the 1925 film resulted
in Ramon Novarro
receiving fan mail
addressed simply to "Mr
Ben-Hur, Hollywood."*

Elizabeth Short

Born July 29, 1924
Died January 14, 1947

A would-be actress who never appeared in a movie, Elizabeth Short would achieve the celebrity she so desired as a result of her horrendous death.

When Elizabeth Short was five years old, her father, Cleo, went bankrupt. He staged his suicide and left Massachusetts to start afresh on the west coast. His wife, Phoebe, struggled to support her five daughters. Eventually Cleo Short notified his family that he was alive and well, and when she was a teenager, Short went to live with him in Vallejo, near San Francisco. She later got an office job at Camp Cooke, where she was popular with the servicemen.

Determined to become a star, Short frequented Hollywood nightclubs and parties in the hope that someone might discover her. With her raven hair, alabaster skin, blood-red lips and nails, and black lace clothing, she attracted a great deal of attention and began to be known as "The Black Dahlia."

There are many conflicting reports about Short's sexuality. Some say she was a lesbian, others say she was a virgin, and there are some stories about her friendly, flirtatious nature being misconstrued by men. She went out with many men and was briefly engaged to Major Matt Gordon, who was killed in a plane crash in 1946. Her final fling was with Robert "Red" Manley, who visited her in the lobby of the Biltmore Hotel on January 9, 1947. He would be the last person to see her alive.

Early on the morning of January 15, 1947, Short's body was found on a vacant lot in Leimert Park, a Los Angeles suburb. The woman who stumbled across the body thought at first that it was a mannequin broken in half, and when she realized it was a human body, she rushed to phone the police. Short had been cut in two, possibly with a butcher's knife, and positioned so that her arms

ABOVE Interest in Elizabeth Short's murder was rekindled when the novelist James Ellroy wrote The Black Dahlia *(1987), which was loosely based on the police investigation of her death.*

were raised above her head, and her legs opened. There were wounds and rope burns all over her body, which had been washed and drained of blood. The cause of death was given as "hemorrhage and shock due to concussion of the brain and lacerations of the face." The report also indicated that sodomy had been performed after her death, and that Short's genital organs were not fully developed, which would have rendered her incapable of full sexual intercourse.

Robert Manley was the major suspect, but he was cleared after passing two polygraph tests. Mark Hansen, in whose home Short had stayed for a time, was also interrogated. A pathetic character named Jack Anderson Wilson (alias Arnold Smith and Al Morrison) was also a possibility, as he was one of the suspects in the unsolved murder of Georgette Bauerdorf, a woman who had befriended Elizabeth Short at the Hollywood Canteen. However, just before he was due to meet with the police, he fell asleep while smoking in bed and died in the resulting fire. The case remains unsolved.

Sharon Tate

Born January 24, 1943
Died August 9, 1969

There is no more gruesome Hollywood murder than the crazed, drug-induced killing by Charles Manson's infamous "Manson Family" of the beautiful and pregnant young actress Sharon Tate.

Sharon Tate was hardly a movie star. Her first foray into Hollywood life was the recurring role of Janet Trego in the television series *The Beverly Hillbillies,* and she had minor roles in the films *Valley of the Dolls* and *Don't Make Waves* (both in 1967), *Rosemary's Baby* (1968), and *Wrecking Crew* (1969). Her greatest role had been her marriage to immensely gifted director Roman Polanski. Having achieved considerable success in Europe with *Repulsion* (1965) and *Cul-de-sac* (1966), Polanski became a Hollywood sensation with *Rosemary's Baby* (1968).

By August 1969, Tate was eight months' pregnant and living in Cielo Drive, Bel Air. On the night of August 9, 1969, Polanski was in Europe and Tate invited three friends over for a small party. They were coffee heiress Abigail Folger and her boyfriend, Voytek Frykowski, as well as celebrity hair stylist Jay Sebring. None of them could possibly know that for months, out on the edges of the desert, a psychopath named Charles Manson had been fueling his cult following with bad drugs and apocalyptic visions of murder and mayhem. The Manson Family was going to leave its mark.

On the night of August 9, Manson's followers drove to Bel Air. Sometime after midnight, nearby residents heard shots; one neighbor reported hearing a scream of "Oh, God, no, please don't! Oh, God, no, don't, don't…." When Winifred Chapman, Tate's housekeeper, arrived at the house early the next morning, she saw the mayhem and ran. The police were later to report that the word "PIG" had been written in blood on one of the walls and that all four people, as well as a teenage visitor (18-year-old Steve Parent), had been murdered in a particularly gruesome fashion. Faces had been smashed in. People had been tied up. Bodies had been stabbed over and over again. Tate had been stabbed 16 times. Folger had been stabbed 28 times.

Eventually the Los Angeles Police Department traced the murders to the Spahn Farm where the Manson Family were living. In 1971, several members of Manson's cult—Susan Atkins, Charles "Tex" Watson, Patricia Krenwinkel, and Linda Kasabian—were found guilty of murder, as was Charles Manson, the man who had organized these callous crimes.

ABOVE Sharon Tate made one movie appearance with her husband, Roman Polanski, in his 1967 film, The Fearless Vampire Killers.

Star Shot

Manson Family member Susan Atkins had once been a member of Anton La Vey's Church of Satan. In 1967, Roman Polanski cast Anton La Vey in *Rosemary's Baby.*

LEFT In Valley of the Dolls *(1967), Sharon Tate (center) played opposite film luminaries Barbara Parkins (left) and Patty Duke (right).*

Drugstore Cowboy

In the fast-paced world of Hollywood, an addiction to drugs such as sleeping pills, barbiturates, alcohol, cocaine, or heroin can not only endanger your career—it can be deadly. Many actors and actresses have turned to drugs to help them overcome performance anxiety or depression, to get them through the rigorous pace of filming set by the studios, or simply to give them a buzz—only to be abandoned by the studios when the addiction begins to take its toll on the star's acting ability or looks.

Painfully shy Gail Russell drowned her stage fright in alcohol, while grief drove Marie Prevost to the bottle. It has long been reputed that Pier Angeli's love for the tragic James Dean caused her to commit suicide by taking an overdose of barbiturates. Judy Garland and Wallace Reid were both given drugs by their studios to combat the fatigue of grueling schedules, while John Belushi and River Phoenix got caught up in the Hollywood party drug scene and paid the ultimate price. In a sad twist, Dorothy Dandridge and Robert Pastorelli were two performers who seemed to have kicked their addictions and were on the comeback trail—only to suffer one deadly lapse into their old ways.

Nick Adams

Born July 10, 1931
Died February 7, 1968

ABOVE When Nick
Adams and Carol
Nugent divorced,
Adams won custody
of their two children,
Allyson and Jeb.

Star Shot

**Nick Adams was the
first person to befriend
Elvis Presley when
Elvis first arrived in
Hollywood in 1956.**

Nick Adams was born in Nanticoke, Pennsylvania, the second son of Ukrainian immigrants. Nick's father was a coal miner, and when Nick's uncle was crushed to death in a mining accident, the family decided to move to Jersey City, New Jersey.

Adams was convinced that an acting career would be the passport out of his bleak working-class existence. When he was 18, he hitchhiked to Los Angeles and eventually was hired for a soft drink commercial in 1950; it starred another aspiring actor, James Dean. He spoke one line in the 1952 film, *Somebody Loves Me*.

After many failed auditions, Adams was drafted into the Coast Guard, but he kept abreast of the Hollywood scene. In 1954, he turned up for an audition wearing his Coast Guard uniform, and so impressed director John Ford with his tenacity and spunk that he was given a part in *Mister Roberts* (1955). This was the springboard for roles in a number of movies including *Rebel Without a Cause* (1955), *Picnic* (1955), *Our Miss Brooks* (1956), and *No Time for Sergeants* (1958), where he received second billing.

The years 1959–1961 were happy and productive ones for Adams: He married actress Carol Nugent, two children were born in quick succession, and he starred in a new television western, *The Rebel*. The role of ex-Confederate soldier Johnny Yuma catapulted Adams to fame and fortune. Unfortunately the series was scrapped after two seasons, not for lack of popularity, but because of studio politics. In 1962 he had minor parts in the movies *The Interns* and *Hell Is for Heroes*, and had another crack at television in the short-lived *Saints and Sinners*. The following year Adams was nominated for the Actor in a Supporting Role Oscar® for his role in *Twilight of Honor* (1963), but despite campaigning vigorously, lost to Melvyn Douglas in *Hud*.

Adams continued to take any jobs he could get, which were often in B-grade horror and sci-fi films such as *Die, Monster, Die!* (1965) and *Mission Mars* (1968). By this time his marriage was falling apart and he was involved in messy legal wrangles.

Adams was well known for his punctuality, and when he failed to appear for a dinner engagement with his lawyer, Ervin Roeder, on February 7, 1968, Roeder became concerned and broke into his house in Coldwater Canyon. He found Adams's dead body—dressed in a plaid shirt, jeans, and boots—propped up against the bedroom wall. The autopsy showed that Adams had overdosed on a cocktail of the anti-anxiety medications paraldehyde and Promazine, and Coroner Thomas Noguchi's report stated that the death was "accidental–suicidal and undetermined." There was much speculation of foul play, because no drugs or needles were found in the bedroom, and no suicide note had been written.

Pier Angeli

Born June 19, 1932
Died September 10, 1971

Star Shot

Pier Angeli had a twin sister, actress Marisa Luisa Pierangeli (Marisa Pavan). Pavan married, divorced, and later remarried French actor Jean-Pierre Aumont.

Born in Sardinia, Italy, Anna Maria Pierangeli studied art in Rome before she embarked on an acting career and changed her name to Pier Angeli. Reflecting her heavenly name, she had an angelic radiance that the camera adored, and after minor roles in two Italian films in the late 1940s, MGM cast her in *Teresa* (1951), in which she played a troubled Italian war bride.

Angeli was lured to Hollywood, where she was hailed as the next Ingrid Bergman. Vincente Minnelli hired her for the part of Rima the Bird Girl in *Green Mansions*, but the project was abandoned; when the film was finally made in 1959, the part went to Audrey Hepburn.

In 1954 Angeli appeared in *The Flame and the Flesh* with Lana Turner, and *The Silver Chalice* with Paul Newman and Jack Palance. That same year she fell hopelessly in love with the man she would later claim was her soul mate, James Dean. Her controlling, devoutly Catholic mother disapproved of Dean because he wasn't Catholic, and instead encouraged her to marry Italian-American crooner Vic Damone. Angeli gave birth to their son, Perry, in August 1955, just a month before Dean's fatal car crash.

Pier Angeli teamed up with Paul Newman again in the successful 1956 biopic of Rocky Graziano, *Somebody Up There Likes Me*. She starred opposite Mel Ferrer in *The Vintage* (1957), a crime drama set in an Italian vineyard, and played a circus acrobat in *Merry Andrew* (1958) co-starring Danny Kaye. It was during this period that Angeli and Damone separated, and a messy divorce and custody battle ensued.

Throughout the 1960s Angeli lived and worked mainly in Europe. She was nominated for a British Academy Film Award for her role in the English drama *The Angry Silence* (1960).

The only Hollywood films she appeared in during this decade were *Sodom and Gomorrah* (1962) and *Battle of the Bulge* (1965). In 1962 she married Italian musician Armando Trovajoli, but they separated not long after their son, Andrew, was born in 1963.

In 1971, Angeli moved back to the United States. Having endured more than her share of personal, professional, and financial disappointments, she was reduced to starring in the low-budget monster movie, *Octaman* (1971), which was to be her last picture. On September 10, 1971, after several previous suicide attempts, Pier Angeli died of a barbiturate overdose in her Beverly Hills home.

LEFT John Belushi's popularity soared when moviegoers were exposed to his irreverent, in-your-face comedic style in National Lampoon's Animal House (1978).

John Belushi

Born January 24, 1949
Died March 5, 1982

From the time he was a child in Wheaton, Illinois, John Belushi discovered that he could make people laugh. As a teenager, he was the co-captain of the high school football team, played drums, performed in variety shows, and was voted homecoming king and "most humorous" of the Class of '67. While at the College of DuPage near Wheaton he formed an improvisational comedy trio, the West Compass Players, modeled on Chicago's Second City troupe.

Like so many in the late 1960s, Belushi acquired a taste for marijuana and hallucinogens, dressed like a hippie, and protested against the Vietnam War. He avoided the draft because of elevated blood pressure (made higher when he ate salt before the physical examination).

In 1971, Belushi became the youngest member of Second City, and people soon began to take notice. On the strength of his Joe Cocker impersonation, he was cast in the off-Broadway musical *National Lampoon's Lemmings* (1973), a send-up of Woodstock. During this time Belushi discovered cocaine and the tranquilizer Quaalude. After *Lemmings*, he remained part of the *Lampoon* team, writing and acting in their syndicated radio program.

BELOW A dubious honor? The street term for a "speedball"— a dangerous mix of cocaine and heroin—is now a "Belushi."

John Belushi became a household name as one of the stars of the New York-based television series *Saturday Night Live*, which premiered in October, 1975. This cutting-edge series launched the careers of many other gifted comedians including Gilda Radner, Dan Aykroyd, Chevy Chase, Bill Murray, and Steve Martin. The program gave Belushi the opportunity to perfect his physical style of comedy, inventing characters such as the Samurai warrior, and irreverently impersonating Elizabeth Taylor and Marlon Brando.

On December 31, 1976, Belushi married Judy Jacklin, a girl he had known since high school and with whom he'd been living for some years. Judy was deeply worried about her husband's progressing cocaine addiction, which nearly got him fired from *Saturday Night Live* on several occasions.

The following year, Jack Nicholson summoned Belushi for a minor part in *Goin' South* (1978). Belushi went on location to Mexico, and it was not a happy experience: he didn't like Nicholson, and the feeling was mutual. His next role was more satisfying—that of the boorish fraternity member "Bluto" in *National Lampoon's Animal House* (1978). The film was a resounding success.

Steven Spielberg offered John Belushi $350,000 to appear in *1941*, released in 1979, but he was concerned about Belushi's drug habit. Belushi was now using everything to excess: food, alcohol, cigarettes, pot, tranquilizers, and especially cocaine. Tired of meeting the demands of both New York and Hollywood, Belushi quit *Saturday Night Live* in order to concentrate on his movie career. His next project was with Dan Aykroyd: *The Blues Brothers* (1980), in which they played characters originally created for *Saturday Night Live*. Both Belushi and Aykroyd loved music, and this upbeat, soulful movie enabled them to work with such R&B greats as Ray Charles, Aretha Franklin, James Brown, and Cab Calloway. The movie is considered a classic.

ABOVE With Japanese actor Toshiro Mifune, in the comedy–action film 1941 *(1979). John Belushi played an out-of-control fighter pilot in this box-office flop.*

Belushi shed 40 pounds (18 kg) to play the romantic lead in *Continental Divide* (1981). However, there was little chemistry with co-star Blair Brown, and the film received a lukewarm response. *Neighbors* (1981), a black comedy with Dan Aykroyd, also failed to live up to expectations. Desperate for a hit movie, Belushi decided to create one himself, a comedy/crime caper entitled *Noble Rot* (a rewrite by Belushi of Paul de Mielche's script *Sweet Deceptions*). He took Paramount Studio's criticism of the screenplay as a personal affront, and with his self-esteem at an all-time low, he flew to Los Angeles, checked into the Chateau Marmont Hotel on Sunset Boulevard, and embarked on a marathon drug binge. Judy stayed behind in New York.

On March 1, 1982, Belushi met up with Los Angeles acquaintance Cathy Smith, a drug addict and dealer who had once been involved with Canadian singer/songwriter Gordon Lightfoot. Smith introduced Belushi to "speedballs," an injection of cocaine and heroin, and he loved the effect. The pair hung out together for several days.

BELOW National Lampoon's Animal House (1978) was filmed at the University of Oregon because there was not enough money to pay for a studio set.

In the early hours of March 5, Belushi and Smith arrived back at the hotel, after having partied all night. Several people joined them, including Robert De Niro and Robin Williams. Belushi wasn't feeling well, but that didn't stop him from consuming even more drugs. Finally, Smith gave Belushi one more shot, he had a shower and went to bed, and she drove off to place a bet on a horse. Several hours later, Belushi's fitness trainer Bill Wallace turned up and found his client lying on the bed, naked, and curled up in the fetal position, his tongue hanging out. Wallace tried to revive him, but it was too late—John Belushi was dead. The coroner's report stated that the death was due to "acute cocaine and heroin intoxication." Belushi was buried on March 9 at Martha's Vineyard, Massachusetts, a place where he had always found peace.

In 1983, Smith was charged with second-degree murder. She was later sentenced to three years in jail for involuntary manslaughter, but only spent 18 months behind bars.

Star Shot
Dorothy Dandridge turned down the role of Tuptim in the film musical *The King and I* (1956); the role eventually went to Rita Moreno.

Dorothy Dandridge

Born November 9, 1922
Died September 8, 1965

Dorothy Dandridge had much in common with fellow actresses Marilyn Monroe and Judy Garland. Born in the 1920s, she experienced an unhappy childhood and disastrous relationships, was addicted to alcohol and pills, and succumbed to a drug-induced death in her prime. But as an African-American, Dandridge had to combat the added challenge of racism.

Her mother Ruby separated from her father Cyril while she was pregnant, and for several years she raised baby Dorothy and her older sister Vivian alone. Intent on a show-business career both for herself and her two small daughters, Ruby and her new partner, Geneva ("Auntie") Williams, trained the girls in singing, dancing, reciting, and piano. As "The Wonder Children," the Dandridge girls began performing in their home town of Cleveland, Ohio, and then traveled throughout the south of the United States with the National Baptist Convention. Dandridge endured all manner of abuse from Williams, who was a jealous and demanding stepparent.

When the Depression hit, Ruby set her sights on Hollywood. The sisters joined with another singer, Etta Jones, becoming "The Dandridge Sisters." They performed in nightclubs and appeared in a number of films including *The Big Broadcast of 1936* (1935) and *A Day at the Races* (1937). Ruby was forging her own movie career, but as an African-American woman, her choice of parts was limited. In 1938, The Dandridge Sisters went to New York to sing at the famous Cotton Club; a few years later Dorothy Dandridge struck out on her own as a solo performer.

The film musical *Sun Valley Serenade* (1941) reunited Dandridge with tap-dancing great Harold Nicholas of the Nicholas Brothers, whom she had previously met at the Cotton Club. They married in 1942, and Dandridge was happy to devote herself to marriage and motherhood. But her dreams of a perfect family were shattered when her daughter Harolyn, born in 1943, was diagnosed as severely intellectually disabled, and her husband turned out to be a notorious womanizer. Dandridge divorced Nicholas in 1949.

ABOVE Dorothy Dandridge was one of the first African-American cinema superstars. Singer Lena Horne called her "our Marilyn Monroe."

Ruby and Geneva looked after Harolyn for a while, but Dandridge later placed her in private nursing care.

During her years with Nicholas, Dandridge appeared in a few films, such as *Atlantic City* (1944) and *Pillow to Post* (1945), and her singing talents attracted a good deal of attention. With her marriage now over, Dandridge put all her energies into her career. She took acting and dancing lessons, and under the guidance of her friend and musical director Phil Moore, she developed a sophisticated nightclub act that took her overseas and to some of the most glamorous entertainment venues in the United States, such as the Mocambo in Hollywood and the Empire Room of The Waldorf-Astoria in New York. Although she was well paid, Dandridge hated the work, and she was often

banned from staying in the hotels where she performed because of her African-American heritage.

Gradually, Dandridge picked up better roles, working her way up from *Tarzan's Peril* and *The Harlem Globetrotters* (both in 1951) to *Bright Road* (1953), in which she played a schoolteacher. Her most memorable film is *Carmen Jones* (1954), a musical based on the Bizet opera, with an all-star cast including Harry Belafonte and Pearl Bailey. Director Otto Preminger turned her down for the leading role, thinking she didn't have enough sex appeal to be convincing. Dandridge went for a second audition, unrecognizable in heavy makeup and tight, seductive clothes. She won not only the part but also the heart of the married director, and they embarked on a tumultuous affair. It was a blow to Dandridge that Preminger had her voice dubbed by opera singer Marilyn Horne. But she was rewarded with an Oscar® nomination for Best Actress (the first African-American to win such an accolade) and was featured on the cover of *Life* magazine.

Unfortunately, due to racial typecasting, it was a long time before Dandridge was offered another decent part: a role in the controversial *Island in the Sun* (1957), again with Harry Belafonte. The European-made *The Happy Road* and *Tamango* (both in 1957) followed. Her last important film was George Gershwin's opera *Porgy and Bess* (1959), co-starring Sidney Poitier and Sammy Davis Jr. and directed by Otto Preminger.

Dandridge's second marriage to white restaurateur/nightclub owner Jack Denison in 1959 was the start of a progressive downward spiral. In just a few years Denison managed to squander most of Dandridge's hard-earned money, and that, combined with some bad investments, left her bankrupt. She was forced to put her now teenage daughter (who had a mental age of four) in a state institution as she could no longer afford to pay the private nurse, and, guilt-ridden, she began drinking heavily and taking prescribed drugs.

In 1965, Dandridge seemed determined to take control of her life and career. She detoxed at a health spa, and some film possibilities and a New York nightclub engagement were in the offing. On September 8, 1965, Dandridge's manager, Earl Mills, came to pick her up at her apartment to take her to the doctor to have a cast put on a minor ankle fracture. When he couldn't get into the apartment, Mills broke in and found Dandridge on the bathroom floor, wearing only a blue headscarf—she had been dead for two hours. At first it was thought that her death was due to an embolism caused by the fracture. A subsequent autopsy revealed that she had overdosed on her antidepressant, Tofranil, and it remains uncertain whether she actually committed suicide. However, just a few months earlier, Dandridge had given her manager a letter that requested, "In case of death … cremate me right away. If I have anything … give it to my mother…." When Dandridge died, she had a total of $2.14 in the bank.

LEFT With Sidney Poitier in Porgy and Bess *(1959). George Gershwin stipulated that only African-American singers were to perform his opera.*

ABOVE Dorothy Dandridge as Jane Richards in a scene from Bright Road *(1953). She once said, "If I were white, I would capture the world."*

LEFT Island in the Sun *(1957), co-starring Harry Belafonte, caused something of a stir as it dealt with the vexed issue of interracial relationships.*

Eric Douglas

Born June 21, 1958
Died July 6, 2004

Eric Douglas explained that "the pressures of being the youngest son in a famous family sometimes got to me. I used to feel I had to compare myself to them." It couldn't have been easy being the son of Kirk Douglas, one of Hollywood's most revered actors, whose career has spanned more than five decades. And not only did Eric have his father's shoes to fill, but his older half-brother, Michael Douglas, has also been a major player in the motion picture industry, both as a producer and actor.

Star Shot

In 1999, an overdose of prescription drugs left Eric Douglas with speech and walking impairments.

Eric was the second son of Kirk Douglas and his second wife, Anne Buydens. His other siblings included half-brother Joel and older brother Peter. He made his acting debut at the age of 13 in *A Gunfight* (1971) starring his father and Johnny Cash. His next film role wasn't until 1982—a television movie set in Israel, *Remembrance of Love*, which also starred Kirk Douglas. When his father attempted to give him some acting advice, Eric replied, "Dad, you're not the director. You're just an actor."

During the 1980s, Eric appeared in such forgettable teenage films as *The Flamingo Kid* (1984) with Matt Dillon, and *Tomboy* (1985). After a minor role in Eddie Murphy's *The Golden Child* (1986), he turned his energies to stand-up comedy and became known for his wry, self-mocking style of humor. Eric joined with his father once again in an episode of HBO's *Tales from the Crypt* (1991), and appeared in *Delta Force 3: The Killing Game* (1991), and another television series, *Alaska Kid* (1993).

LEFT When Michael Douglas placed his hand and footprints in the courtyard of Mann's Chinese Theater in 1997, he was accompanied by his brother, Eric.

Had he persevered, Eric Douglas probably would have matured into a competent character actor. But for years he was troubled by alcoholism and drug addiction, and although he was constantly in and out of rehabilitation centers, he never seemed to achieve any sort of lasting sobriety. As his addiction progressed, Eric was often in the news for drunken driving and other misdemeanors.

On July 6, 2004, Eric's body was discovered by the cleaner who had let herself in to his Manhattan apartment. His death was ruled as accidental, caused by acute intoxication from alcohol, painkillers, and tranquilizers. Police ruled out foul play.

In 1997 Kirk Douglas wrote in his memoir *Climbing the Mountain*: "For my youngest and most troubled son, Eric, I would bless him to learn how to take blame and credit with equanimity and to control his impulsive nature." Alas, his wish never came true.

Chris Farley

Born February 15, 1964
Died December 18, 1997

LEFT Chris Farley was the first choice to play the lead in The Cable Guy *(1996) but because of his busy schedule, the part went to Jim Carrey.*

Star Shot

The animated film *Shrek* was conceived with Chris Farley in mind. Farley recorded most of Shrek's dialogue before he died, but out of respect, the decision was made not to use his voice.

The similarities between Chris Farley and his hero John Belushi are uncanny. They both had gargantuan appetites for anything that made them feel good, they were both Aquarians, and they both followed very similar paths to stardom and self-destruction, both dying at the age of 33.

Christopher Crosby Farley was raised in a close-knit Irish-Catholic family in Madison, Wisconsin. A boisterous, overweight child, he found he could gain acceptance from his peers by being funny. An intelligent young man, Farley received a degree in theater and communications from Marquette University in Milwaukee in 1986. From the ImprovOlympic Theatre it was a natural progression to Chicago's famous Second City troupe.

When *Saturday Night Live* producer Lorne Michaels saw Farley perform, he was so entertained by his outrageous physical comedy that he signed Farley for the 1990 season. During the five years that Farley was a series regular, he made frequent forays into the movies, appearing in *Wayne's World* (1992), *Coneheads* (1993), *Wayne's World 2* (1993), *Airheads* (1994), and *Billy Madison* (1995).

Chris Farley's first leading role was in *Tommy Boy* (1995), where he was teamed with weedy David Spade. The film was a great box office success, and the pair of opposites got together again the following year for *Black Sheep* (1996). Farley was paid handsomely to appear with Chris Rock in *Beverly Hills Ninja* (1997), and his last film, *Almost Heroes* (1998), was the one he enjoyed the most. It was directed by Christopher Guest and co-starred Matthew Perry.

By this time Farley was a wealthy and recognized star, friends and fans adored him, but he was still dissatisfied. He wanted to break out of the oafish, fat-boy stereotype, and was still trying to fill an inner emptiness with food, drugs, alcohol, and prostitutes. For several years he sought help from health farms and rehabilitation centers all over the United States, achieving one year of sobriety before falling back into his old ways again.

Farley's final binge consisted of a week of almost nonstop eating, drinking, cocaine snorting, and more. The last person to see him alive was a stripper who performed for him in his luxury Chicago apartment in the early hours of Thursday, December 18, 1997. Later that day, Farley's brother found him dead. The autopsy revealed the cause of death was an overdose of morphine and cocaine, combined with coronary artery disease.

In memory of their brother, Farley's siblings set up the Chris Farley Foundation, which uses comedy to help instruct young people about drugs and alcohol.

ABOVE With Tom Arnold. To show his range as an actor, Chris Farley dreamed of one day playing Roscoe "Fatty" Arbuckle in a film about his tragic life.

Judy Garland

Born June 10, 1922
Died June 22, 1969

The girl who began her life as Frances Ethel Gumm went on to become one of the most enduring, talented, and charismatic performers of the twentieth century. Her father, Frank, managed a movie theater in Grand Rapids, Minnesota. Her mother, Ethel, played the piano there, and at the age of two, "Baby" Frances joined her two older sisters on the stage during intermissions.

In 1927, Frank purchased a theater in Lancaster, California. A fiercely ambitious mother, Ethel enrolled "The Gumm Sisters" in the prestigious Meglin Kiddies talent school in Los Angeles. Their singing and dancing act would take them to the Chicago World's Fair in 1933 where they changed their name to "The Garland Sisters." "Baby" (by now the star) became Judy Garland.

After years of auditions, Garland finally landed a movie contract with MGM in October 1935; a month later her beloved father died of spinal meningitis. Without Frank, Garland no longer had a buffer between herself and her mother, and not only did she have Ethel's bullying to contend with, but MGM now had control of her whole life. The studio gave Garland amphetamines to enable her to lose weight and work long hours, and then gave her barbiturates to wind down. But despite the grueling schedule, Garland loved acting. Her first

ABOVE With Fred Astaire in the 1948 musical Easter Parade. *Even at an early age, Judy Garland had a mature and distinctive voice and singing style.*

credited movie role was in *Every Sunday* (1936), and she was then loaned to 20th Century Fox for *Pigskin Parade* (1936). In *Broadway Melody of 1938* (1937), Garland charmed audiences with her song to Clark Gable, and after *Thoroughbreds Don't Cry* (1937) and the 1938 film *Love Finds Andy Hardy* (the first of ten films that Garland and Mickey Rooney would do together), Garland was awarded the role that would rocket her to stardom: Dorothy in *The Wizard of Oz* (1939). The screen adaptation of L. Frank Baum's novel has become one of the most treasured movies of all time, due in no small part to Garland's portrayal of the heroine and her emotive rendition of "Over the Rainbow."

Between 1940 and 1942, Garland made seven films, including *For Me and My Gal* (1942), which was Gene Kelly's screen debut. At the age of 19, she married bandleader David Rose. When she became pregnant, the studio coerced her into an abortion because they felt that motherhood didn't fit her image. The marriage lasted only a few years. Throughout the 1940s, Garland starred in one movie after another, including *Meet Me in St. Louis* (1944), *Ziegfeld Follies* (1946), and *Easter Parade* (1948). Somehow she managed to find time

RIGHT Judy Garland will always be remembered as the little girl who followed the yellow brick road. She was 17 when she made The Wizard of Oz *in 1939.*

to marry Italian director Vincente Minnelli in 1945 and give birth to her daughter, Liza, one year later. However, postpartum depression and exhaustion took their toll, and now Garland was using more drugs than ever. After a nervous breakdown and hospitalization in 1950, she made just one more movie for MGM—*Summer Stock* (1950)—before her contract was terminated. Her second marriage ended in 1951, and she made her first suicide attempt.

Garland returned to the stage in 1951 at the London Palladium, encouraged by her new husband, impresario Sid Luft. Her magnificent performance was so well received that it was repeated at the Palace Theater in New York. The early 1950s were happy years for the Lufts: their children, Lorna and Joey, were born in 1952 and 1955 respectively; they were members of the Beverly Hills A-list; and Garland's drug intake was fairly controlled. They produced *A Star is Born* (1954), which earned Garland an Oscar® nomination for Best Actress. But by the end of the decade, a demanding concert, recording, and television schedule meant that Garland needed more drugs to cope. Photographs from this period show an almost unrecognizable Garland with a bloated face and body—and in 1959 she nearly died from liver failure caused by hepatitis.

Ever resilient, Garland bounced back again—her 1961 concert at Carnegie Hall was one of the finest of her career. That year she was nominated again for an Oscar®, for her supporting role in *Judgment at Nuremberg* (1961). But the cracks in her marriage were widening, and she had added the new drugs Ritalin and Valium to her pharmacopeia, mixing them with alcohol. When Garland's own television series was canceled in 1964 after only one season, she was bitterly disappointed. Despite their huge earnings, Garland and Luft were profligate spenders and poor financial managers, so by the time they divorced in 1965, they were both deeply in debt.

Over the next four years, Garland had two more brief marriages (to gay actor Mark Herron in 1965, and nightclub manager Mickey Deans in 1969), and many affairs in between. Garland was addicted to love and romance as much as to any substance. But more than anything else, she was addicted to the applause—and although the pills and the men always let her down, her audiences never did, even when she reached rock bottom.

The week after her 47th birthday and only three months after their marriage, Garland and Deans went to London, her favorite city. On the morning of June 22, 1969, Deans found Garland dead in the bathroom of their apartment. The autopsy confirmed that her death was caused by an accidental overdose of the barbiturate Seconal. Most people who knew her agreed that despite all her turmoil, she loved life and her children too much to have killed herself. Judy Garland's body was flown back to New York, where countless fans and members of the entertainment industry paid tribute to this bright star who had finally found peace.

ABOVE "The Man That Got Away" from A Star is Born (1954) seems to reflect something of Judy Garland's bad luck with marriage.

BELOW The bestselling recording of Garland's 1961 Carnegie Hall concert won a Grammy® for Album of the Year.

Alexander Godunov

Born November 28, 1949
Died May 18, 1995

ABOVE Alexander Godunov's interpretations of the great classical ballet lead roles resulted in a gold medal at the 1973 Moscow International Competition.

RIGHT The popular 1986 comedy The Money Pit, *with Tom Hanks, gave Alexander Godunov the chance to flex his acting muscles.*

The broodingly handsome dancer and actor Alexander Godunov was born on Sakhalin Island, part of the former Soviet Union. He grew up in Latvia, and began dance lessons at the age of nine at the Riga State Ballet School, where he made friends with another aspiring dancer, Mikhail Baryshnikov. Godunov was given the opportunity to tour with the Moscow Classical Ballet, and then in 1971 became principal dancer with the famous Bolshoi Ballet.

In 1973, Godunov went to the United States with the Bolshoi Ballet, and on his next visit five years later he requested political asylum. At the time he was married to fellow Bolshoi member Lyudmilla Vlasova. On August 23, 1979, the KGB put Vlasova on a plane back to Moscow, but the flight was delayed for three days at New York's Kennedy Airport while the American authorities tried to determine whether Vlasova was leaving of her own volition. Eventually Vlasova flew home to the U.S.S.R., and although Godunov tried to get her out again, it never happened.

Godunov became the principal dancer of the American Ballet Theater in 1979, which was run by his old friend Baryshnikov, who ultimately fired him from the troupe in 1982. The dismissal was a bitter disappointment for Godunov, who remarked that Baryshnikov "threw me away like a potato peel." In the same year he divorced his wife and began a six-year relationship with English actress Jacqueline Bisset. A documentary entitled *Godunov: The World to Dance In* was produced in 1983 and won several awards.

With his sights set on an acting career, Godunov left the world of dance and headed for Hollywood, appearing in a total of seven movies. His first film was *Witness* (1985), starring Harrison Ford and Kelly McGillis, in which he played a humble Amish farmer. In *The Money Pit* (1986), with Tom Hanks and Shelley Long, Godunov showed he had a flair for comedy in the role of the egocentric symphony conductor. He was the villain in *Die Hard* (1988) and *The Zone* (1996), and in *North* (1994), Godunov and Kelly McGillis played Amish parents in a spoof of their *Witness* characters.

Godunov had not long returned from Budapest, Hungary, where he had been filming *The Zone*, when he was found dead in his West Hollywood apartment. It was believed that he had been dead for about two days. The official cause of death was given as alcohol-induced hepatitis.

Robert Pastorelli

Born June 21, 1954
Died March 8, 2004

Before he became an actor, New Jersey native Robert Pastorelli was headed for a career as a professional boxer. However, injuries he sustained from a near-fatal car accident on his 19th birthday forced him to trade the boxing ring for the entertainment arena. While searching for work, Pastorelli lived in his car for 18 months in the 1970s until he was offered roles in the New York stage productions of *Death of a Salesman* and *Rebel Without a Cause*.

Pastorelli went to Hollywood in 1982, and over the next few years appeared in numerous television series such as *Cagney and Lacey, Barney Miller, St. Elsewhere, Hill Street Blues,* and *Miami Vice*. His first movie roles were in *I Married a Centerfold* (1984) and *California Girls* (1985). He was usually cast as the "rough diamond." From 1988 to 1994 he played the philosophical house painter, Eldin, in the hugely successful sitcom *Murphy Brown,* and left when he stopped enjoying it. His own sitcom, *Double Rush* (1995), was short-lived.

Pastorelli maintained that he went where the work was, and there was work aplenty for this versatile character actor. From the late 1980s onward he co-starred in a wide variety of films in many different genres, including *Outrageous Fortune* (1987), *Beverly Hills Cop II* (1987), *Dances with Wolves* (1990), *Sister Act 2: Back in the Habit* (1993), *Michael* (1996), *Eraser* (1996), and *A Simple Wish* (1997). He continued to accept interesting television roles as well, such as *Cracker* (1997), a U.S. version of a U.K. hit series, and a remake of *South Pacific* (2001) with Glenn Close. He joined with Close again in the London stage production of *A Streetcar Named Desire* in 2002.

From living in his car at the start of his career, Pastorelli now owned three Cadillacs, as well as homes in Los Angeles, the Hollywood Hills, and Sea Girt, New Jersey. However, all was not well in his life. In 1999, Pastorelli's 25-year-old girlfriend, Charemon Jonovich, shot herself in front of him—they had had a baby daughter, Gianna, just over a year before Jonovich's death.

On the morning of March 8, 2004, Pastorelli's assistant entered his Hollywood Hills home and found him slumped over on the toilet, with vomit on his clothes and a syringe in his arm. The coroner declared that the cause of death was an accidental overdose of morphine and cocaine. What made his death such a tragedy was that Pastorelli had been off drugs for many years, and was a highly regarded member of Hollywood's film community. Interestingly, just before his death, the police re-opened Jonovich's case, and Pastorelli was named as "a person of interest," but the case was closed again when he died.

ABOVE Actor Robert Pastorelli had a number of tattoos, including roses, a wolf, a dragon, an angel, and some children's faces.

Star Shot

When he died, Pastorelli had just completed shooting *Be Cool*, the sequel to *Get Shorty* (1995) starring John Travolta and Uma Thurman, released early in 2005.

River Phoenix

Born August 23, 1970
Died October 31, 1993

ABOVE River Phoenix valued the support of his family. He once said, "We all wanted to be entertainers and our parents did whatever they could to help us."

RIGHT River Phoenix and Wil Wheaton (right) in Stand by Me *(1986). This film was based on a semiautobiographical story by Stephen King.*

The first child of flower children John Bottom and Arlyn Dunetz Bottom, River Jude was born on a farm in Madras, Oregon. After some years of wandering, John and Arlyn's quest led them to the Children of God, a radical cult that recruited many of its members from the hippie community.

The family moved from Texas to Mexico to Puerto Rico to South America, where John was appointed "Archbishop of Venezuela." This position paid no money, however, and five-year-old River and his three-year-old sister Rain often had to sing on the streets to keep their family (which by now included brother Joaquin and sister Liberty) from starving. The Bottoms became disenchanted with the cult and in 1978 stowed away on a freighter bound for the United States. Their last child, Summer Joy, was born in Florida, and with high hopes for the future, the family changed their last name to Phoenix.

The children supplemented the meager family income by singing and winning talent shows. Arlyn was guided to Los Angeles, believing that if her gifted children became famous, they could make the world a better place. With the same zeal that she approached spirituality and vegetarianism, Arlyn set about getting her children into show business. She got a job as a secretary at NBC, and met high-profile children's agent Iris Burton, who immediately sensed that River had star quality. With Burton's help, River and Rain got small spots singing on kids' television programs. River appeared in a few commercials, but stopped doing them because he felt they were "phony."

In 1982, 11-year-old River was cast in the television series *Seven Brides for Seven Brothers*, which only ran for one season. River then got dramatic parts in some television movies and in the miniseries *Robert Kennedy and His Times* (1984), in which he played a youthful Robert Kennedy, Jr. From there, he landed the role of the owlish scientist in his first feature film, *Explorers* (1985), which was also Ethan Hawke's first movie. For the first time, River made friends outside of his family, but because of his eccentric upbringing and lack of formal education, he still felt different and apart.

River was chosen from over 300 hopefuls for the coming-of-age film *Stand by Me* (1986), blossoming under Rob Reiner's relaxed style of directing, and enjoying the camaraderie on set. During this time River first sampled beer, cigarettes, and marijuana. Later that year, River and his father traveled to Belize to film *The Mosquito Coast* (1986), a story that echoed the Phoenix family's own life. Director Peter Weir could see in him "something apart from the

acting ability." The wisdom of an old soul combined with childlike vulnerability shone through. Three movies were released in 1988: *A Night in the Life of Jimmy Reardon*, *Little Nikita*, and *Running on Empty*. River's performance in *Running on Empty* earned him an Oscar® nomination for Actor in a Supporting Role. He then did *Indiana Jones and the Last Crusade* (1989).

Arlyn's dream had come true: River was a star, and was able to use his fame to speak out for animal rights and the environment. But John was concerned that Hollywood was a corrupting influence, so they bought a 20-acre (8-hectare) property near Gainesville, Florida, a college town with a strong alternative culture. In between movies, River formed a rock band called Aleka's Attic and began drinking and using cocaine in earnest. Nevertheless, his career continued apace, in such diverse and interesting films as *I Love You to Death* (1990), *My Own Private Idaho* (1991), *Dogfight* (1991), *Sneakers* (1992), and *Silent Tongue* (1993). In 1992 he bought his father a retreat in Costa Rica, as well as 800 acres (324 hectares) of rainforest on the Panama/Costa Rica border to protect it.

By 1993, River was thin and pale, and his natural intensity had turned dark and edgy. During the filming of *The Thing Called Love* (1993) he was often under the influence of a chemical substance. He stayed clean and sober for two months during the shooting of *Dark Blood* (1993) in Utah, so when he came back to Los Angeles he was ready to party.

On the evening of October 30, 1993, Joaquin, Rain, and River's girlfriend Samantha Mathis joined River in his room at the Hotel Nikkon, and after a few hours of drinking, they adjourned to The Viper Room on Sunset Boulevard, a trendy nightclub owned by Johnny Depp. Having already consumed various drugs, River went into the bathroom and snorted some heroin. He immediately began vomiting and shaking, and someone gave him a Valium to relax. When he started to have trouble breathing, his companions helped him outside onto the sidewalk, where he went into violent convulsions. By the time the ambulance arrived, River had gone into cardiac arrest; he was quickly taken to Cedars-Sinai Medical Center, where the doctors vainly attempted to revive him. Sadly, 23-year-old River Phoenix died at 1:50 A.M. on Halloween morning of what was later called "acute multiple drug intoxication." The world had lost one of its finest young actors and a sensitive human being.

LEFT With Keanu Reeves in My Own Private Idaho *(1991). During filming, River Phoenix received a humanitarian award from People for the Ethical Treatment of Animals.*

Last Words

"I'm gonna die, dude."

BELOW During filming of The Mosquito Coast *(1986), Harrison Ford commented that 15-year-old River Phoenix was "very workman-like and professional."*

Elvis Presley

Born January 8, 1935
Died August 16, 1977

The man who would be "King"—Elvis Aaron Presley—was born in a two-room house in Tupelo, Mississippi. His parents, Vernon and Gladys, were both children of sharecroppers, with roots that go back to Scotland and the Cherokee nation. Elvis's twin brother, Jesse Garon, died at birth.

Elvis loved singing in church, and at the age of ten he won a $5.00 prize at the state fair for his rendition of "Old Shep." Gladys encouraged his interest in music, buying him a $12.95 guitar for his 12th birthday. The following year, the Presleys moved to Memphis, Tennessee, birthplace of "the blues." After Elvis completed high school, Vernon encouraged him to become an electrician, but once Elvis made a "demo" at Sun Records as a gift for Gladys, his fate was sealed. Sun Records' owner Sam Phillips had never heard anything like his rich, soulful voice and his unique blending of country, gospel, and R&B styles. His first single, "That's All Right," was released in July 1954, and once Elvis began touring the south and making regular appearances on the live radio program *Louisiana Hayride*, his popularity rapidly grew.

In 1955, Elvis signed with RCA—"Heartbreak Hotel" soon reached number one; his eponymous first album was released a few months later. His vibrant, sensual performance on *The Ed Sullivan Show* in 1956 caused a furor, and by now the whole country was talking about the new teen idol from Tennessee.

The hit records kept coming, and on the strength of Elvis's stage presence and sexual magnetism, he was cast in the first of his 33 motion pictures, *Love Me Tender* (1956). His next films, *Jailhouse Rock* (1957) and *King Creole* (1958), were well received by audiences and critics alike. Elvis was making more money than he ever thought possible, and no sooner did he purchase his Memphis mansion, Graceland, than he was drafted into the U.S. Army. In August 1958, while Elvis was stationed at Fort Hood, Texas, his mother died; it is thought that his use of amphetamines possibly began around this period.

After his return from overseas duty in Germany, Elvis's career picked up where it left off, with a new movie—*G.I. Blues* (1960). His next film, *Flaming Star* (1960), was considered his best, and *Blue Hawaii* (1961) his most popular, but Elvis gradually became tired of grinding out one film after another. He wanted to realize his potential as a dramatic actor, but his manager, "Colonel" Tom Parker, insisted that he continue with the tried and true musical formula because of the huge profits generated from the soundtrack albums. According to Elvis, "they keep trying to make *G.I. Blues* and *Blue Hawaii* over and over again, and all they do is move the scenery around a little."

In May 1967, Elvis married Priscilla Beaulieu, who was only 14 when they first met in Germany. Nine months later their daughter, Lisa Marie, was born. The year 1969 was a big one

for Elvis: "Suspicious Minds" was the first number one single he'd had for years; he made his last movie (*Change of Habit*); and he went back to doing what he loved best—performing for his many fans. The Las Vegas concert that year was a sell-out, and the historic Aloha Concert in Hawaii, which was broadcast via satellite to millions around the world in January 1973, was nothing short of a triumph.

The demands of touring, as well as his divorce in 1973, exacerbated Elvis's progressing drug addiction. By the mid-1970s he was consuming massive amounts of amphetamines, painkillers, and sedatives prescribed by his personal physician, Dr. George Nichopolous. Strangely enough, Elvis strongly disapproved of recreational drugs, and he barely touched alcohol. The medications, combined with a long-standing pattern of crash dieting and binge eating, were having a disastrous effect on Elvis's health. Soon after he turned 40, he entered hospital suffering from liver damage, a spastic colon, and glaucoma. Emotionally, he was becoming more introspective and isolated, regretful that he had so little control over his life and career. Nevertheless, Elvis was still the top touring act in the United States in 1977. Although his once-handsome face and body were bloated and he sometimes slurred his words, he hadn't lost the ability to captivate an audience.

In the early hours of August 16, 1977, at Graceland, Elvis took a handful of sleeping pills and went to bed. Around 2:00 P.M. that afternoon, his fiancée, Ginger Alden, found him unconscious on the bathroom floor. Elvis was rushed to the Baptist Memorial Hospital in Memphis, but all the medical techniques possible failed to revive him. The King was dead. Initially, the cause of death was given as cardiac arrhythmia, but blood tests later confirmed that Elvis had a mixture of several narcotics in his system.

The public outpouring of grief over Elvis's death was phenomenal. He was buried alongside his beloved mother at the Forest Hills Cemetery in Memphis, but both bodies were later moved to the Meditation Garden at Graceland. Hundreds of thousands of pilgrims visit Graceland every year to honor one of the most influential entertainers of the twentieth century, who just months before he died, had said, "All I ever wanted was to help people; love them, lift them up, spread some joy."

ABOVE When the Beatles visited the United States in 1965, they wanted to meet The King. They spent the day of August 27 at his home in California.

LEFT Although Priscilla and Elvis Presley were divorced in 1973, he remained a devoted father to his only child, Lisa Marie, born in February 1968.

Marie Prevost

Born November 8, 1898
Died January 23, 1937

One of the loveliest actresses of the silent movie era, Marie Prevost was born Mary Bickford Dunn in Sarnia, Ontario, Canada. The Dunns moved to Denver, Colorado, and following her husband's death, Mrs. Dunn and her two daughters settled in Los Angeles.

In 1917, Mary became one of Max Sennett's "Bathing Beauties," and at Sennett's suggestion, she changed her name to the more French-sounding Marie Prevost. In seven years, Prevost appeared in 26 Keystone comedies, and it was clear that she had star potential. After making eight comedies with Universal Studios, Prevost signed a contract with Warner Bros. Her first serious dramatic role was as Gloria in the adaptation of F. Scott Fitzgerald's Jazz Age novel, *The Beautiful and the Damned* (1922). Prevost fell in love with her co-star, Kenneth Harlan, and they married in 1924. Harlan and Prevost became one of Hollywood's golden couples.

In the same year as her marriage, Prevost starred with Adolphe Menjou in *The Marriage Circle* (1924), directed by Ernst Lubitsch. German-born Lubitsch became renowned for films displaying his unique brand of subtle humor, sexual innuendo, and sophistication. Prevost and Lubitsch would work together again in *Three Women* (1924) and *Kiss Me Again* (1925).

Prevost was devastated when, in 1926, her mother was killed in a car accident. When her marriage ended the following year, she began to drink heavily. Cecil B. DeMille's *The Godless Girl* (1929) was Prevost's first "talkie," and, like many silent stars, Prevost did not adapt well to the new medium. Her voice was considered too nasal, and as she began to gain more and more weight, she was relegated to minor roles. A cycle of starvation diets, overeating, and binge drinking developed. When the work slowed down in the mid-1930s, Prevost was forced to sell her home and move into a seedy Hollywood apartment.

In January 1937, Prevost's neighbors were disturbed by her dachshund's barking. The police found the actress's dead body, with the arms and legs eaten away by the dog. No one knows whether the animal was attempting to wake her, or just trying to survive. Marie Prevost drank and starved herself to death—a tragic ending for a woman who had once been so vibrant and beautiful.

Star Shot

The sister of actress Peggy Prevost, Marie Prevost's first job was as a stenographer.

BELOW The Marriage Circle (1924) shot Marie Prevost to stardom. In 1932, Lubitsch remade the film as One Hour With You, starring Jeanette MacDonald.

Wallace Reid

Born April 15, 1891
Died January 18, 1923

Last Words

"God.... I.... Please!"

It would have been almost impossible for Wallace Reid to have escaped a career in show business. His mother was a stage actress, and his versatile father had been a playwright and actor before becoming a pioneer in the fledgling motion picture industry.

In 1910 Reid traveled to Chicago to join his father, who was employed as a writer and director at Selig Studios. Young Wallace Reid was soon working as a stuntman and doing bit parts. He continued to learn the movie craft in New York, and, barely out of his teens, became involved in all aspects of filmmaking. Reid arrived in the new film community of Hollywood in 1912 and settled into a career as a cameraman and director. But because he was tall, athletic, and handsome, it wasn't long before he was in great demand as a leading man.

In 1913, Reid married 17-year-old actress Dorothy Davenport. By the time he was cast as the blacksmith in D. W. Griffiths's landmark historical epic, *The Birth of a Nation* (1915), he had appeared in more than 100 films. In the same year, Reid signed a contract with Famous Players-Lasky (Paramount) Studios, and for the next eight years he was in constant demand, making one film after another. Some of his memorable early Paramount films include *Carmen* (1915) and *Joan the Woman* (1917), both co-starring Geraldine Farrar and directed by Cecil B. DeMille.

Reid sustained back and head injuries in a train derailment while filming *The Valley of the Giants* (1919) in Oregon. It is generally believed that the studio arranged for Reid to be given morphine so he could keep working. Unfortunately, he gradually became addicted to the drug and also drank heavily, yet he continued to keep up the frenetic pace that was set for him. Among his many films were *The Affairs of Anatole* and *Don't Tell Everything* (both in 1921) co-starring screen goddess Gloria Swanson, and the racing-car features *The Roaring Road* (1919), *Double Speed* (1920), and *Excuse My Dust* (1920).

In 1922, Reid had a physical and nervous collapse while on the set of *Thirty Days* and was admitted to a sanitarium. His weight had dropped from 170 to 120 pounds (77 to 54 kg), and his severely weakened system was not able to cope with an attack of influenza. He died in the sanitarium on January 18, 1923, leaving behind his two small children, Wallace Jr. and Betty.

Wallace Reid was one of the most likable and popular actors of his era, and was greatly missed by colleagues and fans. His wife, Dorothy Davenport, became an avid anti-drug crusader, producing and starring in a film entitled *Human Wreckage* (1923) that warned of the dangers of narcotics. She remained devoted to the memory of her husband, and died in 1977.

ABOVE Wallace Reid (right) with Eddie Heffernan in the 1922 action film, Across the Continent. *Reid made seven other films that year, so it was no surprise when he collapsed on the set of his last film,* Thirty Days *(1922).*

Rachel Roberts

Born September 20, 1927
Died November 26, 1980

ABOVE With husband
Rex Harrison, while
recording Much Ado
About Nothing (1963).
They appeared together
in the film A Flea in
Her Ear (1968).

Rachel Roberts was born in Llanelli, Wales, the daughter of a Baptist minister. She managed to escape the confines of her provincial religious upbringing once she arrived in London to study at the Royal Academy of Dramatic Art.

Roberts launched herself on the professional stage in 1951 at Stratford-upon-Avon as Ceres in *Twelfth Night*. Other Shakespearean roles followed in 1954 and 1955 with the Old Vic Company. It turned out that the classically trained actress also had a flair for musical comedy, and throughout the 1950s and 1960s she performed in such productions as *Talk of the Night, Keep Your Hair On*, and *Maggie May* (written by Lionel Bart, of *Oliver!* fame).

In 1953, her first three films were released: *Valley of Song, The Weak and the Wicked,* and *The Limping Man*. There would be several more movie roles throughout the 1950s, but it wasn't until *Saturday Night, Sunday Morning* (1960) that Roberts would find her film niche. Based on the novel by Alan Sillitoe, *Saturday Night, Sunday Morning* earned Roberts a British Academy Film Award and made young Albert Finney a star.

The early 1960s was an exciting and creative time for British cinema, spawning a new wave of gritty, working-class dramas that suited Roberts's intense acting style and unique beauty. Another such vehicle was *This Sporting Life* (1963) co-starring Richard Harris, which would reward Roberts with another British Academy Film Award and an Oscar® nomination for Best Actress. During this busy period, she divorced her husband of six years, actor Alan Dobie, and became the fourth wife of actor Rex Harrison, who was then at the peak of his career.

Roberts continued to act in a wide variety of films, plays, and television programs, both in Britain and the United States. Some of the highlights include *Blithe Spirit* (television, 1969), *O Lucky Man!* (1973), *Murder on the Orient Express* (1974), *Picnic at Hanging Rock* (1975), *Habeas Corpus* (Broadway, 1975), *The Tony Randall Show* (television, 1976), *Once a Catholic* (Broadway, 1979), and *Yanks* (1979).

After her bitter divorce from Harrison in 1971, Roberts settled in Los Angeles. Throughout her life she had suffered from intermittent bouts of depression and heavy drinking, which worsened as time went on. On November 26, 1980, she no longer had the strength to fight her demons, and ingested a lethal combination of barbiturates and a caustic poison. Had she lived, Roberts could have had a successful literary career: her diaries were published after her death as the insightful, witty, and poignant *No Bells on Sunday: The Rachel Roberts Journals* (1984).

Gail Russell

Born September 21, 1924
Died August 26, 1961

A sensitive, shy, and artistic young girl, Gail Russell was born in Chicago, and when she was 12 (some sources say 14) her family moved to Santa Monica, California. A high-school friend knew a Paramount executive, and told him of Russell's exceptional beauty. Despite her lack of experience, and pushed by her ambitious mother, Russell signed a seven-year contract in 1942.

Paramount set about grooming their new starlet, and cast her in her first film, a teenage comedy *Henry Aldrich Gets Glamour* (1943), soon followed by *Lady in the Dark* (1944) with Ginger Rogers. Russell experienced severe panic attacks while filming the supernatural thriller *The Uninvited* (1944) with Ray Milland, and she learned to steady her nerves with alcohol. Her next film was the very successful romantic comedy *Our Hearts Were Young and Gay* (1944), but its sequel, *Our Hearts Were Growing Up* (1946), did not fare as well at the box office. In 1947, Russell starred in *Calcutta*, and had a brief encounter with the director, John Farrow, who was married and a devout Catholic. She began dating ruggedly handsome actor Guy Madison (who became television's *Wild Bill Hickok*), and was also rumored to be involved with John Wayne, her co-star in *Angel and the Badman* (1947), although he insisted their relationship was platonic.

Wayne and Russell teamed up again in the adventure/romance *Wake of the Red Witch* (1948). By now, Russell's pattern of anxiety and drinking was getting worse, and marriage to Guy Madison and several mediocre films in 1949 did little to alleviate it. Russell was becoming unreliable, and in 1950 Paramount terminated her contract. Her marriage ended in 1954.

From 1950 to 1961, Russell appeared in only six movies, including *Seven Men from Now* (1956), a Western produced by John Wayne, and *The Tattered Dress* (1957), a film noir drama starring Jeff Chandler and Jeanne Crain. During this period she had several psychiatric admissions and repeated arrests for driving under the influence of alcohol. One of the hospitalizations occurred when John Wayne's wife was suing for divorce, and accused Russell of adultery with him.

Despite several attempts to dry out, Gail Russell kept sinking deeper and deeper into an alcoholic morass. At the very end, she had imprisoned herself in her small apartment and refused to respond to any of her neighbors' attempts to help her. The police were called, and found that 36-year-old Gail Russell had drunk herself to death. Although many people believed she died of an alcohol-related heart attack, the autopsy revealed that she died from liver damage and malnutrition.

ABOVE Our Hearts Were Young and Gay *(1944), about two girls visiting Europe, was based on the book by actress and writer Cornelia Otis Skinner.*

Star Shot

Gail Russell made only two notable appearances on television: in a 1956 episode of *Studio 57* and a 1960 episode of *The Rebel*.

LEFT Gail Russell (center), with Irene Rich (left) and John Wayne in Angel and the Badman *(1947), which Wayne also produced. Today it is considered a classic, but the film was poorly received when it was first released.*

Peggy Shannon

Born January 10, 1910
Died May 11, 1941

Peggy Shannon was born Winona Sammon in Pine Bluff, Arkansas, in January 1910 (according to some sources, 1906). While visiting an aunt in New York, Shannon met Florenz Ziegfeld. The legendary showman was so impressed with the pert redhead that he immediately hired her as a chorus girl in the *Ziegfeld Follies* of 1924.

The following year, Shannon joined Earl Carroll's *Vanities*, a production to rival *Ziegfeld Follies*, and in 1927 she was chosen as the leading actress in Carroll's Broadway play, *What Ann Brought Home*. She appeared in several more Broadway comedies. One day, Paramount producer B. P. Schulberg was in the audience, and convinced Shannon to come to Hollywood.

Shannon signed a contract with Paramount, and her first assignment was to replace the ailing "It Girl," Clara Bow, in *The Secret Call* (1931). It looked as though Shannon was going to be a big star. She was in a continual stream of films from 1931 to 1933 including *False Faces* (1932), a black comedy about cosmetic surgery; and *Society Girl* (1932) and *Painted Woman* (1932), both co-starring the rookie Spencer Tracy.

BELOW Peggy Shannon was buried at the Hollywood Forever Cemetery in California. Her headstone reads, "That Red Headed Girl, Peggy Shannon."

In spite of her talent and good looks, Shannon lacked that certain charisma necessary to be a movie star. She was also reputed to be drinking heavily, something that would have contributed to her dramatic mood swings and unprofessional attitude. When Hollywood didn't live up to her expectations (and vice versa), Shannon returned to the New York stage to star in *Page Miss Glory* (1934) and *The Light Behind the Shadow* (1935), but had to leave the latter production due to illness, possibly alcohol-related.

When she came back to Hollywood in 1935 she made on average two films a year until 1940, but they were mainly B-grade movies: *Youth on Parole* (1937), *Girls on Probation* (1938), *Fixer Dugan* (1939), and the "Little Rascals" short *All About Hash* (1940). On the rare occasions that she got to appear in a quality film such as George Cukor's classic *The Women* (1939) or *The House Across the Bay* (1940) with Joan Bennett and George Raft, she was given only bit parts.

Shannon married cameraman Albert G. Roberts in October 1940 (it was her second marriage). Seven months later, her husband came home to their modest North Hollywood apartment to find his wife slumped across the kitchen table, an empty bottle not far away. The coroner ruled that the cause of death was heart attack brought on by liver failure. A few weeks later, Albert Roberts shot himself in the very same chair where his wife had died. His suicide note read, "I am very much in love with my wife, Peggy Shannon. In this spot she passed away, so in reverence to her, you will find me in the same spot."

Robert Walker

Born October 13, 1918
Died August 28, 1951

Robert Walker was born in Salt Lake City, Utah. A somewhat restless and rebellious youth, Walker found an outlet for his energies in high school drama. At the American Academy of Dramatic Arts in New York he fell in love with fellow student Phyllis Isley (who later became Jennifer Jones). They married in 1939, and their sons, Robert Jr. and Michael, came along in quick succession. Walker worked as a script reader, acted in radio soap operas, and got a number of bit parts in the early 1940s before he was offered his first supporting roles in *Bataan* (1943) and *Madame Curie* (1943). In 1944 he starred in *See Here, Private Hargrove*.

ABOVE Robert Walker with his wife, Jennifer Jones. Walker was admired for his comic timing in films such as Her Highness and the Bellboy *(1945).*

Director David O. Selznick cast Walker and his wife together in the wartime love story *Since You Went Away* (1944). It was a bitter irony that during the shooting, they separated because Jones and Selznick had embarked on a passionate affair. Walker threw himself into his work, displaying his versatility in films such as *Thirty Seconds over Tokyo* (1944) with Spencer Tracy, *The Clock* (1945) with Judy Garland, and *Till the Clouds Roll By* (1946), in which he played composer Jerome Kern.

RIGHT Following in the theatrical steps of their parents, Robert Walker, Jr., and Michael Walker both became actors.

Over the next few years, Walker's behavior became increasingly erratic. Because he was naturally prone to depression and was so devoted to his sons, his divorce had a devastating effect. He would disappear for days at a time, was involved in a hit-and-run accident, and impulsively married actress Barbara Ford (the marriage only lasted six weeks). Four more movies made in just over a year left Walker depleted, and when he was arrested for drink driving in 1948, MGM threatened to cancel his contract unless he got help. At the studio's expense, Walker spent six months at the Menninger Clinic in Topeka, Kansas.

Walker returned to Hollywood with renewed vigor. He made several more films, including the Western *Vengeance Valley* (1951) and Alfred Hitchcock's critically acclaimed thriller *Strangers on a Train* (1951). At only 32, it seemed that Walker still had his best roles ahead of him—but unfortunately, that was not to be.

On August 28, 1951, Walker's housekeeper telephoned his psychiatrist because she thought he seemed particularly agitated. Dr. Frederick Hacker arrived, accompanied by his associate, Dr. Sidney Silver, and, after a struggle, the doctors injected the patient with seven and a half grains of the sedative sodium amytal, a dose he'd had several times before. Almost instantly, Walker became unconscious and stopped breathing. The emergency squad arrived at the Pacific Palisades home and, along with the doctors, they tried to resuscitate him, but within the hour Walker had died of respiratory failure due to an unusual reaction to the drug. Walker was making *My Son John* (1952) when he died—it was finished using extra footage from *Strangers on a Train* (1951).

Dangerous Liaisons

From illicit love affairs and claims of rape to criminal trials and suicides, the sordid scandals that rock the cradle of Hollywood have one thing in common—death. Although it occurred over 80 years ago, one of the strangest liaisons in Hollywood history is still talked about today—the death of actress Virginia Rappe after a weekend of partying with Roscoe "Fatty" Arbuckle.

Broken hearts, illness, and depression have overwhelmed many of Hollywood's finest, and they decided that suicide was the only answer. Barbara Bates and Charles Boyer could not face a life without their beloved life partner, while tragic dalliances left Carole Landis and Lupe Velez reaching for the barbiturate Seconal. Richard Farnsworth, Brian Keith, and Hervé Villechaize suffered agonizing health problems and ended their misery through suicide. And depression over a career in rapid descent saw Karl Dane, Alan Ladd, and Helen Twelvetrees take their own lives.

A few actors were reported to have committed suicide, but doubts remain. A question mark still hangs over the deaths of Margaux Hemingway, George Reeves, and George Zucco.

Roscoe Arbuckle

Born March 24, 1887
Died   June 29, 1933

O ver the years, many scandals have rocked the entertainment industry, but probably none have achieved quite the notoriety of the case involving comedy king Roscoe "Fatty" Arbuckle and his alleged murder of model and aspiring actress Virginia Rappe.

Roscoe Conkling Arbuckle was the youngest of William and Mary Arbuckle's nine children. Because Roscoe was such a huge baby compared with his siblings, his father suspected that he may have been the proverbial "milkman's son" and never really accepted him. When Roscoe was one year old, the family moved from Kansas to Santa Ana, California. In 1899, Roscoe's mother died, and William Arbuckle virtually abandoned his 12-year-old son, leaving him to fend for himself much of the time.

While Roscoe was working in the kitchen of a San José hotel, a customer heard him singing and suggested that he enter a talent contest. He won first prize—as much for his comical antics as for his singing—and he was soon performing on the vaudeville circuit. In 1909, Arbuckle made his movie debut in the silent short *Ben's Kid*. The same year, he married 17-year-old singer Araminta ("Minty") Durfee.

Arbuckle's career in motion pictures progressed slowly and steadily. He joined Mack Sennett's studio as one of the madcap Keystone Cops. After a couple of years, Arbuckle began to command starring roles, and he was especially popular in the "Fatty and Mabel" films with Mabel Normand, including *Mabel, Fatty, and the Law* (1915) and *Mabel and Fatty Viewing the World's Fair at San Francisco* (1915). As well as being a gifted comic actor, Arbuckle was also interested in writing and directing. With Joseph M. Schenck, he set up a production company known as Comique Film Corporation. It is generally thought that the Comique films, such as *Butcher Boy* (1917) with Buster Keaton, and *The Garage* (1919), were Arbuckle's best. It was during this period that Minty left Arbuckle because of his drinking.

In 1921, Arbuckle signed a three-year contract with Paramount Studios. On a salary of $1 million per year, Arbuckle was one of the highest-paid stars in Hollywood, and he worked incessantly; at one point he was making three films at once. Needing a vacation, Arbuckle and his friend Fred Fishbach decided to take a trip to San Francisco on a weekend in September 1921.

ABOVE His contract stipulated that Arbuckle had to weigh more than 250 pounds (113 kg); he consistently maintained a weight of over 300 pounds (136 kg).

RIGHT With Molly Malone in a scene from A Desert Hero (1919). Arbuckle also wrote and directed the film.

Immediately after settling into their suites at the St. Francis Hotel, Arbuckle and his friends embarked on a weekend of heavy partying. Some of the people to turn up were Maude Delmont (a woman who had a record of fraud and other criminal activities) and 26-year-old model and would-be actress Virginia Rappe, who had a history of prostitution, venereal disease, and multiple abortions.

On the afternoon of September 5, 1921, Arbuckle found Rappe on the floor of his bathroom in considerable pain and distress. He helped her to the bed and tried to settle her down by giving her a glass

LEFT A 1920 studio portrait of Roscoe Arbuckle. After the Rappe scandal, Arbuckle directed about 35 films under the pseudonym of William Goodrich.

Star Shot

John Belushi, Chris Farley, and John Candy were all considered for the role of Roscoe Arbuckle in a movie of his life, but they all died at a young age due to their excesses.

of water and placing ice on her abdomen. Later, Rappe began groaning and tearing at her clothes. Arbuckle summoned his companions, and they put Rappe in a cold bath, which seemed to calm her. They then called the hotel management, who arranged for a doctor to visit—his diagnosis was that she was merely drunk. Arbuckle left the hotel for a time, and when he returned, the hotel physician came in to see Rappe and gave her some morphine. Assuming that all was well, Arbuckle and his friends returned to Los Angeles on Tuesday. Later that week, Rappe was admitted to the hospital, and she died on Friday, September 9, from acute peritonitis and a ruptured bladder, possibly caused by venereal disease.

Arbuckle was charged with rape and murder, and the charge was later reduced to manslaughter. Fueled by the sensational press, all sorts of false rumors abounded. Arbuckle was painted as a monster who sadistically raped Rappe with a Coke bottle, and moralists used Arbuckle as their scapegoat for all of Hollywood's depravity and immorality. Not only was Arbuckle's Paramount contract canceled and his movies taken out of distribution, the actor was also blacklisted from films. Many people stood by him, though, including his estranged wife, Minty, and his good friend, Buster Keaton.

After three trials within five months, Arbuckle was finally acquitted on April 12, 1922. Although he won the case and the blacklisting was subsequently lifted, Arbuckle was a pariah. Financially he was nearly ruined, having had to sell most of his assets to pay the exorbitant legal fees. As the decade progressed, Arbuckle remarried (he and his second wife divorced after three years because of his drinking), and he was able to earn some money as a film director working under an assumed name.

Ten years after the incident, Arbuckle seemed to find happiness again. He married a lovely young actress named Addie McPhail and had signed a contract with Warner Bros. Sadly, after returning home from a wedding anniversary dinner with his wife, he died of a heart attack in his sleep at the age of only 46.

ABOVE By 1914, both Roscoe "Fatty" Arbuckle and fellow comedian Charlie Chaplin were appearing regularly in many of Mack Sennett's popular comedies.

Barbara Bates

Born August 6, 1925
Died March 18, 1969

RIGHT Barbara Bates (left) prevents Anne Baxter from using the telephone in All About Eve *(1950). Bates played a small but pivotal role in the film.*

Star Shot

During 1954, Barbara Bates appeared regularly on the television show *It's a Great Life.* **She also made guest appearances on** *Studio 57* **(1955) and** *The Saint* **(1962).**

Barbara Bates was born and raised in Denver, Colorado. As a young girl she studied ballet, and at the age of 19 she won a trip to Hollywood as the first prize in a local beauty contest. She took her mother along as a traveling companion, but Mrs. Bates returned to Denver alone. While they were in Hollywood, Barbara had met Cecil Coen, a United Artists publicist more than twice her age, and he convinced her to remain in Los Angeles.

Coen arranged for Bates to meet producer Walter Wanger, who cast her as one of the seven dancing girls in *Salome Where She Danced* (1945), starring Yvonne DeCarlo. Over the next few years, Bates kept busy with small, uncredited parts in a number of movies, such as *Lady on a Train* (1945) and *The Crimson Canary* (1945). In March 1945, Cecil Coen divorced his wife, and he and Bates married just a few days later. That same year, Bates appeared on the cover of several magazines, including *Life*.

Bates's career really began to take off in the late 1940s. Highlights include *June Bride* (1948), with Bette Davis and Robert Montgomery; *One Last Fling* (1949), with Alexis Smith; *The Inspector General* (1949), with Danny Kaye and Walter Slezak; *All About Eve* (1950), with Bette Davis and Anne Baxter; *Cheaper by the Dozen* (1950), with Clifton Webb, Jeanne Crain, and Myrna Loy; and its sequel *Belles on Their Toes* (1952).

Unfortunately, Bates wasn't able to physically and emotionally cope with the demands of Hollywood. She was often ill, and suffered bouts of depression and low self-esteem. In 1956, Coen accepted a job as publicity director for United Artists in London, and while overseas, Bates's condition worsened. She made a few films with Rank Studios—*House of Secrets* (1956) with Michael Craig, and *Town on Trial* (1957) with John Mills—but because of her fragile state of mind, Rank canceled her contract.

Back in the United States, Bates co-starred with Rory Calhoun in *Apache Territory* (1958) before fading from the movie scene. When Coen died of cancer in January 1967, Bates was devastated and returned to Denver. Although she attempted to build a new life with Denver sportscaster William Reed, she never really recovered from Coen's death. She gassed herself in her car on March 18, 1969, just four months after her second marriage. Her body was found by her mother, and her death was ruled as suicide by carbon monoxide poisoning.

LEFT A promotional portrait for the 1948 film Always Together, *in which Barbara Bates, in an uncredited performance, plays a ticket seller.*

Clara Blandick

Born June 4, 1880
Died April 15, 1962

Best remembered for her role as Dorothy's careworn Auntie Em in *The Wizard of Oz* (1939), Clara Blandick was a hardworking character actress of both stage and screen. In 40 years she appeared in a total of 120 motion pictures.

Blandick was born on an American ship docked in Hong Kong harbor. She spent much of her childhood in Hong Kong and appeared in her first silent movie in 1911. She later concentrated on the theater, traveling to Hollywood with the advent of the talkies. Since she was middle-aged by 1930, she was often typecast as an aunt, grandmother, or domestic servant.

Some of her career highlights include *Tom Sawyer* (1930) and *Huckleberry Finn* (1931) with Jackie Coogan (in which she played Aunt Polly); *Ever in My Heart* (1933) with Barbara Stanwyck; *Sisters under the Skin* (1934) with Frank Morgan (who would later play "the great and powerful Oz" in *The Wizard of Oz*), *The Girl from Missouri* (1934) with Jean Harlow and Lionel Barrymore; *The Trail of the Lonesome Pine* (1936) with Fred MacMurray and Henry Fonda; *Anthony Adverse* (1936) with Fredric March and Olivia de Havilland; the original *A Star is Born* (1937) with Janet Gaynor and Fredric March; and *You Can't Have Everything* (1937) with Alice Faye and the Ritz Brothers.

Blandick was again cast as Aunt Polly in *Tom Sawyer, Detective* (1938), and as Miss Watson in *The Adventures of Huckleberry Finn* (1939), with Mickey Rooney in the title role. After *The Wizard of Oz* (1939), she appeared in *Swanee River* (1939) with Don Ameche and Al Jolson; *Anne of Windy Poplars* (1940); *Rings on Her Fingers* (1942) with Henry Fonda and Gene Tierney; *People Are Funny* (1946), in which she played the grandmother of Jack Haley, the "Tin Man" in *The Wizard of Oz*; *A Stolen Life* (1946) with Bette Davis and Glenn Ford; and *Key to the City* (1950) with Clark Gable and Loretta Young. Her last film was *Love That Brute* (1950).

By the time she reached her eighties, she was crippled with arthritis, going blind, and had lost the will to live. On Palm Sunday, 1962, she went to church as was her custom. She then returned to her apartment and wrote a note, stating that she could endure the pain no longer. Blandick took an overdose of sleeping pills and placed a plastic bag over her head.

Last Words

"I pray the Lord my soul to take. Amen."
(From Clara Blandick's suicide note.)

RIGHT Clara Blandick (far right) in The Wizard of Oz *(1939). The movie provided Blandick with just one week's work.*

LEFT With Marlene Dietrich in The Garden of Allah (1936). His debonair manner and good looks made Charles Boyer one of the biggest sex symbols of his time.

Star Shot

Although nominated four times, Charles Boyer never won an Oscar® for his acting. He did, however, receive a special Academy Award® in 1942 for his "progressive cultural achievement."

Charles Boyer

Born August 28, 1899
Died August 26, 1978

French actor Charles Boyer made a name for himself in Hollywood as an intense, passionate lover, and the circumstances surrounding his death were more tragic and romantic than anything a screenwriter could have imagined.

Born in Figeac in the southwest of France, Boyer studied philosophy at the Sorbonne. Acting, however, had always been his greatest love, and he abandoned philosophy to pursue drama at the Paris Conservatory. After working for a number of years in French theater and films, Boyer was approached by MGM to star in French versions of American motion pictures. He subsequently learned English and was then cast in his first English-speaking film, *The Magnificent Lie* (1931), with Ruth Chatterton and Ralph Bellamy. For the next few years, Boyer moved back and forth between Hollywood and Europe. He met and married British stage actress Pat Paterson in 1934, and they eventually settled in the United States.

BELOW Throughout his career, Charles Boyer continued to work in the theater. He is pictured here during the 1963 season of Terence Rattigan's Man and Boy in Brighton, England.

Throughout the late 1930s and 1940s, Boyer went from strength to strength. He received Academy Award® nominations for his roles in *Conquest* (1937), with Greta Garbo; *Algiers* (1938), with Hedy Lamarr; and *Gaslight* (1944), with Ingrid Bergman. Other highlights include *Love Affair* (1939), with Irene Dunne; *All This, and Heaven Too* (1940), with Bette Davis; and *The Constant Nymph* (1943), with Joan Fontaine. Although his film persona was often that of a play-boy and he starred with some very desirable actresses, off-screen he was content to lead a quiet life with Pat and their son, Michael, who was born in December 1943.

In the 1950s, Boyer was excited by the new medium of television. He was one of the creators of Four Star Productions, and as well as starring in many episodes of *Four Star Playhouse*, he appeared in *Playhouse 90*, *Alcoa Theatre*, and a hilarious episode of *I Love Lucy*. Now in his sixties, he received a fourth Academy Award® nomination for *Fanny* (1961), co-starring Leslie Caron and Maurice Chevalier. Tragedy struck in 1965 when his only child, Michael, shot and killed himself over a broken engagement at the age of 21.

Boyer continued to work in his senior years in varied films such as *Casino Royale* (1967), *Barefoot in the Park* (1967), *The April Fools* (1969), and *Lost Horizon* (1973). His last motion picture was *A Matter of Time* (1976), with Ingrid Bergman and Liza Minnelli.

On August 24, 1978, Pat died of cancer, and Boyer could not face the prospect of living without his partner of 44 years. Two days later he deliberately overdosed on the barbiturate Seconal. He was found unconscious and rushed to the hospital, where he died later that day.

Jonathan Brandis

Born April 13, 1976
Died November 12, 2003

Jonathan Gregory Brandis was born in Danbury, Connecticut. A bright little boy with a cute elfin face and crystal blue eyes, Brandis began his show business career when he was just a tiny tot, appearing in numerous television commercials. From there he progressed to the television soap opera *One Life to Live*. The family moved to Los Angeles, and throughout the 1980s and early 1990s Brandis appeared in a variety of popular television dramas and sitcoms, including *L.A. Law*; *Who's the Boss?*; *Full House*; *Murder, She Wrote*; *The Wonder Years*; and *Blossom*.

Brandis had bit parts in a few films before landing the starring role of Bastian in *The NeverEnding Story II: The Next Chapter* (1990). This was followed by the comedy *Ladybugs* (1992) with Rodney Dangerfield, and the action-adventure film *Sidekicks* (1992) with Beau Bridges and Chuck Norris. He was best-known for his portrayal of Lucas Wolenczak in Steven Spielberg's sci-fi series *SeaQuest DSV*, which ran for two seasons in 1993 and 1994. On the strength of this role, Brandis became a great favorite with young teenage girls, and won the Youth in Film Awards' "Best Youth Actor in a Leading Role in a Television Series."

In 1994, Brandis went to the Czech Republic for the filming of the television movie *Good King Wenceslas*, co-starring Stefanie Powers and Leo McKern. He then appeared in several more television films, including *Born Free: A New Adventure* (1996), *Fall into Darkness* (1996), and *Two Came Back* (1997). He was cast in supporting roles in a number of feature films, including the Farrelly Brothers' *Outside Providence* (1999); *Ride with the Devil* (1999), a Civil War drama starring Jewel Kilcher and Tobey Maguire; *Hart's War* (2002), with Bruce Willis; and *Puerto Vallarta Squeeze* (2003), starring Scott Glenn and Harvey Keitel. He missed out on the coveted role of Anakin Skywalker in *Star Wars: Episode II—Attack of the Clones* (2002).

Brandis was also hoping to branch out as a writer and director. He had written one episode of *SeaQuest DSV*, and had just finished directing a short film, *The Slainesville Boys* (2004).

On November 11, 2003, a friend arrived at Brandis's Los Angeles apartment to find that he had hanged himself. At that point he was still alive, and was rushed to the hospital where he died the next day. Investigations showed that Brandis's death was suicide, and that there were no drugs in his system. He didn't leave a note, and no one knows why the 27-year-old chose to end his life.

BELOW An effervescent Jonathan Brandis as the scientifically gifted Lucas Wolenczak in the futuristic hit television series, SeaQuest DSV (1993).

Charles Butterworth

Born July 26, 1896
Died June 14, 1946

Thin, sensitive, intelligent, and effeminate, Charles Butterworth was born in the unlikely setting of South Bend, Indiana. On Broadway and in Hollywood Butterworth became a beloved comic actor, especially in films of the 1930s. He was known for his screen persona as an eccentric blueblood aristocrat, playing characters with names such as Ludwig Pfeffer, Floppy Phil Montague, the Duke of Ephesus, and Professor Lippincott.

Butterworth graduated from Notre Dame with a law degree, then worked as a reporter for a few years before discovering acting in the late 1920s. Buoyant after the popularity of a show he both wrote and performed at a press club, Butterworth was quickly snapped up by Broadway. After playing in numerous musical comedies, Butterworth joined the actors' migration to Hollywood in 1930 and made his credited debut in *The Life of the Party* (1930)—although he did work as an extra in *Ladies of Leisure* in the same year. Butterworth dug himself a niche as the protagonist's joking sidekick, playing support to such luminaries as John Barrymore in *The Mad Genius* (1931), Maurice Chevalier and Jeanette MacDonald in *Love Me Tonight* (1932), Laurel and Hardy in *Hollywood Party* (1934), and Henry Fonda and Margaret Sullavan in *The Moon's Our Home* (1936). Butterworth gained his only starring vehicle as Willie Harrington in *Baby Face Harrington* (1935), directed by the greatly respected Raoul Walsh.

Directors were keen to use Butterworth in the same way as Robin Williams is used today—due to his penchant for wisecracks, screenwriters would only write a portion of his dialogue, hoping Butterworth would add his own wit during

ABOVE Charles Butterworth appeared with many Hollywood luminaries, including Mae West in Every Day's a Holiday *(1937) and Nelson Eddy in* Let Freedom Ring *(1939).*

shooting. Butterworth became jaded with this treatment; he was more comfortable with the rigid professionalism of Broadway. Butterworth's popularity began to fade in the late 1930s, and by the advent of the 1940s he was only getting work at "B" studios, with the notable exception of the Warner Bros. movie *This is the Army* (1943) with Joan Leslie.

Two years after his last forgettable film, the musical *Dixie Jamboree* (1944), in which he provided the comic relief, an official report came to light that stated Butterworth had died in an automobile accident in Los Angeles, California. The real story is that Charles Butterworth committed suicide, driving the car off a cliff after the death of his friend, humorist and actor Robert Benchley. Charles Butterworth is interred at St. Joseph Valley Cemetery, South Bend, Indiana.

RIGHT Charles Butterworth co-starred with Fred MacMurray (left) and Carole Lombard in the 1937 motion picture Swing High, Swing Low.

Capucine

Born January 6, 1931
Died March 17, 1990

Capucine, the chic European model, was always known as a mysterious and alluring femme fatale. Her sexuality was a topic of much speculation: magazines suggested she was a lesbian, bisexual, or even a transsexual, but she was never interested in coming out to the media. Despite her sexual ambiguity, she had a power over men. Capucine wasn't the greatest actress, but perhaps her looks accounted for her charm with the camera.

Born Germaine Lefebvre in Toulon, France, during her modeling career she adopted the name Capucine, the French name for the flower nasturtium, apparently an aphrodisiac. At the age of 19, Capucine married Pierre Trabaud after meeting him on the set of her first movie, *Rendez-vous de juille* (1949). Their relationship lasted seven months, and she never married again despite relationships with many of Hollywood's leading men.

In the 1950s Charles Feldman contracted her to Hollywood, and she ended up appearing in a handful of Hollywood films, including a starring role in *The Pink Panther* (1963). In the late 1960s and 1970s she appeared mainly in obscure French and Italian films, though she had a part in Federico Fellini's *Satyricon* (1969). During her residence in Hollywood she was linked with David Niven and romanced William Holden. Holden left his wife, Brenda Marshall, for her. Their romance ended, but when Holden died in 1981 he bequeathed $50,000 to Capucine.

The film that added to speculation in the United States about Capucine's sexuality was the

oddity *Walk on the Wild Side* (1962), a film that tried to explore homosexuality while working within the confines of the archaic Production Code. Feldman got Capucine the role as the lost love turned prostitute, Hallie, in love with the bordello madam played by Barbara Stanwyck. Feldman insisted Capucine be dressed in the latest Pierre Cardin fashion, despite the film being set in the 1930s. In an on-set argument, Capucine declared leading man Laurence Harvey's kisses weren't manly enough for her. He replied, "Honey, kissing you is like kissing the side of a beer bottle."

From 1962 until the end of her life, Capucine lived in Lausanne, Switzerland. At the age of 59 her depression finally got the better of her, and she threw herself out of her eighth-story apartment window. Her only known survivors were three cats.

Capucine managed to steal one last heart even in death—a young man who had romanced Capucine later in life killed himself a year after her suicide.

Star Shot

Capucine and Audrey Hepburn were friends, and Hepburn saved Capucine's life many times when the depressed actress attempted to commit suicide.

Lindsay Crosby

Born January 5, 1938
Died December 11, 1989

Life for Lindsay Crosby could not have been easy. A strict upbringing by his disciplinarian father, crooner and actor Bing Crosby, was made worse by never living up to his father's immense success. He was reminded of his failures every year when the ubiquitous song "White Christmas" was played in every shopping mall.

Lindsay was one of four sons (along with Gary and twin brothers Dennis and Phillip) from Bing Crosby's first marriage to the alcoholic and reclusive Dixie Lee.

Unlike his father, who enjoyed a successful musical and film career, Lindsay never excelled in show business. The four sons became a nightclub act, The Crosby Boys, in the late 1950s, but disbanded in 1959 after they brawled in their dressing room in Montreal, Canada. At the age of 24, Lindsay appeared in the Rat Pack showcase *Sergeants 3* (1962), with his brothers, Phillip and Dennis. His acting career never went beyond independent exploitation films, especially biker revenge melodramas like *The Girls from Thunder Strip* (1966) and *The Glory Stompers* (1968). His last appearance was in Roger Corman's heist film, *Murph the Surf* (1975).

In the early 1980s Bing's reputation was attacked in son Gary's autobiography, *Going My Own Way*, in which he claimed that Bing beat his four sons until they bled. He also submitted them to verbal abuse, calling Gary "Bucket Butt" and Lindsay "The Head." The gap between the public perception of the man voted Outstanding Screen Father in 1946 and the reality of the alcoholic tyrant scandalized Bing Crosby. The accusations drew a strong reaction from some original family members as well as Crosby's second wife, Kathryn. Lindsay, who was the most favored of Bing's first four sons, said, "Gary said what needed to be said," but outwardly he always remained the most even-tempered of the Crosby boys. Speaking about being the son of Bing Crosby, he said he remembered "all the good things I did with my dad and forgot all the times that were rough."

As Christmas 1989 approached, Lindsay Crosby was in terrible shape. He had been recently hospitalized for depression and had broken up with his long-term girlfriend, Pam Desnon. One source said Crosby would often "tortur[e] himself around Christmas time by listening to his father's records."

On December 11, 1989, less than 24 hours after watching the movie *White Christmas* (1954) on television, Lindsay Crosby shot himself in the head. Dennis Crosby followed suit in 1991.

BELOW Bing Crosby takes center stage in this family portrait taken in the mid-1950s. From left are his sons Dennis, Lindsay, Gary, and Philip.

Karl Dane

Born October 12, 1886
Died April 15, 1934

The new sound technology of the late 1920s destroyed the careers of many stars. Foreign actors especially were, as one writer said, "the immediate and spectacular victims" of talkies. No one suffered the shift to sound more than comedian Karl Dane. Dane was the awkward, hulking partner of George K. Arthur in the comedy duo, "Arthur and Dane," who flourished briefly with MGM at the end of the silent era. Because of his heavy accent, he sadly fell victim to the transition to sound and ended his life soon after.

Born Rasmus Karl Thekelsen Gottlieb in Copenhagen, Denmark, Karl Dane performed on stage as a child. He moved to Los Angeles in 1916 and found work on three anti-German films: *My Four Years in Germany* (1918), *To Hell with the Kaiser!* (1918), and *The Fall of the Hohenzollerns* (1919). But it wasn't until Dane was cast as John Gilbert's tobacco-chewing buddy in King Vidor's *The Big Parade* (1925) that he found his niche playing comic support.

In 1925, Dane first appeared with George K. Arthur in *Lights of Old Broadway*, and two years later they officially became a team in *Rookies* (1927). The duo's appeal was based on their extreme physical differences: Dane was a full 70 pounds (32 kg) heavier and some 9 inches (23 cm) taller than Arthur. "Arthur and Dane" made six more films together before the inevitable emergence of sound.

Neither man's acting career survived, yet Arthur's retreat from the limelight was far more successful. He retired from acting in 1935 and went into business, distributing and producing films (including the Oscar®-winning 33-minute short, *The Bespoken Overcoat,* in 1956), and he died in 1985.

Karl Dane continued to pursue acting work, but his thick Scandinavian accent did not record well on the primitive sound equipment used on *Navy Blues* (1929), his first talking motion picture. Within a year it was obvious that Dane could no longer get lead roles and, by 1931, his career had ground to a halt. After training to become a carpenter, and then a mechanic, he finally became the operator of a hot dog stand located outside MGM. Facing a life without prospects, Dane returned to his home on April 15, 1934, and shot himself. His body lay in the Los Angeles morgue for three days until MGM offered to pay for his funeral costs. Karl Dane is interred in the Hollywood Forever Cemetery.

ABOVE With Buster Keaton (right) in 1928's Brotherly Love. *Karl Dane had been an aviator in the Danish Flying Corps before coming to the United States.*

Star Shot

Karl Dane played the role of Ramadan in *The Son of the Sheik* (1926), the last film Rudolph Valentino made before he died at age 31 from peritonitis and septicemia.

RIGHT Karl Dane as Slim, one of the soldiers who befriends John Gilbert in the World War I film The Big Parade *(1925). Tragically, John Gilbert succumbed to a heart attack in 1936 at the age of just 36.*

Richard Farnsworth

Born September 1, 1920
Died October 6, 2000

ABOVE From the film Sylvester (1985). Richard Farnsworth worked as the stuntman and body double for film cowboy Roy Rogers during the 1940s and 1950s.

By climbing onto his rickety riding lawnmower in *The Straight Story* (1999), wiry Richard Farnsworth began the most successful and, tragically, last journey he would ever take. In this film he played Alvin Straight, a real-life person who crossed Iowa and Wisconsin to visit his estranged brother, who was ironically dying of cancer. The fields of wheat spanning to the horizon must have struck a chord with this ex-stuntman, who was born on the range and would die there. Farnsworth, who only turned to dramatic roles at age 57, garnered a nomination for Best Actor in the 72nd Annual Academy Awards® for the role of Alvin Straight, and at the time he was the oldest actor ever to be nominated.

Farnsworth left school during the Great Depression to help support his widowed mother. He learned to ride horses at age ten, and was working in the stables of a local polo barn by 15. He stumbled into film in 1937 when he rode horses in the Marx Brothers' film, *A Day At The Races*. Back then film credits were brief and he went uncredited, spending many years in Hollywood being alternately trampled by horses and shot off them. "If there was a wagon or something I would be driving it, but they didn't let me say anything," he commented once.

In 1938, he was signed as one of 500 Mongolian horsemen in *The Adventures of Marco Polo*, performing as a stuntman opposite Gary Cooper, and he also drove chariots for Cecil B. DeMille in *The Ten Commandments*. After fighting in World War II, Farnsworth married his true love, Maggie, in 1947. He appeared as Kirk Douglas's body double in Stanley Kubrick's swords and sandals epic *Spartacus* (1960), and in his laconic way joked: "For 16 months I wore this short little skirt with my bony knees knockin' on the back lot of Universal. I looked about as much like a gladiator as my granddaughter, but I held my own." Richard Farnsworth worked as

a stuntman in 49 films and television series, including body doubling for James Garner and Paul Newman. He was a cofounder of the Stuntmen's Association in 1961.

His first screen credit was as "Dick Farnsworth" in *Texas Across the River* (1966), his first speaking role was opposite Goldie Hawn in *The Duchess and the Dirtwater Fox* (1976), and he was nominated for a Best Actor in a Supporting Role Academy Award® opposite Jane Fonda in *Comes a Horseman* (1978). In *The Two Jakes* (1990), Farnsworth had a part as an oil baron; Jack Nicholson said, "he isn't fooling anyone with his Roy Rogers act," but by then Farnsworth had ridden more horses in more films than most of his acting contemporaries.

Westerns in the 1980s were low-budget, introspective affairs yearning for the glory days of the 1950s. Phillip Borsos's *The Grey Fox* (1982) provided Farnsworth with one of his most acclaimed screen roles. He played Bill Miner, a stagecoach robber freed from San Quentin after 33 years, who emerges to a modernized century and turns to robbing trains. In 1985, Richard Farnsworth's beloved Maggie died, and a few years later he met the woman who would be his fiancée for 11 years, flight attendant Jewely Van Valin.

Farnsworth once told an interviewer, "I'm really disappointed in what the people seem to want nowadays: action, sex, violence. I've turned down quite a bit of work because there's too many four-letter words." Given his old-fashioned cowboy ideals, Farnsworth's pairing with controversial director David Lynch seems extraordinary, but when Lynch cast him in the G-rated *The Straight Story* (1999), Farnsworth took this, his last role, for which he won an Academy Award® nomination and a Canadian Independent Spirit Award. Audiences were genuinely touched by the quiet honor Farnsworth brought to Straight's journey. Farnsworth was already suffering from prostate cancer at this point, and he postponed hip-replacement surgery to shoot the film. Though in considerable pain and requiring a cane, the professional Farnsworth never made his pain an issue on the set.

As the cancer advanced, Farnsworth couldn't walk and became paralyzed, and he once said to a friend, "It's been a nice ride, but this old world's gotten too heavy for me." Farnsworth shot himself in the head with a .38 revolver at his New Mexico ranch a month after his 80th birthday. Sheriff Tom Sullivan of Lincoln County stated: "The lady who lives with him [Van Valin] heard a gunshot a little after 5:00 P.M. and she went into the room and saw him. She called a neighbor who was one of my former deputies. He went over and found Farnsworth. This was an obvious self-inflicted gunshot." The old Hollywood cowboy had a bittersweet end on his beloved range.

LEFT Richard Farnsworth with his long-time companion, Jewely Van Valin, in 2000. Farnsworth has a star on the Hollywood Walk of Fame located at 1560 Vine Street.

Star Shot

One of the most beloved characters played by Richard Farnsworth during his 60-year career was Matthew Cuthbert in the 1985 television miniseries, *Anne of Green Gables.*

BELOW Richard Farnsworth as Red Blow in The Natural, *the 1984 baseball film based on the Bernard Malamud novel. The film starred Robert Redford (right).*

Trevor Goddard

Born October 14, 1962
Died June 7, 2003

ABOVE During filming of Hollywood Vampyr *(2002), Goddard is said to have fainted at the sight of fake blood pouring from a woman's arm.*

Star Shot

When he was a teenager, Trevor Goddard was the drummer in a rock band.

Trevor Goddard's shocking death led to the revelation, at his funeral service, that he had been leading a fictitious life.

Goddard had a strong career as a professional boxer before being offered a role in a Budweiser commercial in 1991. He collected the 1992 Los Angeles Drama Critics' Circle Award for Best Lead Performance for his role as a sexually confused boxer in *Cock & Bull Story* (beating actors of such caliber as Sir Ian McKellan and Laurence Fishburne).

His good looks and powerful physique suited action roles, and it wasn't long before he was appearing in films such as *Men of War* (1994). His performance as Kano in *Mortal Kombat* (1995) left an impression on the ongoing line of computer games: Kano gained the Australian accent that Goddard had in the film. In 1998, Goddard found stardom with his role in CBS's hit series *J.A.G.* as Lieutenant Commander Mic Brumby, the love interest for Catherine Bell's character, Mac. His last screen appearance was in Disney's *Pirates of the Caribbean: The Curse of the Black Pearl* (2003), as the evil pirate Grapple.

Yet Goddard's greatest performance was his own life. He was born in Surrey, England, and was raised in Kent, yet when he first auditioned for roles, Goddard found his English accent meant that he was rejected for most parts. Many casting agents confused his English accent with an Australian one, so he claimed he was born in Perth, Western Australia. He even went so far as to fabricate a troubled childhood, telling journalists that he had accumulated criminal convictions in his youth before boxing resurrected his sense of self-worth. As soon as Goddard began lying about his roots, he was immediately picked for more roles; he even ousted a native Australian for a job voicing an animated kangaroo. Goddard also attended functions held by the Australian Film and Television Association in Los Angeles to support "AussieWood."

Goddard dropped his Australian accent for his final appearance in *J.A.G.* in 2001, when, ironically, he had to imitate an Englishman.

In 2003, Trevor Goddard was going through divorce proceedings with his wife of ten years, Ruthann. On June 8, Goddard's girlfriend discovered the actor's body at his home in the Hollywood Hills. There was a note addressed to her but it did not suggest his death was intentional. The Los Angeles coroner's preliminary finding ruled that Goddard's death was suicide, but toxicology reports discovered cocaine and heroin in his system, so the final report ruled his death an apparent accidental overdose. He was 40 years old.

At the memorial service, Goddard's father, Eric, stunned 400 close friends and work colleagues when he revealed his son's subterfuge. However, Goddard's publicist and lawyer continued to claim Goddard was Australian.

LEFT Trevor Goddard was most famous for his role of Mic Brumby in the television series J.A.G. *Goddard also made guest appearances in shows such as* The X Files; Murder, She Wrote; *and* Baywatch.

Spalding Gray

Born June 5, 1941
Died January 10, 2004

Spalding Gray was born in an upper-class family on Rhode Island. Like his mother, Margaret, who killed herself in 1967, Spalding suffered from depression.

Gray became famous in avant-garde theater during the 1970s, especially with his painfully honest, neurotic monologues. He appeared in several films, such as *The Killing Fields* (1984), *King of the Hill* (1993), and *The Paper* (1994), but it was the film version of his monologue *Swimming to Cambodia* (1987) that won him national acclaim. In the film Gray uses his small role in *The Killing Fields* to launch into some commentary on war in East Asia.

In 2001, while holidaying in Ireland, Gray suffered severe injuries when a minivan crashed into his family's car— yet the physical effects were nothing in comparison to the psychological damage. Gray combated his depression with antidepressants and therapy, but his treatment made him no less susceptible to suicide fantasy.

Gray attempted to end his life on several occasions. On October 15, 2003, he threw himself from the Sag Harbor Bridge in New York into calm water and was pulled to land by a policeman.

On January 10, 2004, Gray accompanied his family to see the motion picture, *Big Fish* (2003). By the end Gray was weeping. At 6:30 P.M. Gray left his family, claiming he intended to visit some friends. The night was bitterly cold, with Manhattan's temperature reaching a low of 1°F (−17°C). About 10:30 P.M. he called home and told Theo, his six-year-old son, he was just checking in. He did not return home, and on January 11 his wife, Kathleen Russo, informed the police that Gray was missing.

A day later a Staten Island Ferry worker claimed he'd seen Gray coming off the ferry on the night of January 9. Russo wondered if he was practicing his suicide with a "dry run."

The family waited for two months before the mystery was tragically solved. A body was pulled from New York's East River at 3:00 P.M. on Sunday, March 9. The New York medical examiner identified Spalding Gray from his dental records. The only recognizable feature was his black corduroy pants.

While many never considered Gray a suicide risk because he used his monologues therapeutically, there are passages that suggest an obsession with a watery death in *Swimming to Cambodia*. Gray also used his suicide obsession for comic effect. He provided his own epitaph in a 1997 interview: "An American Original: Troubled, Inner-Directed, and Cannot Type."

ABOVE Monster in a Box *(1992) addresses Spalding Gray's attempts to write a novel. Equally happy and sad, the film is considered by many to be his best work.*

LEFT *Jonathan Hale (far left) in 1938's* Blondie. *In the 1950s, Hale appeared in television shows such as* The Cisco Kid *and* Adventures of Wild Bill Hickok.

Jonathan Hale

Born March 21, 1891
Died February 28, 1966

Ontario-born and originally christened Jonathan Hatley, Jonathan Hale had a prolific film career as a character actor, yet is largely unknown today. He appeared in over 200 films as an authority figure with silver hair and a stern, patrician demeanor. Sometimes credited as Jonathan Hale, Jr. or John Hale, he was a member of the Canadian diplomatic service before discovering a talent for acting, and his peer-of-the-realm attitude allowed him to play a steady stream of military officers, politicians, and business executives. Hale is most recognizable as Dagwood's boss, Mr. Dithers, in the *Blondie* film series, 28 "B" films made from 1938 to 1946.

Jonathan Hale became inextricably linked with the roles of executives and politicians he played. Jovial by nature, he often told the story of how he'd almost been a wealthy man except for the bad monetary decisions of his father. Hale began playing character parts in 1934, and appeared in classics such as *The Raven* (1935); the Marx Brothers' *A Night at The Opera* (1935); and *A Star is Born* (1937), opposite Fredric March. Though stockier and more regal than the gnarly Dithers of the *Blondie* comics, Hale became synonymous with the role, and he last played the character in *Blondie's Lucky Day* (1946). Hale also appeared regularly as Irish Inspector Fernack in RKO's *The Saint* serial (1941). After 1946, Hale played supporting roles and walk-ons, frequently uncredited. He worked prolifically in television in the 1950s, with cameo parts in series such as *The Adventures of Superman* (1953).

Hale also supported in the films *Alice Adams* (1935); *Fury* (1936); *Boys Town* (1938); *Since You Went Away* (1944); *Johnny Belinda* (1948); and *Strangers on a Train* (1951), in which his character is famously assassinated. During the twilight of his career, Hale took on such under-valued screen gems as *Son of Paleface* (1952), *She Couldn't Say No* (1954), *Men of the Fighting Lady* (1954), and *The Three Outlaws* (1956), all sadly uncredited roles.

In February 1966, after a long illness and depressed because of his failing health, Jonathan Hale shot himself, just months before the television premiere of his *Blondie* films. He is buried in the Pierce Brothers Valhalla Memorial Park, North Hollywood, in an unmarked grave.

Jon Hall

Born February 23, 1913
Died December 13, 1979

Jon Hall, the muscular man of action, and Maria Montez, the beautiful, exotic temptress, teamed up for six sand and skin romps including *Arabian Nights* (1942), *Cobra Woman* (1944), and *Sudan* (1945). Once the team broke up, neither ever reached the same box office success again, and Hall's life would end tragically.

Of Tahitian and Swiss ancestry, Jon Hall was born Charles Hall Locher on a train in Fresno, California, in 1913 (some sources say 1915). Hall spent part of his childhood in Tahiti, though he was also educated in England and Switzerland.

Samuel Goldwyn cast Hall in John Ford's *The Hurricane* (1937), as a Polynesian in love with mature beauty Dorothy Lamour. Before long Hall was advertised as "Goldwyn's Gift to Women" and "The King of Technicolor" when he began appearing with Maria Montez in Universal's escapist spectacles. The plot of these "Easterns" usually featured the brawny Hall fighting savages to rescue Montez, who appeared wearing as little as the restrictive Production Code would allow. War-wearied audiences lapped it up.

While playing every woman's fantasy on the cinema screen, Hall's off-screen life was less than romantic. Hall was married to vocalist and actress Frances Langford from 1934 to 1955, and he married and divorced Raquel Torres twice.

Once the success of the Hall/Montez team waned, Hall appeared in the popular television adventure series *Ramar of the Jungle* (1952–54). Overweight and lethargic, he could no longer maintain a career as a leading man, and he moved on to selling photography equipment.

The Beach Girls and the Monster (1965) was Hall's final film, as both actor and first-time director. It features Hall as oceanographer Dr. Otto Lindsay investigating a series of murders that he believes to be the work of a giant, humanoid fish. When the monster is finally cornered, its real identity is revealed to be Dr. Lindsay himself.

Hall attended the premiere of Dino De Laurentiis's insipid remake of *The Hurricane* (1979), despite suffering from crippling bladder cancer. After an operation to remove the cancer, Hall was bedridden in agony for several months. On December 13, 1979, Hall's sister returned to her North Hollywood home, where Hall was staying, and discovered his body. Frustrated with how restricted his life had become, he had shot himself around 7:00 A.M.

Jon Hall is interred at the Forest Lawn (Hollywood Hills) cemetery in Los Angeles, California, not far from Buster Keaton.

RIGHT Aloma of the South Seas (1941) paired handsome Jon Hall (left) once more with the "Queen of the Sarong," Dorothy Lamour.

ABOVE Jon Hall with wife Frances Langford in 1935. Hall and Langford appeared together in only one film, Deputy Marshal *(1949).*

Star Shot

The book from which the story of Jon Hall's 1937 movie *The Hurricane* came was written by Hall's uncle, James Norman Hall.

Margaux Hemingway

Born February 16, 1955
Died July 1, 1996

RIGHT Margaux Hemingway appeared on the cover of Time *magazine in June 1975. Her modeling successes landed her a $1 million contract with the makers of Faberge perfume.*

Star Shot

Margaux Hemingway was named for the Chateau Margaux vineyard in Bordeaux, France. When she became sober, she preferred to spell her name Margot to avoid its association with alcohol.

The Hemingways carry a family tradition of suicide: five members of this famous family have killed themselves. Margaux Hemingway is the most recent of these suicides, ending a life plagued by alcoholism, epilepsy, and bulimia.

Hemingway's bouts of depression may well have been caused by genetics. Her grandfather, the great writer Ernest Hemingway, battled with depression and alcoholism before killing himself on July 2, 1961. Margaux compared her life with that of her grandfather but, unlike him, she sought treatment, saying people could learn from their experiences.

Hemingway also fought the constant comparison between herself and her younger sister, Mariel. Their acting careers commenced simultaneously in the film *Lipstick* (1976). Mariel went on to garner a Best Actress in a Supporting Role Oscar® nomination for Woody Allen's *Manhattan* (1979) in the same year Margaux appeared in *Killer Fish* (also known as *Deadly Treasure of the Piranha*). This paved the way for appearances in oddities such as *They Call Me Bruce?* (1982) and the Spanish film *La Máquina de matar* (1984). By the early 1990s Margaux was appearing in soft-core porn films such as *Inner Sanctum* (1991).

But after Saturday, June 29, 1996, Margaux just disappeared from sight. A friend, Judy Stabile, visited her Santa Monica home on July 1 to check on her. When Margaux didn't answer the door, a handyman climbed up a ladder to her second-floor apartment. He discovered her dead body covered in blankets.

There was no suicide note, but the original coroner's report suggests Margaux's obsessive personality: "The table appears to be set up as an altar. On all four corners of the table is approximately one teaspoon of salt…. Candles are inside a circle enclosed by a white ribbon…. A [knight] is laying on its side just outside the circle. There were pieces of notebook paper shaped in a heart with the words, 'Love, healing, protection for Margot forever.'"

The Los Angeles coroner's office concluded a month later that it was suicide, and that Margaux Hemingway had killed herself by taking an overdose of Klonopin, a barbiturate. Mariel refuted such claims, blaming unfounded media speculation. She also cited her sister's trait of being a drama queen: "If she had committed suicide, she would have left a note … a long note naming everyone who had ever wronged her."

Margaux Hemingway's suicide was almost 35 years to the day that her grandfather took his own life.

LEFT Margaux Hemingway suffered from epilepsy. During her short life, she worked with epilepsy organizations to help raise awareness of the condition.

Brian Keith

Born November 14, 1921
Died June 24, 1997

ABOVE Brian Keith
(right) and the cast of
Family Affair. Keith won
three Emmy Awards®
for his down-to-earth
portrayal of Uncle Bill.

Brian Keith specialized in playing gruff sidekicks and second leads in a career that spanned more than 40 years on stage, television, and film. Keith played resilient characters, but in his later years agonizing chemotherapy and the suicide of his daughter proved too much for him.

Brian Keith, born Robert Keith Richey, Jr., was the son of prominent character actor Robert Keith. His first appearance on screen was at the age of three in the film *Pied Piper of Malone* (1924). Keith served as an aerial machine gunner during World War II, and when his badly damaged plane was attacked by two Japanese Zero fighters he was nearly killed. Because Keith's machine guns jammed, he confused the Japanese pilots by firing a flare pistol at them.

After the war, Keith became a stage actor, branching into live television before his first major film appearance in *Arrowhead* in 1953. Many motion picture roles followed, including a rare romantic lead in *The Parent Trap* (1961), a memorable turn as Lieutenant Colonel Morris Langdon in *Reflections of a Golden Eye* (1967) opposite Marlon Brando and Elizabeth Taylor, and he even played President Theodore Roosevelt in *The Wind and the Lion* (1975). But Keith is remembered best for his role as the gruff rock "Uncle Bill" in the CBS television series *Family Affair* (1966–71). When *Family Affair* was canceled, Brian Keith continued with supporting roles until he picked up his second series role, playing retired Judge Milton in *Hardcastle and McCormick* (1983–86).

The last year of Keith's life was a struggle. He was diagnosed with lung cancer and emphysema (despite quitting smoking in 1987), and the chemotherapy took an emotional toll on the 75-year-old actor. But far more tragic was the death of Keith's daughter in April of that year. Keith was devastated when 27-year-old Daisy died of a self-inflicted gunshot wound, leaving no suicide note.

On Tuesday, June 24, 1997, at 10:13 A.M., family members notified the police, who found Keith's body in his Malibu home. He, too, had placed a gun to his head and pulled the trigger. Johnny Whitaker, one-time child actor in *Family Affair*, had spoken to Keith on the telephone only five days before. "He was not feeling good because he'd been going through the chemotherapy for his cancer," Whitaker said. "And he'd been having other problems."

Brian Keith is buried at Westwood Memorial Park, Los Angeles, California next to his daughter, Daisy Keith.

Star Shot
Brian Keith's young co-star in *Family Affair*, Anissa Jones, died from a drug overdose in 1976 at the age of just 18.

RIGHT Brian Keith was rarely out of work. He appeared in television programs as varied as The Alfred Hitchcock Hour, Wagon Train, 77 Sunset Strip, and Star Trek.

Alan Ladd

Born September 3, 1913
Died January 29, 1964

*A*lan Walbridge Ladd represented on screen an individualistic, iconoclastic heroism. Ladd became a middle-ranking star in the 1940s and 1950s, one of the Top 10 Distributors' moneymakers in 1947, 1953, and 1954, even though he was short for a leading man at only 5 feet, 6 inches (1.68 m) tall. Ladd's leading ladies often had to stand in trenches during shooting. Audiences found Ladd's laidback demeanor and lethal grace affecting and inscrutable; his icy-cool, ethereal presence gave him an iconic status comparable to James Dean. In fact, director George Stevens offered Ladd James Dean's role in *Giant* (1956), but he refused.

ABOVE Alan Ladd with his second wife, Sue Carol, in 1954. Carol began her career as an actress, but became an agent in the late 1930s.

Alan Ladd's mother immigrated from England at 19, and his American father died when he was four. He was a small, sickly child who was cruelly given the school nickname "Tiny." When he was eight years old, Ladd's mother married a house painter and the family migrated to California. At school Ladd discovered athletics, and his light frame became such a benefit that by 1931 he had started training for the Olympics. Unfortunately, disappointment was to follow, as an injury destroyed his dream of competing. Ladd moved between jobs, opened a hamburger stand self-effacingly called "Tiny's Patio," then worked as a grip (scenery and lighting assistant) at Warner Bros. He married his close friend Marjorie Harrold in 1936, but monetary issues meant that the couple could not live together initially. In 1937, the couple shared a friend's apartment, and Marjorie had their son, Alan Jr. Ladd's alcoholic mother moved in with them, and she later committed suicide by ingesting ant poison—her death witnessed by Ladd.

BELOW A scene from Red Mountain (1952). In 1953, Alan Ladd was voted Most Popular Male Star in the Photoplay awards.

Ladd's first screen credit is often given as *Born to the West* (1937). Due to a clerical error in the studio's publicity, Ladd was wrongly included in the cast credits. Talent scout Sue Carol discovered Ladd in 1939, and a string of small parts ensued as he did his time as a studio bit player. Ladd's star finally shone in 1941, when he gained an uncredited speaking part in Orson Welles's immortal *Citizen Kane*, uttering the words "Or Rosebud?" before the sled is incinerated. In the same year Ladd was cast as Raven the psychopath in *This Gun for Hire*, and the role made him a star. Just as Ladd got his break, war was declared and he was drafted in 1943. His war role was just a cameo, as he was discharged the same year with a double hernia and stomach ulcer. In the film *China* (1943), Ladd's character, Mr. Jones, knocks down John Sparrow (William Bendix) on the road to Shanghai, rather than stop to help save the lives of the Chinese from

the invading Japanese army. Like the scarred actor, Jones asserted the right of the hero to do nothing to help if it did not suit him. This rugged individualism brought Ladd a raft of tough-guy protagonists in the 1940s; he packed cinemas, and he was one of the few male stars whose face on a cover would sell magazines. One famous conversation between Ladd, at the height of his fame, and a friend on the Paramount backlot reveals a lot about his persona:

"I hear your new picture starts Monday?"

"Yeah, and I haven't read the script yet."

"That must be kind of disturbing?"

"Sure is, I don't know what I'm going to wear."

In the 1950s Alan Ladd scored undoubtedly his greatest role, in the "superwestern" *Shane* (1953). One fizzing critic declared *Shane* was "fixed in the dreamy clarity of a fairy tale. The hero, Alan Ladd, is hardly a man at all, but something like the Spirit of the West, beautiful in fringed buckskins." In one famous scene, young Joey runs after the hero he idolizes, calling for him to come back. The audience is left to question whether Shane is once again leaving the quiet life with his own charisma intact, or if he is actually dead in the saddle.

By the end of the 1950s, liquor and several flops had taken their toll on his charisma and bankability. In 1961 Ladd was asked, "What would you change about yourself if you could?" He replied, "Everything."

Although his star had faded in the 1960s, Ladd urgently desired the title role in the epic motion picture, *Lawrence of Arabia* (1962), playing another silent, stoic blond enigma, so much so that he personally lobbied the director, David Lean—to no avail, as Peter O'Toole was given the part. In November 1962 Ladd was found unconscious, lying in a pool of blood with a bullet wound near his heart. He survived this suicide attempt, but in January 1964 he was successful. Alan Ladd was found dead due to an overdose of sedatives and alcohol in Palm Springs, California. Ladd was interred at Forest Lawn, Glendale, California, in the Freedom Mausoleum, Sanctuary of Heritage. Apart from his movies, Ladd left another Hollywood legacy: his son, Alan Ladd, Jr., became a film producer.

Alan Ladd has a star on the Hollywood Walk of Fame at 1601 Vine Street.

ABOVE On the set of Shane (1953). At the front of Alan Ladd's tomb is a statue of the actor dressed as Shane, the role for which he will be forever remembered.

Star Shot

The woman who helped make Alan Ladd a star, Sue Carol, became his second wife when he married her in 1942. They had two children, Alana and David.

RIGHT Alan Ladd with Corinne Calvert and Marc Cavell in the 1952 drama Thunder in the East. *The film also featured Deborah Kerr.*

Carole Landis

Born January 1, 1919
Died July 5, 1948

ABOVE Carole Landis comforts Victor Mature in the adventure film, One Million B.C. (1940). The film was Mature's first starring role.

RIGHT Carole Landis in 1943, preparing to marry her third husband, Thomas Wallace. Although she was a talented actress, the critics only seemed to comment on her beauty.

Landis's comments to *Photoplay,* a little before her death in 1948, reveal her tragic, romantic character: "The glamor and the tinsel, the fame and the money, mean very little if there is a hurt in the heart." It would be her unrequited love for actor Rex Harrison, her "hurt in the heart," that would finally drive Landis to suicide.

Soon after Landis's birth as Francis Lillian Mary Ridste, her father abandoned the family. At age 15 Landis eloped with 19-year-old Irving Wheeler to Yuma, Arizona, but, after a few weeks, the marriage was annulled because she was underage. They remarried in August 1934, and the couple moved to California with Landis's mother, Clara. Landis and Wheeler divorced in 1939.

In 1937, Landis could be seen in *A Star is Born* and *A Day at the Races,* but she was plucked out of the chorus for an uncredited role in the musical *Varsity Show* (1937). After her Warner Bros. contract, worth $50 a week, lapsed, Hal Roach cast a new and improved Landis in the 1940 film *One Million B.C.*—Landis had had plastic surgery on her nose, dyed her hair blonde, and dieted for the role. Director Hal Roach quickly sold Landis as the "best legs in town" and "The Ping Girl," a nonsensical name (apparently short for "purring" girl) that Landis strongly protested against. Since Landis's first marriage, she had been married again three times and had pursued numerous affairs, but when Landis met Rex Harrison (married at the time to Lilli Palmer) and the two began a steamy affair, it was the beginning of the end for her.

On July 4, 1948, Harrison joined Landis for dinner at her home in Brentwood Heights, California. Landis was distraught about her financial problems, but Harrison barely heeded her, and he left Landis at 9:00 P.M. The next afternoon Harrison phoned Landis's house. The maid said there was no answer, and Harrison hurried over. At 3:00 P.M. Harrison found Landis dead. She was lying on her side with her cheek resting on her jewel box. Seconal, a powerful barbiturate, and alcohol were found in her bloodstream. Landis was only 29, and had made 49 films.

Carole Landis's funeral was held at Forest Lawn Memorial Park in Glendale, California. She was buried in an evening gown with an orchid pinned to each shoulder strap. The pallbearers included Dick Haynes, Pat O'Brien, and Cesar Romero. Rex Harrison was quickly branded the villain of the affair, and Fox canceled his contract.

Maggie McNamara

Born June 18, 1928
Died February 18, 1978

Maggie McNamara made a promising start to her film career. In only her second film she was cast in the classic *Three Coins in the Fountain* (1954); unfortunately, she only featured in two more films. She had the look that was in vogue, and played both sensuous and wholesome characters. Born in New York City, McNamara began her acting career on stage. One of four children of Irish-American parents, she attended Textile High in New York in preparation for a career in modeling. As a teenager her photograph appeared twice on the cover of *Life* magazine while she took acting classes.

McNamara debuted on Broadway in *The King of Friday's Men* (1951) before she headlined a national production of *The Moon Is Blue* for a year and a half, replacing Barbara Bel Geddes as lead in 1952. She hit Hollywood when Otto Preminger cast her opposite David Niven and William Holden in the film version of *The Moon Is Blue* (1953), where she garnered a nomination for the Best Actress Academy Award®. *The New York Times* stage critic, Brooks Atkinson, commented that McNamara was "remarkably pretty and has a gift for acting." *The New York Times* noted in 1978 that *The Moon Is Blue* aroused controversy because of "indecent" conversations about sex, although in comparison with some of today's films it is very tame. During the film's first exhibition, the Catholic Legion of Decency was unimpressed with it, labeling it "C" for Condemned. McNamara was subsequently signed by 20th Century Fox and starred in *Prince of Players* (1955), opposite Richard Burton.

Maggie McNamara also appeared on television in *The Twilight Zone* (1959–65), *Ben Casey* (1961–66), and *The Alfred Hitchcock Hour* (1962–65). In 1962 she returned to Broadway to play in *Step on a Crack*, and in 1963 she returned to film when Preminger cast her as support in *The Cardinal* (1963), her last film.

Maggie McNamara, 49, committed suicide by overdosing on sleeping pills in New York, the place of her birth, and she is interred at Saint Charles Cemetery, Farmingdale, New York. Her plot—Section 18, Row MM, Grave 165—is unmarked. McNamara worked as a typist after acting, and her obituary in *The New York Times* appeared a whole month after her death. Like Lana Turner, the intelligent McNamara was straitjacketed by her good looks during her brief career.

ABOVE Maggie McNamara (center) with Dorothy McGuire (left) and Jean Peters in the romantic Three Coins in the Fountain *(1954). The film tells the story of three young American women who throw coins into Rome's Trevi Fountain in the hope that their dream of meeting the perfect man would come to pass.*

Star Shot

Just before her death, Maggie McNamara had taken up writing. Her screenplay for the movie *The Mighty Dandelion* was greenlighted by a studio, but the film was never made.

Ona Munson

Born June 16, 1903
Died February 11, 1955

ABOVE Belle Watling, the role made famous by Ona Munson, was originally offered to Tallulah Bankhead, who refused it because the part was "too small."

A slender, diminutive, 5 foot, 2 inch (1.57 m) blonde, Ona Munson achieved recognition as Belle Watling, the heart-of-gold prostitute, in *Gone with the Wind* (1939). A dramatic supporting actress in 1930s and 1940s Hollywood, Munson's background encompassed vaudeville and Broadway. For her *Gone with the Wind* screen test she drawled throatily to secure the part. Producer David O. Selznick had announced that Mae West was to play Belle, but this was merely a publicity stunt. Munson's subsequent film roles were as supporting characters in westerns and melodramas. She is also known for her dubious role as Mother Gin Sling (Hollywood's self-censored name for brothel owner Mother Goddamn) in Josef von Sternberg's *The Shanghai Gesture* (1941).

Born in Portland, Oregon, as Owena Wolcott, at 16 Munson appeared on vaudeville as the title character in *No, No, Nanette* in New York. This made her a star, and in 1926 she opened *Twinkle, Twinkle* with Joe E. Brown. She introduced the song "You're the Cream in My Coffee" in the Broadway play *Hold Everything* (1927), and this became her signature song. In the 1930s, Munson returned to the stage, playing Regina in Alla Nazimova's revival of Ibsen's *Ghosts*, and Lorelei Kilbourne on CBS Radio's *Big Town* (1940–42), replacing Claire Trevor, who incidentally also gained fame by playing a prostitute, in *Stagecoach* (1939). Munson's last motion picture was *The Red House* (1947), with Edward G. Robinson. She was married three times—to director Eddie Buzzell, Stewart McDonald, and artist Eugene Berman—but still managed to find the time to be director Ernst Lubitsch's mistress for five years. In Paris during the 1940s and 1950s, Munson was a close friend of Vera and Igor Stravinsky, was Alla Nazimova's lover and protégé, and had alleged affairs with Marlene Dietrich and Mercedes de Acosta. De Acosta also had torrid affairs with Dietrich, Greta Garbo, and Cecil Beaton.

Ona Munson's career had essentially stalled after the success of *Gone with the Wind* (1939). Her husband, Eugene Berman, found her dead from an overdose of barbiturates in their New York apartment. Ona Munson is buried at the Ferncliff Cemetery and Mausoleum, Hartsdale, Westchester County, New York. Her plot is Unit 8, tier Y, columbarium G, niche 5, next to Berman.

Sadly, Ona Munson was not the only member of the *Gone with the Wind* (1939) cast to commit suicide. George Reeves, who played Stuart Tarleton in the Civil War epic, apparently shot himself in 1959 at the age of only 45.

George Reeves

Born January 5, 1914
Died June 16, 1959

T he death of the star of television's *The Adventures of Superman* (1952) has remained a mystery ever since his body was discovered in his Los Angeles bedroom.

Reeves was born George Keefer Brewer, the son of Don and Helen Brewer, who divorced soon after his birth. Helen then married Frank Joseph Besselo, and maintained to George for many years that his biological father was dead. In the late 1930s, George took on the stage name Reeves, and he was cast as Stuart Tarleton in *Gone with the Wind* (1939). Although he appeared in a few films, his career floundered for many years after the war until he was cast in the hugely successful *The Adventures of Superman* and became a superhero to thousands of baby boomers.

Months before Reeves's "suicide," he received death threats and was involved in a traffic accident that left him needing 27 stitches. On June 15, 1959, Reeves, his fiancée Lenore Lemmon, and their house guest Robert Condon (Reeves's best man) drank heavily before going to bed. At about 12:30 A.M. on June 16, two friends of Reeves and Lemmon, Carol Von Ronkel and William Bliss, interrupted the couple's sleep. Reeves, furious with them, returned to bed and Lenore joked, "He'll probably go up to his room and shoot himself." Shortly afterward, at 1:20 A.M., they heard a loud bang upstairs. Reeves was lying dead on his bed, his .30-caliber Luger pistol next to him.

Was it suicide or murder? Circumstantial evidence originally indicated Reeves committed

suicide, but Reeves's friends were unconvinced. Although Reeves's career had been in stasis, with *The Adventures of Superman* resurrected for 1960 he was in high spirits. Forensic evidence didn't help the case for suicide. The police uncovered one bullet in the ceiling and two bullet holes in the floor; also, the Luger's empty cartridge was found under the body, which is unusual for a suicide.

Who were the suspects? First, there was Toni Mannix, married to Loew's Inc. Vice President Eddie "Bulldog" Mannix, a man with alleged mob connections. Reeves and Toni had been involved for seven years before Reeves ended the relationship in 1958. Lenore Lemmon alleged that Toni harassed Reeves for months. Toni was the only beneficiary in Reeves's will. But Lenore was equally suspect. She, too, had unsavory connections. Apparently Lenore was extremely jealous, and she and Reeves had been arguing that evening. Lenore left California the next day and never returned. Both women are now deceased, so the truth will never be known.

After his death, a myth arose that Reeves believed he was Superman and fell while trying to fly.

George Sanders

Born　July 3, 1906
Died　April 25, 1972

Last Words

"Dear World, I am leaving because I am bored. I feel I have lived long enough. I am leaving you with your worries in this sweet cesspool—good luck. Love, George" (From George Sanders's suicide note.)

Sanders was famous as the cynical British fop, a villainous sneer and the acerbic remark being his stock in trade. He appeared in over 90 motion pictures from the mid-1930s onward, and maintained a debonair style and a ruthless wit up until his death at the age of 65.

Sanders's father was a rope manufacturer and his mother a famous horticulturalist. Sanders had one brother, Tom Conway, who also had a successful career on the screen. The family lived in St. Petersburg, Russia, but left for England during the Bolshevik Revolution of 1917.

In 1934, Sanders made his screen debut in *Love, Life and Laughter*. By 1936, his contract shifted from a British film company to 20th Century Fox. His U.S. debut that same year was as Lord Everett Stacy in *Lloyds of London*. Sanders went on to star in the movie series *The Saint* (1939–41), although most of his career saw him play ruthless cads. The highlight of his career was certainly his Oscar®-winning role as the cynical theater critic, Addison De Witt, in *All About Eve* (1950), which starred Bette Davis. But running a close second has to be his role as Mr. Freeze in the camp television series, *Batman*, in 1966.

Sanders's reputation for cutting wit continued offscreen. He stated, "I hate interviews because I don't get paid for them. I hate to give autographs and never do. I am always rude to people. I am not a sweet person. I am a disagreeable person. I am a hateful person. I like to be hateful." Unsurprisingly, this attitude never mixed comfortably with marriage. He was married four times, two of them to Gabors: Zsa Zsa in 1949, whom he divorced in 1954, and her older sister Magda in 1970. This relationship lasted only a matter of weeks.

RIGHT During 1957, Sanders hosted his own television series, The George Sanders Mystery Theater. It ran for 13 episodes before being canceled.

One of Sanders's last film roles was in the spy thriller *The Kremlin Letter* (1970), where he played an aging drag queen who becomes the darling of the Moscow literati.

By the time he was shooting *Psychomania* (1971), Sanders's health was quickly declining. He was being treated for depression. He sold his beautiful home in Majorca and registered at a hotel in Castelldelfels, 10 miles (16 km) south of Barcelona, Spain. On the night of April 24, 1972, he retired to bed, requesting an early wake-up call. In the morning, when he didn't respond to the call, the hotel manager investigated and found Sanders dead. He had overdosed on vodka and five bottles of the barbiturate Nembutal. In 1937, while talking to David Niven, he promised he would take his own life. On April 25, 1972, he made good on his promise.

Jean Seberg

Born November 13, 1938
Died September 8, 1979

Jean Seberg was plucked from thousands of hopefuls to star in Otto Preminger's *Saint Joan* (1957). For the elfin beauty it should have been the beginning of a fairy-tale rise to stardom. What eventuated was anything but.

Critics universally panned Seberg's performance, but Preminger used her again in *Bonjour Tristesse* (1958). But it was Seberg's role as Patricia in Jean-Luc Godard's New Wave classic *A bout de souffle* (1960) that made her a cultural icon. Over the next few years, Seberg would fly between France and the United States, appearing in films of variable quality on both sides of the Atlantic. Her American career encompassed *Lilith* (1964), with Warren Beatty, Peter Fonda, and Gene Hackman; the musical *Paint Your Wagon* (1969); and the blockbuster film *Airport* (1970), as Burt Lancaster's love interest.

In the late 1960s, Jean Seberg became active in left-wing politics and especially in the cause of the Black Panthers, the militant black rights movement. According to Romain Gary, her second husband, Seberg's political activity drew attention from J. Edgar Hoover and the FBI. In an effort to "neutralize" Seberg, on April 27, 1970, the FBI leaked a fake letter to a Hollywood gossip column syndicated across the United States. The column made insinuations about Seberg, who was seven months' pregnant, claiming that the father was a prominent Black Panther.

Seberg was so traumatized that she attempted suicide with pills. This caused her to go into premature labor, and her baby died only two days after being born. (Some reports state that the baby was stillborn.) At a press conference, Seberg presented her dead white baby to shocked reporters.

Seberg continued to suffer from depression and attempted suicide on the anniversary of her child's death every year.

Despite her ongoing depression and suicidal tendencies, by 1979 she did appear to be more at ease and even considered returning to filmmaking. On August 27, 1979, Seberg disappeared. She was reported missing, and, despite public pleas for her safe return, fans and loved ones feared the worst. Twelve days after her disappearance, Seberg was found naked in the back of her white Renault. The autopsy determined she had taken an overdose of barbiturates.

Jean-Paul Belmondo, Jean-Paul Sartre, and Simone de Beauvoir attended her funeral at the Montparnasse Cemetery in Paris. Seberg is still considered an icon in France.

Romain Gary killed himself a year later with a Smith and Wesson .38 in the mouth.

ABOVE As Saint Joan in the 1957 film. In the burning at the stake scene, Otto Preminger, known for his cruelty to actors, allowed Seberg to be actually burned.

Walter Slezak

Born May 3, 1902
Died April 21, 1983

A powerful and ruggedly handsome man when young, Walter Slezak gained weight during middle age, which helped to establish him as a talented character actor. He could play antagonists or sidekicks with equal zeal.

Born in Vienna, Austria, son of Metropolitan Opera star Leo Slezak, Walter entered films by chance following a career as a bank clerk, after meeting director Michael Curtiz in 1922. Curtiz cast him in the German epic *Sodom and Gomorrah* (1922), and in 1930 Slezak moved to the United States to act on stage and in films. His Broadway debut was in 1931, and he developed into a familiar Broadway face during the 1930s. Slezak made his Hollywood film debut as the Austrian Count married to Ginger Rogers in *Once Upon a Honeymoon* (1942), but made an impact as the cartoonish antagonist in Bob Hope's *The Princess and the Pirate* (1944). Slezak also appeared in *The Fallen Sparrow* (1943), Alfred Hitchcock's *Lifeboat* (1944), *Cornered* (1945), *Sinbad the Sailor* (1947), *The Pirate* (1948), *The Inspector General* (1949), *People Will Talk* (1951), *Call Me Madam* (1953), *The Miracle* (1959), *Emil and the Detectives* (1964), and *Treasure Island* (1972), based on the book by Robert Louis Stevenson.

During the shooting of *Lifeboat* (1944), Hitchcock gave Slezak curly hair to soften his character, as Slezak puts it: "to give my appearance an extra coat of deceptive harmlessness." He would have to sit in the makeup chair for hours every morning, listening to the costume department gossip, and "it was always a letdown to leave this happy little group, go on the sound stage, and listen to Tallulah Bankhead." In 1955, Slezak garnered professional acclaim when he won a Tony Award® for his portrayal of Cesar in the Broadway production of *Fanny*, bagging a New York Drama Critics' Circle Award in the same year. With musical talent inherited from his father, Slezak also sang at the Metropolitan Opera, making his debut in *The Gypsy Baron* in 1959. *What Time's the Next Swan?,* his autobiography, was published in 1962.

At the time of his death, Walter Slezak was survived by three children, including his daughter Erika, who is well-known to audiences of the television soap opera, *One Life to Live.* Slezak actually played his daughter's godfather on the series in 1974. Slezak had been in ill health for some years and he committed suicide in 1983 in Flower Hill, New York. He is buried at the Egern Friedhof cemetery in Munich, Germany, in his family plot. His devoted wife, Johanna Van Ryn, was married to him from 1943 until his untimely death.

ABOVE Walter Slezak with his wife, Johanna. In addition to his acting and singing talents, Slezak also had a gift for art: he was a painter and sculptor.

Star Shot

As well as *One Life to Live*, Walter Slezak made guest appearances on a variety of other television shows, including *Rawhide*, *Dr. Kildare*, *Batman*, and *The Love Boat*.

RIGHT With Ronald Reagan and Bonzo the chimpanzee in Bedtime for Bonzo (1951). Walter Slezak played a college professor in one of his finest comic roles.

Everett Sloane

Born October 1, 1909
Died August 6, 1965

There was another ferry pulling in. And there was a girl waiting to get on. A white dress she had on. She was carrying a white parasol. I only saw her for one second, she didn't see me at all, but I bet a month hasn't gone by since, that I haven't thought of that girl.

Everett Sloane, playing Mr. Bernstein, wistfully utters these words, metaphorically defining Charles Foster Kane (Orson Welles), the title character of *Citizen Kane* (1941). This was Sloane's first screen role, in probably the greatest movie ever made. In the film, Sloane plays a loyal henchman to Kane, and in his career he had a similar relationship with Welles. Sloane's pinched face, short stature, and tiny round glasses gave him a nearsighted look, and he became a character actor dominated by Welles's leading-man status. For Sloane, this role foreshadowed things to come: he saw the greatness of Welles, but could never fully escape from Welles's shadow.

Born in New York, Sloane was already an accomplished stage and radio actor before he moved to Hollywood with Welles's Mercury Theater troupe. He married Luba Herman in 1933, and she was by his side until his death. After *Citizen Kane*, Sloane's next three speaking roles were also in Welles's films: *Journey Into Fear* (1943), *The Lady from Shanghai* (1947), and *Prince of Foxes* (1949), the latter two directed by Welles. This frustrated

ABOVE With Fredric March (right) in the play A Bell for Adano *(1944). Everett Sloane's television appearances included* Gunsmoke, Rawhide, *and* Bonanza.

Sloane and his quest for roles outside the Mercury Theater stalwarts, and when Welles wanted him to play treacherous Iago in Welles's direction of *Othello* (1952), Sloane turned him down. The fact that Welles continually returned to Sloane is a compliment of sorts, but by then Sloane was desperate to forge his own acting career.

To a certain extent he managed it, for Sloane kept working right up to his death. His most critically acclaimed role came in *Patterns* (1956), where he revisited on screen his stage performance as corporate monster Walter Ramsey. He supported Bogart in *Sirocco* (1951), before establishing a new career voicing cartoon characters for television, primarily *Dick Tracy* (1961) and *Mister Magoo* (1964). During Sloane's career he moved from acting in films to sound-only roles, because he was afraid he was going blind. In early August 1965 he overdosed on barbiturates in Brentwood, California, and the verdict was suicide.

Star Shot

Before turning to films, Everett Sloane was a well-respected radio personality, performing in more than 15,000 broadcasts.

Inger Stevens

Born October 18, 1934
Died April 30, 1970

Inger Stevens was born Inger Strensland in Stockholm, Sweden. After her parents divorced, Stevens moved to the United States with her father. At 16, she ran away from home and worked in New York as a showgirl. At the same time she took lessons at the Actors Studio. One of her best-remembered roles was in an episode of the television show *The Twilight Zone* (1960), in which she played a driver who keeps passing the same hitchhiker on the road. The viewer discovers that the ghost is an embodiment of death, and that Stevens's character has been dead the entire time, having been killed in a car accident. Fatalistically, Stevens once said, "A career, no matter how successful, can't put its arms around you. You end up being like Grand Central Station with people just coming and going. And there you are—left all alone."

Stevens was romantically involved with Bing Crosby while playing the second female lead in *Man on Fire* (1957), her Hollywood debut. Their relationship ended badly because Stevens refused to convert to Catholicism. When Bing Crosby married Kathryn Grant in October 1957, Stevens was shattered. Turning back to filmmaking, she was inspiring as the petrified wife in *Cry Terror!* (1958), opposite James Mason; she supported Yul Brynner in *The Buccaneer* (1958). Stevens gained industry recognition as the lead in the television series *The Farmer's Daughter*, winning a Golden Globe® in 1963. She also had roles in *Bonanza* (1959), *The Twilight Zone* (1960), and *The Alfred Hitchcock Hour* (1963).

ABOVE On the red carpet in 1967 Inger Stevens is said to have had affairs with a number of her leading men, including James Mason and Anthony Quinn.

Stevens diced with death three times. She attempted suicide by swallowing a mixture of barbiturates and ammonia; she survived, but suffered temporary blindness, blood clots in her lungs, and swollen legs. While filming in a tunnel during the making of *Cry Terror!* (1958), she and several others were almost overcome by carbon monoxide fumes. She also escaped from a plane moments before it crashed.

Star Shot

Inger Stevens was chairwoman of the California Council of Retarded Children and was on the board of the Neuro–Psychiatric Institute at the UCLA Medical Center.

After her suicide from barbiturate poisoning in Hollywood in 1970, friends and fans alike were stunned to discover that Stevens had been married to African-American character actor Ike Jones since 1961. The marriage was hidden to protect her career, although the couple was estranged when she died. Four weeks after Stevens's death, Jones requested to be made administrator of her estate; her brother supported him in court, and Jones was eventually given half her estate. Jones donated all the funds to charities and other organizations that were involved in child welfare and that cared for those with mental health problems. Inger Stevens was cremated and her ashes were scattered at sea.

RIGHT Just months before her death, Inger Stevens signed up to play the lead in a new television crime show, The Most Deadly Game.

David Strickland

Born October 14, 1969
Died March 22, 1999

D avid Strickland, 29, was a young comedian whose career was just taking off when he ended his life in Room 20 of the Oasis Motel at 1731 Las Vegas Boulevard in Los Angeles at 4:00 A.M. on Monday, March 22, 1999. Strickland was born in Glen Cove, New York. He gained some acting experience in stand-up comedy and soon appeared on episodes of the popular television programs *Roseanne* (1988) and *Dave's World* (1993), as well as earning regular parts on *Sister, Sister* (1994) and *Mad About You* (1992). When he gained a central role on the Brooke Shields vehicle, *Suddenly Susan,* as the insecure music journalist, Todd, the future looked bright.

When Strickland checked into the Oasis Motel in the early hours of March 22, it was at the end of an alcohol and drug binge during which he toured several strip clubs and bars with friend and fellow comedian, Andy Dick. After Strickland failed to answer a checkout phone call, a maid at the Oasis Motel entered his room and found Strickland's body hanging from a bed sheet strung from a ceiling beam, a chair next to the body.

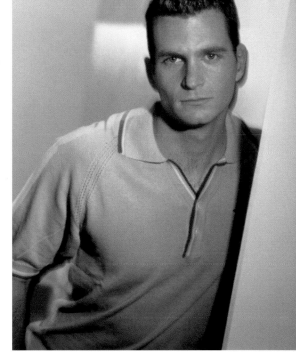

Why did Strickland commit suicide? When detectives began putting the pieces together, they found few clues as to Strickland's motivation. Strickland left no note and made no long-distance calls. His career appeared to be taking off: he had just co-starred with Sandra Bullock and Ben Affleck as Bullock's ex-boyfriend in *Forces of Nature* (1999). At the time of his death, *Forces of Nature* had reached number one at the box office. Only weeks before, Strickland had appeared in a television interview saying, "I'd like to be 38, 39, and doing something really great and sort of have this look back and say, 'He's worked consistently. There's something nice about that.'"

But Strickland had his personal demons. On December 21 of the previous year, Strickland had pleaded no contest to possession of cocaine and had been ordered into a drug rehabilitation program. On the day of his suicide, Strickland was scheduled to appear in Los Angeles Municipal Court for a progress report on this program. Very few people knew of his history of bipolar disorder, and Strickland had recently stopped taking the prescribed lithium to control his mood swings.

His funeral was held at Forest Lawn, Glendale, California. Brooke Shields, Judd Nelson, Julianna Margulies, and Strickland's girlfriend, Tiffani-Amber Thiessen, were among those who attended. He was cremated and his ashes given to his family. Strickland was remembered on a special tribute episode of *Suddenly Susan*.

ABOVE David Strickland appeared in supporting roles in a number of films, including Postcards From America *(1994) and* Delivered *(1998).*

Margaret Sullavan

Born May 16, 1911
Died January 1, 1960

*ABOVE Margaret Sulla-
van with James Stewart
in* The Shop Around
the Corner *(1940). The
film centers on a pen-
pal romance between
the characters played
by Sullavan and Stewart.*

Star Shot

**Had she lived, Margaret
Sullavan would have been
actor Dennis Hopper's
mother-in-law, since he
was married to her daugh-
ter, Brooke Hayward,
from 1961 to 1969.**

Despite appearing the picture of poise and grace in starring roles, Margaret Sullavan hated the motion picture industry and quickly obtained a reputation for being difficult. She had four tempestuous marriages (her husbands included Henry Fonda and director William Wyler) and appeared in only 16 movies. Much of Sullavan's talent remained untapped and unrealized because she was typecast as a tragic, second-rate heroine in soap opera scenarios.

Margaret Sullavan rebelled all her life. Her parents were appalled about her choosing a career as an actress, but she persisted. She appeared on Broadway in Preston Sturges's *Strictly Dishonorable*, and Hollywood director John M. Stahl, recognizing her talents, offered her a star-ring role in the film *Only Yesterday* (1933). She would accept the role only on her terms: $1,200 weekly, with three years' non-exclusive and approval rights. But with this contract came compromise. Because Sullavan was not a regular Hollywood beauty, she underwent many cosmetic changes, including having a mole removed, her hair dyed, and carefully placed lipstick to counteract the downward movement and placement of her mouth.

Sullavan hated the "hullaboo of fame" and preferred theater to the filmmaking process. Her third husband, Leland Hayward, arranged a contract with MGM for her to make six pictures, and she finally had the opportunity to play with substantial material. She received an Oscar® nomination for Best Actress and was the recipient of the New York Film Critics' Award for *Three Comrades* (1938), in which she co-starred with Robert Taylor.

Sullavan was praised for her understated performance in her last film, *No Sad Songs For Me* (1950), playing a woman dying from cancer. Later she earned a reputation for not being dependable when she suddenly pulled out of the making of *The Pilot* in 1956 and checked herself into a sanitarium.

On the day of her death, Margaret Sullavan lay in the bedroom of her New Haven, Connecticut, hotel, nervous and exhausted. A physician was summoned in the wee hours of the morning and then again later in the afternoon. The actress was left resting in her room until her husband at the time, Kenneth Wagg, returned three hours later. Sullavan's door was locked and she did not respond to calls, so the hotel manager was summoned. Eventually it took a hotel engineer to saw through the door chain. They discovered Sullavan's dead body in her bed. She had died from a barbiturate overdose.

Eight days after her death it was discovered that Margaret Sullavan had been fighting permanent hearing loss since 1948. Facing a silent future, she chose to take her own life.

Helen Twelvetrees

Born December 25, 1908
Died February 13, 1958

A temperamental star of the early Hollywood sound era, Helen Twelvetrees was born Helen Jurgens in New York. She attended the American Academy of Dramatic Arts, where she met and married alcoholic actor Clark Twelvetrees and took his less "foreign" surname. Inspired by her love for the screen, she joined the great migration to Hollywood and became one of the actresses to take the place of silent stars who could not adjust to the talkies. Her first job was at Fox, appearing in *The Ghost Talks* (1929). She went on to star with Clark Gable in *The Painted Desert* (1931) and John Barrymore in *State's Attorney* (1932). Twelvetrees signed with Pathé studio after receiving a nod as one of 1929's 13 WAMPAS Baby Stars, briefly becoming Pathé's most bankable female. Ironically, she had a slight lisp, so her fame in Hollywood in the days where sound was paramount is a credit to her tenacity and bullying temperament—and her tears.

As Twelvetrees was a 5 foot, 4 inch (1.63 m) blonde, she was consistently cast in "fallen angel" roles, including her breakthrough role in *Her Man* (1930). Twelvetrees's zenith came in *A Woman of Experience* (1931), where critics compared her favorably to silent screen goddess Lillian Gish. This brought roles in *Bad Company* (1931), *Panama Flo* (1932), and *My Woman* (1933). But one stinging critic snapped that Twelvetrees "was good at crying." Unfortunately, she was not considered very good at acting, and she was quickly dropped.

Accused of overacting in films—and in her life—by the gossip columns, Twelvetrees became increasingly difficult for the studio brass to manage. Twelvetrees was associated with RKO after alienating Pathé and Fox, yet left once über-producer David O. Selznick discovered the more talented Katharine Hepburn. During 1936 and 1937, her deteriorating marriage with stuntman husband Frank Woody was splashed across the tabloids. Her third husband, Conrad Payne, was with her until her death.

In 1937, Twelvetrees co-starred with Buck Jones in *Hollywood Round-Up*, a film that tells the story of the protagonist's rise from lowly stuntman to film star. The reverse occurred for Twelvetrees as she slipped from stardom into obscurity. She became addicted to painkillers and could not cope with the sudden drop in her fame and the dead-end roles she was forced to take. On February 13, 1958, at the age of 49, Helen Twelvetrees committed suicide by taking an overdose of drugs.

ABOVE One of Helen Twelvetrees's favorite roles was as Jean Ogden in Unashamed *(1932), where she played a feisty heroine, rather than a teary one.*

Star Shot
Helen Twelvetrees's co-star in *Hollywood Round-Up* (1937) was Grant Withers, who also committed suicide by taking a drug overdose, a little over a year after Helen Twelvetrees.

LEFT Helen Twelvetrees made her Broadway debut in 1941 in Boudoir *by Jacques Deval. It folded after 11 performances, and Twelvetrees retired from acting altogether.*

Lupe Velez

Born July 18, 1908
Died December 13, 1944

Of all the Mexican entertainers to transfer to Hollywood—including Dolores del Rio, Ramon Novarro, and José Mojica—Lupe Velez is the most famous and dearly beloved. Known variably as the Hot Tamale, the Mexican Wildcat, and the Queen of the Hot-Cha, Velez was famous for her scandalous headlines, sexual aggressiveness, and talent for self-promotion. But in the 1940s, the values of liberal Hollywood would come into direct conflict with her Mexican Catholic upbringing.

Velez was born María Guadalupe Vélez de Villalobos in San Luis Potosi, a suburb of Mexico City. Early in life her parents sent Velez to a convent school in San Antonio, Texas, to try to tame her unruliness. When she was still young, Velez's father was killed in the Mexican Revolution, and, in an effort to support her mother, two sisters, and young brother, Velez decided to go on the

ABOVE On the set of Resurrection *(1931) with director Edwin Carewe (center) and co-star John Boles. Lupe Velez also starred in a Spanish version of the film in 1931.*

stage. In 1926, aged 18, she arrived in Hollywood and danced in the local Music Box Revue starring Fanny Brice. But it was when she won recognition in *The Gaucho* (1927) as a wild mountain girl opposite Douglas Fairbanks and Mary Pickford that Velez's career picked up.

Lupe Velez's crazy screen persona was emphasized by her very public affairs with some of Hollywood's leading men. She began a passionate affair with Gary Cooper before Cooper's parents broke up the romance, and she never really recovered from it. Velez turned to other Hollywood actors such as John Gilbert and Johnny Weissmuller, the Olympic swimmer who would go on to play Tarzan. She married Weissmuller in October 1933. While many of Velez's films were insipid, her marital disputes with Weissmuller were always entertaining fare. They divorced in 1939.

In 1940, Lupe Velez first played the role she would be best remembered for: Carmelita, a fiery Mexican entertainer, in the modest program filler *The Girl From Mexico*. RKO was

RIGHT Lupe Velez pictured in 1939. Her final motion picture was the Spanish-language film Nana *(1944), which she had to return to Mexico to make.*

surprised by the success of the film, which had nothing to do with the script and everything to do with Velez's spirited performance, and they programmed seven more "Mexican Spitfire" movies between 1940 and 1943, such as *Mexican Spitfire* (1940), *Mexican Spitfire Out West* (1940), *Mexican Spitfire Sees a Ghost* (1942), and *Mexican Spitfire's Blessed Event* (1943).

In 1943, Velez met 27-year-old Harold Ramond (also known as Harald Maresch), an unemployed Austrian actor. On November 27, 1944, she announced that she would marry Ramond, but by December 10 she was calling off the wedding plans. Few knew that Velez was four months' pregnant and unconvinced that Ramond loved her. As she was a devout Catholic, abortion was out of the question, so she was considering having one of her sisters raise the child.

On the night of December 13, 1944, Velez dined with two close companions, Estelle Taylor and Benita Oakie. After the meal, Velez revealed her situation: "I'm tired of life. I have to fight for everything. I'm so tired of it all. Ever since I was a baby in Mexico, I've been fighting. I am getting to the place where the only thing I am afraid of is life itself. It's my baby. I couldn't commit murder and still live with myself. I would rather kill myself." Velez returned alone to her Beverly Hills mansion at 732 North Rodeo Drive. Her sisters, with whom she lived, were away. Velez put on her favorite blue silk pajamas and took an overdose of the barbiturate Seconal.

The following day in *The Examiner*, Louella Parsons featured an exclusive farewell to Velez, including a description of the scene at North Rodeo Drive: "Lupe was never lovelier as she lay there, as if slumbering.... A faint smile, like secret dreams.... Looking like a child taking nappy, like a good little girl.... Hark! There are the doggies, there's Chops, there's Chips, scratching at the door.... They're whimpering, they're whining.... They want their little Lupita to take them out to play...."

For a long time afterward, a very different image of Velez's death circulated, influenced by Kenneth Anger's book, *Hollywood Babylon*. This myth suggested Velez's rich meal had mixed disastrously with the Seconal and sent her rushing to the toilet. Rather than dying in peaceful repose in blue pajamas with her hands clasped in prayer, Velez was found with her head in the toilet bowl.

The funeral took place at Forest Lawn Memorial Park's Church of the Recessional in Glendale, California. Four thousand friends and fans passed by her casket. The pallbearers included Johnny Weissmuller, Gilbert Roland, and Arturo de Cordova. Velez was buried at the Pateon Civil de Délores Cemetery in Mexico City. One third of Velez's estate went to her housekeeper, Mrs. Beulah Kinder.

LEFT Lupe Velez with her husband, former Olympian Johnny Weissmuller, in happier days. Their marriage lasted for only five years.

Last Words

"You know the facts for the reason I'm taking my life." (From Lupe Velez's suicide note addressed to Harold Ramond.)

BELOW Lupe Velez as a nightclub singer in Lady of the Pavements *(1928). Velez played dramatic roles before turning her hand to comedy in the 1930s.*

Hervé Villechaize

Born April 23, 1943
Died September 4, 1993

On the day of his death, the 3 foot, 11 inch (1.19 m) Hervé Villechaize tape recorded a message for his lover, Kathy Self: "Kathy, I can't live like this anymore. I've always been a proud man and always wanted to make you proud of me. You know you made me feel like a giant, and that's how I want you to remember me. I'm doing what I have to do."

Villechaize was never at ease with his short stature and undersized lungs, even when they made him a star. He went into the garden and shot himself through a pillow he held to his chest.

Villechaize was born in Paris, but stopped growing early. He studied art at the Beaux-Arts in Paris and orchestrated a successful exhibition of his own work. At 21, he left France for the United States, where he continued painting while dabbling as a novelty film extra, notably as "Midget" in *Chappaqua* (1966) and "Deputy" in *The Last Stop* (1972). Villechaize's breakthrough came in the James Bond film *The Man with the Golden Gun* (1974), where he played Nick Nack, sidekick of assassin Scaramanga, played by Christopher Lee.

His role as Tattoo, servant of Mr. Roarke (Ricardo Montalban), in the television series *Fantasy Island* (1978) cemented his fame. It was here his catchphrase was first heard: "Da plane! Da plane!" The series was a hit, and Villechaize became a wealthy Hollywood star, his fortune peaking at $3.6 million. In 1983, he demanded more money from the show's producers to bring his pay into parity with that of Montalban. The bluff failed, Villechaize was axed, and he broke up with his model wife. The series was canceled within a year.

ABOVE Hervé Villechaize was married only once, to Camille Hagen. The marriage lasted about 12 months.

"It hurts, it hurts....
I'm dying, I'm dying!"

RIGHT With Ricardo Montalban in Fantasy Island *(1978–1983). The show was remade in the late 1990s, but this version was not as successful as its predecessor.*

Villechaize spent his career playing the lackey of tall, strong, tanned leading men, and those roles reaffirmed his low self-esteem about his body and his health. He could never be a "giant." He lost his money on risky investments and fame-hungry women, and contracted near-fatal pneumonia in 1992. Depressed and alcoholic, Villechaize started passing up roles he was offered. Unable to sleep on his back, he started coughing up blood, and one lung finally failed. On the day of his death, after having watched a film, Hervé Villechaize inscribed a suicide note and made *that* recording. Kathy Self was the first to discover his body and call an ambulance. He died at the Medical Center of North Hollywood at 3:40 P.M. He was cremated and his ashes were scattered off Point Fermin, Los Angeles.

Grant Withers

Born January 17, 1904
Died March 27, 1959

Appearing in over 170 films, Grant Withers was a longtime drinking companion of John Wayne. Like Ward Bond, another member of Wayne's Stock Company, he provided support on many of Wayne's westerns but, unlike Bond, he never found success on his own.

Withers worked as a salesman and newspaper reporter before gaining his first role in *The Gentle Cyclone* in 1926. He quickly became one of Hollywood's leading men, a dashing, tall, handsome matinee idol. But when he starred with Loretta Young in *The Second Floor Mystery* (1930), Withers made a disastrous decision. Young was only 17 but had fallen in love with the charming Withers, and they eloped to Yuma, Arizona, in 1930.

The marriage was doomed to failure, and Young's age was only part of the problem. Withers, 25 and recently divorced, was irresponsible and a heavy drinker. He could not control his finances, often refusing to pay bills. During the couple's one year of "wedded bliss," Withers was sued and arrested several times, and his contract at Warner Bros. was not renewed. In 1931, Young and Withers divorced, and, in the following year, Withers declared bankruptcy.

The elopement and the consequent effort by Young's mother to annul the marriage were the fodder of fan and gossip magazines. While the relationship only threatened to destroy Young's career, it crippled Withers's. It was not long before the romantic lead was demoted to supporting parts, predominantly as villains in B-grade movies and serials.

Throughout his troubled times, Withers came to rely on John Wayne. They had become friends in the late 1920s as members of the "Young Men's Purity, Total Abstinence, and Snooker Pool Association." When Withers was broke, Wayne provided him with much-needed character work. In all, Wayne and Withers appeared in nine films together, including *Fort Apache* (1948) and *Rio Grande* (1950).

Withers's last screen appearance was in Roger Corman's B-grade film noir *I Mobster* (1958) as mob boss Paul Moran. By now Wayne was a superstar, and even Ward Bond was starring in his own television show, *Wagon Train* (1957–61). Withers, by all accounts, was an incompetent drunk and totally bankrupt. On the evening of March 26, 1959, he wrote a short note asking for forgiveness from his friends, then washed down a large handful of barbiturates with a bottle of vodka.

Ward Bond suffered a heart attack and died a little over a year later. Both deaths devastated Wayne.

BELOW Grant Withers with Loretta Young in 1930. Ironically, after their marriage ended, they appeared together in the 1931 comedy Too Young to Marry.

RIGHT Gig Young took his name from the character he played in The Gay Sisters *(1942), which starred Barbara Stanwyck and George Brent.*

Gig Young

Born   November 4, 1913
Died   October 19, 1978

Star Shot

Gig Young was nominated three times for a Best Actor in a Supporting Role Oscar®, eventually winning a golden statuette for his character of Rocky in *They Shoot Horses, Don't They?* (1969).

Gig Young, born Byron Elsworth Barr, was a likable, smooth, and charming character actor who made a career in films where women left him in the final reel. Throughout his career, Young lost Jane Greer to Peter Lawford in *You for Me* (1952), Doris Day to Clark Gable in *Teacher's Pet* (1958), and even managed to lose three women (Doris Day, Dorothy Malone, and Elizabeth Fraser) in *Young at Heart* (1954).

Young was also unlucky in love in real life. He married five times. His seven-year marriage to *Bewitched*'s Elizabeth Montgomery ended in an acrimonious split in 1963. He suffered a public breakup with his fourth wife, Elaine Williams, when Young sued for paternity of his only child, Jennifer. His fifth marriage, at 64, to 31-year-old Kim Schmidt lasted three weeks.

Young met Schmidt on the set of *Game of Death* (1978), which starred Bruce Lee (Lee's footage was shot in 1973; director Robert Clouse finished the film several years later with a new cast). It would not only be Young's final film, but also Bruce Lee's. Schmidt and Young's relationship was tempestuous, but they married and moved into their Osborne Hotel apartment in New York.

During mid-morning on October 19, 1978, Young called the doorman to inquire about weather conditions. At noon, Schmidt placed an order for groceries. Between 2:30 P.M. and 3:30 P.M. the Osborne manager thought he heard two gunshots and after some time located the source as Room 1BB. When police officers arrived, they found the couple dead in their bedroom. Schmidt was lying on her back, and a bullet had entered through the base of her skull. Young was face down on the carpet. His hand held a .38 caliber snub-nosed Smith and Wesson pistol. The bullet that killed him had entered through his mouth.

Friends were adamant that even if Young was capable of suicide, he was completely incapable of murder. What could possibly have brought this charming actor to commit such an act?

Friends believed Schmidt had married Young simply to strengthen her own acting career. Young's will was causing friction between them—half of Young's $200,000 estate would go to Schmidt, but she was pressuring the aging actor to give her everything. Perhaps Schmidt was a scapegoat for all the wrongs Young felt women had perpetrated against him. Or, Young may have suffered a psychotic attack because of his withdrawal from drugs and alcohol.

Gig Young was buried in his family grave site at Green Hill Cemetery in Waynesville, North Carolina.

BELOW With Jane Greer in You for Me *(1952). Gig Young was friends with George Reeves and they were signed up by Warner Bros. at the same time.*

George Zucco

Born January 11, 1886
Died May 28, 1960

Despite his sinister name, villainous eyebrows, and piercing dark stare so associated with the rogues he often played on screen, George Zucco was the consummate professional and viewed acting as a serious occupation, never allowing mustache-twirling parody to infiltrate his more dubious later roles. Zucco was born in Manchester, England, and spent years on the stage, including a long run in the West End play *Journey's End* and a critically praised Broadway turn as British Prime Minister Benjamin Disraeli in *Victoria Regina*. Zucco was eventually enticed to the irresistible glitter of Hollywood and appeared in almost 100 films from the 1930s to the 1960s. The diverse range of motion pictures included major studio productions, classic Universal horror films that made him famous, and the inevitable barrel-scraping B-grade movies in the twilight of his career.

After his screen debut in *The Dreyfus Case* (1931) at the age of 45, Zucco quickly developed a reputation as a fine character actor. In *Saratoga* (1937), he received eighth billing amid an all-star cast including Clark Gable, Jean Harlow, Lionel Barrymore, and Walter Pidgeon. He played in the critically acclaimed *The Hunchback of Notre Dame* (1939) opposite Charles Laughton, and as the great detective's genius arch-nemesis, Professor Moriarty, in *The Adventures of Sherlock Holmes* (1939). In an odd twist of fate, he reprised his stage role as a British Prime Minister in *Suez* (1938), although Miles Mander played Disraeli in that particular production. It was Zucco's role—and very fetching costume—as the High Priest of Karnak in the cycle of Universal horrors *The Mummy's Hand* (1940), *The Mummy's Tomb* (1942), and *The Mummy's Ghost* (1944) that cemented his status with fans of the genre.

George Zucco died mysteriously, much like the Egyptian priest who gilded his star, in Hollywood, California, in 1960. The official report on his death was suicide, while informal accounts suggest that there was no reason he would have committed suicide—that he was an old man and simply died of pneumonia or a major stroke.

In a six-degrees-of-traumatic-death epilogue, Johnny Weissmuller starred with Zucco in *Tarzan and the Mermaids* (1948); Weissmuller was once married to Lupe Velez, who also committed suicide. Zucco is interred at Forest Lawn Cemetery in the Hollywood Hills. His grave is hidden away in the bottom corner of the mausoleum, and his last resting place is unmarked.

Star Shot

George Zucco's last screen role was as Professor Lampini in the 1966 film *Doom of Dracula,* which also featured another horror movie veteran, Boris Karloff.

ABOVE Andoheb, the high priest (George Zucco), looks down at Peggy Moran in The Mummy's Hand *(1940), while Tom Tyler (right) looks on. Moran died from injuries sustained in a car accident, and Tyler suffered a fatal heart attack at age 50.*

The Accidental Tourist

Car wrecks, plane crashes, house fires, and other deadly accidents have sent many of Hollywood's sons and daughters on a one-way trip to the next world. Air travel is the choice mode of transport for many a moneyed celebrity, so it is no surprise that quite a few stars—from Carole Lombard and Audie Murphy to Will Rogers and Aaliyah—have fallen from the sky.

Even when actors and actresses keep their feet firmly on the ground, fatal accidents can befall them. The combination of speed, fatigue, or illness and the power of an automobile had devastating consequences for several of Hollywood's favorites—James Dean, Grace Kelly, Jayne Mansfield, and Tom Mix are just a few who perished behind the wheel.

While they may not have had a red-hot career, Jack Cassidy, Linda Darnell, Gloria Dickson, and Butterfly McQueen did manage to go out in a blaze of glory—all four died in house fires. William Holden, Jeffrey Hunter, and Michael Wilding, on the other hand, had a "fall from grace." Each suffered fatal head injuries as a result of a fall. And the story of Frank Silvera's death should be a lesson to us all—electricity can be dangerous!

Aaliyah

Born January 16, 1979
Died August 25, 2001

ABOVE A fourth Aaliyah album, entitled I Care 4 U, *was released posthumously. Her single, "More Than a Woman," topped the U.K. charts in early 2002.*

RIGHT Aaliyah is remembered at the 29th Annual American Music Awards in 2002. The Aaliyah Memorial Fund supports some of the late singer's favorite causes, such as breast cancer research and AIDS awareness.

Aaliyah packed much into her short lifetime. By the time she was just 22 years old, the R&B singer was an established recording artist and was set to become a major movie star.

Aaliyah Dana Haughton was born in Brooklyn, New York, and when she was small, her family moved to Detroit, a city with a rich musical heritage. A hard-working and ambitious child, Aaliyah excelled at her studies while keeping up a busy schedule of singing, dancing, and music lessons. At age nine she appeared on the television talent show *Star Search*, and at 11 she performed with Gladys Knight in Las Vegas. (Aaliyah's uncle, Barry Hankerson, was Knight's former husband and head of Blackground Records.)

While a 14-year-old student at Detroit Performing Arts High School in 1994, Aaliyah released her debut album, aptly titled *Age Ain't Nothing But a Number,* which went platinum; two singles reached the Billboard top ten. At age 15, Aaliyah secretly married R&B performer R. Kelly; the marriage was later annulled. In her senior year of high school she recorded her second album, the funky *One in a Million,* which was even more successful, going double platinum. The 17-year-old Aaliyah was now a superstar.

Aaliyah found a wider audience when she recorded theme songs for two movies: "Are You Somebody" (*Doctor Dolittle,* 1998) and "Journey to the Past" (*Anastasia,* 1997), which she performed at the 70th Annual Academy Awards®, as it was nominated for the Best Original Song Oscar®. Her own movie career took off when producer Joel Silver cast her opposite Jet Li in the spirited action-adventure *Romeo Must Die* (2000). The movie soundtrack was a huge hit, and her single from the soundtrack, "Try Again," saw Aaliyah nominated for a Grammy®. It also won an MTV award. She then starred as the evil vampire Akasha in *Queen of the Damned* (released in 2002, after her death), based on the popular Anne Rice novel.

Her third, self-titled album was released in 2001 and was an instant success. With more movies in the pipeline, Aaliyah was going from strength to strength. But it all literally came crashing down when, on August 25, 2001, she was killed in a plane crash, along with the pilot and several members of her entourage. She had been filming a video on Abaco Island in the Bahamas when the small Cessna, which was heading for Florida, crashed and burned shortly after takeoff.

Aaliyah was a much-loved and respected member of the entertainment industry, and her passing was a great blow to her family, friends, and fans.

Jack Cassidy

Born March 5, 1927
Died December 12, 1976

Jack Cassidy was a consummate entertainer, making a name for himself as an actor in theater, television, and film, and as a recording artist.

The dashing performer was born John Joseph Edward Cassidy in Richmond Hill, New York. At age 16 he got into the chorus of his first Broadway musical, *Something for the Boys* (1943), and throughout the 1940s he continued to pick up small parts on the New York stage and with touring companies. In 1948, he married actress Evelyn Ward, and in 1950 their son, David Cassidy, came along (he later became famous as Keith in *The Partridge Family*).

Jack Cassidy's first starring Broadway role was in *Wish You Were Here* (1952), and he was a continuing presence in theater for over 20 years. He won a Tony Award® in 1964 for *She Loves Me* (1963), and would earn three more Tony Award® nominations during his life. After his divorce from Ward in 1956, he married rising star Shirley Jones, and they had three handsome and talented sons: Shaun, Patrick, and Ryan.

Throughout his career, Jack Cassidy regularly appeared on television in a variety of programs—musical, drama, and comedy—such as *Wagon Train*, *Hawaiian Eye*, *The Alfred Hitchcock Hour*, *Password*, *Bewitched*, *Get Smart*, *The Mary Tyler Moore Show*, *Columbo*, *The Ed Sullivan Show*, *Mission Impossible*, *The Carol Burnett Show*, *The Mod Squad*, and *The Julie Andrews Hour*. He received Emmy® nominations for his starring roles in *He and She* (1967) and the PBS movie, *The Andersonville Trial* (1970), directed by George C. Scott.

Cassidy didn't really begin to hit his stride on the big screen until the mid-1970s. He had memorable roles in the Clint Eastwood action/adventure film, *The Eiger Sanction* (1975); *W. C. Fields and Me* (1976), in which he played his hero, John Barrymore; and *The Private Files of J. Edgar Hoover* (1977), in the part of Damon Runyon.

Following his divorce from Shirley Jones in 1974, Jack Cassidy was living in a penthouse apartment in North Kings Road, West Hollywood. In the early hours of December 12, 1976, he was lying on the sofa, smoking a cigarette. He fell asleep and the cigarette dropped onto the sofa, instantly setting it alight. Before long, the whole building was ablaze, and the apartment was destroyed; five fire engines were needed to quell the inferno. Cassidy's body was unrecognizable, and because his car was missing, his family and friends hoped that he had gone to Palm Springs, as he had previously indicated. As it turned out, however, a friend had borrowed the car. Eventually, Cassidy's remains were identified by his dental records. (In another version of the story, it is stated that Cassidy was identified by an unusual pinky ring he wore that bore his family crest.)

ABOVE In the animated feature Mr. Magoo's Christmas Carol *(1964), which starred the voice of Jim Backus, Jack Cassidy provided the voice for Bob Cratchit.*

Star Shot

Jack Cassidy started writing—but never finished—a play entitled *A Waltz for Willie Ryan*. The main character was based on his working-class father.

Linda Darnell

Born October 16, 1923
Died April 10, 1965

Reflecting on his sister's death, Cal Darnell commented, "Whatever you fear most in life, you will probably meet." That was certainly true for hydrophobic Natalie Wood, who met her death by drowning. And it was also true for Linda Darnell, who had a morbid fear of fire.

Monetta Eloyse Darnell grew up in a rather eccentric family in Dallas, Texas. Her quiet father, Roy (a post office employee), married his extreme opposite, Pearl, who has been described as a "screwball" and a "fire-eating dragon." Pearl wanted an escape from her mundane life and saw pretty, dark-haired Monetta—the most attractive of her six children—as the ticket out. She channeled her formidable energy into preparing Monetta for stardom, pushing her into music, dance, and drama lessons, and entering her into talent shows and beauty pageants. Monetta passively went along with, and gradually began to believe in, her mother's dream. Their persistence eventually led them to Hollywood talent scouts, and at the age of 15, Monetta signed a contract with 20th Century Fox and changed her name to Linda Darnell.

Darnell's first film was *Hotel for Women* (1939), in which she played a model. She was then cast opposite screen idol Tyrone Power in four movies: *Daytime Wife* (1939), *Brigham Young* (1940), *The Mark of Zorro* (1940), and *Blood and Sand* (1941). She was happily making friends with other young actors and enjoying the independence of being in her own apartment. With her considerable earnings, she bought her parents a home in Brentwood, California.

In 1944, 20-year-old Darnell married J. Peverell Marley, a cameraman more than twice her age. After making a cameo appearance as the Virgin Mary in *The Song of Bernadette* (1943), Darnell had a few mediocre performances in *It Happened Tomorrow* (1944) and *Buffalo Bill* (1944). Her career was given a boost when she tied with Gene Tierney, Ingrid Bergman, and Hedy Lamarr as *Look* magazine's most beautiful woman in Hollywood. Fox producer Darryl Zanuck decided it was now time for his star to shed her "good girl" image, and in *Summer Storm* (1944), *Hangover Square* (1945), and *Fallen Angel* (1945), Darnell really turned on the sex appeal. It was also about this time that she realized she was infertile, and she began to eat and drink excessively.

She made three big movies in 1946: *Centennial Summer* with Jeanne Crain and Cornell Wilde, *My Darling Clementine* with Henry Fonda, and *Anna and the King of Siam* with Irene Dunne and Rex Harrison. As the slave girl Tuptim in *Anna and the King of Siam*, she had to be burned at the stake, which was excruciating for someone so terrified of fire. In 1947, Darnell landed the plum role in 20th Century Fox's lavish production of *Forever Amber*, based on the titillating best-selling novel.

BELOW Linda Darnell as Amber St. Clair in Forever Amber *(1947). The film was condemned by many Christian groups as totally immoral.*

Seductive and blonde, she played the mistress of Charles II, and again had to confront her great fear: one of the scenes took place in a re-creation of the great fire of London.

Darnell and her husband reunited after a separation, and in 1948 they adopted a baby daughter, Charlotte Mildred (Lola). In her next two films, Darnell played the "bitch": *Unfaithfully Yours* (1948) and *A Letter to Three Wives* (1949). In *A Letter to Three Wives*, Darnell's acting blossomed under the sensitive direction of Joseph Mankiewicz, who had also written the superb screenplay. She also fell deeply in love with the married director, and they had a lengthy affair. When it ended, Darnell became depressed and turned increasingly to alcohol.

Although Darnell made eight movies from 1950 to 1952, none of them were exceptional, and her career was going downhill. She divorced Marley in 1952, and her 20th Century Fox contract was terminated a year later. Still grieving over her breakup with Mankiewicz, she

ABOVE Terrified of fire, Linda Darnell was convincing as the doomed slave girl being burned at the stake in the film Anna and the King of Siam *(1946).*

impulsively married beer baron Phillip Liebmann in 1954, but the relationship only lasted one year. Throughout the 1950s and 1960s, Darnell made very few films—most of them B-grades—and she tried to earn a decent living by acting in television and regional theater. Her third marriage, to airline pilot Merle Robertson in 1957, ended in 1962 and left her with huge debts.

In April 1965, Darnell was visiting her former secretary, Jeanne Curtis, in Glenview, Illinois. They stayed up one night to watch one of Darnell's early movies, *Star Dust* (1940), and then retired upstairs to their bedrooms. A few hours later, Curtis, her teenage daughter, and Darnell were all woken up by a fire that was raging in the downstairs part of the house. It was

believed to have been started by a lit cigarette. The Curtises managed to jump out the window, but Darnell went downstairs and became trapped in the blazing living room. The fire department managed to rescue her, and she was taken to hospital with second- and third-degree burns over 90 percent of her body. Surgery and a tracheotomy were performed, and Darnell survived for 33 hours, but her lungs finally gave out. She died on April 10, 1965.

LEFT With Laird Cregar in Hangover Square *(1945), based on Patrick Hamilton's novel. The film cemented Linda Darnell's popularity.*

ABOVE A publicity shot of Linda Darnell from 1954. Her last role was with Rory Calhoun in the 1965 western film, Black Spurs.

Last Words

"That guy's got to stop....
He'll see us."

James Dean

Born February 8, 1931
Died September 30, 1955

James Dean's enduring appeal lies in the way he presented the image of the "angry young man," which became a template for the moody adolescent during the years when baby boomers were growing up. The template was established with only three major movies, and it was so powerful that, even to this day, his brooding, handsome, sexually charged image can be found on the walls of rebellious adolescents around the world.

Dean was born in Marion, Indiana, in 1931, and in 1936 the family moved to Santa Monica, California. When Dean was only nine years old his mother died of uterine cancer. His father put him on a train to Fairmont, Indiana, to live with his aunt, Ortense Winslow, and her husband, Marcus, on their farm. Dean was devastated at the loss of his beloved mother and felt rejected by his father. Nevertheless, he grew to love his aunt and uncle, whom he called "Mom" and "Dad."

As a student at Fairmont High School, Dean played basketball and rode motorcycles, but he never really fit in. He felt more comfortable on stage, performing in church and school plays. Another "outsider" in the conservative farming community was Wesleyan minister James DeWeerd. The erudite pastor recognized in Dean a kindred spirit and became his cultural and sexual guide. From the outset, Dean's private life was extremely complicated, and the young man would experience many and varied liaisons with both men and women during his life.

ABOVE James Dean in a trademark pose. In 1996, he was pictured on a commemorative postage stamp issued as part of the "Legends of Hollywood" series.

Following his graduation in 1949, Dean decided to continue his education in California and hopefully build a relationship with his estranged father. He spent a year at Santa Monica City College and later transferred to UCLA. However, he never got close to his father, and he never finished college, choosing instead to join James Whitmore's classes, which taught the "method" style of acting as developed by the Actors Studio.

Over the next few years, Dean landed some small jobs in television, films, and commercials, but was becoming increasingly discouraged. In October 1951, he left Hollywood and was accepted by the prestigious Actors Studio in New York, the *alma mater* of acting greats such as Marlon Brando, Montgomery Clift, and Julie Harris. He made his Broadway debut in *See the Jaguar* (1952), and on the strength of his superb performance in the play *The Immoralist* (1954), director Elia Kazan cast him in the film *East of Eden* (1955), which was based on the John Steinbeck novel.

RIGHT The 1955 film, Rebel Without a Cause, released after Dean's death, challenged audiences with its realistic portrait of disaffected teenagers.

Dean drew on his memories of childhood abandonment to play the part of the anguished Cal Trask, and he was

nominated for an Academy Award® for Best Actor. Around this time he was romantically linked with beautiful Italian actress Pier Angeli, but her domineering mother put an end to the relationship because he was not a Catholic. Angeli would always hold a special place in her heart for Dean, and she never really got over him.

LEFT With Burl Ives (left), Hal Taggart (behind Dean), and Raymond Massey (right) in the iconic Elia Kazan film, East of Eden *(1955).*

Dean's next film role was in the classic tale of teenage angst, *Rebel Without a Cause* (1955), which enhanced his reputation both on- and off-screen as a surly yet vulnerable misfit. He made friends with his teenage co-stars Natalie Wood and Sal Mineo, both of whom would also die young in tragic circumstances; many people believe that the film was cursed. *Giant* (1956), based on Edna Ferber's best-selling novel, was Dean's final film role. It featured a star-studded cast including Elizabeth Taylor and Rock Hudson, and Dean's performance earned him a second Oscar® nomination for Best Actor (which was announced posthumously).

His meteoric success gave him enough money to buy a 1955 Porsche Spyder. He had always wanted to race cars, and here was a vehicle that he could enter in the Palm Springs, Bakersfield, and Santa Barbara road races. On September 30, 1955, he was heading toward the road races at Salinas when he was pulled over for speeding. A little over two hours later, Dean crashed into another car. His passenger, Porsche mechanic Rolf Wuetherich, was thrown clear of the accident and suffered a broken leg and injuries to the jaw; the driver of the other vehicle was only slightly hurt. James Dean died in the ambulance on the way to the hospital—with his death a legend and a myth had been born.

BELOW James Dean's brooding good looks and anguished expressions won him a place in Empire *magazine's 100 Sexiest Stars in Film History.*

Today fans still wonder what happened to the Porsche Spyder. It was bought in 1958, disappeared that year, and, according to rumors, has subsequently led to the deaths of many people who purchased parts from the car when it was broken up for scrap. Dean's legend is so potent that his gravestone has been stolen a number of times, and rumors still abound that he did not actually die in the car accident but was either badly injured or his face was disfigured. The irony of Dean's death was that only 13 days before he died he had made a 30-second commercial for the National Highway Committee to help encourage safe driving. He was allowed to improvise the ending, so he said, "And remember … drive safely … because the life you save may be mine."

Dorothy Dell

Born January 30, 1915
Died June 8, 1934

This lovely Southern belle was born Dorothy Dell Goff in Hattiesburg, Mississippi. Her face was her fortune from the time she won her first beauty contest as a baby. When Dell was ten, she moved with her family to New Orleans—there she met Dorothy Lamour, and the two remained good friends throughout Dell's short life.

Dell continued to do well in beauty contests, and at age 15 she won both the Miss America and Miss Universe crowns. She was also a singer and performed on local radio programs.

In 1931, 16-year-old Dell joined a vaudeville troupe, accompanied by her mother, her sister, and Lamour. After touring throughout the United States, she was chosen for the 1931 season of the *Ziegfeld Follies* (as it turned out, 1931 would be the last year of the *Follies*). Dell was a solo performer, singing a bawdy song entitled "Was I Drunk?" which she would later record. Around this time, Dell's name was linked with that of popular actor and singer Russ Columbo, another star to suffer an early death—he was accidentally shot just three months after Dell's death.

Dell, like so many other Ziegfeld girls (including Barbara Stanwyck, Helen Morgan, Anita Travis, and Marion Davies), went on to pursue a movie career. She appeared in three musical shorts before signing on with Paramount. Her first feature film was *Wharf Angel* (1934), starring Preston Foster and Victor McLaglen, and she received encouraging reviews.

BELOW On the same day that Little Miss Marker *was released in 1934, Dorothy Dell was featured on the cover of* Paramount *magazine.*

In 1934, Dorothy Dell co-starred with tiny Shirley Temple, Adolphe Menjou, and Charles Bickford in *Little Miss Marker*, based on a story by Damon Runyon. Many people consider it to be Temple's best effort, and Dell delivered an excellent performance as Bangles Carson, a nightclub singer with a heart of gold.

Dell's third and final motion picture was *Shoot the Works* (1934), a musical comedy starring Jack Oakie. She was able to put her singing talents to good use, which earned her favorable comparisons with the young Mae West.

In the early hours of June 8, 1934, Dell was being driven home from a party in Altadena by her date, Dr. Carl Wagner. They were heading toward Pasadena when the car skidded out of control and ended up crashing into a boulder in a ditch. Dell was killed instantly, and Wagner hung on for a few hours before he, too, died in Pasadena Hospital.

Dell's last movie premiered on June 29, a few weeks after her death. Had she lived, her next starring role would have been in *Now and Forever* (1934), with Gary Cooper and Shirley Temple. Her part was eventually played by Carole Lombard, another talented actress who would later die in a tragic accident.

Gloria Dickson

Born August 13, 1916
Died April 10, 1945

LEFT The Legion of Decency condemned This Thing Called Love (1941) for its loose morals. The film was banned in Australia and Ireland.

Gloria Dickson was born Thais Alalia Dickerson in Pocatello, Idaho. When she was 12 her father died, and her mother took Thais and her older sister to begin a new life in Long Beach, California.

After Thais graduated from high school in 1935, she joined the Wayside Colony Players in Long Beach. From there, she toured with another theater troupe, and the following year was accepted into the Federal Theaters Project. While performing in the Los Angeles production of *The Devil Passes* (1936), a Warner Bros. talent scout spotted her. After a successful screen test, she signed a three-year contract, changing her name to Gloria Dickson.

Dickson's first movie was *They Won't Forget* (1937), a mystery directed by Mervyn LeRoy and co-starring Claude Rains and Lana Turner. She was approached by other studios, but Jack Warner refused to loan her out. Dickson then appeared on Broadway in *Wise Tomorrow* (1937), and her performance was well received.

From that rather auspicious beginning, it seemed that Dickson would become a major star. She worked in 23 films in a variety of genres—drama, western, musical, and comedy—but never had a lead role in a high-profile movie. Some of her career highlights include *Racket Busters* (1938) with Humphrey Bogart; *They Made Me a Criminal* (1939) with John Garfield and Ann Sheridan; *This Thing Called Love* (1941) with Melvyn Douglas and Rosalind Russell; and *Lady of Burlesque* (1943) with Barbara Stanwyck.

By the time Dickson was 27 she had been married three times. Her first husband was makeup artist Perc Westmore—the marriage ended due to drinking, violence, and infidelity. (Some sources report that he even forced her to have a nose job.) In 1941, she wed Ralph Murphy, the director of her 1940 film, *I Want a Divorce*. Dickson remarried Murphy when she discovered their earlier marriage wasn't legal because her first divorce hadn't been finalized. Murphy was also unfaithful; the marriage lasted only 18 months. She might have been lucky the third time around with a former bodyguard to Jean Harlow, William Fitzgerald, whom she married in May 1944—but fate intervened.

ABOVE Gloria Dickson having fun with John Garfield. She appeared with Garfield in the 1939 crime drama, They Made Me a Criminal.

On the afternoon of April 10, 1945, Dickson's West Hollywood neighbor smelled burning leaves coming from Dickson's yard. A few hours later he looked over to see the house in flames. When the fire department arrived, they found Dickson's body lying face down in the upstairs bathroom. It was believed that Dickson had gone upstairs to have an afternoon nap, as was her custom, and that the fire was started downstairs by a cigarette. Once Dickson awoke, she may have tried to escape from the bathroom window before she was asphyxiated. Her body was covered in first- and second-degree burns.

William Holden

Born April 17, 1918
Died November 16, 1981

With a career that spanned more than 40 years and included over 70 films, three Academy Award® nominations, and one Academy Award®, William Holden can truly be classed as one of Hollywood's greats.

He began his life in O'Fallon, Illinois, as William Franklin Beedle, Jr., and was raised in Monrovia, California. The good-looking, athletic boy was planning to become an industrial chemist like his father. However, while performing with the South Pasadena Playhouse, he was noticed by a Paramount talent scout. Before long, the 20-year-old had signed a seven-year contract and become William Holden.

After a couple of small parts, Holden was loaned to Columbia to play the leading role of a young man torn between music and boxing in *Golden Boy* (1939), which co-starred Barbara Stanwyck.

Holden kept very busy both professionally and personally during the 1940s, appearing in some 18 films, including *Our Town* (1940), *Arizona* (1940), *Young and Willing* (1943), and *Apartment for Peggy* (1948). He married actress Brenda Marshall in 1941; their two sons, Peter and Scott, were born in 1944 and 1946 respectively. (Holden later adopted Marshall's daughter, Virginia, from a previous marriage.) He also served in the U.S. Army during World War II.

ABOVE William Holden with Audrey Hepburn in Sabrina *(1954). He was considered one of the sexiest leading men in Hollywood in the 1950s.*

The movie that would transform Holden from an actor to a star was Billy Wilder's classic *Sunset Boulevard* (1950), in a role that was originally intended for Montgomery Clift. Holden received an Academy Award® nomination for his portrayal of Joe Gillis, the screenwriter turned gigolo. He then displayed his talent and versatility in such vastly different movies as the light-hearted *Born Yesterday* (1950) and the black war comedy *Stalag 17* (1953), for which he won the Academy Award® for Best Actor.

In the mid-1950s, Holden's youthful, all-American looks had weathered (due partly to his increasing alcohol intake), but he was more attractive than ever. The films during this time established the 30-something Holden as a powerful sex symbol: *The Country Girl* (1954) and *The Bridges at Toko-Ri* (1955), both with Grace Kelly; *Sabrina* (1954), with Audrey Hepburn; and *Love is a Many Splendored Thing* (1955), with Jennifer Jones. The dance scene from *Picnic* (1955), in which Holden portrays a romantic drifter

RIGHT William Holden starred with Alec Guinness (left) and Jack Hawkins (right) in The Bridge on the River Kwai *(1957), set in the jungles of Thailand.*

opposite Kim Novak, rates as one of the most sensual movie scenes of all time. He was also involved in steamy affairs off-screen with both Grace Kelly and Audrey Hepburn.

LEFT William Holden with his actress wife, Brenda Marshall, in a Hollywood nightclub in 1955. They divorced after 30 years of marriage.

William Holden's next major film was a complete change of pace—David Lean's war epic *The Bridge on the River Kwai* (1957), co-starring Jack Hawkins and Alec Guinness. An inveterate traveler, Holden fell in love with Africa and its wildlife and bought 2,000 acres (810 hectares) of land in Kenya for preservation. *The Lion* (1962) was set in Kenya and co-starred Trevor Howard and Capucine (who was also a real-life love interest).

During the 1960s, Holden's enthusiasm for acting waned, as he grew more interested in traveling, conservation, and business pursuits. He was drinking heavily and becoming restless, reclusive, and discontented. Some of his films of the 1960s include *Paris—When it Sizzles* (1964), *Alvarez Kelly* (1966), and *The Christmas Tree* (1969). His best role for many years was as an outlaw in Sam Peckinpah's irreverent, violent western *The Wild Bunch* (1969).

In 1971, Holden and Marshall ended their marriage after years of estrangement. He had never done much television, but he won an Emmy® for his role as a police officer in the 1973 television movie *The Blue Knight*. Holden went on to star in the films *The Towering Inferno* (1974) and *Network* (1976), a satire on the television industry. *Network*'s cast included Peter Finch, Faye Dunaway, and Robert Duvall. Holden was honored with a nomination for Best Actor Oscar® for his excellent portrayal of a newsreader, but the award went posthumously to Peter Finch, who died just a few months before the ceremony. Among Holden's last films were *Damien: Omen II* (1978), *Ashanti* (1979), and *S.O.B.* (1981).

BELOW Dedicated to animal conservation, William Holden made many public and television appearances to promote his message.

On November 16, 1981, not long after completing *S.O.B.*, Holden was found dead in his Santa Monica apartment, lying on the bedroom floor and steeped in blood. It was estimated that he had been dead for several days, and the body had already begun to decompose. There were assorted empty bottles in the trash can and a half-full bottle of vodka on the kitchen counter.

Dr. Thomas Noguchi, the Los Angeles County Coroner, performed the autopsy. William Holden had died drunk, with a blood alcohol reading of .22 percent. Noguchi believed that Holden had tripped over a scatter rug while getting out of bed, and hit his head on the bedside table, deeply wounding his forehead. There is no evidence that he tried to reach for the telephone—if he had he phoned someone before he passed out, he most probably would have survived the injury. It was a lonely ending for such a charismatic and talented actor. He lives on in his many films, and in the William Holden Wildlife Foundation, established by his close friend, actress Stefanie Powers.

Leslie Howard

Born April 3, 1893
Died June 1, 1943

RIGHT With Ann Harding in The Animal Kingdom *(1932). Howard was often called "the perfect English gentleman."*

BELOW With Norma Shearer in Romeo and Juliet *(1936). Leslie Howard was 43 years old when he played Romeo.*

Leslie Howard Stainer was born in London in 1893 to Hungarian-Jewish parents. He suffered shellshock during World War I, and was advised to take up a hobby as part of his rehabilitation program. He chose acting.

Before long, Howard was performing professionally on the London stage and in British silent films. His first "talkie" would also be his first American film, *Outward Bound* (1930). Howard was soon in demand as a stage and screen actor in both England and the United States. He was nominated for a Best Actor Academy Award® for the whimsical *Berkeley Square* (1933), and became famous in the costume drama *The Scarlet Pimpernel* (1934) with Merle Oberon and Raymond Massey.

Much of Howard's success stemmed from the fact that he was very selective, choosing the right vehicles for his talent. Some highlights include *Of Human Bondage* (1934), based on the popular W. Somerset Maugham novel; *The Petrified Forest* (1936), with Humphrey Bogart; and *Pygmalion* (1938), which he also directed, and for which he got his second Oscar® nomination for Best Actor. However, it is for the coveted role of the Southern gentleman, Ashley Wilkes, in *Gone with the Wind* (1939), co-starring Clark Gable and fellow Brit Vivien Leigh, that Howard is best remembered. In 1939 he also co-produced and starred in *Intermezzo: A Love Story*, with Ingrid Bergman.

Howard's career ended as it began—as the result of war. When World War II broke out, he returned to England and channeled his acting, producing, directing, writing, and broadcasting energies into helping the Allied cause. Howard's patriotic films include *Pimpernel Smith* (1941), *Forty-Ninth Parallel* (1941), *The First of the Few* (1942), *In Which We Serve* (1942), and *The Gentle Sex* (1943). His last job was as the narrator of *War in the Mediterranean* (1943).

On June 1, 1943, Leslie Howard was a passenger on a British Overseas Airways Corp. (BOAC) DC-3 commercial flight from Lisbon, Portugal, bound for London. Three hours after takeoff, just over the Bay of Biscay north of Spain, the plane was shot down by a squadron of eight Luftwaffe fighters. None of the four crew members or 13 passengers survived. It has been speculated that the plane may have been a decoy: the Germans had planned to assassinate British Prime Minister Winston Churchill and believed he was on that airplane. Some think that Howard himself was a target for the Nazis because of all his propaganda work.

Leslie Howard left behind his wife of 27 years, Ruth Martin Howard, and two children, Ronald and Ruth Leslie.

Jeffrey Hunter

Born November 25, 1926
Died May 27, 1969

Jeffrey Hunter was born Henry Herman McKinnies, Jr., in New Orleans, Louisiana, and grew up in Milwaukee, Wisconsin. As a teenager, Hunter began acting in local radio programs and in amateur theater. After a stint in the U.S. Navy from 1945 to 1946, he studied speech at Northwestern University in Illinois, and went on to do postgraduate work at UCLA.

Talent scouts approached Hunter after seeing him in a college production of *All My Sons*. They were impressed with his stage presence, not to mention his athletic physique, dark hair, blue eyes, and winning smile. Hunter signed a contract with 20th Century Fox in 1950, and in the same year he married actress Barbara Rush—their son, Christopher, was born in 1952.

In his 18-year career, Hunter appeared in some 50 films—his first was *Fourteen Hours* (1951), which also featured beginner Grace Kelly. Other early films include *Red Skies of Montana* (1952), *Belles on their Toes* (1952), and *Princess of the Nile* (1954).

Hunter's most creative period was during the mid- to late 1950s, when he was cast in several westerns: John Ford's classic *The Searchers* (1956), with John Wayne and Natalie Wood; *The Proud Ones* (1956); and *Gun for a Coward* (1957). He also starred in the psychological thriller *A Kiss Before Dying* (1956) and the political drama *The Last Hurrah* (1958). His marriage to Rush ended in 1955, and two years later he married model Joan "Dusty" Bartlett; they had two sons together.

King of Kings (1961)—in which Hunter played the central role of Jesus Christ—is considered his signature film. It was directed by Nicholas Ray (of *Rebel Without a Cause* fame). Hunter then joined an all-star cast in the World War II blockbuster *The Longest Day* (1962).

His career started to go downhill from there. Hunter starred in the short-lived television western *Temple Houston* (1963), and was chosen to portray Captain Pike in the pilot for the *Star Trek* television series. However, he did not continue with the role, choosing instead to concentrate on motion pictures (which at this point were mainly European-made "sword and sandal" epics).

ABOVE Jean Peters co-starred with Jeffrey Hunter in the adventure drama Lure of the Wilderness *(1952), which was set in a Georgia swamp.*

In May 1969, not long after his third marriage, to soap-opera star Emily McLaughlin, Hunter went to Spain to film the crime-adventure *¡Viva América!* (1969). While on the set he suffered facial injuries during an explosion, and shortly afterward he hit the back of his head against a door. The injuries were exacerbated by the long flight from Spain to Los Angeles. When Hunter arrived in Los Angeles he was admitted to hospital. After he was discharged he experienced a cerebral hemorrhage and fell down a flight of stairs in his house, causing further head injuries. He never woke up after surgery and died on May 27, 1969.

Grace Kelly

Born November 12, 1929
Died September 14, 1982

ABOVE Grace Kelly appeared as Georgie Elgin in The Country Girl *(1954), opposite Bing Crosby as her husband, a singer who has fallen on hard times.*

RIGHT It is against the law in Monaco to screen any of Grace Kelly's films. Prince Rainier (right) banned them after their marriage.

Grace Patricia Kelly was aptly named: graceful and patrician are two words that are often used to describe this extraordinarily beautiful woman who lived such an extraordinary life.

Unlike most actresses of her time, Kelly came from a privileged background. Her father, Jack—the son of an Irish laborer—epitomized the American dream, becoming very wealthy in the building industry. Her mother, Margaret, had been a physical education teacher before she married and had four children. Grace, the third child, was artistic and introspective—more like her playwright uncle, George Kelly, than her competitive and athletic parents and siblings. Jack clearly favored his oldest daughter, Peggy, and Grace spent her life trying to win her father's love and approval.

Kelly knew from an early age that she wanted to be an actress. After she graduated from Stevens Academy in Philadelphia in 1947, her parents grudgingly allowed her to attend the American Academy of Dramatic Arts. Her professional acting debut was with the Bucks County Playhouse in Pennsylvania, in her uncle's play *The Torch Bearers*. She soon progressed to the Broadway stage, playing the daughter in Strindberg's drama *The Father* (1949), with Raymond Massey in the title role.

In 1951, Kelly was cast in the film *Fourteen Hours*. Her next role was in the classic western *High Noon* (1952). It is not surprising that, given her father complex, she began an intense affair with her co-star, 51-year-old Gary Cooper.

The African adventure-love story *Mogambo* (1953) made Grace Kelly a star. She was nominated for an Academy Award® for Best Actress in a Supporting Role and developed a close relationship with Clark Gable, who was also twice her age. While working in a television drama, *The Way of an Eagle* (1953), she had a fling with French cast member Jean-Pierre Aumont.

The year 1954 was an important one for Kelly. She was featured on the cover of *Life* magazine and made the best-dressed list (thanks to her involvement with fashion designer and playboy Oleg Cassini). In *Dial M for Murder* (1954), she began a mutually beneficial professional association with director Alfred Hitchcock. Her co-star, Ray Milland, separated from his wife because he was so infatuated with Kelly, but he went back to his wife for financial reasons. Kelly went on to star in another Hitchcock thriller, *Rear Window* (1954), with James Stewart.

In *The Bridges at Toko-Ri* (1955), there was a lot of chemistry, both on- and off-screen, with sexy leading man William Holden. Kelly and Holden worked together again in *The Country*

Girl (1954). The star, Bing Crosby, thought that Kelly was too pretty for the role of his drab, downtrodden wife (although her looks weren't a drawback in their subsequent romance). However, she got the part, and won the Academy Award® for Best Actress that year. Her third Hitchcock film, *To Catch a Thief* (1955) with Cary Grant, was very popular and received good reviews.

Kelly's next scheduled motion picture was *The Swan* (1956) about a commoner who falls in love with a prince. By strange coincidence, while attending the 1955 Cannes Film Festival, she was introduced to Prince Rainier Grimaldi of Monaco, and there was instant attraction between them. The prince had been looking for a high-profile wife to help boost tourism in his financially beleaguered country. Several months later, he came to the United States to propose marriage, contingent on Kelly passing a fertility test and, allegedly, her family supplying a $2 million dowry.

High Society (1956) was Grace Kelly's last film before she became Princess Grace of Monaco. On April 18, 1956, she and the prince were married in a civil ceremony, and the following day a fairytale wedding took place in the Catholic Cathedral of St. Nicholas in Monaco. The televised service was watched by millions around the world.

After a difficult period of adjustment, Kelly gradually settled into royal life, especially once her first two children, Caroline (1957) and Albert (1958), were born. Her father's death in 1960 caused her to become depressed. She knew that acting would lift her spirits, but the Monaco public refused to let her appear on screen again. After several miscarriages, her third child, Stephanie, was born in 1965.

Kelly devoted much of her life to charitable causes, and was on the board of 20th Century Fox. During the 1970s the cracks began to widen in her marriage: she kept her own apartment in Paris, and it was rumored that the prince was seeing other women and that she was drinking heavily. Her daughter Caroline's escapades were making the headlines, and Kelly struggled to maintain a brave and dignified front.

On September 13, 1982, Kelly and Stephanie were driving from their home at Roc Agel to Kelly's dressmaker in Monaco. Kelly was not comfortable behind the wheel and usually employed a chauffeur, but because the car was so full of clothes, she decided to drive herself. As she was negotiating a sharp bend on the Moyenne Corniche, Kelly lost control of the car, which plummeted down a steep embankment. Both mother and daughter were rushed to hospital. Stephanie escaped serious injury, but Kelly had a collapsed lung, brain hemorrhage, and broken right leg. Tests showed that Kelly had also suffered a stroke, which had caused her to become disoriented while driving. The following day, the family agreed to take her off life support, and she died in the hospital that bore her name: Princess Grace.

LEFT To Catch a Thief *(1955) paired suave Cary Grant with sophisticated Grace Kelly. Set in the French Riviera, it was a huge hit at the box office.*

Star Shot

Little did Grace Kelly know that 27 years after filming the car scene in *To Catch a Thief* (1955), she would be fatally injured on the same stretch of road.

BELOW Before her marriage, Grace Kelly was considered for the role of Maggie in the film version of Cat on a Hot Tin Roof. *The role went to Elizabeth Taylor in 1958.*

Ernie Kovacs

Born January 23, 1919
Died January 13, 1962

Known for his trademark mustache and Havana cigar, Ernie Kovacs was an inventive and influential television pioneer and sometime film actor.

After attending the American Academy of Dramatic Arts in New York, Kovacs returned to his home town of Trenton, New Jersey, where he worked at a local radio station for several years. Kovacs's foray into television began on a cooking show, *Deadline for Dinner* (1950). His Philadelphia-based program, *Ernie in Kovacsland* (1951), was taken up by the NBC network. He fell in love with a cast member, the singer and actress Edie Adams, and married (for the second time) in 1954. *Kovacs Unlimited* (also known as *The Ernie Kovacs Show*) featured on CBS in 1952, and another series aired in 1956.

As well as performing, Kovacs was a writer and producer, and he explored the technical and creative potential of television. He specialized in sight gags, experimented with sound effects, and invented memorable characters such as a group of musical apes known as The Nairobi Trio, and silent Eugene, reminiscent of Chaplin's "Little Tramp."

Kovacs appeared in 11 motion pictures from 1956 to 1961, and proved to be a competent character actor. Some of his best films are: *Bell, Book and Candle* (1958), with Jack Lemmon and James Stewart; *Our Man in Havana* (1959), with Alec Guinness and Maureen O'Hara; *Strangers When We Meet* (1960), with Kirk Douglas and Kim Novak; and *North to Alaska* (1960), with John Wayne and Stewart Granger.

On January 12, 1962, Kovacs went directly from the television studio to a party at Billy Wilder's house—his wife had driven her own car and met him there. They both left the party after 1:00 A.M., and for some reason they switched cars—Kovacs took Adams's new Corvair station wagon, and she went home in his Rolls. He asked Yves Montand if he'd like a lift home, but perhaps Montand felt that Kovacs had had a bit too much to drink, and he refused.

It had been raining, and Kovacs was probably speeding along Santa Monica Boulevard when he lost control of the Corvair. The car hit a concrete island and then wrapped itself around a pole. Kovacs died from a fractured skull—the death was violent but blessedly quick. An unlit cigar was found close to his hand—it is believed that he was trying to light it when the car spun out of control.

When Kovacs died, he left his widow with a mountain of debts due to his extravagant lifestyle, gambling, and unpaid taxes. With a small daughter to support, Adams had to work hard to pay off his debts. Ironically, she became well known for her Muriel Cigar commercial, singing "Hey, Big Spender."

ABOVE Ernie Kovacs with his wife, Edie Adams. In 1984, Jeff Goldblum starred in the made-for-television Ernie Kovacs: Behind the Laughter.

Star Shot

Ernie Kovacs's and Edie Adams's daughter, Mia Susan, was killed in a car accident in Los Angeles in 1982. She was just 22 years old.

RIGHT Ernie Kovacs was a loved and respected entertainer. Among the pallbearers at his funeral were Frank Sinatra, Jack Lemmon, and Dean Martin.

Ormer Locklear

Born October 28, 1891
Died August 2, 1920

Ormer Locklear holds a unique place in film history. He was not an actor as such, but became a silent movie star because of his incredible talents in aviation acrobatics.

Locklear was born in Greenville, Texas, and was raised in Forth Worth. Always fascinated with vehicles and engines, he worked as a mechanic and builder before joining the Army Air Service when the United States entered World War I in 1917. Locklear found that he had a natural aptitude for flying and became a flight instructor at Barron Field, Texas, rising quickly to the rank of Second Lieutenant.

In an attempt to make adjustments and repairs to his JN4 "Jenny" biplane while in midair, Locklear became proficient in the dangerous skill of "wing walking." He expanded his daredevil repertoire by doing handstands on the wing, jumping from a moving car to a plane, and jumping from one plane to another. He began to make quite a name for himself, and, instead of reenlisting, left the service in 1919 and embarked on an extremely lucrative career as a stunt pilot and "barnstormer," helped along by promoter William Pickens. Barnstorming shows were aviation exhibitions usually held in open fields or county fairs, and were especially popular in southern California.

Because he had good looks and a flamboyant showman's personality, Locklear became a favorite on the barnstorming circuit. He traveled around the United States performing death-defying stunts, and soon earned enough money to purchase his own plane and set up "Lieut. Ormer Locklear's Flying Circus." Aviators such as Locklear, Charles Lindbergh, and Bessie Coleman were the equivalent of today's superstars, and it wasn't long before Locklear was discovered by some "important people" in Hollywood. Early moviemakers such as Mack Sennett recognized that flying could be used to great effect in motion pictures.

Locklear's first role was in *The Great Air Robbery* (1920), which told the story of an intrepid pilot who overcomes villains and treacherous weather to deliver the mail. He then signed a contract with 20th Century Fox to star in their next aviation movie, *The Skywayman* (1920).

While performing a maneuver for *The Skywayman* with "Skeets" Elliott at DeMille Airfield in Los Angeles, the plane spun out of control and crashed—both men died. One explanation for the accident is that Locklear was blinded by studio searchlights, which should have been turned off so that he could see when to pull out of the dive; the crew simply forgot to turn off the lights. The movie showed the death scene as it actually happened, in all its horror.

ABOVE A still from the 1920 film, The Skywayman, *starring Ormer Locklear. There is no copy of the film in existence today.*

Carole Lombard

Born October 6, 1908
Died January 16, 1942

By 1942, Carole Lombard was one of the darlings of Hollywood, when she was tragically killed in a plane crash at the age of only 33. Born in Indiana in 1908, she made her first movie, *A Perfect Crime,* in 1921. In 1926, Lombard was involved in a car accident, which caused scarring to the left side of her face. However, after plastic surgery and with the clever use of makeup, this had little impact on her film career. Over the years she developed a reputation as a fine comedienne in films such as *Twentieth Century* (1934) and *My Man Godfrey* (1936). She married Clark Gable in 1939 and became the toast of Hollywood.

All airline tragedies have an "if only …" component, and Carole Lombard's death was no exception. She had been raising money for the U.S. war effort and had managed to sell over $2 million worth of war bonds. How could such success lead to her death? The plane she caught back to Hollywood departed from Indianapolis at 4:00 A.M. on Friday, January 16, 1942. It was a military aircraft. In those days it took 17 hours to fly from Indianapolis to Los Angeles. When the plane stopped at Albuquerque, there were nine officers waiting to climb aboard. The plane was full, but the officers had orders that allowed them to take the seats of civilians flying on the plane. By rights Lombard should have been left at Albuquerque, but she claimed that she was a special case.

Using all her charm and wit, she argued that, having sold so many U.S. war bonds, she had an honorary rank. The officials gave in and she was allowed to continue on the flight with her mother and a friend. The plane made another stop at Las Vegas and shortly afterward, at 7:07 P.M., about 35 miles (56 km) west of Las Vegas, it hit the rocky top of a nearby mountain, burst into flames, and crashed. Clark Gable and a number of studio executives immediately flew to the crash site, but it was too late. Lombard's body had been burned beyond recognition and was headless. A grieving Gable accompanied the body back to Hollywood, where he purchased three plots in the Forest Lawn cemetery: one for Lombard, her mother, and himself. Carole Lombard is still remembered as Hollywood's first war casualty.

ABOVE Carole Lombard starred in the 1942 film, To Be or Not to Be, *which was in post-production at the time of her death.*

LEFT Clark Gable and Carole Lombard after their 1939 marriage. They appeared in only one film together, No Man of Her Own *(1932).*

Star Shot

In 1936, Carole Lombard received her only Oscar® nomination, for the role of Irene Bullock in *My Man Godfrey.* The award went to Luise Rainer for *The Great Ziegfeld.*

Butterfly McQueen

Born January 7, 1911
Died December 22, 1995

Butterfly McQueen will be forever remembered as Prissy, the naïve and muddle-headed maid in *Gone with the Wind* (1939). Her squeal of distress, "Miss Scarlet, I don't know nothin' 'bout birthin' babies!" is one of the classic film lines of all time. However, there was much more to Butterfly McQueen than Prissy.

Born Thelma McQueen in Tampa, Florida, she grew up in Georgia. She moved to New York and was dancing professionally at age 13 with a Harlem youth dance troupe. When she was 24, she danced the butterfly ballet in *A Midsummer Night's Dream*, and decided to legally change her name from Thelma to Butterfly.

McQueen made her Broadway debut in *Brown Sugar* (1937). Her next stage role was in the comedy *What a Life!* (1938). In the film *The Women* (1939), McQueen had a minor role as a cosmetics counter girl before she went on to *Gone with the Wind* (1939). Unfortunately, in most of the movies she made afterward, such as *Affectionately Yours* (1941), *Flame of Barbary Coast* (1945), and *Mildred Pierce* (1945), she was typecast as a maid. McQueen went on to appear in several more films, including *Duel in the Sun* (1946) with Jennifer Jones and Gregory Peck. She also appeared as Oriole in the television series *Beulah* from 1950 to 1952, and when she left was replaced by Ruby Dandridge, Dorothy Dandridge's mother.

Refusing to play the "handkerchief head" parts then offered to African-American women, McQueen acted only sporadically on stage. Moving between Augusta, Georgia, and New York, she worked in a variety of occupations such as dancing teacher, maid, personal companion, waitress, and receptionist. She had long been interested in politics and civil rights, and at age 64, she graduated with a BA in political science from City College in New York.

In the 1970s and 1980s, McQueen experienced a career resurgence of sorts. She had a cameo role in an African-American comedy, *Amazing Grace* (1974), starring Moms Mabley; was in the 1975 television adaptation of *The Adventures of Huckleberry Finn;* won an Emmy Award® for her role as the fairy godmother, Aunt Thelma, in the television movie *Seven Wishes for a Rich Kid* (1979); and was cast by director Peter Weir in *The Mosquito Coast* (1986), with Harrison Ford and River Phoenix.

On December 22, 1995, McQueen was trying to light a kerosene heater in her tiny one-bedroom home in Augusta when her clothes caught fire. Some people passing by noticed the flames and dragged her out of the house. When she arrived at Augusta Regional Medical Center she had second- and third-degree burns to over 70 percent of her body, and she died ten hours later. She was nearly 85 years old.

ABOVE Butterfly McQueen is unforgettable as Vivien Leigh's scatty maid in the classic 1939 Civil War drama, Gone with the Wind.

Jayne Mansfield

Born April 19, 1933
Died June 29, 1967

ABOVE Jayne Mansfield's greatest role was as a mother. Her children always accompanied her when she went away to film on location.

RIGHT On the set of the 1960 crime drama, Too Hot to Handle. *In this film, Jayne Mansfield plays Midnight Franklin, a sultry nightclub singer.*

In the 1950s, directly as a result of the huge success of Marilyn Monroe, a blonde bombshell with an hourglass figure was guaranteed lots of work and almost certain success in the movie industry. England had Diana Dors, and America offered the world the curvaceous Vera Jayne Palmer, who dyed her hair platinum blonde and became known, rather unkindly, as "the poor man's Marilyn Monroe."

In contrast to the flashy, dumb-blonde image that she later cultivated, Vera Jayne was actually highly intelligent and came from a professional family in Bryn Mawr, Pennsylvania. Her mother, Vera, was a teacher and her father, Herbert, a lawyer. In a somewhat eerie foreshadowing of her own death, her father died of a heart attack while behind the wheel of a car; both three-year-old Vera Jayne and her mother were passengers, and they miraculously survived the subsequent accident. When Vera Jayne was six years old, her mother married a Texan and they moved to Dallas.

Vera Jayne married high school sweetheart Paul Mansfield in January 1950, and her first child, Jayne Marie, was born in November that year. Motherhood did not stop Mansfield from pursuing her dreams of becoming a star. She took acting courses at the University of Texas in Austin, and after appearing in several beauty contests and local television shows, she moved to Los Angeles. Paul Mansfield was not very supportive of his wife's ambitions, and their marriage ended just as her career was beginning to take off.

With the help of agent James Byron, Mansfield became skilled in the art of blatant self-promotion. She used various publicity stunts to attract attention to herself, but it was the title of Playboy Playmate of February 1955 that brought her to the notice of the movie studios. That same year, Mansfield had small parts in three movies: *Pete Kelly's Blues, Illegal,* and *Hell on Frisco Bay.*

Mansfield enjoyed rave reviews with the 1955 Broadway play *Will Success Spoil Rock Hunter?* (she acted in both the play and the 1957 movie, which starred Tony Randall and Joan Blondell). Her next vehicle was the rock 'n' roll classic *The Girl Can't Help It* (1956), starring Tom Ewell, and featuring performances by Little Richard, Fats Domino, and The Platters. This was followed by *The Wayward Bus* (1957), with Dan Dailey and Joan Collins, based on John Steinbeck's novel.

In 1958, Mansfield married a well-known Hungarian bodybuilder and Mr. Universe of 1956, Mickey Hargitay. When they met, Hargitay had been part of Mae West's stage act. Mansfield and Hargitay had three children—Miklos Jr., Zoltan, and Mariska. They bought a large house

on Sunset Boulevard in Beverly Hills, had the exterior painted pink, and garishly decorated it in pink throughout. Unlike most of today's film stars who scorn the paparazzi, the Mansfield-Hargitays welcomed media intrusion into their lives—the more publicity, the better. Unfortunately, the attention now seemed to work against Mansfield. Her career had been based on playing blonde bimbos and, very quickly, she became marginalized and almost a caricature of herself.

Mansfield kept herself busy in the early 1960s, making guest appearances on popular television shows such as *Burke's Law*, *The Steve Allen Show*, and *The Jack Benny Program*. She also signed up for some well-paid Las Vegas engagements at The Tropicana and The Dunes. However, the standard of movie offers deteriorated to B-grades such as Italian-made *The Loves of Hercules* (1960), semi-pornographic *Promises! Promises!* (1963), and *Primitive Love* (1964)—all co-starring Hargitay.

In 1964, Mansfield divorced Hargitay and married novice film director Matt Cimber, who became her manager. Cimber's decisions proved detrimental to Mansfield's career: he advised her against accepting the role of Ginger in television's *Gilligan's Island*, which ended up being one of the most popular sitcoms of the 1960s. Their relationship lasted long enough to produce a son, Anthony, born in 1965; Mansfield and Cimber divorced in 1966. As the 1960s progressed toward the hippie era, Mansfield's bouffant, glitzy, glamor-girl style became unfashionable, although she did win the hearts of the U.S. servicemen when she visited Vietnam with Bob Hope in 1967.

In the early hours of June 29, 1967, Mansfield was traveling from a nightclub engagement in Biloxi, Mississippi, to New Orleans, Louisiana. About 20 miles (32 km) from New Orleans, the 1966 Buick Electra she was in slammed into the back of and went underneath a tractor-trailer. All three people in the front seat—Mansfield, her current boyfriend Sam Brody, and the 20-year-old driver, Ronnie Harrison—were killed instantly. Her three Hargitay children, who were in the back seat, suffered only minor injuries. For years an urban myth insisted that Mansfield had been decapitated in the accident, but in reality she was scalped, losing the top part of her skull in a particularly gruesome death.

Mansfield's last film—*Single Room, Furnished*—was directed by her third husband and released posthumously in 1968.

LEFT Jayne Mansfield with Mickey Hargitay in 1963. After her death, Hargitay had a heart-shaped headstone placed on her grave.

BELOW This 1960 publicity photograph was shot in the lavishly decorated pink bathroom of Jayne Mansfield's Beverly Hills home.

Tom Mix

Born January 6, 1880
Died October 12, 1940

Star Shot

In 1929, Tom Mix attended the funeral of legendary lawman Wyatt Earp, and was one of the pallbearers.

BELOW Tom Mix with his wife, Victoria, and daughter, Thomasina. Mix epitomized the clean-cut cowboy hero and was the model for later actors in the genre.

In his 25-year career as a cowboy star, Tom Mix starred in over 300 silent films and ten "talkies," and he was also a talented writer, producer, and director.

Although he hailed from rural Pennsylvania and not the actual "West," Mix grew up around horses and spent hours practicing equestrian tricks. He had an adventurous spirit, and after a stint in the U.S. Army (from which he went AWOL in 1902), he headed for the Oklahoma Territory. Mix spent some years honing his skills as a cattle wrangler and performing in Wild West shows and rodeos before he was hired by Selig Polyscope Company for their film *Ranch Life in the Great Southwest* (1910).

Mix served his apprenticeship with Selig for seven years, but he wouldn't actually achieve stardom until he signed with Fox Films in 1917. This led to a long string of westerns, including *The Untamed* (1920), *The Lone Star Ranger* (1923), *Riders of the Purple Sage* (1925), *The Great K and A Train Robbery* (1926), *Outlaws of Red River* (1927), *Hello Cheyenne* (1928), and *Son of the Golden West* (1928). Strangely enough, one of Mix's best films, *Dick Turpin* (1925), is not about a cowboy but an English highwayman, although it contains similar elements: it is fast-paced and action-packed, with heroes and villains, and showcases daredevil stunts.

Off-screen, too, Mix loved excitement. He enjoyed fast cars, entertained lavishly, and had a mansion in Hollywood and a ranch in Arizona. He also had a weakness for beautiful women, and married five times and had two daughters.

In the 1920s, Mix was one of the most popular stars of the day, and a favorite with children (along with his horse, Tony.) As the silent era drew to a close, Mix was approaching his fifties; he made another ten films before retiring from films in 1935 with the serial *The Miracle Rider*. He returned to his first love—performing in front of live audiences—in the Tom Mix Circus (1936–38), and remained in the limelight through his comic books and radio program.

On October 12, 1940, Mix was driving his 1937 Cord roadster approximately 80 miles per hour (130 kph) along Highway 79 between Florence and Tucson, Arizona. He didn't heed the signs warning that a bridge had been washed away, and his car went into a ravine. Mix's metal-framed suitcase slipped off the back shelf and hit him in the back of the head, causing instant death. The Tom Mix Museum in Dewey, Oklahoma, houses the suitcase and other memorabilia, and the Tom Mix Death Site Marker—a 7-foot (2.1-m) black iron horse on Highway 79—pays tribute to the "King of the Cowboys."

Grace Moore

Born December 5, 1898
Died January 26, 1947

Dubbed "The Tennessee Nightingale" and described by Florenz Ziegfeld as one of the world's most beautiful women, Mary Willie Grace Moore was born in Slabtown (now Gough), Tennessee, in 1898 (some sources say 1901). As a child she sang in the church choir and attended Jellico High School.

Moore began her musical training at Wilson-Greens School of Music in Chevy Chase, Maryland, and continued her studies in New York. In the early 1920s, she appeared in a number of Broadway musicals, including *Hitchy Koo* written by Jerome Kern, and Irving Berlin's *The Music Box Review*. She went on to Europe for further tuition, and in 1928 made her Parisian operatic debut at the Opera Comique as Mimi in *La Bohème*, returning to New York in the same year to play Mimi again at the Metropolitan Opera House.

In 1930, Moore made her motion picture debut in *A Lady's Morals*, based on the life of singer Jenny Lind; this was soon followed by *New Moon* (1931) with Adolphe Menjou. The following year she married Spanish actor Valentin Parera in France. Throughout the 1930s, Moore starred in six more films: *One Night of Love* (1934), which earned her an Academy Award® nomination; *Love Me Forever* (1935); *The King Steps Out* (1936) with Franchot Tone; *When You're in Love* (1937) with Cary Grant; *I'll Take Romance* (1937); and *Louise* (1939).

After *Louise* in 1939, Moore appeared in no more movies, choosing instead to concentrate on her singing career. She was an elegant and charismatic entertainer, and performed to packed opera houses and concert halls throughout the United States and Europe. So greatly was she admired in France that she was awarded the title of "Chevalier of the Legion of Honor" in 1939. During World War II, Moore was involved in the USO (United Service Organizations), entertaining American troops in Europe, and in 1944 she managed to find the time to write her autobiography, *You're Only Young Once*.

On January 26, 1947, the day after playing to an audience of 4,000 in Copenhagen, Denmark, Moore was killed in a plane crash. Bound for Stockholm in Sweden, the DC-3 had just taken off and had reached an altitude of 150 feet (46 m) when it stalled in midair, crashed, and exploded into flames. Sweden's Prince Gustav Adolf was also among those killed in the accident. Moore's remains were buried in her native Tennessee.

ABOVE Grace Moore as Jenny Lind in A Lady's Morals *(1930). In her operatic career, Moore sang all the major soprano roles, including Carmen and Tosca.*

Peggy Moran

Born October 23, 1918
Died October 25, 2002

When she was six years old, Mary Jeanette ("Peggy") Moran was told by a famous Hollywood psychic that she would grow up to become an actress. She certainly had the makings of an artist: her mother, Louise, had been a dancer, and her father, Earl Moran, was a famous pin-up artist and illustrator.

Peggy Moran was born in Clinton, Iowa, but after her parents' divorce in 1924, she and her mother and siblings eventually settled in Los Angeles, California. As a student she excelled in drama, and her dreams (and the psychic's prediction) soon came true: she was offered a contract with Warner Bros. only weeks after graduation. After several bit parts in Warner movies and as a freelance actress, Moran's first featured role was in the Gene Autry western *Rhythm of the Saddle* (1938). This was soon followed by small parts in several films including *Ninotchka* (1939), starring Greta Garbo.

Moran obtained an interview with producer Joe Pasternak and director Henry Koster in 1939. She so impressed both men with her friendly personality and girl-next-door loveliness that she secured a contract with Universal Studios, and would later go out with Koster. Moran's Universal debut was in *First Love* (1939), starring Deanna Durbin.

Over the next four years, Moran made one movie after another, including *Argentine Nights* (1940), with the Ritz Brothers and Andrews Sisters; *One Night in the Tropics* (1940), with Abbott and Costello; and *Trail of the Vigilantes* (1940), with Franchot Tone. But Moran's claim to fame would be as a "scream queen" in *The Mummy's Hand* (1940) and *Horror Island* (1941).

In 1942, Moran married Henry Koster, and while pregnant with her first son, Nicolas, she starred in what was to be her final film: *King of the Cowboys* (1943), with Roy Rogers. Another son, Peter, soon followed, and Moran was happy to give up acting to become a full-

ABOVE Peggy Moran (right) posing with Elaine Morey. Famous for her "scream queen" role in The Mummy's Hand *(1940), Moran's favorite film was* King Kong *(1933).*

time mother to her boys (including a stepson, Bob). Koster had a long and successful career as a director and was nominated for an Academy Award® for *The Bishop's Wife* (1947). They were married for 46 years until Koster's death in 1988.

Moran kept her glowing good looks well into her senior years, and she was a popular attraction at movie nostalgia conventions. On August 26, 2002, she was a passenger in a friend's car—the friend lost control of the vehicle on the freeway near Oxnard, California, and Moran sustained severe injuries to her leg, neck, ribs, and lung. She battled for two months, managing to make it to her 84th birthday, but died two days later on October 25, 2002.

Herbert Mundin

Born August 21, 1898
Died March 5, 1939

Many people today may not be familiar with the name Herbert Mundin, but they would surely recognize the face. This short, chubby British character actor appeared in 54 films between 1930 and 1939, and would probably have continued for many more years had it not been for his untimely death at the age of 40.

Mundin was born on a farm in Lancashire, England in 1898. After serving in World War I, he joined a traveling musical theater troupe and was later cast in *Charlot's Revue* (1925). Mundin appeared in several British films, including *Ashes* (1930), before heading to Hollywood. His first credited U.S. role was in *The Trial of Vivienne Ware* (1932).

Throughout the 1930s, Mundin made one motion picture after another in a variety of genres. Some of his early efforts include *Chandu the Magician* (1932); *Sherlock Holmes* (1932); and *Cavalcade* (1933), which won the 1933 Academy Award® for Best Picture. Other highlights were *Shanghai Madness* (1933), starring Spencer Tracy and Fay Wray; *Hoop-La* (1933), with Clara Bow; *Orient Express* (1934), based on a Graham Greene novel; and *Bottoms Up* (1934), again with Spencer Tracy.

In 1935, Mundin played the role of Barkis in *The Personal History, Adventures, Experience, and Observation of David Copperfield, the Younger* (otherwise known as *David Copperfield* and starring Lionel Barrymore, Basil Rathbone, and Freddie Bartholomew as the young David). From there he went on to sail the high seas with Charles Laughton and Clark Gable in *Mutiny on the Bounty* (1935) as the ship's steward.

Mundin was fortunate that *Tarzan Escapes* (1936) had to be completely remade because the original version was thought to be too violent for children. The writers added the character of Jiggs Rawlins for comic relief, and Mundin stole the show with his line "Miss Jane, 'e's the finest gentleman I've ever 'ad the privilege of knowin' … trousers or no trousers!" The film grossed $2 million, but some thought that it was jinxed: 37-year-old producer Irving Thalberg died a week after completion, supporting actor John Buckler was killed in a car accident a week before release, and Mundin's own death occurred just three years later.

After *Tarzan Escapes*, Herbert Mundin appeared in *Angel* (1937) with Marlene Dietrich, and *The Adventures of Robin Hood* (1938) with Errol Flynn. In *Robin Hood*, he played one of the Merry Men, Much the Miller's Son. His last film was *Society Lawyer* (1939), with Walter Pidgeon, before he was killed in a car accident in Van Nuys, California, just north of Los Angeles.

Star Shot

Herbert Mundin worked as a wireless operator during World War I.

BELOW Herbert Mundin (left) as Layton the butler in Society Lawyer *(1939), which starred Walter Pidgeon and Virginia Bruce.*

Audie Murphy

Born June 20, 1924
Died May 28, 1971

ABOVE The Red Badge of Courage *(1951), the coming-of-age film set in Civil War America, is probably Audie Murphy's most famous role.*

RIGHT With Elaine Stewart in Night Passage *(1957). Audie Murphy was inducted into Oklahoma's National Cowboy Hall of Fame in 1996.*

Many Hollywood actors have come from humble beginnings, but very few would have had a beginning quite as humble as Audie Leon Murphy. He was born and raised in the cotton belt just north of Dallas, Texas, where his parents worked as sharecroppers. His mother, Josie, gave birth to 12 children, but only nine survived. His father, Emmett, left home when Audie was only ten years old, at the height of the Depression. Young Audie had to grow up very quickly, leaving school to help run the farm and provide food for his family. Times got even tougher when his mother died in 1941.

Rejected by the Navy and Marines because of his short 5 foot, 5 inch (1.65 m) stature, Murphy enlisted in the U.S. Army in 1942. After completing his basic training at Camp Wolters, Texas, and Fort Meade, Maryland, he was assigned to the 15th Infantry Regiment, Third Infantry Division, and served in North Africa, France, Italy, and Germany. In his three years of active duty, Murphy rose through the ranks and won a battlefield commission while becoming the most decorated American soldier of World War II. He received a total of 33 awards, including three Purple Hearts and the prestigious United States Congressional Medal of Honor. This high tribute was in recognition of Murphy's bravery in the Colmar Pocket campaign in northeastern France in January 1945. As well as all the medals and citations, he also took home with him hip wounds and a serious case of battle fatigue, now known as Post-Traumatic Stress Disorder, that would haunt him the rest of his life.

Audie Murphy was hailed as a national hero, gracing the pages of many newspapers and magazines. His picture on the cover of *Life* magazine in July 1945 shows a handsome 21-year-old with a boyish grin and just the faintest hint of sadness in his eyes. Actor James Cagney intuitively picked Murphy as having the makings of a star, and suggested that he might like to come to Hollywood. Murphy took the actor's advice, but he wasn't an overnight success—he had to endure a few lean years and lots of rejections. He was used to hardship, but was relieved when he received his first small parts in *Texas, Brooklyn, and Heaven* (1948), with Guy Madison and Irene Ryan, and *Beyond Glory* (1948), with Alan Ladd and Donna Reed. His first feature role

was as a juvenile delinquent in *Bad Boy* (1949). Throughout his 25-year career he would make a total of 45 films.

In 1951, Murphy starred in John Huston's *The Red Badge of Courage*, based on the Civil War novel by Stephen Crane. In the early 1950s he appeared in a string of westerns, including *Sierra* (1950), co-starring Wanda Hendrix (who became his first wife for a short time), and *The Cimarron Kid* (1952), with Hugh O'Brian. He was teamed with brunette beauty Susan Cabot in three cowboy movies: *The Duel at Silver Creek* (1952), *Gunsmoke* (1953), and *Ride Clear of Diablo* (1954). Shortly after his divorce from Hendrix, he married airline hostess Pamela Archer in 1951, and their two sons came along in 1952 and 1954.

Between 1955 and 1960, Murphy was at the peak of his career. In 1955, he played himself in the film version of his 1949 autobiography *To Hell and Back* (1955); the book was a bestseller and is still in print today, and the picture was a huge hit for Universal. Other important movies include *Night Passage* (1957), with James Stewart; *The Quiet American* (1958), with Michael Redgrave (the first American movie to be made in Vietnam); and John Huston's *The Unforgiven* (1960), co-starring Burt Lancaster and Audrey Hepburn. With his newfound prosperity, Murphy bought ranches in Texas, Arizona, and California, and developed a passion for racehorse breeding and training.

Unfortunately, the 1960s weren't so kind to Murphy. With the demise of the studio system and the waning popularity of westerns, good roles were harder to come by. And along with his love of horses came a love of gambling, which had dire financial consequences. Worst of all, Murphy's war demons continued to plague him, manifesting themselves in depression, insomnia, and drug and alcohol dependence. He tried to use his own misfortunes to help others, becoming an outspoken advocate for the improvement of health services and benefits for veterans.

Murphy's last role was as Jesse James in *A Time for Dying* (1971). At age 46, there were indications that some good work was in store for him—he was offered a part in Clint Eastwood's *Dirty Harry* (1971). But this was not to be. On May 28, 1971, he was a passenger in a private plane with four others. The weather conditions were bad—fog, rain, and thunder—and the aircraft crashed into the side of a mountain 12 miles (19 km) from Roanoke, Virginia. Everyone on board—including the pilot—was killed instantly. Murphy was buried in Arlington National Cemetery in Virginia, and people continue to come to pay their respects to the sharecropper's son who became a war hero and movie star.

LEFT Audie Murphy (right) starred as himself in the autobiographical film To Hell and Back *(1955). He is pictured here with Marshall Thompson.*

Star Shot

Audie Murphy was a well-respected songwriter. His songs have been recorded by many artists, including Eddy Arnold, Teresa Brewer, Harry Nilsson, and Charley Pride.

BELOW Audie Murphy was not only honored by his countrymen, he was also awarded five military decorations from France and Belgium.

Will Rogers

Born November 4, 1879
Died August 15, 1935

Last Words

"Well, Wiley's got her warmed up. Let's go!"

W ill Rogers was a multimedia personality long before the term was invented. As well as acting in both silent movies and "talkies," he performed in Wild West shows, circuses, vaudeville, and on the Broadway stage. Rogers also had a wide audience for his radio broadcasts, books, newspaper articles, and records.

Born in the northeastern part of the Indian Territory that later became Oologah, Oklahoma, William Rogers came from a large, close-knit family. His father, Clement Rogers, was a cattle rancher and judge who was instrumental in drafting the Oklahoma constitution. Mary America Schrimsher Rogers, his mother, was of Cherokee ancestry. She had eight children but only four survived. When Will was only ten, Mary died and his father later remarried.

Rogers learned the skills of roping and riding from a former slave who was employed on his father's ranch. He left school at 15 to work on a cattle drive from Texas to Kansas. His itchy feet took him to Argentina and then South Africa in 1902, where, billed as "The Cherokee Kid," he performed rope tricks and riding maneuvers in Texas Jack's Wild West Show. Show business was now well and truly in his blood. He returned to the United States in 1904 to appear in the rodeo at the St. Louis World's Fair, and became one of the star attractions when the rodeo went to New York's Madison Square Garden the following year. From rodeos, it was a natural progression to the vaudeville circuit, where Rogers charmed spectators not only with his clever lasso tricks, but also with his gentle humor and simple folk philosophy. In 1908, Will Rogers married his long-time sweetheart, Betty Blake, and they had four children: Will Jr., Mary, Jimmy, and Fred (who died of diphtheria at the age of two).

Showman Florenz Ziegfeld was impressed by Rogers's stage performance and offered him a spot in his revue, and then in the *Ziegfeld Follies* in 1916, where Rogers worked his cowboy magic on sophisticated New York audiences. Rogers was then lured by Samuel Goldwyn into his first silent motion picture, *Laughing Bill Hyde* (1918), which was made in New Jersey. This was the start of a long and successful film career, in which Rogers

BELOW Will Rogers (far right) with movie personalities (from left to right) Slim Somerville, Richard Cromwell, Jane Darwell, George Marshall, and Rochelle Hudson in 1935.

would star in a total of 54 movies. In 1919, Rogers went to Hollywood and became part of the burgeoning film industry there. Some of his silent films include *Almost a Husband* (1919); *Jubilo* (1919), an "Our Gang" comedy; *The Ropin' Fool* (1921); *The Cowboy Sheik* (1924); and *A Texas Steer* (1927) also featuring Douglas Fairbanks, Jr.

Although Rogers's silent movies were well received, it was with sound that his talent and personality really emerged. His first "talkie" was *They Had to See Paris* (1929), and this would be followed by another 20 films between 1929 and 1935. Highlights include *So This Is London* (1930) and *A Connecticut Yankee* (1931), both co-starring Maureen O'Sullivan; *Business and Pleasure* (1932), with Joel McCrea; *State Fair* (1933), with Janet Gaynor; *Handy Andy* (1934), with Peggy Wood; and *Doubting Thomas* (1935), with Billie Burke. Rogers's last film was *In Old Kentucky* (1935), in which Bill "Bojangles" Robinson teaches Rogers how to tap dance. Along with Shirley Temple, Rogers was the most popular movie star of the Depression era. Both entertainers exuded the optimism and confidence that were sorely needed in a nation ravaged by unemployment.

Rogers's energy, enthusiasm, and interest in people and the world were boundless. Throughout the 1920s and 1930s, in addition to his movie career, he wrote thousands of articles for *The New York Times*, which were syndicated in over 500 newspapers. Crowds thronged to his lectures to hear his humble wisdom peppered with funny observations. He is probably more quoted than any other American, and some of his sayings are legendary: "It's great to be great, but it's greater to be human" and "I love a dog. He does nothing for political reasons." Although he rubbed shoulders with world leaders and the crowned heads of Europe, Rogers always identified with the common man. He railed at the disparity between rich and poor, and was a supporter of the Salvation Army and Red Cross.

An inveterate traveler, Rogers was passionate about aviation, often flying around the country in U.S. Mail planes. He was friends with Charles Lindbergh, and in 1935 he jumped at the chance to join famous aviator Wiley Post on a trip from Alaska to Siberia. Funded by Rogers and accompanied by much fanfare and publicity, they took off on August 15, 1935, from Fairbanks, Alaska. A few hundred miles from the Arctic Circle near Point Barrow, the engine failed and the plane crashed straight into a riverbank, killing both pilot and passenger.

The world mourned the passing of the "Indian Cowboy" who never met a man he didn't like. Rogers is remembered at the Will Rogers Museum in Claremore, Oklahoma, the magnificent Will Rogers State Park in Pacific Palisades, California (which was once his ranch and was donated by his children after their mother died), and at Will Rogers World Airport in Oklahoma City.

ABOVE Such was his prowess with the lasso that Will Rogers once made it into the Guinness Book of Records for throwing three lassos at once.

LEFT Will Rogers appeared on the cover of Time *magazine in July 1926. A genuine man of the people, he once said, "Everybody is ignorant, only on different subjects."*

Frank Silvera

Born July 24, 1914
Died June 11, 1970

J amaican-born Frank Silvera grew up in Boston, Massachusetts. He began to study law at Northeastern University, but left to pursue his passion for acting.

As a member of the American Negro Theatre in Harlem and the Theatre of America, Silvera performed with some of the leading African-American actors of the day, such as Harry Belafonte, Ossie Davis, Ruby Dee, and Sidney Poitier. He was also involved in the prestigious Actors Studio and acted in a number of Broadway plays, including *A Hatful of Rain* and Tennessee Williams's *Camino Real*.

Silvera made his film debut as a Mexican in *Viva Zapata!* (1952). Silvera's appearance crossed ethnic boundaries, and throughout his career he would convincingly portray Italians, Hispanics, African-Americans, and Polynesians. He was a sought-after character actor throughout the 1950s and 1960s. As well as *Viva Zapata!*, his motion pictures during this time include *The Fighter* (1952), with Lee J. Cobb; *The Cimarron Kid* (1952), with Audie Murphy; Stanley Kubrick's *Fear and Desire* (1953) and *Killer's Kiss* (1955); *Heller in Pink Tights* (1960), starring Anthony Quinn, Sophia Loren, and an aging Ramon Novarro; and *Mutiny on the Bounty* (1962), with Marlon Brando, Trevor Howard, and Richard Harris.

Throughout this busy period, Silvera became actively involved in the civil rights movement, and founded the Frank Silvera

ABOVE Frank Silvera in a scene from Viva Zapata! *(1952). He was nominated for a Tony Award® in 1963 for his role in the Broadway production of* The Lady of the Camellias.

Theater of Being in Los Angeles. The theater was set up to foster the talents of young African-Americans and espoused the "method acting" principles of the Actors Studio. He also appeared in dozens of television programs, including *Perry Mason, Bat Masterson, The Rebel, The Twilight Zone, Bonanza, Marcus Welby, M.D.*, and *Hawaii Five-O*, and was a regular on *The High Chaparral*. Among Silvera's later motion pictures are *The Appaloosa* (1966), with Marlon Brando; *Hombre* (1967), with Paul Newman; *The St. Valentine's Day Massacre* (1967), with Jason Robards and George Segal; and *Che!* (1969), with Omar Sharif.

On June 11, 1970, Frank Silvera died in a bizarre accident in his home in Pasadena, California. Seemingly he was electrocuted while cleaning the garbage disposal unit. Nobody was there to witness the accident, and by the time he was found, it was too late. His last film, *Valdez is Coming* (1971), was released after his death. In 1973, the Frank Silvera Writers' Workshop was established in Harlem by a group of dedicated artists including actor Morgan Freeman, and named in honor of the man who did so much to further the cause of African-Americans, especially in the performing arts.

Michael Wilding

Born July 23, 1912
Died July 8, 1979

Although he is probably most famous for becoming the second of Elizabeth Taylor's seven husbands, Michael Wilding had a long and fruitful acting career of his own, appearing in some 50 films over a period of 40 years.

Wilding was born in Westcliff-on-Sea, in Essex, England, and after completing his schooling he became a commercial artist. While working in the art department of a film studio in London, he decided he'd prefer to work in front of the camera rather than behind the scenes. He obtained bit parts in a number of British films of the 1930s, and his first credited role was in *There Ain't No Justice* (1939).

Throughout the early 1940s, Wilding was kept continually employed in supporting roles in British films. Some highlights include *Sailors Three* (1940); *Spring Meeting* (1941); *Kipps* (1941); and *In Which We Serve* (1942), the wartime drama written by Noel Coward, directed by Coward and David Lean, and starring Coward, Celia Johnson, and John Mills.

Wilding's first lead role was in *English without Tears* (1944). He had good screen chemistry with Anna Neagle, and they would go on to star together in *Piccadilly Incident* (1946); *The Courtneys of Curzon Street* (1947); *Spring in Park Lane* (1948); *Maytime in Mayfair* (1949); and *The Lady with the Lamp* (1951). Other important movies during this prolific period include Alfred Hitchcock's *Under Capricorn* (1949) and *Stage Fright* (1950), as well as U.S.-made *The Law and the Lady* (1951) and *Torch Song* (1953), with Joan Crawford.

At the height of his success, 39-year-old Wilding met 19-year-old Elizabeth Taylor. Their London wedding on February 21, 1952, was a media event. They had two sons—Michael Jr. in 1953 and Christopher in 1955—and divorced in 1957.

Wilding appeared in several more films throughout the 1950s and early 1960s—*The Egyptian* (1954), *The Glass Slipper* (1955), and *The World of Suzie Wong* (1960), to name but a few. He left acting for medical reasons and became an agent, but in the early 1970s came out of retirement to play minor roles in *Waterloo* (1970), *Lady Caroline Lamb* (1972), and the television film *Frankenstein: The True Story* (1973). His wife of 12 years, British actress Margaret Leighton, lost her battle against multiple sclerosis in 1976.

Michael Wilding died in Chichester, England, on July 8, 1979. All his life, he had suffered from epilepsy, and during a seizure he fell down a flight of stairs and sustained severe head injuries from which he never recovered.

ABOVE Debonair Michael Wilding played a sophisticated con man in the 1951 film, The Law and the Lady, *co-starring Greer Garson and Fernando Lamas.*

Star Shot

In 1952, Michael Wilding and Elizabeth Taylor were on a plane that was about to take off. Taylor felt a strong urge to disembark, and soon after takeoff the aircraft exploded in midair.

RIGHT Wilding's sons with Elizabeth Taylor (pictured here in 1956) both joined the movie industry: Michael Wilding, Jr., is an actor and Christopher Wilding works behind the scenes.

Lights! Camera! Death!

Move over *Earthquake, Titanic,* and *Armageddon.* There's a new type of Hollywood disaster movie—and it involves the real-life deaths of actors and actresses involved in filming. Some of these celebrities—Bela Lugosi, Oliver Reed, and Tyrone Power—died of natural causes during the making of a film, throwing producers and directors into a nightmare of epic proportions as they faced the lengthy and expensive task of rewriting or reshooting the film. Other movie sets seemed to be plagued by misfortune, which ultimately led to the demise of the star—Brandon Lee was accidentally shot while making *The Crow* (1994), and Vic Morrow was decapitated while filming *Twilight Zone: The Movie* (1983).

Perhaps more sinister are rumors of death curses attached to certain films or movie serials. *Rebel Without a Cause* (1955) is the classic example, with four major stars dying prematurely (James Dean, Sal Mineo, Natalie Wood, and Nick Adams—all of whom appear individually in this book). Eight of the *"Our Gang" ("Little Rascals")* child stars died before the age of 50 (including three before the age of 20), and 91 members of the cast and crew of *The Conqueror* (1956) succumbed to cancer caused by the fallout from atomic bomb testing near the film's Utah set.

Ben-Hur (1925 and 1959)

Given that the chariot race in the 1959 version of *Ben-Hur* is still regarded by many aficionados as the finest sustained piece of action ever brought to the movie screen, it is hardly surprising that it has been associated with drama and death. For years it was believed that during what appears to be a genuinely thrilling and very dangerous scene a stuntman, filling in for Stephen Boyd who played Messala, was killed. It's a good, plausible story. The only problem is that it is almost certainly wrong. So potent was the myth that when Charlton Heston wrote his autobiography he specifically emphasized the falseness of the statement. Yakima Canutt, the second-unit director and stunt coordinator for the film, also denied that anyone had died while the chariot scene was being filmed. He claimed that the only injury that occurred—a cut on the chin—was sustained by his son, one of the stuntmen.

How do rumors like this get started? It would appear that in the case of *Ben-Hur* it was just a simple case of confusion. To date there have been three cinematic versions of Lew Wallace's famous book —1907, 1925, and 1959—and an animated television version in 2003. The chariot race for the 1925 version was first shot in Rome, and there is good documentation that one of the extras was killed during filming. The actor who played Messala, Francis X. Bushman, produced an account of the

*ABOVE Racing chariots
in the 1959 film. In
2003, Charlton Heston
played Ben-Hur again,
when he provided the
voice for the character
in the animated made-
for-television feature.*

filming which notes: "During one take, we went around the curve and the wheel broke on the other fellow's chariot. The hub hit the ground and the guy shot up in the air about thirty feet. I turned and saw him up there—it was like a slow-motion film. He fell on a pile of lumber and died of internal injuries." After the accident, filming of the chariot race was moved to California.

There is also some debate about another scene involving a sea battle in the 1925 version of *Ben-Hur.* In some reports, some extras drowned when one of the ships caught fire and the men were forced to leap into the water clothed in heavy armor; they had lied about their ability to swim in order to gain the extra work. Other stories deny that the deaths occurred.

If the extras did indeed die, this shouldn't be surprising given that the movie promotion bragged that a cast of 125,000 had been used, and that the stunt coordinator was known for taking unnecessary risks. He probably considered a few deaths in a cast of 125,000 good odds.

The Conqueror (1956)

This historical adventure film based on the dramatic life of twelfth-century Mongolian warlord Genghis Khan was a disaster of epic proportions—financially, artistically, and, ultimately, morally.

In 1948, eccentric and obsessive entrepreneur Howard Hughes purchased RKO studios, and set about producing overblown films such as *Jet Pilot* (1951), *Son of Sinbad* (1955), and *Underwater!* (1955).

At the cost of $6 million, *The Conqueror* was the most expensive of Hughes's endeavors and was beset with problems from the very start. First of all, Dick Powell was hired as the film's director, but Powell (as competent a director as he was as an actor) had only previously directed one other film. Blue-eyed cowboy star John Wayne and red-haired Susan Hayward were hopelessly miscast as the Mongol and his Tartar bride (the *LA Times* commented that it was "the most improbable piece of casting unless Mickey Rooney were to play Jesus in *King of Kings*"). Although the story moves along at an entertaining pace, the screenplay is full of ridiculously bad dialogue in quasi-Shakespearean English.

During filming in the harsh Utah desert, the company had to endure temperatures of up to 120°F (49°C), made even worse for those actors who were in full costume and makeup. Then a flash flood nearly wiped everyone out. The cast and crew may have escaped heatstroke and drowning, but an even more insidious death would await many of them.

While it has been suggested that Hughes may have been aware of possible dangers, everyone else involved in the motion picture were ignorant of the fact that the picturesque location of Snow Canyon, Utah, could prove hazardous to their health. In 1953, the U.S. government had tested 11 atomic bombs in Yucca Flat, Nevada, 137 miles (220 km) from the film set. Much of the dust settled in Snow Canyon. Not only were the workers exposed to the contamination for 13 weeks on location, but they had to revisit it back at the studio: Hughes had arranged to ship 60 tons (61 tonnes) of dirt back to the sound stage for retakes.

Of the 220 members of *The Conqueror* community, 91 developed cancer (this percentage is three times greater than in a normal sampling of people), and 46 died from the disease. It is undetermined how many Native American extras from the nearby Shivwit reservation became sick or died as a result of the fallout. Most of the major players were affected: director Dick Powell died at age 58 of stomach cancer; John Wayne at 72 of lung and stomach cancer; Susan Hayward at 56 of brain tumors; and Agnes Moorehead at 73 of lung cancer. On the day that 51-year-old Pedro Armendáriz found out that his kidney cancer had spread to his lymphatic system, he committed suicide.

ABOVE Millionaire film producer and businessman Howard Hughes also designed aircraft. Director Martin Scorsese's The Aviator *(2004) is based on Hughes's fascinating life.*

Star Shot

The screenwriter for *The Conqueror*, Oscar Millard, envisaged Marlon Brando playing the role of Temujin (Genghis Khan).

LEFT John Wayne is said to have loved the script used for The Conqueror *(1956). Director Dick Powell had wanted a revised script, but gave in to Wayne's wishes.*

The Crow (1994)

What was it about the star-crossed and tragic Lee family? First Bruce Lee, the great *kung fu* action actor, died in Hong Kong of a brain edema at the height of his success when he was only 32, and then his son Brandon Lee, at the tender age of 28, was accidentally killed just as his career was starting to take off. Bruce and Brandon Lee were two considerable talents who died before they reached their full potential.

Brandon Lee was never embarrassed about his famous father. Although he was born in the United States, he was fluent in Cantonese by the age of eight and quickly learned the art of *kung fu* which had made his father so famous. His acting career started in 1986 when he made *Kung Fu: The Movie* (1986) for television. He followed it with *Kung Fu: The Next Generation* (1987) before making the big screen movies *Laser Mission* (1990), *Showdown in Little Tokyo* (1991), and *Rapid Fire* (1992). His biggest role was to be that of Eric Draven in the horror-thriller *The Crow* (1994), about a man who is murdered and comes back to life to avenge his murder and that of his fiancée.

From the beginning of the shoot, *The Crow* was plagued by minor accidents. Eventually they came to film the scene where the bad guy, Funboy, played by Michael Massee, shoots Draven (Brandon Lee) a number of times. Although the scene was filmed using blank cartridges, a cap from one of the blanks penetrated Lee's stomach and became lodged in his spine. Lee immediately dropped to the floor in agony. Although at first the crew was riveted by what they thought was an outstanding piece of acting, it soon became obvious that Lee was injured and that the situation was life-threatening.

Lee was rushed to the hospital where, after five hours of emergency surgery, he was pronounced dead on March 31, 1993. He was due to be married less than three weeks later. It was appropriate that his body was flown from Wilmington, North Carolina, to Seattle, Washington, where he was buried—dressed in his wedding tuxedo—in Lake View Cemetery beside his father. *The Crow* was finished as a tribute to Lee, using a body double with Lee's face digitally added to the scenes, and the footage of Lee's fatal accident was destroyed before it could be developed.

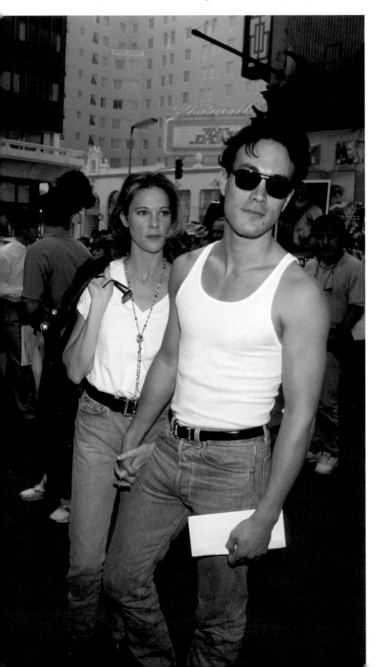

LEFT Brandon Lee was the original choice to play his father, Bruce Lee, in a 1993 biopic. Jason Scott Lee (no relation) ended up playing the martial arts hero.

Star Shot

One of Oliver Reed's most memorable characters is the menacing Bill Sikes in the musical film *Oliver!* (1968), which was directed by Reed's uncle, Sir Carol Reed.

Gladiator (2000)

It is always a problem when an actor dies of natural causes during the making of a film. Imagine the distress felt by Ridley Scott when, on May 2, 1999, he learned that the larger-than-life Oliver Reed (a man whose drinking escapades had become legendary around the world), who was an integral part of his huge Roman Empire spectacular, *Gladiator*, had died of a heart attack. When it was discovered that Reed's heart attack was the result of drinking three bottles of rum and, just to test his 61-year-old body, arm-wrestling five sailors in a bar in Malta, it is difficult to believe that the makers of *Gladiator* were exactly amused by the wild antics of this remarkable actor. At the time of his death, Reed had only five days left on the set, and was celebrating his last full week of shooting.

Scott, like Reed's fans around the world, probably believed that Reed was either immortal or an accident waiting to happen. That didn't stop him deciding that Reed, who was looking suitably jowly and dissipated, would be perfect as Antonius Proximo, the hardened gladiator trainer. Reed was paid $1 million for the role, and was happy to be part of such a fascinating project and to be working alongside bright young stars Russell Crowe and Joaquin Phoenix, and another old hell-raiser, Richard Harris (who died just three years later).

What Scott didn't anticipate was the cost and complexity of either reshooting the Reed scenes with another actor or, as actually happened, creating the face of Reed for the still unshot scenes by employing the miracle of computer graphics. In the end he had to change the storyline (Proximo was supposed to live—he was now killed off), use a body double, and insert Reed's head on the filmed image. Scott likened the process to a jigsaw puzzle—a very expensive jigsaw puzzle—that added $3 million to the movie's $100 million budget. Proximo's death scene was tactfully shot from behind.

Visual effects director John Nelson modestly downplayed his technical feats. He said that "Oliver gave an inspiring, moving performance. All we did was help him finish it." The film was nominated for a total of 12 Academy Awards® and won five, including awards for Best Picture, Best Actor (Russell Crowe), Visual Effects, Sound, and Costume Design. The closing credits of *Gladiator* include a dedication: "To our friend, Oliver Reed."

ABOVE *In addition to* Gladiator *(2000), English director Ridley Scott is best known for his films* Alien *(1979),* Blade Runner *(1982), and the ground-breaking* Thelma & Louise *(1991).*

"Our Gang" ("Little Rascals")

Whether you know them as "Our Gang" or the "Little Rascals," the series of 221 comedy shorts produced between 1922 and 1944 delighted generations of children.

Created by producer Hal Roach (best known for his Laurel and Hardy films), the first "Our Gang" childhood adventures were silent movies up until 1929, and happily made the transition to "talkies." The Hal Roach talkie years are generally considered to be the most entertaining, and feature the most memorable characters: Scotty, Darla, Farina, Wheezer, Jackie, Porky, Butch, Spanky, Alfalfa, and Buckwheat, along with Pete the lovable pooch. In 1938, Roach sold "Our Gang" to MGM, and when the rights were then sold to television in the 1950s, the series became known as the "Little Rascals."

Although the "Little Rascals" episodes are considered politically incorrect by today's standards (some episodes have even been censored), the films were actually ahead of their time in portraying racial integration, and there is no denying that the best of them are clever, charming, and very funny. But sadly, a number of the young actors suffered the fate of many a child star—they were no longer wanted in Hollywood once they grew up—and several of them met a tragic or untimely end. The most heartbreaking example is Carl "Alfalfa" Switzer.

Star Shot

Robert Blake (who played Mickey Gubitosi) became famous in the 1970s in television's *Baretta*. In April 2002, Blake was arrested for the 2001 murder of his wife; he was acquitted in March 2005.

Alfalfa was the lanky kid with freckles, a cowlick, and an hilarious singing style who starred in some 60 episodes between 1935 and 1940. Off-screen, he was a troubled and hot-tempered youngster, often getting into scrapes and playing cruel and dangerous practical jokes. After leaving the series, he had small (often uncredited) parts in a number of 1940s films, including *The Human Comedy* (1943), *Going My Way* (1944), and *The Courage of Lassie* (1946).

Good roles were even harder to come by in the 1950s, and Switzer had to work as a bartender and hunting guide in order to supplement his irregular income. He was often in financial trouble, a situation which could have been alleviated had he been paid royalties for his "Little Rascals" episodes. Alas, neither Switzer nor the other young actors ever received a cent from television syndication.

However, in 1958, things were starting to look promising for the 31-year-old: he landed a role in *The*

LEFT A 1929 portrait of "Our Gang." At top are Harry Spear (left), Alan Hoskins, and Shirley Jean Rickert. Pete the Pup, Mary Ann Jackson, Norman "Chubby" Chaney, and Robert Hutchins are seated.

Defiant Ones (1958), which could have led to a comeback. But until he got paid for the film, he was still broke. On January 21, 1959, Switzer was desperate for cash, and after a heavy drinking session, he worked out how he could get some. Some weeks prior, Switzer had borrowed a hunting dog from one Moses "Bud" Stiltz. When the dog disappeared, Switzer offered a $35 reward. A few days later someone returned the dog, and Switzer duly paid up and also bought the rescuer $15 worth of drinks. However, Switzer later decided that, as the owner of the dog, Stiltz should reimburse him the money. Switzer and his friend, Jack Piott, went to Stiltz's Mission Hills, California, home, demanding the $50. Fighting ensued, and eventually

Stiltz shot Switzer in the lower abdomen. Switzer died from internal bleeding before he reached the hospital. When Stiltz appeared before a court, he claimed that Switzer threw a knife at him and that the shot was fired in self-defense. The jury ruled that the killing was "justifiable homicide," and Stiltz was freed.

ABOVE Matthew "Stymie" Beard in 1932. Stymie's character was originally going to be known as Hercules.

Other "Little Rascals" also died young. Carl Switzer's brother, Harold "Slim" Switzer, a regular cast member, made no more movies after 1940. He committed suicide in 1967 at the age of 42.

Norman "Chubby" Chaney was more than chubby—when barely in his teens he weighed close to 300 pounds (136 kg). After a glandular operation he lost more than half his weight, but in 1936, at the age of 18, he died from complications.

Robert "Wheezer" Hutchins was a military casualty, dying in a plane crash during the last hour of his basic training in 1945. He was 19 years old.

William "Froggy" Laughlin was only 16 when he died in a motor scooter accident in 1948.

Darla Hood continued in show business, providing background vocals and singing in commercials. At the age of 47, while in the hospital for an operation, she contracted a fatal bout of hepatitis. She died in 1979.

BELOW Child actors often do school work between scenes. This photograph from 1930 shows the children still in costume.

Scotty Beckett had a reasonably successful career in film and television. However, he died in 1968 at age 38 of a barbiturate overdose.

William "Buckwheat" Thomas died of a heart attack in 1980, aged 49.

A few of the "Our Gang" ("Little Rascals") made it to their fifties. Mickey Daniels, Jr., died from cirrhosis of the liver at 55, Matthew "Stymie" Beard succumbed to pneumonia at 56, and cancer took Mary Kornman at 57 and Allen "Farina" Hoskins at 59.

Producer Hal Roach had a very long and satisfying career in the entertainment industry, and he died of pneumonia in 1992 at the ripe old age of 100 years.

Plan 9 from Outer Space (1959)

RIGHT Tor Johnson and Mona McKinnon in Plan 9 From Outer Space *(1959). Johnson also stars in Ed Wood's* Bride of the Monster *(1955).*

Star Shot

On viewing Bela Lugosi's caped body before his funeral, Peter Lorre said, "Do you think we should drive a stake through his heart, just in case?"

BELOW Bela Lugosi remains the definitive Dracula. When the film was released in 1931, Lugosi received thousands of letters from his female fans.

One of the great fears of all actors is that they will become typecast. This happened to Bela Lugosi who, even today, nearly 50 years after his death, is still known for only one role—that of Count Dracula.

Born Béla Ferenc Dezsō Blaskó in Hungary in 1882, Lugosi emigrated to the United States after a long and successful career in both Hungarian theater and movies. He arrived in New York in 1921, and in 1927 was cast in the role of Count Dracula on Broadway. This fateful casting was to determine his public persona for the rest of his life. In 1931, the famous Hollywood film *Dracula* appeared, and Bela Lugosi became a household name around the world. He became famous for playing monster figures, appearing in early horror classics such as *Murders in the Rue Morgue* (1932), *White Zombie* (1932), *Son of Frankenstein* (1939), *Return of the Vampire* (1944), and *Abbott and Costello Meet Frankenstein* (1948).

Lugosi died of a heart attack on August 16, 1956, aged 73. He was buried in his Dracula costume, complete with one of his capes. At the time of his death he was playing the Ghoul Man in *Plan 9 from Outer Space,* a now-famous movie which some critics have dubbed "the worst film ever made," written and directed by the hilariously incompetent Ed Wood. The budget was so low that the flying saucers were made out of paper plates and hubcaps, the tombstones were made of cardboard, and the "aliens" were dressed in pajamas.

Lugosi had appeared in two previous Wood productions: as the scientist in *Glen or Glenda?* (1953), based on Ed Wood's personal experiences as a transvestite; and *Bride of the Monster* (1955). The aging, morphine-addicted Lugosi was in such dire financial straits that he was forced to accept any work that was offered to him.

Unfortunately for Wood, shooting for *Plan 9 from Outer Space* had just started when Lugosi died, but this did not stop him— he used a chiropractor acquaintance to fill in for Lugosi. The chiropractor was obliged to hold the Dracula-like cape over his face for the entire movie. For Bela Lugosi, it was a sad finale to an impressive career.

After receiving the "Golden Turkey" award in 1980, *Plan 9 from Outer Space* became a cult classic, and it gained even more exposure when Tim Burton's motion picture, *Ed Wood* (1994), was released. Johnny Depp was a charismatic Wood, and Martin Landau earned the Academy Award® for Best Actor in a Supporting Role for his sensitive portrayal of Bela Lugosi.

Solomon and Sheba (1959)

A handsome, swashbuckling, romantic hero of the movies, Tyrone Power was only 45 years old when he died of a heart attack on November 15, 1958. Was there some hidden and darker explanation for his death, or was he just an unlucky man struck down before he reached old age?

Power started his career in Hollywood in 1925, and by the 1930s his good looks and acting talent ensured that he was being sought to play romantic lead roles. He appeared in movies as diverse as *Alexander's Ragtime Band* (1938), *Marie Antoinette* (1938), *The Rains Came* (1939), *The Mark of Zorro* (1940), and *The Luck of the Irish* (1948). In 1957, 32 years into his career, he was still making films as memorable as *The Sun Also Rises* and *Witness for the Prosecution*. In 1958, he traveled to Spain where he was to star as King Solomon in King Vidor's Biblical epic, *Solomon and Sheba*.

On the day of Power's death everyone agreed he was looking fit and healthy. Vidor decided to shoot a scene where Power and George Sanders were engaged in a dramatic sword fight on an elevated landing. Both men were wearing heavy robes and the swords they were swinging weighed about 15 pounds (7 kg). It is claimed that Sanders asked for the scene to be shot at least eight times until Power, obviously exhausted, threw down his sword and said, "If you can't find anything there you can use, just use the close-ups of me. I've had it!"

ABOVE Dashing hero Tyrone Power with Linda Darnell in The Mark of Zorro *(1940). Power's tombstone bears the words "Good night, sweet prince."*

Power was taken off the set to his dressing room where he started shaking violently. A doctor was called for, but he was not on the set. Only an hour later Power died from a heart attack. He was replaced by Yul Brynner, and when the film appeared, Tyrone Power's name was not listed in the credits. His funeral in Spain turned into a voyeuristic circus, leaving his new wife of only six months, Debbie Ann Minardos, horrified that she had not been given the opportunity to express her grief in private.

Some stories state that Power's heart attack was brought on by having to film a scene where he carried his co-star, Gina Lollobrigida, up and down a staircase up to 40 times. Regardless of the cause, it seems that Power was destined to suffer the same fate as his father—Tyrone Power, Sr., died of a heart attack in 1931.

Star Shot

Over half of *Solomon and Sheba* had been shot when Tyrone Power died. Yul Brynner refilmed most of Power's scenes, but Power can still be seen in some long shots.

LEFT Yul Brynner and Marisa Pavan in a scene from Solomon and Sheba *(1959). A heavy smoker throughout his life, Brynner succumbed to lung cancer in 1985 at the age of 65.*

Twilight Zone: The Movie (1983)

It was July 1982, and the Hollywood community was not amused. A young hotshot director, John Landis, who had achieved fame with his massive car pile-up in the film *The Blues Brothers* (1980), had gone too far in his quest for reality and three people were now dead—including two innocent children. A barrage of criticisms came thick and fast. What had happened? Was it a tragic accident, or a dreadful case of safety violations on the movie set? A well-known actor, Vic Morrow, had been decapitated by the rotor of a crashing helicopter, and two Vietnamese children—Renee Shin-Yi Chen and My-ca Dinh Le—had also been killed. Morrow was 53 at the time.

Vic Morrow had been a part of the Hollywood scene since his impressive screen debut as Artie West in *The Blackboard Jungle* (1955). Throughout the

ABOVE An exuberant John Landis outside a theater screening The Blues Brothers *(1980). Landis also directed the Michael Jackson video* Thriller *(1983).*

1950s he'd had important roles in movies like *King Creole* (1958) and *God's Little Acre* (1958), but by the 1970s he was mostly working in television. The high-profile film version of *Twilight Zone*, produced by Steven Spielberg and featuring four segments directed by John Landis, Spielberg, George Miller, and Ron Dante, was a definite high point in a career that had been going nowhere for many years. But Morrow didn't fully appreciate what he was getting himself into by agreeing to star in Landis's segment of the motion picture. Many years before he had had a premonition that he was going to die in a helicopter crash—little did he know how soon this prediction was to become fact.

Rumors about what happened abound to this day. Some say that director John Landis kept screaming at the helicopter pilot, "Fly lower! Lower!" despite the inherent safety risks. The helicopter crash may have been caused by shrapnel from exploding pyrotechnics. Other rumors say that virtually everyone on the set was either drunk or on cocaine. Some blame Steven Spielberg who, as producer of the film, could have reined in Landis's excesses.

It was obvious that Landis knew that he had committed a grave error of judgment. At Morrow's funeral, unannounced and unwelcome, he stood up and delivered a rambling eulogy in which, to the fury of many who blamed him for Morrow's death, he declared that he was "proud to have directed Vic in what Vic, himself, considered the best performance of his career." Later charged with manslaughter, Landis was eventually acquitted. One of the saddest ironies of the whole debacle is that Morrow's last words before he was killed are believed to be, "I've got to be crazy to do this shot. I should have asked for a double."

RIGHT Vic Morrow in 1971. Morrow achieved lasting fame with his portrayal of Sgt. Chip Saunders in the World War II television drama, Combat *(1962–67).*

Picture Credits

The Publisher would like to thank Getty Images and the other copyright owners for permission to reproduce their images. Every attempt has been made to obtain permission for use of all images from the copyright owners, however, if any errors or omissions have occurred, Global Book Publishing would be pleased to hear from copyright owners.

Key: (t) top of page; (b) bottom of page; (l) left side of page; (r) right side of page; (c) center of page.

AFP/Getty Images

13(t), 17(t), 48(l), 203(tr), 229(r), 260(tl), 266(tl), 267(l), 296–297(b).

Getty Images

1, 2–3, 4–5, 6, 8, 9, 10–11, 12(tl), 12(cr), 12(bl), 14(t), 14(b), 15(c), 15(b), 16(t), 16(b), 16–17(b), 17(cr), 20(l), 20(b), 20–21(t), 21(b), 22(l), 22–23(b), 23(r), 24–25(b), 25(r), 26(tl), 27(br), 28(l), 28–29(b), 29(r), 30(bl), 30(r), 31(r), 32(bl), 33(tr), 34(l), 34–35(b), 35(r), 36(l), 36(br), 36–37(t), 37(r), 38(br), 39(tl), 40(l), 40–41(b), 41(r), 42(l), 42(br), 43(tr), 44–45(t), 46(bl), 47(tr), 48–49(b), 50(l), 50–51(t), 51(r), 52(l), 52–53(b), 53(tr), 54(tr), 54(br), 55(r), 56(bl), 56–57(t), 57(br), 58(l), 58–59(b), 60(l), 61(tr), 61(br), 62(l), 62–63(t), 62–63(b), 63(r), 64(bl), 65(tr), 66(l), 66–67(b), 67(t), 68(bl), 68(r), 69(bl), 69(tr), 70–71(b), 71(t), 72(bl), 72–73(c), 73(tr), 74–75(b), 75(r), 76(l), 76(r), 77(br), 78(l), 78–79(c), 79(r), 80(l), 80–81(t), 82(bl), 82(r), 83(l), 83(tr), 84(bl), 84–85(t), 85(tr), 85(br), 86(l), 86(br), 87(r), 88(tl), 89(tl), 89(br), 90(tl), 90(bl), 91(tr), 91(br), 92(l), 94(tl), 94(bl), 95(br), 96(l), 96(br), 97(tr), 98(tl), 98–99(c), 99(br), 100(bl), 100–101(b), 102(l), 102(t), 104(l), 104(tr), 105(tr), 105(br), 107(bl), 107(r), 108(l), 108–109(b), 110(l), 110–111(b), 111(r), 112(bl), 113(t), 113(r), 114(tr), 116–117(t), 117(br), 118(l), 118(r), 119(b), 121(r), 122(br), 123(l), 124(l), 124–125(b), 125(t), 126(bl), 126–127(t), 127(br), 128(r), 129(l), 129(br), 130(l), 130(t), 131(l), 132(bl), 132–133(t), 133(bl), 133(r), 134(l), 135(tl), 135(br), 136(l), 138(bl), 138–139(t), 139(cr), 139(br), 140(l), 140(tr), 141(tr), 142(bl), 142–143(t), 143(r), 144(l), 144–145(b), 145(r), 146(l), 146(br), 146–147(t), 147(br), 148(tl), 149(r), 150(bl), 150(r), 151(tr), 152(bl), 152–153(t), 153(r), 154(bl), 154(tr), 155(r), 156–157(b), 158(bl), 158(tr), 159(r), 160(l), 161(tl), 161(br), 162(l), 163(tr), 164(br), 164–165(t), 167(tr), 168(bl), 168–169(t), 170(l), 171(bl), 172(l), 172–173(b), 173(r), 174(l), 175(br), 176(l), 176–177(t), 177(br), 178–179(b), 179(tr), 180(bl), 180(tr), 181(l), 181(r), 182(bl), 183(l), 184(l), 185(tl), 185(br), 186(l), 186–187(b), 187(r), 188(tr), 189(l), 189(tr), 190–191(t), 191(br), 192(bl), 192(tr), 193(l), 193(r), 194(bl), 194(tr), 195(l), 195(tr), 196(l), 196–197(b), 198(l), 198–199(b), 199(r), 200(bl), 200–201(t), 201(r), 202(l), 203(l), 204–205(b), 205(r), 206–207, 208(l), 208–209(b), 209(r), 210(tr), 211(br), 212(l), 212–213(t), 213(br), 214(l), 215(bl), 215(tr), 216(l), 216(tr), 216(br), 217(r), 218–219, 220(l), 221(r), 222–223(b), 224–225(t), 225(br), 226(l), 227(bl), 227(tr), 228(l), 228–229(b), 230–231, 232(l), 233(bl), 233(tr), 234(tl), 234(bl), 235(tr), 235(br), 236–237(b), 238(bl), 240(l), 240(r), 241(tr), 241(br), 242–243(b), 243(tr), 244(tl), 244(bl), 245(tl), 245(br), 246(tr), 247(bl), 247(tr), 248(tl), 248–249(b), 249(r), 250(l), 250–251(b), 252(bl), 254–255, 256(l), 256(br), 257(tl), 258(bl), 258–259(t), 259(br), 260(bl), 262(l), 262–263(b), 263(tr), 264(bl), 265(tr), 265(br), 266(cl), 267(br), 268(tl), 268(bl), 270(tl), 271(tr), 271(br), 272(bl), 273(tr), 274(tl), 274(bl), 274–275(t), 275(r), 276(l), 276(br), 278(l), 278–279(b), 279(r), 280(bl), 280–281(t), 281(r), 282–283(b), 284(l), 285(r), 286(l), 286–287(b), 287(r), 288(l), 288(r), 289(tl), 289(br), 290(l), 290(r), 291(br), 292(bl), 292(tr), 293(r), 294–295, 297(r), 298–299(t), 299(bl), 299(r), 300(br), 300–301(t), 301(br), 302(bl), 303(tl), 303(r), 304(l), 304(r), 305(tl), 305(br), 306(bl), 306(tr), 307(r), 308(r), 308–309(t), 309(br), 310(tl), 311(r), 312(bl), 312(tr), 313(r), 314(br), 315(tl), 316(bl), 316(tr), 317(r), 318(l), 319(tl), 319(tr), 320(l), 320(br), 321(tl), 322(bl), 322(tr), 323(r), 325(tr), 325(br), 326–327, 328(l), 329(bl), 329(tr), 331(tl), 332(bl), 332(tr), 333(tr), 333(br), 334(bl), 334(r), 335(l), 335(tr), 336(br).

Stuart Scott

Cover (with thanks to our model, Pia Andersen).

Time Life Pictures/Getty Images

13(b), 15(t), 18–19, 24(l), 26(b), 27(tl), 32(r), 38(l), 39(br), 43(br), 44(tl), 44(bl), 45(r), 47(l), 49(tr), 56(tl), 59(br), 60(br), 64(tl), 65(bl), 70(l), 74(l), 77(tl), 81(r), 88(bl), 92–93(b), 93(r), 101(r), 103(r), 106(l), 109(r), 110(tr), 114(bl), 115(bl), 115(r), 116(l), 119(tl), 120(l), 120–121(t), 123(r), 126(tl), 128(tl), 136(br), 136–137(t), 137(br), 140–141(b), 148–149(b), 151(l), 156(l), 157(r), 163(bl), 164(l), 165(r), 166(l), 166–167(b), 169(r), 171(r), 174(r), 175(tl), 178(l), 183(r), 188(bl), 190(l), 197(r), 204(l), 210(bl), 212(br), 220–221(b), 222(tr), 223(r), 224(l), 224(br), 236(l), 237(tl), 237(r), 238–239(t), 239(r), 242(l), 246(l), 251(r), 253(tl), 253(r), 257(r), 261(br), 269(r), 272(r), 273(br), 277(r), 282(l), 283(tr), 284–285(b), 296(l), 298(bl), 300(l), 308(l), 310(br), 314(l), 315(br), 321(l), 323(l), 324(l), 330(bl), 331(r), 336(l).

Variety

33(l).

Captions for preliminary pages and chapter openers

Page 1: George Reeves in costume as Superman

Pages 2–3: Dorothy Dandridge and Harry Belafonte in a scene from *Carmen Jones* (1954)

Pages 4–5: Sal Mineo, James Dean, and Natalie Wood in a scene from *Rebel Without a Cause* (1955)

Page 6: Studio portrait of Elvis Presley

Page 8: Humphrey Bogart and Marilyn Monroe at the premiere of *How to Marry a Millionaire* (1953)

Page 9: John-Michael Howson at a cocktail party

Pages 10–11: Jayne Mansfield photographed in 1965

Pages 18–19: Errol Flynn relaxing on his yacht during a fishing trip

Pages 206–207: Marilyn Monroe and Eli Wallach on the set of *The Misfits* (1961)

Pages 218–219: Anthony Dawson and Grace Kelly in a scene from *Dial M for Murder* (1954)

Pages 230–231: Elvis Presley in military uniform, lying on an army cot

Pages 254–255: Alan Ladd and Veronica Lake in a scene from *The Blue Dahlia* (1946)

Pages 294–295: The wreck of James Dean's Porsche Spyder

Pages 326–327: The filming of the chariot race in the 1925 version of *Ben-Hur*

Produced by
Global Book Publishing Pty Ltd
1/181 High Street, Willoughby,
NSW 2068, Australia
Phone (612) 9967 3100
Fax (612) 9967 5891
Email rightsmanager@globalpub.com.au
Publication, arrangement, and text
© Global Book Publishing Pty Ltd 2005

Film Star Table

Ideal for movie fans and trivia buffs alike, this fascinating table comprises at-a-glance information for each actor and actress featured in *Cut!*, from the date and place of their birth to the date and place of their death, the cause of their death, and their place of burial. In addition, the star's birth name, nickname, and any spouses or partners are included. The age at death column reveals just how young many of these Hollywood celebrities were when they died.

Professional Name	Birth Name	Nickname	Date of Birth	Place of Birth	Date of Death
Aaliyah	Aaliyah Dana Haughton	—	January 16, 1979	Brooklyn, New York, USA	August 25, 2001
Nick Adams	Nicholas Aloysius Adamschock	—	July 10, 1931	Nanticoke, Pennsylvania, USA	February 7, 1968
Renée Adorée	Jeanne de la Fonte	—	September 30, 1898	Lille, France	October 5, 1933
Frank Albertson	Frank Albertson	—	February 2, 1909	Fergus Falls, Minnesota, USA	February 29, 1964
Pier Angeli	Anna Maria Pierangeli	—	June 19, 1932	Cagliari, Sardinia, Italy	September 10, 1971
Roscoe Arbuckle	Roscoe Conkling Arbuckle	"Fatty," The Prince of Whales	March 24, 1887	Smith Center, Kansas, USA	June 29, 1933
Pedro Armendáriz	Pedro Gregorio Armendáriz Hastings	—	May 9, 1912	Mexico City, Mexico	June 18, 1963
Agnes Ayres	Agnes Eyre Hinkle (Henkel)	—	April 4, 1898	Carbondale, Illinois, USA	December 25, 1940
Lex Barker	Alexander Crichlow Barker, Jr.	Sexy Lexy	May 8, 1919	Rye, New York, USA	May 11, 1973
Diana Barrymore	Diana Blanche Barrymore Blythe	—	March 3, 1921	New York, New York, USA	January 25, 1960
John Barrymore	John Sidney Blythe	The Great Profile	February 14, 1882	Philadelphia, Pennsylvania, USA	May 29, 1942
James Baskett	James Baskett	—	February 16, 1904	Indianapolis, Indiana, USA	September 9, 1948
Barbara Bates	Barbara Bates	—	August 6, 1925	Denver, Colorado, USA	March 18, 1969
Warner Baxter	Warner Leroy Baxter	—	March 29, 1889	Columbus, Ohio, USA	May 7, 1951
Matthew Beard	Matthew Beard, Jr.	"Stymie"	January 1, 1925	Los Angeles, California, USA	January 8, 1981
Scotty Beckett	Scott Hastings Beckett	—	October 4, 1929	Oakland, California, USA	May 10, 1968
John Belushi	John Adam Belushi	—	January 24, 1949	Chicago, Illinois, USA	March 5, 1982
William Bendix	William Bendix	—	January 14, 1906	New York, New York, USA	December 14, 1964
Constance Bennett	Constance Campbell Bennett	—	October 22, 1904	New York, New York, USA	July 24, 1965
Clara Blandick	Clara Blandick	—	June 4, 1880	On an American ship in Hong Kong harbor	April 15, 1962
Humphrey Bogart	Humphrey DeForest Bogart	Bogie, Bogey	December 25, 1899	New York, New York, USA	January 14, 1957
Ward Bond	Wardell Bond	—	April 9, 1903	Benkelman, Nebraska, USA	November 5, 1960
Olive Borden	Sybil Tinkle	—	July 14, 1907	Richmond, Virginia, USA	October 1, 1947
Clara Bow	Clara Gordon Bowtinelli	The "It" Girl, The Brooklyn Bonfire	July 29, 1905	Brooklyn, New York, USA	September 27, 1965
Stephen Boyd	William Millar	—	July 4, 1928	Glengormley, Northern Ireland	June 2, 1977
Charles Boyer	Charles Boyer	—	August 28, 1899	Figeac, Lot, Midi-Pyrénées, France	August 26, 1978
Alice Brady	Alice Brady	—	November 2, 1892	New York, New York, USA	October 28, 1939
Jonathan Brandis	Jonathan Gregory Brandis	—	April 13, 1976	Danbury, Connecticut, USA	November 12, 2003
Geraldine Brooks	Geraldine Stroock	—	October 29, 1925	New York, New York, USA	June 19, 1977

Place of Death	Age at Death	Cause of Death	Place of Burial	Spouse(s)/Partner(s)
Abaco Island, Bahamas	22	Plane crash	Ferncliff Cemetery and Mausoleum, New York, USA	R. Kelly
Beverly Hills, California, USA	36	Drug overdose	Saints Cyril & Methodius Ukrainian Church Cemetery, Pennsylvania, USA	Carol Nugent
Tujunga, California, USA	35	Tuberculosis	Hollywood Forever Cemetery, California, USA	Tom Moore, Sherman Gill
Santa Monica, California, USA	55	Natural causes	Holy Cross Cemetery, Culver City, California, USA	Virginia Shelley, Grace Gillern
Beverly Hills, California, USA	39	Barbiturate overdose	Cimetière des Bulvis, Rueil Malmaison, France	Vic Damone, Armando Trovajoli
New York, New York, USA	46	Heart attack	Cremated, ashes scattered over the Pacific Ocean	Araminta Durfee, Doris Deane, Addie McPhail
Los Angeles, California, USA	51	Suicide (gunshot)	Unknown	Carmelita Bohr
Los Angeles, California, USA	42	Cerebral hemorrhage	Hollywood Forever Cemetery, California, USA	Frank P. Schuker, Manuel Reachi
New York, New York, USA	54	Heart attack	Cremated	Constanze Thurlow, Arlene Dahl, Lana Turner, Irene Labhart
New York, New York, USA	38	Heart failure	Woodlawn Cemetery, Bronx, New York, USA	Bramwell Fletcher, John R. Howard, Robert Wilcox
Los Angeles, California, USA	60	Bronchial pneumonia, cirrhosis of the liver	Mount Vernon Cemetery, Philadelphia, Pennsylvania, USA	Katherine Corri Harris, Blanche Oelrichs, Dolores Costello, Elaine Jacobs (Barrie)
Los Angeles, California, USA	44	Heart disease	Crown Hill Cemetery, Indianapolis, Indiana, USA	Unknown
Denver, Colorado, USA	43	Suicide (carbon monoxide poisoning)	Crown Hill Cemetery, Lakewood, Colorado, USA	Cecil Coen, William Reed
Beverly Hills, California, USA	62	Bronchial pneumonia	Forest Lawn Memorial Park, Glendale, California, USA	Viola Caldwell, Winifred Bryson
Los Angeles, California, USA	56	Pneumonia	Evergreen Cemetery, Los Angeles, California, USA	—
Los Angeles, California, USA	38	Barbiturate overdose	San Fernando Mission Cemetery, Mission Hills, California, USA	Beverly Baker, Sunny Vickers
Hollywood, California, USA	33	Cocaine and heroin overdose	Abel's Hill Cemetery, Chilmark, Massachusetts, USA	Judy Jacklin
Los Angeles, California, USA	58	Lobar pneumonia	San Fernando Mission Cemetery, California, USA	Theresa Stefanotti
Fort Dix, New Jersey, USA	60	Cerebral hemorrhage	Arlington National Cemetery, Virginia, USA	Chester Hirst Moorhead, Philip Morgan Plant, Henri de la Falaise, Gilbert Roland, John Theron Coulter
Hollywood, California, USA	81	Suicide (drug overdose and asphyxiation)	Forest Lawn Memorial Park, Glendale, California, USA	—
Los Angeles, California, USA	57	Throat cancer	Forest Lawn Memorial Park, Glendale, California, USA	Helen Menken, Mary Philips, Mayo Methot, Lauren Bacall
Dallas, Texas, USA	57	Heart attack	Cremated, ashes scattered over the Pacific Ocean	Doris Sellers Childs, Mary Louise May
Los Angeles, California, USA	40	Stomach problem	Forest Lawn Memorial Park, Glendale, California, USA	John Moeller, Theodore Spector
Los Angeles, California, USA	60	Heart attack	Forest Lawn Memorial Park, Glendale, California, USA	Rex Bell
Granada Hills, California, USA	48	Heart attack	Oakwood Memorial Park, Chatsworth, California, USA	Mariella di Sarzana, Elizabeth Mills
Phoenix, Arizona, USA	78	Suicide (drug overdose)	Holy Cross Cemetery, Culver City, California, USA	Pat Paterson
New York, New York, USA	46	Cancer	Sleepy Hollow Cemetery, Tarrytown, New York, USA	James Crane
Los Angeles, California, USA	27	Suicide (hanging)	Cremated	—
Riverhead, New York, USA	51	Heart attack	Washington Memorial Park Cemetery, Coram, New York, USA	Herbert Sargent, Budd Schulberg

Professional Name	Birth Name	Nickname	Date of Birth	Place of Birth	Date of Death
Richard Burton	Richard Walter Jenkins	—	November 10, 1925	Pontrhydyfen, Wales	August 5, 1984
Charles Butterworth	Charles Butterworth	—	July 26, 1896	South Bend, Indiana, USA	June 14, 1946
Susan Cabot	Harriet Shapiro	—	July 9, 1927	Boston, Massachusetts, USA	December 10, 1986
John Candy	John Franklin Candy	—	October 31, 1950	Toronto, Canada	March 4, 1994
Capucine	Germaine Lefebvre	—	January 6, 1931	Toulon, France	March 17, 1990
Jack Carson	John Elmer Carson	—	October 27, 1910	Carman, Canada	January 2, 1963
Nell Carter	Nell Ruth Hardy	—	September 13, 1948	Birmingham, Alabama, USA	January 23, 2003
Katrin Cartlidge	Katrin Cartlidge	—	May 15, 1961	London, England	September 7, 2002
Jack Cassidy	John Joseph Edward Cassidy	—	March 5, 1927	Richmond Hill, New York, USA	December 12, 1976
Ted Cassidy	Theodore Crawford Cassidy	—	July 31, 1932	Pittsburgh, Pennsylvania, USA	January 16, 1979
Peggie Castle	Peggie Castle	—	December 22, 1927	Appalachia, Virginia, USA	August 11, 1973
John Cazale	John Cazale	—	August 12, 1935	Boston, Massachusetts, USA	March 12, 1978
Helen Chandler	Helen Chandler	—	February 1, 1906	Charleston, South Carolina, USA	April 30, 1965
Jeff Chandler	Ira Grossel	—	December 15, 1918	Brooklyn, New York, USA	June 17, 1961
Lon Chaney	Leonidas Frank Chaney	The Man of a Thousand Faces	April 1, 1883	Colorado Springs, Colorado, USA	August 26, 1930
Norman Chaney	Norman Chaney	"Chubby"	January 18, 1918	Baltimore, Maryland, USA	May 30, 1936
Charley Chase	Charles Joseph Parrott	—	October 20, 1893	Baltimore, Maryland, USA	June 20, 1940
Lana Clarkson	Lana Clarkson	—	April 5, 1962	Long Beach, California, USA	February 3, 2003
Montgomery Clift	Edward Montgomery Clift	—	October 17, 1920	Omaha, Nebraska, USA	July 23, 1966
Colin Clive	Colin Clive-Greig	—	January 20, 1900	St. Malo, France	June 25, 1937
James Coco	James Coco	—	March 21, 1930	New York, New York, USA	February 25, 1987
Gary Cooper	Frank James Cooper	Coop	May 7, 1901	Helena, Montana, USA	May 13, 1961
Lou Costello	Louis Francis Cristillo	—	March 6, 1906	Paterson, New Jersey, USA	March 3, 1959
Laird Cregar	Samuel Laird Cregar	—	July 28, 1916	Philadelphia, Pennsylvania, USA	December 9, 1944
Richard Cromwell	LeRoy Melvin Radabaugh	—	January 8, 1910	Los Angeles, California, USA	October 11, 1960
Lindsay Crosby	Lindsay Harry Crosby	—	January 5, 1938	Los Angeles, California, USA	December 11, 1989
Alan Curtis	Harry Ueberroth	—	July 24, 1909	Chicago, Illinois, USA	February 2, 1953
Dorothy Dandridge	Dorothy Jean Dandridge	—	November 9, 1922	Cleveland, Ohio, USA	September 8, 1965
Karl Dane	Rasmus Karl Thekelsen Gottlieb	—	October 12, 1886	Copenhagen, Denmark	April 15, 1934
Mickey Daniels, Jr.	Richard Daniels, Jr.	—	October 11, 1914	Rock Springs, Wyoming, USA	August 20, 1970
Bobby Darin	Walden Robert Cassotto	—	May 14, 1936	Bronx, New York, USA	December 20, 1973
Linda Darnell	Monetta Eloyse Darnell	—	October 16, 1923	Dallas, Texas, USA	April 10, 1965
Joan Davis	Madonna Josephine Davis	—	June 29, 1907	St. Paul, Minnesota, USA	May 22, 1961
Marguerite de la Motte	Marguerite de la Motte	—	June 22, 1902	Duluth, Minnesota, USA	March 10, 1950
Lya De Putti	Amalia Putty	—	January 10, 1899	Vecsés, Zemplen, Hungary	November 27, 1931
James Dean	James Byron Dean	Jimmy Dean	February 8, 1931	Marion, Indiana, USA	September 30, 1955

Place of Death	Age at Death	Cause of Death	Place of Burial	Spouse(s)/Partner(s)
Geneva, Switzerland	58	Cerebral hemorrhage	Protestant Churchyard, Céligny, Switzerland	Sybil Williams, Elizabeth Taylor (married twice), Susan Hunt, Sally Hay
Los Angeles, California, USA	49	Suicide/car accident	St. Joseph Valley Cemetery, South Bend, Indiana, USA	Unknown
Encino, California, USA	59	Homicide (bashed to death)	Hillside Memorial Park, Culver City, California, USA	Martin Sacker, Michael Roman
Durango, Mexico	43	Heart attack	Holy Cross Cemetery, Culver City, California, USA	Rosemary Hobor
Lausanne, Switzerland	59	Suicide (fall from window)	Cremated	Pierre Trabaud
Encino, California, USA	52	Stomach cancer	Forest Lawn Memorial Park, Glendale, California, USA	Elizabeth Lindy, Kay St. Germain, Lola Albright, Sandra Jolley
Beverly Hills, California, USA	54	Heart disease and diabetes complications	Hillside Memorial Park, Culver City, California, USA	Georg Krynicki, Roger Larocque
London, England	41	Pneumonia and septicemia	Unknown	—
Hollywood, California, USA	49	House fire	Cremated, ashes scattered over the Pacific Ocean	Evelyn Ward, Shirley Jones
Los Angeles, California, USA	46	Complications after open-heart surgery	Cremated	Margaret Helen Jesse
Hollywood, California, USA	45	Cirrhosis of the liver and a heart condition	Cremated	Revis Call, Robert H. Rains, William McGarry, Arthur Morgenstern
New York, New York, USA	42	Bone cancer	Holy Cross Cemetery, Malden, Massachusetts, USA	Meryl Streep (fiancée)
Hollywood, California, USA	59	Heart attack after surgery for bleeding ulcer	Cremated, ashes stored at the Chapel of the Pines Crematory, Los Angeles, California, USA	Cyril Hume, Bramwell Fletcher, Walter Piascik
Los Angeles, California, USA	42	Blood poisoning	Hillside Memorial Park, Culver City, California, USA	Marjorie Hoshelle
Hollywood, California, USA	47	Bronchial cancer	Forest Lawn Memorial Park, Glendale, California, USA	Frances Creighton, Hazel Hastings
Baltimore, Maryland, USA	18	Complications from glandular problem	Baltimore Cemetery, Baltimore, Maryland, USA	—
Hollywood, California, USA	46	Heart attack	Forest Lawn Memorial Park, Glendale, California, USA	Bebe Eltinge
Alhambra, California, USA	40	Homicide (gunshot)	Hollywood Forever Cemetery, California, USA	—
New York, New York, USA	45	Heart attack	Friends Religious Society of Prospect Park, Brooklyn, New York, USA	Lorenzo James (companion)
Los Angeles, California, USA	37	Tuberculosis	Cremated	Jeanne De Casalis
New York, New York, USA	56	Heart attack	St. Gertrude's Roman Catholic Cemetery, Colonia, New Jersey, USA	—
Beverly Hills, California, USA	60	Spinal cancer	Sacred Heart Cemetery, Southampton, New York, USA	Veronica Balfe
Los Angeles, California, USA	52	Heart attack	Calvary Cemetery, Los Angeles, California, USA	Anne Battlers
Los Angeles, California, USA	28	Heart attack	Forest Lawn Memorial Park, Glendale, California, USA	—
Hollywood, California, USA	50	Cancer	Santa Ana Cemetery, California, USA	Angela Lansbury
Las Vegas, Nevada, USA	51	Suicide (gunshot)	Holy Cross Cemetery, Culver City, California, USA	Barbara Frederickson, Janet Schwartze, Susan Crosby
New York, New York, USA	43	Complications after surgery	Memorial Park Cemetery, Skokie, Illinois, USA	Gwen Herman, Sandra Lucas, Priscilla Lawson, Betty Dodero, Ilona Massey
Hollywood, California, USA	41	Barbiturate overdose	Forest Lawn Memorial Park, Glendale, California, USA	Harold Nicholas, Jack Denison
Los Angeles, California, USA	47	Suicide (gunshot)	Hollywood Forever Cemetery, California, USA	Thais Valdemar
San Diego, California, USA	55	Cirrhosis of the liver	Forest Lawn Memorial Park, Glendale, California, USA	—
Los Angeles, California, USA	37	Heart failure after open-heart surgery	Body donated to UCLA Medical Center	Sandra Dee, Andrea Joy Yeager
Chicago, Illinois, USA	41	House fire	Union Hill Cemetery, Kennett Square, Pennsylvania, USA	J. Peverell Marley, Phillip Liebmann, Merle Roy Robertson
Palm Springs, California, USA	53	Heart attack	Holy Cross Cemetery, Culver City, California, USA	Si Wills
San Francisco, California, USA	47	Cerebral thrombosis	Olivet Memorial Park, Colma, California, USA	John Bowers, Sidney H. Rivkin
New York, New York, USA	32	Lobar pneumonia	Ferncliff Cemetery and Mausoleum, Hartsdale, New York, USA	Zoltan de Szepessy, Louis Jahnke
Cholame, California, USA	24	Car accident	Park Cemetery, Fairmount, Indiana, USA	—

Professional Name	Birth Name	Nickname	Date of Birth	Place of Birth	Date of Death
Albert Dekker	Albert Dekker	—	December 20, 1905	Brooklyn, New York, USA	May 5, 1968
Dorothy Dell	Dorothy Dell Goff	—	January 30, 1915	Hattiesburg, Mississippi, USA	June 8, 1934
Sandy Dennis	Sandra Dale Dennis	—	April 27, 1937	Hastings, Nebraska, USA	March 2, 1992
Gloria Dickson	Thais Alalia Dickerson	—	August 13, 1916	Pocatello, Idaho, USA	April 10, 1945
Divine	Harris Glenn Milstead	—	October 19, 1945	Baltimore, Maryland, USA	March 7, 1988
Richard Dix	Ernest Carlton Brimmer	—	July 18, 1893	St. Paul, Minnesota, USA	September 20, 1949
Robert Donat	Friedrich Robert Donath	—	March 18, 1905	Manchester, England	June 9, 1958
Diana Dors	Diana Mary Fluck	The Siren of Swindon, Hurricane in Mink	October 23, 1931	Swindon, England	May 4, 1984
Eric Douglas	Eric Anthony Douglas	—	June 21, 1958	Los Angeles, California, USA	July 6, 2004
Paul Douglas	Paul Douglas	—	April 11, 1907	Philadelphia, Pennsylvania, USA	September 11, 1959
Dominique Dunne	Dominique Ellen Dunne	—	November 23, 1959	Santa Monica, California, USA	November 4, 1982
Josh Ryan Evans	Joshua Ryan Evans	—	January 10, 1982	Hayward, California, USA	August 5, 2002
Myrna Fahey	Myrna E. Fahey	—	March 12, 1933	Carmel, Maine, USA	May 6, 1973
Douglas Fairbanks	Douglas Elton Ulman	—	May 23, 1883	Denver, Colorado, USA	December 12, 1939
Chris Farley	Christopher Crosby Farley	—	February 15, 1964	Madison, Wisconsin, USA	December 18, 1997
Frances Farmer	Frances Elena Farmer	The Bad Girl of West Seattle	September 19, 1913	Seattle, Washington, USA	August 1, 1970
Richard Farnsworth	Richard Farnsworth	—	September 1, 1920	Los Angeles, California, USA	October 6, 2000
Marty Feldman	Marty Feldman	—	July 8, 1933	London, England	December 2, 1982
Betty Field	Betty Field	—	February 8, 1913	Boston, Massachusetts, USA	September 13, 1973
Errol Flynn	Errol Leslie Thomson Flynn	The Baron	June 20, 1909	Hobart, Tasmania, Australia	October 14, 1959
Sean Flynn	Sean Leslie Flynn	—	May 31, 1941	Unknown	April 6, 1970?
Clark Gable	William Clark Gable	The King of Hollywood	February 1, 1901	Cadiz, Ohio, USA	November 16, 1960
John Garfield	Jacob Julius Garfinkle	—	March 4, 1913	New York, New York, USA	May 21, 1952
Judy Garland	Frances Ethel Gumm	—	June 10, 1922	Grand Rapids, Minnesota, USA	June 22, 1969
Peggy Ann Garner	Peggy Ann Garner	—	February 3, 1932	Canton, Ohio, USA	October 16, 1984
Gladys George	Gladys Anna Clare	—	September 13, 1900	Patten, Maine, USA	December 8, 1954
John Gilbert	John Cecil Pringle	—	July 10, 1899	Logan, Utah, USA	January 9, 1936
Trevor Goddard	Trevor Goddard	—	October 14, 1962	Croydon, Surrey, England	June 7, 2003
Alexander Godunov	Boris Alexandrovich Godunov	—	November 28, 1949	Sakhalin Island, USSR	May 18, 1995
Betty Grable	Ruth Elizabeth Grable	The Pin-Up Girl, The Girl with the Million Dollar Legs	December 18, 1916	St. Louis, Missouri, USA	July 2, 1973
Gloria Grahame	Gloria Grahame Hallward	—	November 28, 1923	Los Angeles, California, USA	October 5, 1981

Place of Death	Age at Death	Cause of Death	Place of Burial	Spouse(s)/Partner(s)
Hollywood, California, USA	62	Asphyxiation	Garden State Crematory, North Bergen, New Jersey, USA	Esther Guirini, Geraldine Saunders (fiancée)
Altadena, California, USA	19	Car accident	Metairie Cemetery, New Orleans, Louisiana, USA	—
Westport, Connecticut, USA	54	Ovarian cancer	Lincoln Memorial Park, Lincoln, Nebraska, USA	Gerry Mulligan (partner)
Hollywood, California, USA	28	House fire	Hollywood Forever Cemetery, California, USA	Perc Westmore, Ralph Murphy, William Fitzgerald
Los Angeles, California, USA	42	Enlarged heart	Prospect Hill Park Cemetery, Towson, Maryland, USA	—
Los Angeles, California, USA	56	Heart ailment	Forest Lawn Memorial Park, Glendale, California, USA	Winifred Coe, Virginia Webster
London, England	53	Cerebral hemorrhage caused by asthma	St. Marylebone Crematorium, Finchley, England	Ella Annesley Voysey, Renée Asherson
Windsor, England	52	Ovarian cancer	Sunningdale Catholic Cemetery, Berkshire, England	Dennis Hamilton, Richard Dawson, Alan Lake
Manhattan, New York, USA	46	Drug overdose	Westwood Memorial Park, Los Angeles, California, USA	—
Hollywood, California, USA	52	Heart attack	Garden of Actors Churchyard, London, England	Geraldine Higgins, Susie Welles, Elizabeth Farnesworth, Virginia Field, Jan Sterling
Los Angeles, California, USA	22	Homicide (strangulation)	Westwood Memorial Park, Los Angeles, California, USA	John Sweeney (partner)
San Diego, California, USA	20	Complications from congenital heart condition	Forest Lawn–Hollywood Hills, Los Angeles, California, USA	—
Santa Monica, California, USA	40	Cancer	Mount Pleasant Cemetery, Bangor, Maine, USA	—
Santa Monica, California, USA	56	Heart attack	Hollywood Forever Cemetery, California, USA	Anna Beth Sully, Mary Pickford, Sylvia Ashley
Chicago, Illinois, USA	33	Drug overdose	Resurrection Cemetery, Madison, Wisconsin, USA	—
Indianapolis, Indiana, USA	56	Throat cancer	Oaklawn Memorial Gardens Cemetery, Fishers, Indiana, USA	Leif Erickson, Alfred Lobley, Leland Mikesell
Lincoln, New Mexico, USA	80	Suicide (gunshot)	Forest Lawn–Hollywood Hills, Los Angeles, California, USA	Maggie Farnsworth, Jewely Van Valin (fiancée)
Mexico City, Mexico	49	Heart attack after food poisoning	Forest Lawn–Hollywood Hills, Los Angeles, California, USA	Lauretta Sullivan
Hyannis, Massachusetts, USA	60	Cerebral hemorrhage	Cremated	Elmer Rice, Edwin Lukas, Raymond Olivare
Vancouver, British Columbia, Canada	50	Heart attack	Forest Lawn Memorial Park, Glendale, California, USA	Lili Damita, Nora Eddington, Patrice Wymore
Chi Pou, Cambodia	28	Disappeared, believed murdered	Body never recovered	—
Los Angeles, California, USA	59	Heart attack	Forest Lawn Memorial Park, Glendale, California, USA	Josephine Dillon, Maria Langham, Carole Lombard, Sylvia Ashley, Kay Spreckles
New York, New York, USA	39	Heart attack	Westchester Hills Cemetery, Hastings-on-Hudson, New York, USA	Roberta Siedman
London, England	47	Barbiturate overdose	Ferncliff Cemetery and Mausoleum, Hartsdale, New York, USA	David Rose, Vincente Minnelli, Sidney Luft, Mark Herron, Mickey Deans
Woodland Hills, California, USA	52	Pancreatic cancer	Cremated	Richard Hayes, Albert Salmi, Kenyon Foster Brown
Los Angeles, California, USA	54	Cerebral hemorrhage or stroke	Pierce Brothers Valhalla Memorial Park, Hollywood, California, USA	Ben Erway, Edward Fowler, Leonard Penn, Kenneth Bradley
Los Angeles, California, USA	36	Heart attack	Forest Lawn Memorial Park, Glendale, California, USA	Olivia Burwell, Leatrice Joy, Ina Claire, Virginia Bruce
Hollywood, California, USA	40	Accidental drug overdose	Cremated	Ruthann Goddard
Hollywood, California, USA	45	Alcohol-induced hepatitis	Cremated, ashes scattered over the Pacific Ocean	Lyudmilla Vlasova, Jacqueline Bisset (partner)
Santa Monica, California, USA	56	Lung cancer	Inglewood Park Cemetery, Inglewood, California, USA	Jackie Coogan, Harry James
New York, New York, USA	57	Breast cancer	Oakwood Memorial Park, Chatsworth, California, USA	Stanley Clements, Nicholas Ray, Cy Howard, Tony Ray

Professional Name	Birth Name	Nickname	Date of Birth	Place of Birth	Date of Death
Gilda Gray	Marianna Michalska	The Shimmy Queen, The Queen of the Shimmy Shakers	October 24, 1901	Krakow, Poland	December 22, 1959
Spalding Gray	Spalding Gray	—	June 5, 1941	Providence, Rhode Island, USA	January 10, 2004
Mitzi Green	Mitzi Green	—	October 22, 1920	Bronx, New York, USA	May 24, 1969
Sigrid Gurie	Sigrid Gurie Haukelid	Siren of the Fjords, The Norwegian Garbo	May 18, 1911	Brooklyn, New York, USA	August 14, 1969
Joan Hackett	Joan Ann Hackett	—	March 1, 1934	East Harlem, New York, USA	October 8, 1983
Jean Hagen	Jean Shirley Verhagen	—	August 3, 1923	Chicago, Illinois, USA	August 29, 1977
Jonathan Hale	Jonathan Hatley	—	March 21, 1891	Ontario, Canada	February 28, 1966
Jon Hall	Charles Hall Locher	The King of Technicolor	February 23, 1913	Fresno, California, USA	December 13, 1979
Carrie Hamilton	Carrie Louise Hamilton	—	December 5, 1963	New York, New York, USA	January 20, 2002
Jean Harlow	Harlean Carpenter	The Platinum Blonde	March 3, 1911	Kansas City, Missouri, USA	June 7, 1937
Cassandra Harris	Sandra Colleen Waites	—	December 15, 1952	Sydney, New South Wales, Australia	December 28, 1991
Mildred Harris	Mildred Harris	—	November 29, 1901	Cheyenne, Wyoming, USA	July 20, 1944
Phil Hartman	Philip Edward Hartmann	The Sultan of Smarm	September 24, 1948	Brantford, Ontario, Canada	May 28, 1998
Laurence Harvey	Hirshke Skikne	—	October 1, 1928	Jonischkis, Lithuania	November 25, 1973
Allison Hayes	Mary Jane Hayes	—	March 6, 1930	Charleston, West Virginia, USA	February 27, 1977
Susan Hayward	Edythe Marrener	—	June 30, 1918	Brooklyn, New York, USA	March 14, 1975
Margaux Hemingway	Margot Louise Hemingway	—	February 16, 1955	Portland, Oregon, USA	July 1, 1996
Wanda Hendrix	Dixie Wanda Hendrix	—	November 3, 1928	Jacksonville, Florida, USA	February 1, 1981
Sonja Henie	Sonja Henie	—	April 8, 1912	Kristiania (Oslo), Norway	October 12, 1969
Gregory Hines	Gregory Oliver Hines	Pied Piper of Tap	February 14, 1946	New York, New York, USA	August 9, 2003
John Hodiak	John Hodiak	—	April 16, 1914	Pittsburgh, Pennsylvania, USA	October 19, 1955
William Holden	William Franklin Beedle, Jr.	The Golden Boy	April 17, 1918	O'Fallon, Illinois, USA	November 16, 1981
Judy Holliday	Judith Tuvim	—	June 21, 1921	New York, New York, USA	June 7, 1965
Darla Hood	Darla Jean Hood	—	November 8, 1931	Leedey, Oklahoma, USA	June 13, 1979
Allen Hoskins	Allen Clayton Hoskins	"Farina"	August 9, 1920	Boston Massachusetts, USA	July 26, 1980
Leslie Howard	Leslie Howard Stainer	—	April 3, 1893	London, England	June 1, 1943
Rock Hudson	Roy Harold Scherer, Jr.	Beefcake Baron	November 17, 1925	Winnetka, Illinois, USA	October 2, 1985
Jeffrey Hunter	Henry Herman McKinnies, Jr.	—	November 25, 1926	New Orleans, Louisiana, USA	May 27, 1969
Robert Hutchins	Robert E. Hutchins	"Wheezer"	March 29, 1925	Tacoma, Washington, USA	March 17, 1945
Jim Hutton	Dana James Hutton	—	May 31, 1934	Binghamton, New York, USA	June 2, 1979
Michael Jeter	Michael Jeter	—	August 26, 1952	Lawrenceburg, Tennessee, USA	March 30, 2003
Rita Johnson	Rita McSean	—	August 13, 1913	Worcester, Massachusetts, USA	October 31, 1965
Carolyn Jones	Carolyn Sue Baker	—	April 28, 1929	Amarillo, Texas, USA	August 3, 1983

Place of Death	Age at Death	Cause of Death	Place of Burial	Spouse(s)/Partner(s)
Hollywood, California, USA	58	Heart attack	Holy Cross Cemetery, Culver City, California, USA	John Gorecki, Gaillard T. Boag, Hector de Briceno
New York, New York, USA	62	Suicide (drowned)	Cremated	Renée Shafransky, Kathleen Russo
Huntington Beach, California, USA	48	Cancer	Eden Memorial Park, San Fernando, California, USA	Joseph Pevney
Mexico City, Mexico	58	Embolism	Unknown	Thomas H. Stewart, Dr. Lawrence Spangard, Lynn Abbott
Encino, California, USA	49	Ovarian cancer	Hollywood Forever Cemetery, California, USA	Richard Mulligan
Los Angeles, California, USA	54	Throat cancer	Chapel of the Pines Crematory, Los Angeles, California, USA	Tom Seidel
Woodland Hills, California, USA	74	Suicide (gunshot)	Pierce Brothers Valhalla Memorial Park, Hollywood, California, USA	Unknown
Hollywood, California, USA	66	Suicide (gunshot)	Forest Lawn–Hollywood Hills, Los Angeles, California, USA	Frances Langford, Raquel Torres
Los Angeles, California, USA	38	Pneumonia, and lung and brain cancer	Westwood Memorial Park, Los Angeles, California, USA	Mark Templin
Los Angeles, California, USA	26	Kidney failure and uremic poisoning	Forest Lawn Memorial Park, Glendale, California, USA	Charles Fremont McGrew, Paul Bern, Harold Rosson, William Powell (fiancé)
Los Angeles, California, USA	39	Ovarian cancer	Cremated	Dermot Harris, Pierce Brosnan
Hollywood, California, USA	42	Pneumonia	Hollywood Forever Cemetery, California, USA	Charles Chaplin, Eldridge T. McGovern, William K. Fleckenstein
Encino, California, USA	49	Homicide (gunshot)	Cremated, ashes scattered over Catalina Island	Gretchen Lewis, Lisa Strain, Brynn Hartman
London, England	45	Cancer	Santa Barbara Cemetery, Santa Barbara, California, USA	Margaret Leighton, Joan Perry, Pauline Stone
La Jolla, California, USA	46	Blood poisoning	Holy Cross Cemetery, Culver City, California, USA	Unknown
Hollywood, California, USA	56	Brain tumors	Our Lady of Perpetual Help Cemetery, Carrollton, Georgia, USA	Jess Barker, Floyd Eaton Chalkley
Santa Monica, California, USA	41	Suicide (overdose of barbiturates)	Ketchum Cemetery, Ketchum, Idaho, USA	Erroll Wetson, Bernard Foucher
Burbank, California, USA	52	Pneumonia	Forest Lawn–Hollywood Hills, Los Angeles, California, USA	Audie Murphy, James Stack, Steve LaMonte
En route by plane to Oslo from Paris	57	Leukemia	Hilltop near Henie–Onstad Museum, Oslo, Norway	Dan Topping, Winthrop Gardner, Niels Onstad
Los Angeles, California, USA	57	Liver cancer	Saint Volodymyr's Ukrainian Catholic Cemetery, Oakville, Ontario, Canada	Patricia Panella, Pamela Koslow, Negrita Jayde (fiancée)
Tarzana, California, USA	41	Heart attack	Calvary Cemetery, Los Angeles, California, USA	Anne Baxter
Santa Monica, California, USA	63	Head injury from fall	Cremated, ashes scattered over the Pacific Ocean	Brenda Marshall, Stefanie Powers (partner)
New York, New York, USA	43	Breast cancer	Westchester Hills Cemetery, Hastings-on-Hudson, New York, USA	Dave Oppenheim
Hollywood, California, USA	47	Hepatitis	Hollywood Forever Cemetery, California, USA	José Granson
Oakland, California, USA	59	Cancer	Evergreen Cemetery, Oakland, California, USA	—
Bay of Biscay	50	Plane crash	Body never recovered	Ruth Evelyn Martin
Beverly Hills, California, USA	59	AIDS complications	Cremated, ashes scattered at sea	Phyllis Gates, Marc Christian (partner)
Los Angeles, California, USA	42	Head injury from fall	Glen Haven Memorial Park, Sylmar, California, USA	Barbara Rush, Joan Bartlett, Emily McLaughlin
Merced, California, USA	19	Plane crash	Trinity Lutheran Church, Tacoma, Washington, USA	—
Los Angeles, California, USA	45	Liver cancer	Westwood Memorial Park, Los Angeles, California, USA	Maryline Adams
Los Angeles, California, USA	50	Epileptic seizure	Cremated	—
Hollywood, California, USA	52	Brain hemorrhage	Holy Cross Cemetery, Culver City, California, USA	L. Stanley Kahn, Edwin Hutzler
Hollywood, California, USA	54	Colon cancer	Melrose Abbey Memorial Park, Anaheim, California, USA	Aaron Spelling, Herbert S. Greene, Peter Bailey-Britton

Professional Name	Birth Name	Nickname	Date of Birth	Place of Birth	Date of Death
Bobby Jordan	Robert Jordan	—	April 1, 1923	Harrison, New York, USA	September 10, 1965
Richard Jordan	Robert Anson Jordan	—	July 19, 1938	New York, New York, USA	August 30, 1993
Raul Julia	Raul Rafael Carlos Julia y Arcelay	—	March 9, 1940	San Juan, Puerto Rico	October 24, 1994
Madeline Kahn	Madeline Gail Wolfson	—	September 29, 1942	Boston, Massachusetts, USA	December 3, 1999
Brian Keith	Robert Keith Richey, Jr.	—	November 14, 1921	Bayonne, New Jersey, USA	June 24, 1997
Grace Kelly	Grace Patricia Kelly	—	November 12, 1929	Philadelphia, Pennsylvania, USA	September 14, 1982
Kay Kendall	Kay Justine Kendall McCarthy	—	May 21, 1926	Withernsea, England	September 6, 1959
Mary Kornman	Mary Kornman	—	December 27, 1915	Idaho Falls, Idaho, USA	June 1, 1973
Ernie Kovacs	Ernest E. Kovacs	—	January 23, 1919	Trenton, New Jersey, USA	January 13, 1962
Barbara La Marr	Reatha Dale Watson	The Too Beautiful Girl	July 28, 1896	Yakima, Washington, USA	January 30, 1926
Alan Ladd	Alan Walbridge Ladd	—	September 3, 1913	Hot Springs, Arkansas, USA	January 29, 1964
Veronica Lake	Constance Frances Marie Ockleman	The Peek-a-boo Girl	November 14, 1922	Brooklyn, New York, USA	July 7, 1973
Elissa Landi	Elizabeth Marie Christine Kühnelt	—	December 6, 1904	Venice, Italy	October 21, 1948
Carole Landis	Frances Lillian Mary Ridste	The Ping Girl, The Sweater Girl	January 1, 1919	Fairchild, Wisconsin, USA	July 5, 1948
Michael Landon	Eugene Maurice Orowitz	—	October 31, 1936	Forest Hills, New York, USA	July 1, 1991
Mario Lanza	Alfredo Arnold Cocozza	The Tiger, The Service Caruso	January 31, 1921	Philadelphia, Pennsylvania, USA	October 7, 1959
William Laughlin	William Robert Laughlin	"Froggy"	July 5, 1932	San Gabriel, California, USA	August 31, 1948
Gertrude Lawrence	Gertrude Alexandria Dagmar Lawrence-Klasen	—	July 4, 1898	London, England	September 6, 1952
Brandon Lee	Brandon Bruce Lee	—	February 1, 1965	Oakland, California, USA	March 31, 1993
Bruce Lee	Lee Jun-Fan	—	November 27, 1940	San Francisco, California, USA	July 20, 1973
Vivien Leigh	Vivian Mary Hartley	—	November 5, 1913	Darjeeling, India	July 7, 1967
Ormer Locklear	Ormer Locklear	—	October 28, 1891	Greenville, Texas, USA	August 2, 1920
Carole Lombard	Jane Alice Peters	The Profane Angel, The Hoosier Tornado	October 6, 1908	Fort Wayne, Indiana, USA	January 16, 1942
Peter Lorre	László Löewenstein	The Walking Overcoat	June 26, 1904	Rózsahegy, Hungary	March 23, 1964
Bela Lugosi	Béla Ferenc Dezsõ Blaskó	—	October 20, 1882	Lugos, Hungary	August 16, 1956
Diana Lynn	Dolores Loehr	—	October 7, 1926	Los Angeles, California, USA	December 18, 1971
Hattie McDaniel	Hattie McDaniel	The Colored Sophie Tucker	June 10, 1895	Wichita, Kansas, USA	October 26, 1952
Lawrence McKeen	Lawrence David McKeen, Jr.	Sunny McKeen	September 1, 1924	Los Angeles, California, USA	April 2, 1933
Nina Mae McKinney	Nannie Mayme McKinney	The Black Garbo	June 12, 1912	Lancaster, South Carolina, USA	May 3, 1967
Maggie McNamara	Margaret McNamara	—	June 18, 1928	New York, New York, USA	February 18, 1978
Butterfly McQueen	Thelma McQueen	—	January 7, 1911	Tampa, Florida, USA	December 22, 1995
Steve McQueen	Terence Steven McQueen	The King of Cool	March 24, 1930	Indianapolis, Indiana, USA	November 7, 1980
Silvana Mangano	Silvana Mangano	—	April 21, 1930	Rome, Italy	December 16, 1989

Place of Death	Age at Death	Cause of Death	Place of Burial	Spouse(s)/Partner(s)
Los Angeles, California, USA	42	Cirrhosis of the liver	Los Angeles National Cemetery, California, USA	Lee Jordan
Los Angeles, California, USA	55	Brain tumor	Cremated, ashes scattered on his Californian property	Kathleen Widdoes, Blair Brown (partner), Marcia Cross (partner)
Mahasset, New York, USA	54	Stroke	Buxeda Cemetery, San Juan, Puerto Rico	Magda Vasallo, Merel Poloway
New York, New York, USA	57	Ovarian cancer	Cremated	John Hansbury
Malibu, California, USA	75	Suicide (gunshot)	Westwood Memorial Park, Los Angeles, California, USA	Frances Helm, Judy Landon, Victoria Young
Monte Carlo, Monaco	52	Car accident	Cathedral of St. Nicholas, Monte Carlo, Monaco	Prince Rainier of Monaco
London, England	33	Leukemia	Saint John's Churchyard, London, England	Rex Harrison
Glendale, California, USA	57	Cancer	Linn Grove Cemetery, Greeley, Colorado, USA	Leo Tover, Ralph McCutcheon
Beverly Hills, California, USA	42	Car accident	Forest Lawn–Hollywood Hills, Los Angeles, California, USA	Bette Lee Wilcox, Edie Adams
Altadena, California, USA	29	Anorexia	Hollywood Forever Cemetery, California, USA	Jack Lytell, Lawrence Converse, Phil Ainsworth, Ben Deeley, Jack Dougherty
Palm Springs, California, USA	50	Suicide (drug overdose)	Forest Lawn Memorial Park, Glendale, California, USA	Marjorie Harrold, Sue Carol
Burlington, Vermont, USA	50	Hepatitis	Cremated, ashes scattered in the sea around the Virgin Islands	John S. Detlie, André de Toth, Joseph A. McCarthy, Robert Carleton-Munro
Kingston, New York, USA	43	Cancer	Oak Hill Cemetery, Newburyport, Massachusetts, USA	John Cecil Lawrence, Curtiss Thomas
Pacific Palisades, California, USA	29	Suicide (drug overdose)	Forest Lawn Memorial Park, Glendale, California, USA	Irving Wheeler, Willis Hunt, Jr., Thomas C. Wallace, W. Horace Schmidlapp
Malibu, California, USA	54	Pancreatic cancer	Hillside Memorial Park, Culver City, California, USA	Dodie Frasier, Marjorie Lynn Noe, Cindy Clerico
Rome, Italy	38	Heart attack	Holy Cross Cemetery, Culver City, California, USA	Betty Hicks
La Puente, California, USA	16	Motor scooter accident	Rose Hills Memorial Park, Whittier, California, USA	—
New York, New York, USA	54	Liver cancer	Lakeview Cemetery, Upton, Massachusetts, USA	Francis Gordon-Howley, Richard Aldrich
Wilmington, North Carolina, USA	28	Accidental gunshot wound	Lake View Cemetery, Seattle, Washington, USA	Eliza Hutton (fiancée)
Hong Kong	32	Cerebral edema	Lake View Cemetery, Seattle, Washington, USA	Linda Emery
London, England	53	Tuberculosis	Cremated, ashes scattered on a lake on her property in Sussex, England	Herbert Leigh Holman, Laurence Olivier, John Merivale (partner)
Los Angeles, California, USA	28	Plane crash	Greenwood Memorial Park, Fort Worth, Texas, USA	Viola Dana, Ruby Graves
Table Rock Mountain, Nevada, USA	33	Plane crash	Forest Lawn Memorial Park, Glendale, California, USA	William Powell, Clark Gable
Los Angeles, California, USA	59	Stroke	Hollywood Forever Cemetery, California, USA	Celia Lovsky, Kaaren Verne, Annemarie Brenning
Los Angeles, California, USA	73	Heart attack	Holy Cross Cemetery, Culver City, California, USA	Ilona Szmik, Ilona von Montagh, Beatrice Weeks, Lilian Arch, Hope Lininger
Los Angeles, California, USA	45	Stroke	Episcopal Church of the Heavenly Rest, Manhattan, New York, USA	John C. Lindsay, Mortimer W. Hall
Woodland Hills, California, USA	57	Breast cancer	Angelus Rosedale Cemetery, Los Angeles, California, USA	George Langford, Howard C. Hickman, James Lloyd Crawford, Larry Williams
Los Angeles, California, USA	8	Blood poisoning	Forest Lawn Memorial Park, Glendale, California, USA	—
New York, New York, USA	54	Heart attack	Unknown	Jimmy Monroe
New York, New York, USA	49	Suicide (drug overdose)	Saint Charles Cemetery, Farmingdale, New York, USA	David Swift
Augusta, Georgia, USA	84	Burns from a faulty heater	Body donated to medical science	Unknown
Juárez, Mexico	50	Lung cancer	Cremated, ashes scattered over the Pacific Ocean	Neile Adams, Ali MacGraw, Barbara Minty
Madrid, Spain	59	Lung cancer	Pawling Cemetery, Pawling, New York, USA	Dino De Laurentiis

Professional Name	Birth Name	Nickname	Date of Birth	Place of Birth	Date of Death
Jayne Mansfield	Vera Jayne Palmer	The Poor Man's Marilyn Monroe	April 19, 1933	Bryn Mawr, Pennsylvania, USA	June 29, 1967
Marilyn Maxwell	Marvel Marilyn Maxwell	—	August 3, 1921	Clarinda, Iowa, USA	March 20, 1972
Sal Mineo	Salvatore Mineo, Jr.	The Switchblade Kid	January 10, 1939	Bronx, New York, USA	February 12, 1976
Carmen Miranda	Maria do Carmo Miranda da Cunha	The Brazilian Bombshell	February 9, 1909	Marco de Canavezes, Portugal	August 5, 1955
Tom Mix	Thomas Hezikiah Mix	King of the Cowboys	January 6, 1880	Mix Run, Pennsylvania, USA	October 12, 1940
Marilyn Monroe	Norma Jean Mortenson	—	June 1, 1926	Los Angeles, California, USA	August 5, 1962
Maria Montez	Maria Africa Antonia Gracia Vidal de Santo Silas	The Caribbean Cyclone, The Queen of Technicolor	June 6, 1912	Barahona, Dominican Republic	September 7, 1951
Cleo Moore	Cleouna Moore	—	October 31, 1928	Baton Rouge, Louisiana, USA	October 25, 1973
Grace Moore	Mary Willie Grace Moore	The Tennessee Nightingale	December 5, 1898	Slabtown, Tennessee, USA	January 26, 1947
Agnes Moorehead	Agnes Robertson Moorehead	The Lavender Lady	December 6, 1900	Clinton, Massachusetts, USA	April 30, 1974
Peggy Moran	Mary Jeanette Moran	—	October 23, 1918	Clinton, Iowa, USA	October 25, 2002
Frank Morgan	Francis Philip Wuppermann	—	June 1, 1890	New York, New York, USA	September 18, 1949
Vic Morrow	Victor Morrow	—	February 14, 1929	Bronx, New York, USA	July 23, 1982
Herbert Mundin	Herbert Mundin	—	August 21, 1898	St. Helens, Lancashire, England	March 5, 1939
Janet Munro	Janet Neilson Horsburgh	—	September 28, 1934	Blackpool, Lancashire, England	December 6, 1972
Jules Munshin	Jules Munshin	—	February 22, 1915	New York, New York, USA	February 19, 1970
Ona Munson	Owena Wolcott	—	June 16, 1903	Portland, Oregon, USA	February 11, 1955
Audie Murphy	Audie Leon Murphy	—	June 20, 1924	Kingston, Texas, USA	May 28, 1971
Haing S. Ngor	Haing S. Ngor	—	March 22, 1940	Samrong Young, Cambodia	February 25, 1996
Barbara Nichols	Barbara Marie Nickerauer	—	December 30, 1929	Queens, New York, USA	October 5, 1976
Mabel Normand	Mabel Ethelreid Normand	Queen of Comedy	November 16, 1892	New Brighton, New York, USA	February 22, 1930
Ramon Novarro	Ramón Gil Samaniego	The Latin Lover	February 6, 1899	Durango, Mexico	October 30, 1968
Cathy O'Donnell	Ann Steely	—	July 6, 1925	Siluria, Alabama, USA	April 11, 1970
Heather O'Rourke	Heather Michele O'Rourke	—	December 27, 1975	San Diego, California, USA	February 1, 1988
Helen Parrish	Helen Parrish	—	March 12, 1924	Columbus, Georgia, USA	February 22, 1959
Robert Pastorelli	Robert Joseph Pastorelli	—	June 21, 1954	New Brunswick, New Jersey, USA	March 8, 2004
Luana Patten	Luana Patten	—	July 6, 1938	Long Beach, California, USA	May 1, 1996
Alice Pearce	Alice Pearce	—	October 16, 1917	New York, New York, USA	March 3, 1966
Anthony Perkins	Anthony Perkins	—	April 4, 1932	New York, New York, USA	September 12, 1992
Susan Peters	Suzanne Carnahan	—	July 3, 1921	Spokane, Washington, USA	October 23, 1952
River Phoenix	River Jude Bottom	—	August 23, 1970	Madras, Oregon, USA	October 31, 1993
Jack Pickford	John Charles Smith	—	August 18, 1896	Toronto, Ontario, Canada	January 3, 1933
Dick Powell	Richard Ewing Powell	—	November 14, 1904	Mountain View, Arkansas, USA	January 2, 1963
Tyrone Power	Tyrone Edmund Power, Jr.	—	May 5, 1913	Cincinnati, Ohio, USA	November 15, 1958
Elvis Presley	Elvis Aaron Presley	The King of Rock 'n' Roll	January 8, 1935	Tupelo, Mississippi, USA	August 16, 1977

Place of Death	Age at Death	Cause of Death	Place of Burial	Spouse(s)/Partner(s)
near New Orleans, Louisiana, USA	34	Car accident	Fairview Cemetery, Pen Argyl, Pennsylvania, USA	Paul Mansfield, Mickey Hargitay, Matt Cimber
Beverly Hills, California, USA	50	Heart attack	Cremated, ashes scattered at sea	John Conte, Andy McIntyre, Jerry Davis
Hollywood, California, USA	37	Homicide (stabbing)	Cemetery of the Gate of Heaven, Hawthorne, New York, USA	Jill Haworth (fiancée)
Beverly Hills, California, USA	46	Heart attack	Cemitério São João Batista, Rio de Janeiro, Brazil	David Sebastian
Florence, Arizona, USA	60	Car accident	Forest Lawn Memorial Park, Glendale, California, USA	Grace Allin, Kitty Jewel Perinne, Olive Stokes, Victoria Forde, Mabel Hubbard Ward
Los Angeles, California, USA	36	Drug overdose	Westwood Memorial Park, Los Angeles, California, USA	James Dougherty, Joe DiMaggio, Arthur Miller
Paris, France	39	Heart attack	Cimetière du Montparnasse, Paris, France	William McFeeters, Jean-Pierre Aumont
Inglewood, California, USA	44	Heart attack	Inglewood Park Cemetery, Inglewood, California, USA	Palmer Long, Herbert Heftler
Copenhagen, Denmark	48	Plane crash	Forest Hills Cemetery, Chattanooga, Tennessee, USA	Valentin Parera
Rochester, Minnesota, USA	73	Lung cancer	Dayton Memorial Park, Dayton, Ohio, USA	Jack G. Lee, Robert Gist
Camarillo, California, USA	84	Injuries received in earlier car accident	Cremated, ashes scattered at sea	Henry Koster
Beverly Hills, California, USA	59	Natural causes (in his sleep)	Green–Wood Cemetery, Brooklyn, New York, USA	Alma Muller
Indian Dunes, California, USA	53	Helicopter accident	Hillside Memorial Park, Culver City, California, USA	Barbara Turner
Van Nuys, California, USA	40	Car accident	Inglewood Park Cemetery, Inglewood, California, USA	Unknown
London, England	38	Acute myocarditis	Golders Gate Crematorium, London, England	Tony Wright, Ian Hendry
New York, New York, USA	54	Heart attack	Long Island National Cemetery, New York, USA	Bonnie Brandon
New York, New York, USA	51	Suicide (drug overdose)	Ferncliff Cemetery and Mausoleum, Hartsdale, New York, USA	Edward Buzzell, Stewart McDonald, Eugene Berman
near Roanoke, Virginia, USA	46	Plane crash	Arlington National Cemetery, Virginia, USA	Wanda Hendrix, Pamela Archer
Los Angeles, California, USA	55	Homicide (gunshot)	Rose Hills Memorial Park, Whittier, California, USA	Huoy Ngor
Hollywood, California, USA	46	Liver disease	Pinelawn Memorial Park, Pinelawn, New York, USA	—
Monrovia, California, USA	37	Tuberculosis	Calvary Cemetery, Los Angeles, California, USA	Mack Sennett (fiancé), Lew Cody
Hollywood, California, USA	69	Homicide (beaten to death)	Calvary Cemetery, Los Angeles, California, USA	—
Los Angeles, California, USA	44	Cerebral hemorrhage	Forest Lawn Memorial Park, Glendale, California, USA	Robert Wyler
San Diego, California, USA	12	Cardiopulmonary arrest	Westwood Memorial Park, Los Angeles, California, USA	—
Hollywood, California, USA	34	Cancer	Hollywood Forever Cemetery, California, USA	Charles Lang, Jr., John Guedel
Hollywood, California, USA	49	Accidental drug overdose	St. Catharine's Cemetery, Sea Girt, New Jersey, USA	Charemon Jonovich (partner)
Long Beach, California, USA	57	Respiratory failure	Forest Lawn–Long Beach, California, USA	John Smith
Hollywood, California, USA	48	Ovarian cancer	Cremated, ashes scattered at sea	John Rox, Paul Davies
Hollywood, California, USA	60	AIDS-related pneumonia	Cremated	Berry Berenson
Visalia, California, USA	31	Starvation, kidney ailment, pneumonia	Forest Lawn Memorial Park, Glendale, California, USA	Richard Quine
Hollywood, California, USA	23	Drug overdose	Cremated, ashes scattered at the family's ranch in Florida, USA	—
Paris, France	36	Progressive multiple neuritis	Forest Lawn Memorial Park, Glendale, California, USA	Olive Thomas, Marilyn Miller, Mary Mulhern
Los Angeles, California, USA	58	Stomach cancer	Forest Lawn Memorial Park, Glendale, California, USA	Maude Maund, Joan Blondell, June Allyson
Madrid, Spain	45	Heart attack	Hollywood Forever Cemetery, California, USA	Anabella Power, Linda Christian, Debbie Ann Minardos
Memphis, Tennessee, USA	42	Drug-induced heart attack	Graceland Estate, Memphis, Tennessee, USA	Priscilla Ann Beaulieu, Ginger Alden (fiancée)

Professional Name	Birth Name	Nickname	Date of Birth	Place of Birth	Date of Death
Marie Prevost	Mary Bickford Dunn	—	November 8, 1898	Sarnia, Ontario, Canada	January 23, 1937
Gilda Radner	Gilda Radner	—	June 28, 1946	Detroit, Michigan, USA	May 20, 1989
Charles Ray	Charles Edgar Alfred Ray	—	March 15, 1891	Jacksonville, Illinois, USA	November 23, 1943
Oliver Reed	Robert Oliver Reed	—	February 13, 1938	Wimbledon, England	May 2, 1999
Robert Reed	John Robert Rietz	—	October 19, 1932	Highland Park, Illinois, USA	May 12, 1992
Christopher Reeve	Christopher Reeve	—	September 25, 1952	New York, New York, USA	October 10, 2004
George Reeves	George Keefer Brewer	—	January 5, 1914	Woolstock, Iowa, USA	June 16, 1959
Wallace Reid	William Wallace Reid	—	April 15, 1891	St. Louis, Missouri, USA	January 18, 1923
Lee Remick	Lee Remick	—	December 14, 1935	Quincy, Massachusetts, USA	July 2, 1991
John Ritter	Jonathan Southworth Ritter	—	September 17, 1948	Burbank, California, USA	September 11, 2003
Hal Roach	Harry Eugene Roach	—	January 14, 1892	Elmira, New York, USA	November 2, 1992
Rachel Roberts	Rachel Roberts	—	September 20, 1927	Llanelli, Wales	November 26, 1980
Will Rogers	William Penn Adair Rogers	—	November 4, 1879	Oologah, Oklahoma (was Indian Territory), USA	August 15, 1935
Ruth Roland	Ruth Roland	Queen of the Thriller Serials	August 26, 1892	San Francisco, California, USA	September 22, 1937
Gail Russell	Gail Russell	—	September 21, 1924	Chicago, Illinois, USA	August 26, 1961
Sabu	Sabu Dastagir	—	January 27, 1924	Karapur, Mysore, India	December 2, 1963
George Sanders	George Sanders	—	July 3, 1906	St. Petersburg, Russia	April 25, 1972
Zachary Scott	Zachary Thomson Scott, Jr.	—	February 24, 1914	Austin, Texas, USA	October 3, 1965
Dorothy Sebastian	Dorothy Sabiston	Little Alabam	April 26, 1903	Birmingham, Alabama, USA	April 8, 1957
Jean Seberg	Jean Seberg	—	November 13, 1938	Marshalltown, Iowa, USA	September 8, 1979
Peter Sellers	Richard Henry Sellars	—	September 8, 1925	Southsea, Hampshire, England	July 24, 1980
Peggy Shannon	Winona Sammon	—	January 10, 1910	Pine Bluff, Arkansas, USA	May 11, 1941
Robert Shaw	Robert Shaw	—	August 9, 1927	Westhoughton, Lancashire, England	August 28, 1978
Ann Sheridan	Clara Lou Sheridan	The Oomph Girl	February 21, 1915	Denton, Texas, USA	January 21, 1967
Elizabeth Short	Elizabeth Short	The Black Dahlia	July 29, 1924	Hyde Park, Massachusetts, USA	January 14, 1947
Milton Sills	Milton Sills	—	January 12, 1882	Chicago, Illinois, USA	September 15, 1930
Frank Silvera	Frank Silvera	—	July 24, 1914	Kingston, Jamaica	June 11, 1970
Walter Slezak	Walter Slezak	—	May 3, 1902	Vienna, Austria	April 21, 1983
Everett Sloane	Everett Sloane	—	October 1, 1909	New York, New York, USA	August 6, 1965
Inger Stevens	Inger Stensland	—	October 18, 1934	Stockholm, Sweden	April 30, 1970
Anita Stewart	Anna Stewart	—	February 7, 1895	Brooklyn, New York, USA	May 4, 1961
David Strickland	David Gordon Strickland, Jr.	—	October 14, 1969	Glen Cove, New York, USA	March 22, 1999
Margaret Sullavan	Margaret Brooke Sullavan	—	May 16, 1911	Norfolk, Virginia, USA	January 1, 1960

Place of Death	Age at Death	Cause of Death	Place of Burial	Spouse(s)/Partner(s)
Hollywood, California, USA	38	Alcoholism and malnutrition	Unknown (pauper's grave)	Kenneth Harlan
Los Angeles, California, USA	42	Ovarian cancer	Long Ridge Union Cemetery, Stamford, Connecticut, USA	G. E. Smith, Gene Wilder
Los Angeles, California, USA	52	Tooth infection	Forest Lawn Memorial Park, Glendale, California, USA	Clare Grant, Yvonne Guerin
Valletta, Malta	61	Heart attack	Bruhenny Graveyard, Buttevant, Ireland	Kate Burn, Jackie Daryl, Josephine Burge
Pasadena, California, USA	59	Colon cancer	Memorial Park Cemetery, Skokie, Illinois, USA	Marilyn Rosenberg
Mount Kisco, New York, USA	52	Cardiac failure	Cremated	Gae Exton (partner), Dana Morosini
Beverly Hills, California, USA	45	Suicide (gunshot)	Mountain View Cemetery, Altadena, California, USA	Ellanora Needles, Lenore Lemmon (fiancée)
Los Angeles, California, USA	31	Drug addiction and influenza	Forest Lawn Memorial Park, Glendale, California, USA	Dorothy Davenport
Los Angeles, California, USA	55	Cancer of the kidney and lungs	Cremated	William Colleran, William "Kip" Gowans
Burbank, California, USA	54	Aortic dissection	Forest Lawn–Hollywood Hills, Los Angeles, California, USA	Nancy Morgan, Amy Yasbeck
Los Angeles, California, USA	100	Pneumonia	Woodlawn Cemetery, Elmira, New York, USA	Marguerite Nichols, Lucille Prin
Los Angeles, California, USA	53	Barbiturate poisoning	Cremated, ashes scattered over the Thames River, London, England	Alan Dobie, Rex Harrison
near Point Barrow, Alaska, USA	55	Plane crash	Will Rogers Memorial Museum, Claremore, Oklahoma, USA	Betty Blake
Hollywood, California, USA	45	Cancer	Forest Lawn Memorial Park, Glendale, California, USA	Lionel T. Kent, Ben Bard
Los Angeles, California, USA	36	Alcohol-induced liver damage and malnutrition	Pierce Brothers Valhalla Memorial Park, Hollywood, California, USA	Guy Madison
Chatsworth, California, USA	39	Heart attack	Forest Lawn–Hollywood Hills, Los Angeles, California, USA	Brenda Julien (fiancée), Marilyn Cooper
Barcelona, Spain	65	Suicide (overdose of Nembutal)	Cremated, ashes scattered over the English Channel	Susan Larson, Zsa Zsa Gabor, Benita Hume, Magda Gabor
Austin, Texas, USA	51	Brain tumor	Austin Memorial Park, Austin, Texas, USA	Elaine Anderson, Ruth Ford
Woodland Hills, California, USA	53	Cancer	Holy Cross Cemetery, Culver City, California, USA	William Boyd, Herman Shapiro
Paris, France	40	Suicide (barbiturate overdose)	Cimetière du Montparnasse, Paris, France	François Moreuil, Romain Gary, Dennis Berry, Ahmed Hasmi
London, England	54	Heart attack	Golders Green Crematorium, London, England	Anne Howe, Britt Ekland, Miranda Quarry, Lynne Frederick
Hollywood, California, USA	31	Acute alcoholism	Hollywood Forever Cemetery, California, USA	Alan Davis, Albert G. Roberts
Tourmakeady, Ireland	51	Heart attack	Cremated, ashes scattered near his Irish home	Jennifer Bourke, Mary Ure, Virginia Jansen
Woodland Hills, California, USA	51	Cancer of the liver and esophagus	Chapel of the Pines Crematory, Los Angeles, California, USA	Edward Norris, George Brent, Scott McKay
Hollywood, California, USA	22	Homicide (beaten to death)	Mountain View Cemetery, Oakland, California, USA	Matt Gordon, Jr. (fiancé)
Santa Barbara, California, USA	48	Heart attack	Rosehill Cemetery and Mausoleum, Chicago, Illinois, USA	Gladys Wynne, Doris Kenyon
Pasadena, California, USA	55	Accidental electrocution	Long Island National Cemetery, New York, USA	Unknown
Flower Hill, New York, USA	80	Suicide (gunshot)	Egern Friedhof, Munich, Germany	Johanna Van Ryn
Brentwood, California, USA	55	Suicide (barbiturate poisoning)	Angelus Rosedale Cemetery, Los Angeles, California, USA	Luba Herman
Hollywood, California, USA	35	Suicide (barbiturate poisoning)	Cremated, ashes scattered at sea	Anthony Soglio, Ike Jones
Beverly Hills, California, USA	66	Heart attack	Forest Lawn Memorial Park, Glendale, California, USA	Rudolph Cameron, George Peabody Converse
Las Vegas, Nevada, USA	29	Suicide (hanging)	Cremated	—
New Haven, Connecticut, USA	48	Suicide (drug overdose)	Saint Mary's Whitechapel Episcopal Churchyard, Lancaster, Virginia, USA	Henry Fonda, William Wyler, Leland Hayward, Kenneth Wagg

Professional Name	Birth Name	Nickname	Date of Birth	Place of Birth	Date of Death
Carl Switzer	Carl Dean Switzer	"Alfalfa"	August 7, 1927	Paris, Illinois, USA	January 21, 1959
Harold Switzer	Harold Frederick Switzer	"Slim"	January 16, 1925	Paris, Illinois, USA	April 14, 1967
Lilyan Tashman	Lilyan Tashman	—	October 23, 1896	Brooklyn, New York, USA	March 21, 1934
Sharon Tate	Sharon Marie Tate	—	January 24, 1943	Dallas, Texas, USA	August 9, 1969
Estelle Taylor	Estelle Boylan	—	May 20, 1894	Wilmington, Delaware, USA	April 15, 1958
Robert Taylor	Spangler Arlington Brugh	The Man with the Perfect Profile	August 5, 1911	Filley, Nebraska, USA	June 8, 1969
William Desmond Taylor	William Cunningham Deane-Tanner	—	April 26, 1872	Carlow, Ireland	February 1, 1922
Irving Thalberg	Irving Grant Thalberg	The Boy Wonder	May 30, 1899	Brooklyn, New York, USA	September 14, 1936
William Thomas	William Thomas, Jr.	"Buckwheat"	March 12, 1931	Los Angeles, California, USA	October 10, 1980
Thelma Todd	Thelma Todd	The Ice Cream Blonde	July 29, 1905	Lawrence, Massachusetts, USA	December 16, 1935
Helen Twelvetrees	Helen Marie Jurgens	—	December 25, 1908	Brooklyn, New York, USA	February 13, 1958
Tom Tyler	Vincent Markowski	—	August 9, 1903	Port Henry, New York, USA	May 1, 1954
Robert Urich	Robert Urich	—	December 19, 1946	Toronto, Ohio, USA	April 16, 2002
Rudolph Valentino	Rodolfo Alfonzo Raffaelo Pierre Filibert Guglielmi di Valentina d'Antonguolla	The Sheik	May 6, 1895	Castellaneta, Italy	August 23, 1926
Conrad Veidt	Hans Walter Conrad Weidt	—	January 22, 1893	Potsdam, Germany	April 3, 1943
Lupe Velez	María Guadalupe Vélez de Villalobos	The Mexican Spitfire	July 18, 1908	San Luis Potosi, Mexico	December 13, 1944
Vera-Ellen	Vera-Ellen Westmeyer Rohe	—	February 16, 1921	Cincinnati, Ohio, USA	August 30, 1981
Bobby Vernon	Sylvion de Jardin	—	March 9, 1897	Chicago, Illinois, USA	June 28, 1939
Hervé Villechaize	Hervé Jean-Pierre Villechaize	—	April 23, 1943	Paris, France	September 4, 1993
Robert Walker	Robert Hudson Walker	—	October 13, 1918	Salt Lake City, Utah, USA	August 28, 1951
Deborah Walley	Deborah Walley	—	August 12, 1943	Bridgeport, Connecticut, USA	May 10, 2001
John Wayne	Marion Michael Morrison	The Duke	May 26, 1907	Winterset, Iowa, USA	June 11, 1979
Pearl White	Pearl Fay White	—	March 4, 1889	Green Ridge, Missouri, USA	August 4, 1938
Michael Wilding	Michael Wilding	—	July 23, 1912	Westcliff-on-Sea, Essex, England	July 8, 1979
Warren William	Warren William Krech	The Poor Man's John Barrymore	December 2, 1894	Aitkin, Minnesota, USA	September 24, 1948
Grant Williams	John Grant Williams	—	August 18, 1930	New York, New York, USA	July 28, 1985
Marie Wilson	Katherine Elizabeth Wilson	—	August 19, 1916	Anaheim, California, USA	November 23, 1972
Grant Withers	Granville G. Withers	—	January 17, 1904	Pueblo, Colorado, USA	March 27, 1959
Anna May Wong	Wong Liu Tsong	—	January 3, 1905	Los Angeles, California, USA	February 2, 1961
Natalie Wood	Natalia Nikolaeuna Zakharenko	—	July 20, 1938	San Francisco, California, USA	November 29, 1981
Diana Wynyard	Dorothy Isobel Cox	—	January 16, 1906	London, England	May 13, 1964
Gig Young	Byron Elsworth Barr	—	November 4, 1913	St. Cloud, Minnesota, USA	October 19, 1978
George Zucco	George Zucco	—	January 11, 1886	Manchester, England	May 28, 1960

Place of Death	Age at Death	Cause of Death	Place of Burial	Spouse(s)/Partner(s)
Mission Hills, California, USA	31	Homicide (gunshot)	Hollywood Forever Cemetery, California, USA	Diane Collingwood
Glendale, California, USA	42	Suicide	Hollywood Forever Cemetery, California, USA	—
New York, New York, USA	37	Brain tumor	Washington Cemetery, Brooklyn, New York, USA	Al Lee, Edmund Lowe
Bel Air, California, USA	26	Homicide (stabbed)	Holy Cross Cemetery, Culver City, California, USA	Jay Sebring (fiancé), Roman Polanski
Los Angeles, California, USA	63	Cancer	Hollywood Forever Cemetery, California, USA	Kenneth Malcolm Peacock, Jack Dempsey, Paul Small
Santa Monica, California, USA	57	Lung cancer	Forest Lawn Memorial Park, Glendale, California, USA	Barbara Stanwyck, Ursula Thiess
Los Angeles, California, USA	49	Homicide (gunshot)	Hollywood Forever Cemetery, California, USA	Ethel May Harrison
Santa Monica, California, USA	37	Pneumonia	Forest Lawn Memorial Park, Glendale, California, USA	Norma Shearer
Los Angeles, California, USA	49	Heart attack	Inglewood Park Cemetery, Inglewood, California, USA	Unknown
Pacific Palisades, California, USA	30	Carbon monoxide poisoning	Bellevue Cemetery, Lawrence, Massachusetts, USA	Pasquale DiCicco
Harrisburg, Pennsylvania, USA	49	Suicide (drug overdose)	Middletown Cemetery, Middletown, Pennsylvania, USA	Clark Twelvetrees, Frank Woody, Conrad Payne
Hamtramck, Michigan, USA	50	Heart attack	Mount Olivet Cemetery, Detroit, Michigan, USA	Jeanne Martel
Thousand Oaks, California, USA	55	Cancer (synovial cell sarcoma)	Cremated	Barbara Rucker, Heather Menzies
New York, New York, USA	31	Peritonitis and septicemia	Hollywood Forever Cemetery, California, USA	Jean Acker, Natacha Rambova
Hollywood, California, USA	50	Heart attack	Golders Green Crematorium, London, England	Gussy Holl, Felicitas Radke, Ilona Präeger
Beverly Hills, California, USA	36	Suicide (drug overdose)	Panteon Civil de Dólores, Mexico City, Mexico	Johnny Weissmuller, Harold Ramond (fiancé)
Los Angeles, California, USA	60	Cancer	Glen Haven Memorial Park, Sylmar, California, USA	Robert Hightower, Victor Rothschild
Hollywood, California, USA	42	Heart attack	Forest Lawn Memorial Park, Glendale, California, USA	Angela Vernon
Hollywood, California, USA	50	Suicide (gunshot)	Cremated, ashes scattered off Point Fermin, California, USA	Camille Hagen, Kathy Self (partner)
Los Angeles, California, USA	32	Fatal reaction to prescription drugs	Washington Heights Memorial Park, Ogden, Utah, USA	Jennifer Jones, Barbara Ford
Sedona, Arizona, USA	57	Cancer of the esophagus	Cremated	John Ashley
Los Angeles, California, USA	72	Lung and stomach cancer	Pacific View Memorial Park, Corona del Mar, California, USA	Josephine Alicia Saenz, Esperanza Baur, Pilar Palette
Neuilly-sur-Seine, France	49	Cirrhosis of the liver	Cimetière de Passy, Paris, France	Victor Sutherland, Wallace McCutcheon
Chichester, Sussex, England	66	Head injury from fall	Cremated	Kay Young, Elizabeth Taylor, Susan Neill, Margaret Leighton
Hollywood, California, USA	53	Multiple myeloma	Cremated, ashes scattered over Long Island Sound, New York, USA	Helen William
Los Angeles, California, USA	54	Peritonitis and septicemia	Los Angeles National Cemetery, California, USA	—
Hollywood Hills, California, USA	56	Cancer	Forest Lawn–Hollywood Hills, Los Angeles, California, USA	Nick Grinde, Allan Nixon, Robert Fallon
Hollywood, California, USA	55	Suicide (drug overdose)	Forest Lawn Memorial Park, Glendale, California, USA	Gladys Joyce Walsh, Loretta Young, Estelita Rodriguez
Santa Monica, California, USA	56	Heart attack	Angelus Rosedale Cemetery, Los Angeles, California, USA	—
Off Catalina Island, California, USA	43	Drowning	Westwood Memorial Park, Los Angeles, California, USA	Robert Wagner (married twice), Richard Gregson
London, England	58	Kidney problem	Unknown	Carol Reed
New York, New York, USA	64	Suicide (gunshot)	Green Hill Cemetery, Waynesville, North Carolina, USA	Sheila Stapler, Sophia Rosenstein, Elizabeth Montgomery, Elaine Williams, Kim Schmidt
Hollywood, California, USA	74	Suicide or pneumonia/stroke	Forest Lawn–Hollywood Hills, Los Angeles, California, USA	Frances Hawke

Index

This index contains references to people, films and other productions, and causes of death. Films all have dates; titles without dates are television programs, stage musicals, or plays. Page numbers in *italics* indicate references in star shots or captions, while page numbers in plain text indicate references in the main body of text. Titles starting with a numeral are listed at the beginning of the index, while numbers spelled out are in the appropriate alphabetical sequence.